How Leaders Reason

To Jan and Sabrina

How Leaders Reason

US Intervention in the Caribbean Basin and Latin America

Alex Roberto Hybel

Basil Blackwell

First published 1990

Basil Blackwell Ltd
108 Cowley Road, Oxford OX4 1JF, UK

Basil Blackwell, Inc.
3 Cambridge Center
Cambridge, Massachusetts 02142, USA

British Library Cataloguing in Publication Data
A CIP catalogue record for this book is available from the British Library.

Library of Congress Cataloging in Publication Data
Hybel, Alex Roberto.
    How Leaders Reason : US intervention in
    the Caribbean Basin and Latin America / Alex Hybel.
        p.   cm.
    Includes bibliographical references.
    ISBN 0–631–16937–7
    1. United States – Foreign relations – 1945–   – Decision making.
2. United States – Foreign relations – Latin America.   3. Latin
America – Foreign relations – United States.   4. United States –
Foreign relations – Caribbean Area.   5. Caribbean Area – Foreign
relations – United States.   I. Title.
JX1417.H93   1990   90–150
327.7308 – dc20   CIP

Typeset in 10 on 11 pt Ehrhardt by
Wearside Tradespools, Fulwell, Sunderland
Printed in Great Britain by
TJ Press Ltd, Padstow, Cornwall

Contents

List of Figures and Tables

List of Figures and Tables

Acknowledgments

This book marks the convergence of two drives – one emotional, the other intellectual. When I left Argentina in 1965, I embarked on a journey convinced that I would never return to the land of my birth or to any other South American country, and that I would distance myself emotionally from the environment in which I had been brought up. I was wrong on both counts.

During my final years as a graduate student at Stanford in the early 1980s, I was finally able to accept that one rarely breaks with the past. It was Jan, my wife, who helped me realize that my past was not behind me, but was part of my present and my future. Her love of the Spanish language and her desire to assimilate the differences that one encounters as one travels across the polymorphous Latin American landscape, rekindled my emotional attachment to the land of my youth.

As my interest in Latin America intensified, I started to think how I could link it to my academic work. I was not a Latin American expert, and had no desire to become one. Since my return from Vietnam, where I served in the US Army as a combat photographer, I had focused a significant portion of my academic life on trying to understand how political leaders reason. Two persons helped me build a bridge between these two interests: Robertico Croes and Dwain Mefford.

When I first met Mr Croes, he was a graduate student at the University of Southern California trying to develop a better understanding of what motivated the United States to behave in the Caribbean Basin as it did. To him, this issue was critical, for upon completion of his studies in California he would return to Aruba to serve in its office of foreign affairs. It was with him that I was once again able to experience the long-lost exhilaration of spending countless hours talking into the night about US intervention, Marxism, dependencia, and revolution.

It was Dwain Mefford, however, who helped me finally decide that much could be gained by applying decision-making theory to the analysis of US intervention in the Caribbean Basin and Latin America. From almost my first day at USC, he and I debated incessantly about how to study foreign policy, and the role analogies play in decision-making. To Jan, Robertico, and Dwain I extend my warmest thanks.

Many other individuals have also been very helpful with their time and their thoughts in the creation and completion of this book. Ward Edwards and Thomas Eppel deserve special acknowledgments. Edwards, as Director of the Social Science Research Institute at USC, was kind enough to invite me to participate in many of his own projects, and ensured that I had all the technical help necessary to complete this work. Thomas Eppel, a colleague at the Institute, helped me broaden my understanding of rational choice models and analogical reasoning.

This book also benefited from the comments of scores of friends, colleagues, and students. From Ronald Steel, John Odell, Thomas Biersteker, Abraham Lowenthal, Ralph Di Muccio, Tom Jacobsen, and various anonymous readers, I received many helpful observations, all of which I considered with great care and many of which led to significant changes. Viken Hovsepian and Pamela Starr also deserve special recognition. They both spent countless hours helping me gather the data, analyse the literature on US intervention, and offering extensive and very constructive criticisms of both the empirical and theoretical chapters.

There are four other people who deserve being mentioned by name. As was the case with my first book, Barbara Peurifoy, my mother-in-law, typed earlier drafts and ensured that my writing style did not distort the content of my ideas. Judith Webb and Nancy Raman accepted with great fortitude my reluctance to give up the yellow pad, and translated my scribbles into the word processor. And finally, Amy Mekelburg was kind enough to agree to spend many weekends typing the final draft in order to ensure that I would meet my deadline. To the four of them I am deeply indebted.

I have also accumulated a number of debts of gratitude to several institutions during the four years of research and writing. During the earlier stages I benefited from my position as a research associate in the Social Science Research Institute. A grant from the National Science Foundation enabled me to conduct extensive research on theories of analogies and to gather part of the data. A second grant from the Pew Foundation helped me put together the chapter on US intervention in Nicaragua. And finally, the School of International Relations at USC, and especially its director, Gerald Bender, provided the needed support to complete the manuscript.

This book is dedicated to my wife Jan as a token of appreciation for being a truly "human" human being, and to our daughter Sabrina in the hope that she will possess the depth to appreciate life's delights, and the fortitude to realize that although her path will be paved with broken dreams, it is a path worth travelling.

Alex Roberto Hybel

1

The Nature of the Puzzle

All the perception of truth is the detection of an analogy.
H. D. Thoreau, *Journal*

REASONING AND LEARNING BY ANALOGY

We are all captives of the past. Whether as individuals who must cope with
mundane problems or as foreign policy-makers who must defuse the most
recent international crisis, our decisions are anchored to lessons inferred from
previous occurrences. How we interpret the past, however, can vary significantly, even when our lives are affected by the same events. Just as two drivers
caught in the same gridlock might deduce different lessons from their common
experience, so might two foreign policy-makers absorbed by the demands of the
same international political crisis reach different conclusions regarding the
nature of the problem.

Decision-making is a process that involves the identification and definition of
problems and the ordering and choosing among alternatives (Mefford,
1985: 3). Most decision analysts have channeled their efforts to the second task.
They define the problem in advance and then identify a hierarchy of available
options by referring to the values of the decision-makers (Raiffa, 1968; Keeney
and Raiffa, 1976). Recently, however, analysts have argued that the initial
formulation of a problem can have a decisive effect on the decision actually
reached (Tversky and Kahneman, 1981). They have proposed that the solution
to a problem is not simply the function of a hierarchically ordered set of values,
but is also the function of the way in which the problem itself is interpreted.

Contextual factors associated with past events impose interpretations on new
issues (Polya, 1954; Simon and Hayes, 1979; Carbonell, 1983). This relationship has been acknowledged by foreign policy students. Neustadt and May
(1986), Larson (1985), Lebow (1981), Jervis (1970, 1976), and May (1973),
have argued that foreign policy leaders use historical examples to define
problems, to formulate options, or to argue against proposed policies. Some of
these studies have viewed the use of historical analogies critically, as a source of
illusion and error in the decision-making process. As explained by Robert

Jervis, analogies tend to "obscure aspects of the present case that are different from the past one" (Jervis, 1976: 220).

The claim is justified. History is filled with instances in which leaders sought to resolve new problems by resorting to solutions used in earlier times, quite ignorant of the fact that the differences between the cases stretched far beyond variance in time. In the early 1980s it was not unusual to suggest that the lessons of Vietnam should be studied before concluding that it was imperative to send troops into Nicaragua to topple the newly established Sandinista regime. Too often these arguments were voiced without recognizing that the two problems were very different. Likewise, twenty years earlier, John F. Kennedy, convinced that Barbara Tuchman's book, *The Guns of August*, articulated some important lessons about the First World War, used some of them to design the way he would respond to the Soviet deployment of nuclear missiles in Cuba. Although another major world war was averted, careful analyses of the two problems would have revealed that their differences outweighed their similarities. And finally, little historical insight is required to recognize the inappropriateness of President Harry Truman's reference in 1950 to the Munich debacle to define the problem posed by the invasion of South Korea by its northern counterpart.

Analogies can be sources of error and illusion in decision-making processes; but they are also the means most commonly used for defining problems which, in turn, influence the way alternatives are abstracted and choices made. As linguists and theorists who focus on the formal and computer replication of human reason have noted, analogies are among the most powerful mechanisms devised by the human mind for coping with uncertainty and value complexity (Lakoff and Johnson, 1980; Lehnert and Ringle, 1982).

This study's principal objective is to derive an analogical theory of foreign policy-making that reaches beyond the two-step proposition typically advanced by various students of foreign policy. Their basic contention has been that behavior is the function of decisions derived from lessons inferred from past events.[1] Analogical reasoning, however, entails a significantly more complex process.

The Alexandrian school of grammarians in Ancient Greece was the first to use analogy as a mathematical and logical term for "equality of ratios," as in $a:b = c:d$. Grammarians several centuries before and after Christ were concerned with prescibing "good" grammar. They did this by assembling noun and verb stems, classifying them according to similarities, and then establishing rules for their similarities and differences in inflection. When first applied to inflectional paradigms, the term "analogy" was used to reflect regularities that appeared in grammar, as mathematical proportions between individual forms of individual words. This view was subsequently contested by the Stoics, who proposed that analogy was not founded on logical considerations but was the product of usage, and that it did not always reflect "equality of ratios" but, more precisely, "similarity of ratios" (Esper, 1973: 1–2).

These two conceptions of analogy have survived the challenges of history. Robert Sternberg has developed a theory of analogical reasoning in which he proposes a mechanism to map out logically the component mental operations that sustain a series of related information-processing tasks and "to discover the organization of these component operations in terms of their relationships both to each other and to a higher-order constellation of mental abilities" (1977: 65). Based on the assumption that limitations exist on the human ability to process vast amounts of information, Sternberg proposes that the behavior of a human cognitive system can be depicted as a mechanism designed to delineate the nature of a problem as it surfaces, sort out the information needed to address it, and structure the type of inferences that are derived from the information gathered. For Sternberg, reasoning by analogy in the form of "A is to B as C is to D," in which the first pair relationship is discovered and then mapped according to a particular rule to outline a second identical structural relationship, is such a type of mechanism.

The addressing of a problem involves more than reasoning. As an individual is confronted with a new situation, he will seek to define the problem in some familiar context. Thus, reasoning by analogy in the form "A is to B as C is to D" may or may not remain constant. Jaime Carbonell has proposed that learning by analogy is the most common learning mechanism and that it involves solving problems incrementally as the analyst derives generalizations from the discovery of commonalities among previous and present situations. Past behavior, however, is not incorporated automatically into the current problem, but is adapted to meet its special demands. Responses to earlier problems, in other words, bring about the formation of what Carbonell (1983: 151–2) refers to as "familiar problem space."

The two theories approach analogy from significantly different perspectives. Moreover, individually they do not capture the overall process involved in problem structuring. Sternberg's theory proposes a sophisticated mechanism for describing the inference, mapping, and application of a hierarchical relationship between four or more concepts, some of which symbolize inferences derived from the information processed. The model, however, is static. Each process is presented as if it were a new beginning, as if each problem had been structured outside its historical context. Carbonell's theory, on the other hand, while unable to explain how an initial structure is inferred, mapped, and linked in a hierarchical relationship, helps explain by the concept of "familiar problem space" how a past problem structure is transformed to fit the criteria of the new problem.

This study combines Carbonell's and Sternberg's theories in order to create one that can explain the dynamic, differentiated process of foreign policy-making. Referring to analogy as the similarity of relationships, the new theory explains how policy-makers initially structure the relationships between several ideas, and subsequently infer new relationships from the existing structures. These new relationships affect the selection of alternatives and the means to implement them. The successful solution to a problem leads to the creation of a "problem space." This concept provides the theory with a dynamic context and, as a result, the means to assess whether policy-makers refer to the newly designed "problem space" when a problem arises at a later time.

US INTERVENTION IN THE CARIBBEAN BASIN AND LATIN AMERICA

This study's second objective is to capture the extent to which reasoning and learning by analogy explains US intervention in the Caribbean and Latin America. Political developments in the 1950s and 1960s in Guatemala and Cuba signaled the birth of a new outlook among certain Caribbean and Latin American leaders. The commitment of their respective governments to political, economic, and social reforms conveyed the view that their policies would no longer conform to the expectations of the leaders in Washington. The United States responded to these challenges by attempting to overthrow the challengers. It succeeded in Guatemala; it failed in Cuba. Failure in Cuba did not stop the United States from further intervention, as attested by subsequent events in the Dominican Republic, Chile, Peru, Nicaragua, and Grenada.

The policies carried out by the United States toward these and other sovereign states raise a number of very important questions that are directly related to the elements that bound the concept of analogy. The empirical analysis will focus on two questions: (1) How have the rationale for and form of US intervention against Caribbean and Latin American states been affected by previous experiences; and (2) In instances in which changes in both rationale and form are evident, how were they manifested and to what extent can they be attributed to learning?

A COMPARATIVE APPROACH TO THE ANALYSIS OF US INTERVENTION: FIVE ALTERNATIVE PERSPECTIVES

Proposing a theory involves more than creating an analytical framework and applying it to a set of cases. It is indispensable, as a third task, to identify the puzzles the theory can address.

From the analysis of the literature addressing the causes of US intervention in the Caribbean and Latin America, three major arguments surface repeatedly. The most commonly proposed thesis is that the United States is committed to maintaining its position of predominance in the region and, as a result, will intervene whenever its strategic interests are threatened. A second argument that has received wide attention since the 1960s is that US actions towards it southern counterparts are dictated by the capitalist economic needs of the United States. This general proposition has followed two distinct, often contradictory, paths. The initial thesis was that some of Washington's most important foreign policy-makers were prisoners of the interests of the main companies investing in the Caribbean and Latin America. These foreign policy-makers, according to the thesis, were either major stockholders, former employees, or relatives of former employees.[2]

The latter argument has been challenged by a more generalized structural economic proposition. Based on the contention that the interests of US companies investing abroad do not always converge and that this conflict frees Washington's policy-makers from having to respond to any particular demand, it has been argued that foreign policy formulators are primarily committed to ensuring the stability of a region's economic system. The economy of the United States, it has been noted, depends on the continued existence of an open economic system – that is, an economic system conducive to trade and foreign investment, and one in which the United States can have access to cheap labor and non-human natural resources.[3]

These arguments, as posited, are too general and, thus, are difficult to evaluate. It is possible, however, to logically derive from them a common, testable, hypothesis:[4]

If intervention by the United States is the function of the amount of threat posed to its strategic or economic interests;

Then, the greater the threat posed by an international actor, the greater the force used by the United States.

This study will rely on the above hypothesis to demonstrate that neither a strategic nor an economic paradigm can give an accurate account for US intervention in the Caribbean Basin and Latin America. More specifically, it will show that strategic and economic theories of intervention cannot explain, for instance, why in 1961 Washington sought to overthrow the rulers of Cuba by using almost the same rationale and set of instruments it employed in 1954 to topple the government of Guatemala when the strategic and economic values of the former to the United States were measurably greater than those of the latter. Nor can these theories explain why in 1983 the United States used direct military intervention against an island of limited strategic and economic value – Grenada – but was unwilling to respond in a more forceful fashion against a much more threatening adversary – Nicaragua.

The theoretical challenge just posed will seem reasonable to students who for long have been very critical of our tendency to disregard the foreign policy formulating process. For these analysts it never made much sense to try to understand why a foreign policy was chosen without first attempting to understand the decision-making process that had led to its selection. But their acknowledgment is likely to be followed by the question: what can be explained by an analogical theory of foreign policy-making that cannot be learned from the application of decision-making models derived from other theories designed by social-psychologists, such as cognitive consistency theory or attribution theory?

The 1970s saw the flourishing of a variety of foreign policy-making models. Alexander George's operational code, John Steinbruner's cognitive paradigm, and Robert Axelrod's cognitive mapping convinced us that there was much to be gained by rejecting the unrealistic premises of rationalism. Each of them delineated with some level of precision distinct analytical frameworks, and each showed ways it could be applied to the study of foreign policy-making. Then the well seemed to run dry. Many of these analysts changed the orientation of their intellectual endeavors and their disciples seemed reluctant to lift the dropped banners. But, finally, just a few years ago, Deborah Larson engaged in a valiant and largely successful attempt to show the value of understanding the type of cognitive processes foreign policy-makers engage in as they try to resolve international problems (Larson, 1985). Her success can be attributed to her decision not to rely on existing foreign policy-making models that used cognitive psychological concepts but to focus on different psychological theories (Larson, 1985: 24–65).

As shown by Larson, the main problem with most foreign policy-making models that use cognitive psychological concepts is that they lack a precise theoretical root.[5] Without a well-delineated theoretical framework, a model might be able to uncover relationships between certain cognitive elements and decisions but will not be able to explain them. Part of this problem can be resolved by concentrating on specific theories that are derived from differing assumptions about the way individuals approach the task of resolving problems.

The preferred strategy in any study that seeks to combine theoretical with empirical analysis is to compare the proposed theory with alternative theories. In this present study the task is partially impaired by the fact that the testing of alternative decision-making theories conducted across several cases demands such a detailed analysis that it would be nearly impossible to carry out the work thoroughly without almost doubling its already voluminous content. This problem could be simplified if there were other studies of US intervention in the Caribbean and Latin America that relied on decision-making theories. If such were the case, all that would be required from this present work would be the comparison of those explanations with the ones derived here. Such studies, however, are almost non-existent.[6]

These constraints have been identified not for the purpose of relinquishing responsibility for the comparison of the different decision-making theories, but of highlighting the difficulties of conducting a systematic comparison across seven cases. With these constraints in mind, this study will attempt to ascertain in a general and not always systematic way whether the explanatory value of the analogical theory is greater than the explanatory reach of two cognitive psychological theories: cognitive consistency theory and attribution theory. These two theories by no means reflect the universe of cognitive psychological theories. But along with schema theory, from which the theory of reasoning and learning by analogy is partly derived, they represent competing ways of interpreting how decision-makers address problems and try to resolve them.

At one end of the spectrum stands cognitive consistency theory, which proposes that the individual is driven by the need to maintain a certain level of consistency in his beliefs.[7] This general need, in turn, affects the way the decision-maker processes information as he attempts to define the nature of problems he encounters and seeks to find solutions to them. In some cases, the end result of this tendency will be to purposely overlook, or simply discard as irrelevant, information that might perturb the cognitive balance. Moreover, the theory assumes that trade-offs between competing values affected by the same problem are typically averted by disclaiming their interconnection. Based on this theory, it could be argued that US policy-makers were so determined in 1954 to perceive the Arbenz government in Guatemala as a communist regime that they discarded any information which brought into doubt such inference. From the same theory, it could also be inferred that Washington was so driven by the desire to topple the Guatemalan govenment that it did not estimate the effect intervention might have on general relations between the United States and Caribbean and Latin American governments.

At the opposite end of the same spectrum stands attribution theory. This theory does not claim that the individual works his way into a problem by dissecting it into various interrelated parts, following the careful evaluation of vast amounts of information, and that this process leads him to the deliberate assessment of various alternatives. In fact, it concedes that the individual will, on occasion, preserve an interpretation or explanation of reality beyond the point justified by the available evidence. But this mistake, note advocates of attribution theory, is not the result of the emotional commitment an individual has to a set of values, but the outcome of an analytical process that reflects insufficient understanding of the steps that need to be taken to arrive systematically at a causal explanation (see Larson, 1985: 34–42). The analyst, in other words, might not be a "scientist," but neither is he a "consistency-seeker;" he is, instead, a "naive-scientist." As such, he will try to formulate causal explanations by trying to ascertain the extent to which an effect is precipitated by one potential cause instead of others, how often other people respond in the same way to the presence of the various potential causes, and how much of the effect is actually experienced under the presence of the divergent potential causes (see Kelley, 1964: 194).

Attribution theory, thus, would postulate a rationale different from that forwarded by cognitive consistency theory as to why Washington defined the situation in Guatemala as a communist threat and decided to intervene covertly to overthrow the Arbenz regime. It would propose that US policy-makers concluded that the Arbenz government would pave the way for the establishment of a communist regime only after they had established that such regimes had come into existence in the past whenever they had been preceded by the same conditions that had surfaced in Guatemala. US policy-makers, moreover, chose to launch the covert invasion only after they had established that the same policy had been an effective instrument under similar conditions with a variety of targets.

Between these two extremes lie schema theory and its derivative, reasoning and learning by analogy. Schema theory shares with attribution theory the assumption that the individual is not driven by an internal need to maintain a balance between his beliefs and actions (see Larson, 1985: 50–7). But schema theory has fewer illusions about the individual's analytical capabilities. According to schema theory, the individual commits errors when he handles information not because he is ignorant but because his analytical capabilities are lin..ited. He derives inferences on the basis of sparse information, haphazardly combined in terms of "matched" concepts, which he stores in his memory and uses whenever needed. Thus, the user of schema theory would argue that the definition of the Guatemalan situation as a communist problem was the result of a past experience in which US policy-makers matched the concepts "some government officials are communists" with "the state is in danger of being ruled by a communist regime." The decision to intervene covertly, in turn, involved a similar process: US policy-makers concluded that since covert action in an earlier case against leaders attempting to put together a communist regime had resulted in the birth of a pro-US government, a similar result could be expected from the implementation of a similar strategy.

A THEORETICAL AND EMPIRICAL COMPARISON

This study will demonstrate, as already stated, that there is no direct correspondence between the means of intervention used by different US governments against Caribbean and Latin American regimes, and the intensity of the threat posed by these regimes to the strategies and/or economic interests of the United States, or to the economic interests of US corporations investing abroad. It will also show that although US policy-makers rarely analyzed systematically the information available, it cannot be argued that they were all driven by the need to maintain cognitive consistency or that they just simply lacked the expertise to conduct quasi-scientific analyses. As an alternative explanation it will be proposed that the most effective way to capture the reasoning process behind the definition of problems and the selection of alternatives is by focusing on beliefs and the effect they have on the formation of analogies. The last argument takes a definite form with regard to the Caribbean Basin and Latin America.

Intervention by the United States in the Caribbean Basin and Latin America between 1944 and 1983 was dictated by the lessons US policy-makers inferred from previous actions designed to prevent the formation of communist regimes. Changes in the definition of problems and selection of policies and policy means were in line with the inferences the ruling administration in Washington was convinced should have been derived from former attempts either to pressure a dictatorial regime to transfer power to a moderate, preferably democratic, government; prevent the formation of a political regime dominated by communists; or topple a communist regime.

US policy-makers did not always share a common vision about the lessons they should infer. Inferences were affected by the costs they or others had experienced in some other similar situations, and their attitudes toward intervention. From this general contention, three sub-arguments are elicited. In those instances in which intervention could have been a viable option but the administration chose not to intervene, the decision was the result of the belief that it was morally reprehensible for the United States to dictate the affairs of other states via military and/or economic force. In one instance, this belief was closely related to an earlier experience. Second, the decisions to delay the use of means of intervention and, when used, to apply them gradually and often covertly were the functions either of the low costs believed to have been accrued in the past while relying on the same strategy, or of the high costs assumed to have resulted from intervening too early and too forcefully. Whenever this strategy ensued, the policy-makers placed an uncharacteristically high worth on the need to minimize the chances that the United States would be perceived as an interventionist actor. And, finally, the decisions to resort to very aggressive means of intervention and to use them at the earliest possible time were the functions of the high costs estimated to have been absorbed in the past while relying on less harmful means and implementing them gradually, and of the belief that it is preferable to be perceived as an arrogant power than as one incapable of acting as a hegemon.

The relevance of and appropriateness of these conclusions, *vis-à-vis* those posited by alternative theories, can be gauged according to standard rules of inquiry. The issue, thus, is how to conduct an empirical analysis in which cognitive and non-cognitive theories are compared within and across sets. The first step is to find the appropriate unit of analysis; in this case, it is the scenario. The construction of the scenario consists of the narration of a story as it unfolds over time. Analysis of the sequence of past events must consider not only the decisions that were made but also what problems were being addressed and how objectives and alternatives were evaluated and ordered at different points in time. Each identified event in a scenario, therefore, is designed to capture information that ranges from the identification of the policy implemented to the description of the specific content of the policy, to the specification of the objectives sought by different parties, and finally to the characterization of how each major party rationalized its choice. By systematically comparing this information within one case across time, a pattern is likely to emerge. This pattern, in turn, can be compared with the patterns that are likely to emerge from other cases. From this comparison, it should be possible to structure the different forms that reasoning and learning assume.

To capture the nature of the decision-making process, and to identify the international and domestic conditions under which different policy instruments are used, it is necessary to have a clear understanding of the object under investigation. Intervention is one of those concepts that can rarely be encapsulated by a small number of terms. The simplest way to define it is by identifying the means used and objectives sought by the intervening party against its various targets. This way it is feasible to delineate empirically a set of patterns about the nature of the aggressor's actions and, in turn, to judge whether they were interventionist in content and intent.

The strategy to be used in this study – breaking the concept of intervention into different components – relies extensively on a method proposed by R. J. Vincent. Vincent argues (1974) that intervention is made up of six component parts. Four of these parts refer to: (i) the actor that intervenes; (ii) the target of the act of intervention; (iii) the activity itself; and (iv) the context in which the act takes place. The nature of these component parts need not be discussed at this moment.[8] It is important, however, to look briefly at the two remaining components: types and purposes of intervention.

Historically, intervention has had many different forms. Intervention has entailed the overt deployment of military forces in a foreign sovereign territory, the setting up of a naval blockade, the imposition of an economic embargo, the assassination of a foreign political leader, and so on. Each of these instruments was chosen for a reason. To understand such a rationale, it is first necessary to differentiate and categorize the different possible instruments used by the intervening party to affect the domestic affairs of another state.

Instruments are chosen for the purpose of achieving an objective or set of objectives. Objectives generally have been defined in terms of national interest. Analysts, however, have not always been successful in coming up with a description of the content of the national interest of the United States that could be used effectively to explain the wide range of instruments used by the leaders in Washington to intervene in the affairs of other states. A more promising approach has been suggested by Barry Blechman and Stephen Kaplan. Their basic argument is that the national interest exists at such a high level of abstraction that it cannot be used by policy-makers as a guide for behavior unless it is decomposed into measurable values. In their view, actors define their objectives in the context of the types of actions that they would like to elicit from their targets. The objectives sought by decision-makers are referred to as "operational objectives" (see Blechman and Kaplan, 1978).[9] This study follows Blechman and Kaplan's advice and describes in extensive detail the potential "operational objectives" the US might seek to fulfill in a foreign policy of intervention, and how.

The criteria used to select cases are critical to any empirical analysis that seeks to compare competing theoretical explanations. The study of US actions toward Latin America and Caribbean states with differing capabilities to undermine the strategic and economic interests of the United States facilitates the task of gauging the explanatory reach of the strategic and economic theories. This comparison, however, is not always as simple as it sounds. One of the most obvious problems is that it is not always feasible to bound the contesting theses in non-overlapping variables. For instance, how is one to prove that US determination to undermine the stability of the Allende regime in Chile in the early 1970s was the function of the commitment by US foreign policy-makers to protect the economic interests of the United States in the region and not of their concern that the strategic interests of the United States would be undermined by such a regime, when the two arguments coexist in some measure with one another in that particular case?

The methodological strategy adopted to deal with this problem is centered on one condition. Since some of the factors that define the central concept that represents one theory might help define the central concept that represents another theory, an attempt will be made to make sure that each concept is defined by at least one factor that is not part of another concept and that has a value for the case under analysis that differs significantly from that of the factor that functions as the principal definer of another concept.

The criteria of selecting countries with different strategic and economic capabilities cannot simply be adopted without considering its effects on the conditions necessary for testing the other theories. The systematic analysis of reasoning and learning by analogy, for instance, requires the consideration of cases bounded by a set of interrelated problems and by a time frame. In other words, an analogical theory of foreign policy-making does not assume that decision-makers seek analogies indiscriminately. This means that cases cannot be selected randomly. Naturally, when this criterion is imposed, the possibility exists that there might be insufficient variance among a set of potentially relevant factors within the cases. In other words, by limiting the types of cases that are amenable to the analysis required to assess the explanatory value of an analogical theory of foreign policy-making, one increases the danger that the selection of cases migh bias the conclusion. Luckily, this problem does not surface in this study. The cases selected represent intervention by the United States under different leaders, in significantly different ways, at different times, and against states in the Caribbean and Latin America that differed measurably in terms of their strategic and economic value, the nature of the threat they posed, and their forms of government.

Along with the variances just considered, there are other factors that need to be introduced to test the cognitive theories. The cases selected include instances that describe the way the same group of decision-makers faced the need to decide whether to intervene against the regimes of two different countries, and the way two different decision-making groups went about deciding whether to intervene against the same regime in the same country. Although no definitive answer can be derived from those limited comparisons, it will be feasible to concentrate on a set of extremely pertinent issues. By focusing on the responses generated by the same group to two similar problems at different times, it will be possible to gauge the effect the earlier experience had on the group's ability to approach the new problem in a semi-methodical manner. In turn, by analyzing the reactions of two groups to the same problem, it will be feasible to evaluate the impact beliefs had on their respective definitions of the situation and selections of solutions. Needless to say, in each case an attempt will be made also to ascertain to what extent different decision-making groups tried to evaluate the effect their policies might have on some of their most important values, and whether their success or failure to carry out such an assessment can be attributed to some cognitive need, shortness of time and/or mental capability, or simply to an unawareness that their analyses did not follow strict epistemological rules.

THE STRUCTURE OF THE BOOK

Chapter 2 is the book's theoretical core. It discusses both the various theories that are tested against the theory of reasoning and learning by analogy, and their respective intellectual precursors. Its initial focus is on the nature of the strategic–realist perspective and of Marxist-derived theories of intervention. Contending that these theories share as a common assumption the notion of rationality, the remainder of the chapter reflects on alternative ways of interpreting the way that problems are defined and decisions made. After a brief description of cognitive consistency theory and attribution theory, the analysis switches to the detailed discussion of schema theory and reasoning and learning by analogy.

Chapter 3 complements chapter 2, and sets up the groundwork for the empirical analysis. Following a discussion of how the concept of intervention has been defined and is applied in this study, the focus is placed on the scenario, as the unit of analysis, and how it is structured to capture both the nature of the interaction between states, and the decision-making process within a state. The chapter closes with a presentation of the type of indices that are used to compare the strategic and economic explanations, and the rationale for selecting the various cases.

The empirical analysis consists of three sets of historical cases arranged chronologically. The cases are:[10]

1   US – Guatemala: 1944–1954
2   US – Cuba: 1953–1961
3   US – Dominican Republic: 1958–1965
4   US – Peru: 1963–1975
5   US – Chile: 1964–1973
6   US – Nicaragua: 1976–1983
7   US – Grenada: 1979–1983

These seven cases can be divided into two categories: US intervention in states in the Caribbean Basin versus US intervention in states in South America. Historically, and due to geographical conditions, the United States has always been more inclined to intervene in the domestic affairs of its closest neighbors than in those of South American states. US actions in the Caribbean Basin, however, also require differencing. Intervention against the first three targets, for instance, came at a time when the power of the United States was at its zenith and Vietnam had not wedged itself into the American conscience. But by the time US policy-makers were confronted with the need to respond to the Nicaraguan and Grenadian problems, the Vietnam experience had taken its toll, the United States was no longer the world undisputed hegemon, and almost two decades of new experiences had attenuated the significance of the Bay of Pigs fiasco.

Hence, although an overall comparison of the seven cases of intervention remains one of this study's priorities, it is preceded by a more detailed comparison of the cases in each category. The practical implications of this division are several. A detailed analysis of the first three scenarios is too voluminous to include as part of a single chapter; the same problem does not arise with the cases defining the other two categories. For this reason, the first three cases are presented as separate chapters, while Peru and Chile, as well as Nicaragua and Grenada, are arrayed in pairs. This variance in presentation requires that the chapters be organized somewhat differently. The five empirical chapters have the same first three sections. The first section discusses various attempts to rationalize the actions by the United States and presents the questions that drive the empirical analysis for that case or pair of cases. The second section describes the unfolding of the scenario(s) and represents the rationale behind the critical decisions in the form of analogies. The third section formalizes the main arguments posited in the previous section in terms of well-defined conceptual categories.

The fourth section fulfills one of two possible tasks, depending on whether the chapter focuses on one or two cases. In the first three empirical chapters the objective of the last section is simply to reach some tentative conclusions and to set up the groundwork for the subsequent cases. At the end of the Domincan Republic analysis, however, the study does not move directly to the cases of Peru and Chile; instead, there is a new chapter that focuses on a small set of questions, all pertaining to the first three scenarios, in order to evaluate the strategic and economic theories, and contrast the explanatory values of cognitive consistency theory and attribution theory with schema theory. This same task, but with regard to Peru and Chile in one instance, and Nicaragua and Grenada in the other, is conducted in the concluding section of the two remaining empirical chapters.

In sum, the empirical analysis takes the following form. Chapter 4, which deals with US reaction to developments in Guatemala mainly during the Truman and Eisenhower administrations, sets the tone for the consideration of the remaining cases. The Cuban case, covered in chapter 5, explains how and the extent to which Washington's reasoning processes under Dwight Eisenhower and John F. Kennedy were influenced by the Guatemalan incident. The analysis includes the comparison of the dynamic pattern of objectives, decisions, and policies of the Cuban case with the pattern elicited from the analysis of the Guatemalan case.

US foreign policy toward the Dominican Republic between 1958 and 1965 is analyzed in chapter 6. The Dominican case is different from the two previous ones in one important respect. In Guatemala and Cuba the United States found itself having to deal with governments that were perceived as being committed to undermining the authority, prestige, and power of the United States in the Caribbean Basin. In the Dominican Republic, the United States became obsessed with ensuring that no anti-US government would be established. The interplay between the various theories and their relevance to the first three empirical cases is described and evaluated in chapter 7.

In chapter 8, US actions toward Chile and Peru are analyzed on a comparative basis. These two cases are important in that although they shared many similar conditions, including an approximate time period, US actions were significantly different. The critical task, therefore, is to isolate those conditions that might indicate why Washington believed it was sensible to seek objectives and use policy means so dissimilar. The empirical analysis closes with the comparison of the Nicaraguan and Grenadian cases in chapter 9. These two cases are particularly relevant in that they help determine, among other things, the degree to which US objectives and policy instruments that were born during the Guatemala incident have survived the test of time.

Chapter 10 draws ashore the various theoretical nets. It begins by summarizing the central weaknesses that emanate from attempts to explicate US intervention by using the strategic and economic paradigms. The subsequent section addresses the theoretical problems that spring from reliance on attribution theory and cognitive consistency theory. The penultimate section captures the relationship between beliefs and the forms adopted by different analogies, in the shape of differentiated hypotheses. The chapter concludes with reflections on future research needs.

2

The Calculation of Interests and the Definition of Problems

INTRODUCTION

In a somewhat perverted way, Latin America and the Caribbean Basin have been an exciting and rich laboratory for the construction of theories of US intervention. The general tone of these studies has been that the United States ordinarily intervenes to protect its strategic or economic interests, or the economic interests of US corporations investing in both regions. Part of this chapter's objective is to delineate the conceptual frameworks on which one strategic and two economic theories stand.

Dissatisfied with the mechanistic models which view states as actors responding similarly to the same external challenges, students of foreign policy began to search for answers in the environment defined by the human mind. Aided by theories developed by social psychologists, foreign policy analysts started to promote new ways of envisioning the analysis of foreign policy. Specifically, they argued that cognitive theories explain why rational responses to foreign policy problems are so uncommon, and provide alternative explanations of foreign policy-making. This chapter's second objective is to discuss three of these theories: cognitive dissonance, attribution, and schema theory and its derivative, reasoning and learning by analogy.

THE INTERNATIONAL MILIEU

The strategic–realist perspective

The role of reason in human affairs has been the subject of some of the most intensive philosophical debates in Western civilization. Socrates, Aristotle, the Stoics, and the Epicurians were among the first to propose that with perfect knowledge humans would do the correct and moral things which, in turn, would lead to happiness and the good life. It was within the boundaries of this general idea that Adam Smith promoted the notion of "efficiency," and Jeremy Bentham the concept of "utility."

Adam Smith in *The Wealth of Nations* proposed that society is well served by a man who seeks to act in self-interest, for his action promotes efficiency. Bentham, one of the foremost utilitarians in the nineteenth century, sought to reconcile self-interest and social interest by proposing that an individual acts in the general good because it is in his self-interest to avoid social recrimination and eternal punishment upon death.[1] Although great thinkers of past ages often promoted rationality, rarely did they think that the action of the common man was based on reason. The rational man, such as the merchant capable of seeing his own best economic interests and acting on them dispassionately, was not a precise depiction of the real individual but an "ideal" useful for bounding certain of man's decisions for theoretical purposes in economics (see Marshall, 1920).

It was this type of "ideal" rational man that captured the interest of foreign policy analysts. Since the end of the Second World War, the study of foreign policy has been dominated by one school of thought – political realism. Adherents to political realism have been among the most vehement supporters of the view that rationality is an assumption intrinsic to foreign policy. Decision-makers comprising the official, bureaucratic manifestation of the state are assumed to act as a unitary actor and to formulate external policies based on rational calculations of costs and benefits. Political realism, however, is not a precise replica of rational models of decision-making. In decision theory, the rational individual is one who, when confronted with a problem, makes the choice that has the best chance of bringing about a consequence that is highly desired by him. That same consequence, however, might not be as attractive to an individual with a different rank-order of preferences. In the realist paradigm, it is assumed that all states have as their most valued objective the protection or augmentation of power. States seek power – both the ability to influence others and the resources that can be used to exercise influence – by rationally calculating their interests in terms of power (see de Mesquita, 1981: 29–33; Keohane, 1983: 508). The connection between power and rationality was explained by Hans Morgenthau when he noted that to give meaning to the raw material of foreign policy, i.e., power, political reality must be approached with a rational outline (Morgenthau, 1983: 5).

The realist perspective has undergone significant modifications since Morgenthau first attempted to give it a theoretical form. For the most part the focus of these changes has been on its three central concepts: national interest, power, and rationality. According to Stephen Krasner, the concept of national interest can be studied from two perspectives: logical–deductive and empirical–inductive (1978: 35). The clearest modern articulation of the logical–deductive perspective comes from Morgenthau, who contends that the national interest "is not defined by the whim of a man or the partisanship of party but imposes itself as an objective datum upon all men applying their rational faculties to the conduct of foreign policy" (1983: 33). From the contention that states always strive to protect their sovereignty in an anarchic world, the following predictions or prescriptions for actions can be deduced: states resist or should resist efforts by other states to gain domination; the demise of opponents will or should be averted if permanent disequilibrium could ensue; the balance of power in the system will or should be maintained even when it requires changing allies (Krasner, 1978: 37).

One of the central problems with Morgenthau's conception of the national interest is that it has limited applicability. As Krasner explains, a logical–deductive perspective is of some use when the territorial and political integrity of the state are at stake. The main problem is likely to arise when dealing with issues that are not directly linked to these two concerns. Under such circumstances it is very difficult to infer from the national interest the forms an actor's actions will take (Krasner, 1978: 41). A different but related challenge was advanced by Robert Keohane who argued that "states concerned with self-preservation do not seek to maximize their power when they are not in danger . . . they recognize that a relentless search for universal domination may jeopardize their own autonomy" (1983: 515).

Charles Beard once wrote, "The question – what is national interest? – can be answered, if at all, only by exploring the use of the formula by responsible statesmen and publicists and by discovering the things and patterns of conduct – public and private – embraced within the scope of the formula" (1966: 26). Beard's argument fits nicely within the boundaries of the empirical–inductive approach. This approach assumes that it is possible to induce the national interest from the statements and behavior of central decision-makers. Krasner (1978) argues that in order to differentiate the national interest from other interests that might be attributed either to the administration in power or to particular interest groups, two criteria must be fulfilled. First, the preferences that compose the national interest must not consistently benefit or hurt a particular group. And second, the rank-ordering of the goals that are sought by the central decision-makers must persist over time (p. 35). For Krasner, therefore, the critical task is not to identify a priori a set of objectives from which expected actions can be logically derived, but to uncover empirically both the context and structure of goals that delineate the national interest.

Since the concepts of power and national interest are linked in a dynamic relationship, it should not come as a great surprise that the former also underwent some significant modifications. According to Keohane, power in politics was assumed to be like money in economics, fungible. But, as he adds, when tested, the fungibility assumption turns out to be a weak one: a great amount of military power does not guarantee leverage on all foreign policy matters. To account for this inconsistency, Keohane suggests a relaxation of the fungibility assumption in order to allow for issue-specific appraisals of state power. This means gauging a state's power according to its capability to influence specific issues: military, economic, political, etc. This conceptual modification, however, leaves unresolved the problem generated by the need to develop a priori a power measure that can be used to compare the power of different states across different issues. Keohane attempts to overcome this obstacle by reformulating the core assumptions of the realist approach. He proposes that while power should still be considered a major state objective, it should not be viewed as the "overriding interest in all cases . . . Under different systemic conditions states will define their interests differently" (1983: 529). In other words, a sort of means–ends calculation would be necessary to appraise a state's power relative to the goals it was pursuing.

The strategic–realist perspective, even with some of its conceptual modifications, is not accepted universally. One challenge views all political phenomena as projections of underlying economic forces. The significance of this interpretation is specifically relevant to capitalist states. The capitalist state is regarded as an apparatus of the ruling capitalist class that exploits and represses subordinate classes, i.e. the proletariat, at both the domestic and international levels, for economic gain. This alternative interpretation can be referred to as the Marxist–Leninist perspective.

The Marxist–Leninist perspective

In Marxist–Leninist analysis, power is a crucial *instrument* of state behavior. Hegemonic powers rise to dominant positions in the international system through the use of economic and military resources to secure their interests. However, the prime *motivating factor* for capitalist state behavior lies in the conditions of the *economic substructures* of the international system. Based on this contention, it is inferred that those who control the economic system control the political system.

The conceptual core of the Marxist–Leninist approach can be found in the body of "The Communist Manifesto," written in 1848 by Karl Marx and Friedrich Engels. The intent of the authors was to view history from a materialist perspective, i.e., "the history of class struggles" (Marx and Engels, 1977: 222). The crucial variables in their analysis are capital, class, and state. Marx and Engels note that the "essential condition" for the growth and development of the bourgeois class is the "formation and augmentation of capital" (1977: 231). Fluctuations in capital levels are obtained either through changes in productivity or, more frequently, changes in the price of labor. Since the price of labor depends exclusively on the competition for wages between laborers, capital is "that kind of property which exploits wage-labor, and which cannot increase except upon condition of begetting a new supply of wage-labor for fresh exploitation" (p. 232).

The concepts of *class* and *state* provide the structures within which foreign policies are formulated and executed. In the Marxist perspective, class antagonisms (rooted in the effects of the development of capitalism), create the revolutionary, motivating dynamics of systemic change. The bourgeoisie controls the wealth; the proletariat is merely a factor in its production. Consequently, the *state* is but a bureaucratic, "official" manifestation of the interests of the dominant, i.e. bourgeois capitalist, class. In turn, unlike the realist notion of the state's reason for being (preservation of the national interest defined in terms of power), the Marxist notion posits the basis of the state's existence on the protection and advancement of the interests, defined in terms of profit maximization, of the wealthy class. From this perspective, there is no such thing as a *national* interest, *per se*; only the narrow *material* interests of the bourgeoisie are assumed to guide state behavior. In other words, the state's primary purpose, internally, is to uphold a particular material order and, externally, to perpetuate that order through the expansion and conquest of new markets to absorb excess capital.

The dynamics of the global marketplace provide an essentially independent driving variable in the Marxist framework, the dependent outcome of which is the external behavior of capitalist states. The capitalist states' drive for domination follows a fundamentally deterministic logic of global economic expansion. The need to secure "consistently expanding markets for its products" forces the bourgeois state to extend its relations "over the whole surface of the globe" (Marx and Engels, 1977: 224). Marx, however, never developed fully the extent to which his argument applied to the international arena. To this end, one would have to look at the works of various analysts who sought to develop economic theories of imperialism. This task, however, lies well beyond the scope of this study. For present purposes it is necessary only to focus on Lenin and on some of the more contemporary attempts to restructure his argument.

In the preface of *Imperialism, The Highest Stage of Capitalism*, Lenin asserts that in order to "understand and appraise modern war and modern politics" it is necessary to study the "question of the economic essence of imperialism" (1982: 8). Such an undertaking would, ostensibly, lead the analyst of international affairs to discover the causes of capitalist state behavior.

According to Lenin, modern capitalism is characterized by the "enormous growth of industry and the remarkable rapid process of concentration of production in ever larger enterprises" (1982: 16). A crucial feature of capitalism in an advanced stage is the phenomenon of combined production, involving "the grouping in a single enterprise of different branches of industry, which either represent the consecutive stages in the working up of raw materials . . . or are auxiliary to one another" (p. 18). This feature of capitalism inevitably leads systems of enterprise along the road to monopoly, thus concentrating profits and capital in the hands of a small, yet powerful, capitalist class. Eventually, cartels arise in the international economic system which develop agreements on the conditions of sale and terms of payment (p. 22). The cartels attempt to create a system in which they "divide the markets among themselves, . . . fix the quantity of good to be produced, . . . fix prices, . . . divide the profits among the various enterprises" (p. 22). In turn, the growth of cartels results in the transformation of capitalism into imperialism, for "cartelization" makes possible over-accelerating rates of profit. As the capitalist economic system develops, and profits accumulate, capital begins to flow abroad (p. 29). Thus imperialism is viewed as an inevitable outgrowth of capital "overflows." It follows that a capitalist state's external policies will be conditioned by the need to find new markets towards which the flow of capital can be directed, and to preserve or create economic structures that are conducive to such international expansion.

The "consolidation" of the international capitalist structure is achieved through the activities of banks dealing in finance capital. As capital and revenues become centralized by banking monopolies, a tendency toward the consolidation of separate enterprises into a "single national, capitalist, and then into an international, capitalist, economic unit" becomes evident (p. 34). Close links between banks and industry are established through mergers and the appointment of bank directors to the boards of industrial and commercial enterprises and vice versa (pp. 41–2). These personal ties are then completed among the banks, industry, and the state through crossover of government officials to positions of responsibility in the private business sector. The banks, through their connections and ability to extend or withdraw credit, are able to control considerably the activities of certain industries. Consequently, the importance of the role of finance capital increases.

Theories of international relations rarely remain unaltered. The Marxist–Leninist approach is no exception. Although it is difficult to encapsulate the various variants of the central Marxist–Leninist analysis of economic imperialism into a precise set of categories, it is generally acknowledged that the instrumental-Marxist and structural-Marxist approaches come close to achieving such a goal. These two approaches differ fundamentally from each other in their interpretations of the concept of the national interest and in their consequent analysis of the role of the state in pursuing foreign policies to serve that interest. Both perspectives differ from the central Marxist–Leninist approach in their use of a general definition of imperialism as an essentially expansionary foreign policy, pursued by a national government in order to establish a relationship of domination and control over the ogvernment and/or people "of another nation over which the imperialist government has no traditional claim to sovereignty" (Weisskopf, 1974: 58). Furthermore, the role of surplus finance capital, while relevant, is viewed by both structural- and instrumental-Marxist analysts as only one of several motivating factors in a state's decision to pursue imperialistic foreign policies.

Thomas Weisskopf writes that "one can distinguish alternative motivations for imperialism according to the alternative kinds of interests that might be promoted by imperialist activity" (1974: 58). Thus, the analyst of neo-imperialist policies must distinguish between: (a) the *national* interest, in which case imperialist policies are "expected to benefit the imperialist nation as a whole;" and (b) *class* interests, in which case imperialist policies are expected to "result in net benefits for a particular class of people from among the citizens of the imperialist nation" (p. 59).

In the instrumental-Marxist approach, *class* interests, even at the expense of *national* interests, play or seem to play the primary role in guiding a state's foreign policy behavior. Instrumental-Marxist analysts argue that specific class interests, in which the members of the dominant class attempt to "increase their *particular economic gains* from international economic relations" will pressure a state to follow imperialistc policies "whether or not the net benefits to the nation as a whole are positive" (Weisskopf, 1974: 65). In other words, it is not inconceivable to the instrumental-Marxist analyst that the state might act in ways contrary to the national interest.

Paul Baran and Paul Sweezy submit that one of the tasks of a theory of imperialism is to "analyze the composition and interests of the dominant classes in the dominant countries" (1966: 158). According to these authors, the dominant classes are no longer composed solely of industrialists and bankers. Instead, multinational corporations (MNCs) have become the "basic units of monopoly capitalism in its present stage; their (big) owners and functionaries constitute the leading echelon of the ruling class" (1966: 159). The role of the MNCs in the global marketplace in this century has superseded that of export capital; indeed, many corporations – due to their immense profits from overseas operations – have become *importers* of capital into their own countries. Because MNCs prefer unimpeded access to markets on a transnational basis, the instrumental-Marxist analyst can assume that they will lobby against domestic protectionist measures, trade restrictions, etc. And yet, because they have diverse interests in several countries, many of which are often contradictory rather than complementary, the instrumental-Marxist approach is not conducive to simple generalizations. In other words, although the instrumental-Marxist proposition that the interests of MNCs are embodied in expanding markets is a plausible one, the link between such interests and a capitalist state's foreign policy might in some instances be drawn with a flair for creative speculation. As Andrew Mack (1974) notes, the student of US foreign policy using the analytical framework of economic imperialism must be prepared to answer the question: "Did the foreign policy elite – *regardless* of their subjective philosophies – act in the broad general interest of that section of the corporate elite that has a large stake in overseas trade and investment?" (p. 52).

Weisskopf proposes that the extent to which particular classes will motivate a government to pursue imperialist policies "depends upon the distribution of power among various classes in the society in question" (1974: 66). Since the capitalist classes, wielding disproportionate power and influence in economic and political terms, are likely to tip the balance of power in their own favor, Weisskopf concludes that they will be able to gain government support "in favor of class-based imperialism ... unless the aggregate costs of a given activity become so high as to weigh heavily and obviously on large segments of the population, or unless the activity involves a sharp conflict of interest among powerful classes themselves" (p. 75). Although it is intuitively implausible to suggest that the state will pursue the interests of specific corporate groups in *all* cases of foreign policy, empirical evidence shows – at least tentatively – that the instrumental-Marxist framework is of some analytical utility. Krasner draws the following conclusion from an empirical test of hypotheses drawn from theories of economic imperialism:

> Recent experience in international commodity markets does not support the proposition that capitalist states act to satisfy aggregate economic needs ... but does indicate the corporate interests are supported. (1978: 194)

The structural-Marxist variant develops from a basic proposition in the theory of economic imperialism which contends that the major determinants of the foreign policy of a capitalist state are economic, "imposed by the capitalist system" (Kurth, 1974: 3). It assumes that a capitalist state's external behavior is driven by the "pro-capitalist imperative." In other words, interventionist policies, especially against Third World nations, are undertaken ostensibly as "efforts by American capitalists to protect their investments and markets abroad" (1974: 9). In the structural-Marxist view, however, certain *class* interests are always encompassed in the *national* interest, although the national interest is not necessarily inherent in particular class interests. The primary objective of the national interest in the structural-Marxist approach is the maintenance of macroeconomic prosperity for the capitalist system.

In the pursuit of macroeconomic prosperity, the state may undertake a foreign policy of military adventures and intervention in order to justify high levels of military spending which in turn help to "maintain a high level of aggregate demand" for surplus capital (Weisskopf, 1974: 60). This policy may consequently help to ensure stable foreign markets for direct investment and domestic export goods, and to ensure continued imports of vital raw materials. The state's primary role in the structural-Marxist perspective is to create and maintain structural conditions in the global economic system that will prove conducive to the expansion of the domestic capitalist economy.

Studies that have attempted to corroborate or falsify either Marxist version have not been successful in deriving precise answers. The central criticism postulated against both Marxist perspectives is that the economic variable cannot carry the tremendous explanatory weight assigned to it (Waltz, 1979: 24–37; Holsti, 1985: 74; Viotti and Kauppi, 1987: 416). At first encounter this criticism seems justified, particularly if one's analytical framework is built on the assumption that the international environment is riddled with complexity. However, some formulations of power politics can also be said to have been shortsighted by confining explanations to power variables. Of much greater concern should be that both the strategic–realist and the Marxist–Leninist perspectives are based on the assumption that decision-makers approach international problems and formulate solutions to them rationally.

For many years, students of foreign policy-making have questioned the emphasis placed on rationality and its relationship to either power or economic interests. They agree with John Steinbruner that the "mind of man, for all its marvels, is a limited instrument" (1974: 13). In response to this concern, they proposed using a variety of theories designed by social psychologists that adopt competing perspectives on how the individual approaches and resolves a problem. Three of these theories are: schema theory, cognitive consistency theory, and attribution theory. Since this study's principal objective is to develop a theory of reasoning and learning by analogy, derived partly from schema theory, the latter will be discussed after cognitive consistency and attribution theory have been considered.[2] Such an analysis, moreover, will be more detailed than the analyses of the other two.

COGNITIVE CONSISTENCY AND ATTRIBUTION THEORY

In the 1950s various social psychologists proposed that individuals are incapable of carrying out tasks associated with the rational process of decision-making and, instead, process and interpret information so that they will be able to keep their beliefs, feelings, and cognitions mutually consistent.[3] A consistent structure is one in which: "All relations among 'good elements' [i.e. those that are positively valued] are positive (or null), all relations among 'bad elements' [i.e. those that are negatively valued] are positive (or null), and all relations among good and bad elements are negative (or null)" (Jervis, 1976: 117). The mind, in other words, is a veritable inference-making machine which actively, but unconsciously, manipulates the information it receives to give structure to an ambiguous reality (Steinbruner, 1974: 90 and 111).

Confronted with situations of uncertainty, decision-makers impose on reality a structure such that events have a clear, coherent meaning. Through the use of categorical (rather than probable) judgments, policy-makers believe they can predict decision outcomes with some degree of certainty and not feel the need to evaluate a range of possible alternatives. These judgments rest on strongly held beliefs derived not via the gathering of objective evidence but by reference to a reinforcing experience. This process is called the *assumption of a single outcome calculation* (1974: 123). Moreover, faced with a problem involving conflicting values, decision-makers will separate them, deny that any connection exists between them, and make choices in terms of one value alone without estimating how the other values might be affected. This tendency is best known as *the assumption of value separation* (p. 108).

During the second half of the 1960s, the "consistency-seeker" school of thought began to face some challenges. A group of social psychologists questioned the assumption that the decisions arrived at by an individual were motivated by his need to achieve cognitive consistency. Man began to be seen as a person engaged in "a quest for meaning, not cognitive harmony: for validity, not consistency" (Larson, 1985: 35).

In 1967, Harold Kelley proposed that the decision-maker be perceived as a lay scientist, as an individual who tries to "infer causes for the effects he observes" (Nisbett et al., 1976: 101). According to Kelley, the lay attributor, in an attempt to attribute causes for events of the form "Actor responds in fashion to situation A," will react to three types of information: "distinctiveness," "consistency," and "consensus." Distinctiveness information refers to whether the actor responds in fashion in all situations of the general type, or only in situation A. The second, consistency information, focuses on whether the actor responds in fashion at all times, under a broad variety of circumstances, or only occasionally. And the third type, consensus information, refers to whether other actors also respond in fashion to A, or whether the response is relatively rare (Kelley, 1967: 194). Richard Nisbett and Lee Ross developed further the metaphor of the naive scientist by proposing that the latter must, like the regular scientist, describe accurately an event or object, characterize a sample of data, generalize from the sample to the population of objects or events, measure the covariation between events, propose causal explanations, predict the future, and test theories (Nisbett and Ross, 1980: 8–9; Larson, 1985: 36).

Attribution theory acknowledges that the decision-maker often attempts to confirm his hypotheses by searching for consistent evidence. This form of behavior, contend supporters of attribution theory, need not be ascribed to an assumed tendency by the decision-maker to focus only on that information that is consistent with his beliefs. The reason an individual will process information in such a way is that often he is unaware that the most effective and systematic manner to gauge the soundness of a proposition is by attempting to falsify it (Larson, 1985: 41).

SCHEMA THEORY, AND REASONING AND LEARNING BY ANALOGY

The use of analogies is pervasive in everyday experience (Sternberg, 1977: 99). People resort to analogical thinking whenever they are confronted with new situations by drawing parallels to old experiences. The pattern followed in the preparation of legal cases, for instance, is reasoning by analogy, and it involves a three-step process. First, similarities and differences between present and past cases are uncovered; subsequently, the rule of law inherent in the appropriate previous cases is identified; and then the rule of law is made applicable to the present case (Levi, 1949: 1–2). Not only the identification of similarities is critical to legal reasoning, but also the classification of differences. As noted by E. H. Levi, in analogical reasoning the rules change from case to case and are recreated with each case (1949: 2). More specifically, the fundamental property of analogical reasoning is the changing of rules, in the sense that the determination of a rule is a function of the stipulation of which facts are identified as being similar to those in existence when the rule was first designed.

Social psychologists, relying on concepts and hypotheses used in cognitive psychology, have given a specific theoretical form to some of these ideas. Under the rubric of schema theory, the individual is viewed as a decision-maker overwhelmed by sensations and information who, in an attempt to define and resolve a problem, will resort to shortcuts. Rather than following quasi-scientific rules and procedures when making inferences and decisions, the individual searches for a generic concept stored in his memory that might seem appropriate to the problem at hand. In other words, to understand the world, the problem-solver tries to match "what he is experiencing to past incidents stored in memory ... he searches until he has found a schema that summarizes and categorizes one or more similar stimulus configurations in the past" (Larson, 1985: 52).

Attempts to explain the matching process between concepts have been carried out from at least two perspectives: the information-processing approach and the componential approach (see Sternberg, 1977: chs 3 and 4). The information-processing view of human cognition maintains that in order to understand the behavior of a human cognitive system as it focuses on a problem, one must discover the processes used to solve it and to identify the plan that integrates specific processes into a functional package that produces the desired results (Kail and Pellegrino, 1985: 52–3). The central weakness of models that rely on an information-processing perspective is that they lack a "mapping" operation that helps, on the one hand, to identify the analogy between the pair terms in the first group and the pair terms in the second group and, on the other hand, to communicate the established solution (Sternberg,

1977: 112). This shortcoming can be remedied by using a componential approach. The general purpose of this approach is to identify the mental operations underlying a series of information-processing tasks and to discover the organization of these operations in terms of their relationships to each other and to high-order mental functions. The relationship and significance of these two approaches require some discussion.

H. Shalom and I. M. Schlesinger (1972), seeking to extend the theory of analogical reasoning designed by C. Spearman in 1923, define an analogy item as a relationship between one or more ordered pairs. Each relationship, they add, is structured by a "domain" and a "range." For instance, let us assume that many of the impressions derived about Latin American regimes by Washington are functions of how those regimes treat US companies investing in their respective countries. In a relationship specifying actions initiated by the host country toward US companies investing abroad and inferences derived by Washington about these actions, the domain could consist of stricter labor laws (sll), expropriation (e), or preferential tax treatment (ptt); while the range could include two inferences made by the United States: host government is anti-US (hgaUS), or host government is pro-US (hgpUS).

The Cartesian product in a relationship consists of all possible sets of ordered pairs between the domain and the range. If the actions just proposed describe the universe of possible steps by the host country and inferences derived from these actions by the United States, then the Cartesian product would have the following format: {(sll, hgaUS), (sll, hgpUS), (e, hgaUS), (e, hgpUS), (ptt, hgaUS), (ptt, hgpUS)}.

As presented, the Cartesian product describes all possible sets of ordered pairs without identifying the relationships that are pertinent to analogical reasoning. In analogical reasoning it is critical to distinguish between the rule that refers to the logical relationship among analogical terms, and the rule that refers to the particular formula used by the analyst to solve the analogy. The first rule is generally referred to as the selection rule (SR), while the second rule is commonly identified as the connection formula (CF). The selection rule and the connection formula need not be the same. Moreover, to the extent that politics is not always animated by logic, stipulation of the selection rule might not be a requirement. For all practical purposes, therefore, solving an analogy in politics involves forming a connection formula and applying it. Since relationships in politics cannot be assumed to remain constant, the connection formula used to solve an analogy at one point in time need not be the same subsequently. Going back to the earlier example, it could be suggested that whenever a host government in Latin America begins either to enforce stricter labor laws on US companies or to engage in a policy of expropriation, Washington is likely to label such a government as anti-US. From this connection formula, the following relationships can be inferred:

$$sll:hgaUS :: e:hgaUS$$
$$sll:hgaUS :: ptt:hgpUS$$
$$e:hgaUS :: ptt:hgpUS$$

The difference between the above format and the Cartesian product is that in the latter the modes of action by the host government are not paired with all possible modes of inference by Washington, but only with those established by the connection formula. Moreover, the rule of relations in the second pair of the analogy, i.e., e:hgaUS, corresponds to the inference of the rule relating the two elements of the first half of the analogy. Whether this relationship remains constant or is replaced by a different one depends on whether Washington introduces a different connection formula. The introduction of a different connection formula could be the function of a new lesson learned from a new experience, or it could be the presence of a new administration in Washington.

It should be noted that although the information-processing model of analogical reasoning proposed by Shalom and Schlesinger is very detailed, it does not include an explanation of how the pair terms in the first and second group are identified and the solution communicated. This problem, proposes Robert Sternberg, can be dealt with by creating a mechanism that identifies the mental operations, delineates their relationships to one another, and "maps" a higher-order relation of equivalence between two lower-order relationships (1977: 112).

Sternberg defines analogy as a hierarchy of relationships that takes the form "A is to B as C is to D." The terms "domain" and "range" are also part of Sternberg's componential theory of analogical reasoning, but he uses them differently from the way they are used in the theory proposed by Shalom and Schlesinger. In the new theory the "domain" refers to the terms A and B, while the "range" pertains to C and D. Thus,

A:B :: C:D
Domain   Range

For Sternberg (1977), "an analogy exists when there is a rule, Y, that maps a domain rule, X, into a range rule, Z" (p. 112). In other words, the first lower-order relationship is discovered in the domain of the analogy, which is then mapped to the range of the analogy through the formation of an isomorphic relationship, that is, an identical structural relationship. However, the relationships within the domain and the range are not the products of independent instances but are linked to higher-order relationships that are not time bound. There are three critical components in Sternberg's componential theory of analogical reasoning: attribute identification, attribute comparison, and control (1977: 135). The first step in the analogical process is the translation of the stimulus into some type of mental representation from which additional mental inferences can be subsequently carried out. The mental representation is stored in the working memory and has a value component. The attribute process is referred to as encoding. Placed in terms of the example discussed earlier, encoding could consist of comprehending and storing in memory the following analogical terms: sll, e, ptt, hgaUS, and hgpUS.

At the attribute comparison stage, four steps are generally executed. The first step is the "inference" by which a rule, X, that related the terms in the domain is discovered. The outcome of this inference is then stored in the decision-maker's memory. In the example analogy, inference could be represented as the discovery of the relationship between sll (stricter labor laws) and hgaUS (host government is anti-US). The required second step in the attribute comparison is referred to as "mapping," and it involves the discovery of a higher-order rule, Y, that maps the domain of the analogy into the range. In other words, mapping requires discovery of a rule that relates the first term of the domain to the first term of the range (1977: 136). In the example analogy, mapping could be represented as the discovery of the relationship between sll (stricter labor laws) and e (expropriation). The higher-order rule that addresses the relationship between the first terms of the domain and the range is also stored in memory. "Application" is the third step in the attribute comparison, and it calls for the generation of a rule, Z, that forms a second term for the range that is an expression of the correct answer. In the example analogy, application is the creation of a rule that enables the decision-maker to decide that hgaUS (host government is anti-US) correctly completes the relationship between the domain and the range. The fourth and final step, "justification," is optional. This process is required only in those instances in which none of the terms available is an exact expression of the correct answer and, thus, it is necessary to find an option which can be justified to be the closest to the initially visualized answer.

Control, the third and final component in Sternberg's componential theory of analogical reasoning, involves primarily the translation of the solution of the problem into a response. The response in the example analogy could entail a reduction in financial aid by Washington to the country that expropriated US companies. A schematic representation of this process is presented in figure 1. In addition, table 1 offers a summary of the key elements of the componential model of analogical reasoning.

Figure 1   *Schematic representation of analogical reasoning theory*

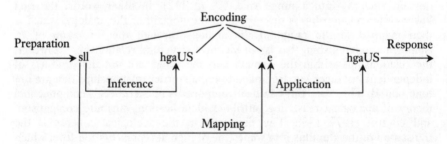

Sternberg's componential theory is useful in the sense that all major processes are explicitly stated in their relationships to each other. Moreover, it is specific in its description of the operations of the three critical components: attribute identification, attribute comparison, and control. Finally, the theory achieves a considerable degree of parsimony by specifying all operations with a minimum number of components.

The putative importance of analogy in problem-solving, however, must

Table 1   Components of analogical reasoning theory

Parameter	Process	Description
1 Attribute identification	1 Encoding	1 Attributes and value of terms in problem identified
2 Attribute comparison	2 Inference	2 Rule, X, relating two terms in domain identified
	3 Mapping	3 Rule, Y, relating first two terms in domain and range generated
	4 Application	4 Rule, Z, to form the second term in the range generated
3 Control	5 Response	5 Solution in attribute comparison translated into response

transcend the issue of reasoning. First, the theory must attempt to explicate how the rule, X, which relates the terms in the domain, is discovered. Or, as explained by Mark Keane (1985), this type of theory does not explain how the terms in the domain are initially identified as being related to one another. Solving this problem is critical, for if the matching of terms is not based on hypothesis, the potential permutations of matches regarding one problem can be enormous (1985: 450). It is no difficult to envision, for instance, different decision-makers addressing the same problem and coming up with different matches. Second, Sternberg's theory is static and does not account for learning. More specifically, it cannot explain possible changes in the inference, mapping, and/or application rules at the attribute comparison stage due to different lessons inferred from past experiences by various leaders.

Analogies are the functions of purposes. Different individuals arrive at different interpretations of the same problem, depending on their current goals (Madison, 1982; Schank, 1982). Similarly, different individuals with different goals, drawing analogies as they confront a common problem, will be inclined to select different matching terms for the domain, even in instances in which they refer to the same past experience. Sternberg's componential theoretical framework can be extended by adding two aspects to it: purpose and learning.

Purpose, as Mark Keane suggests, can be defined in terms of an individual's goal or subgoal at the time he is addressing a problem (1985: 450). Purpose, however, does not exist entirely independently of learning. Past experience can alter not only the way in which individuals attempt to solve new problems, but also their goals and subgoals.[4]

According to Jaime Carbonell, experience in problem-solving is gained incrementally (1983: 137). A decision-maker, when encountering a new problem situation, is reminded of past situations at different levels of abstraction that resemble the present problem. The problem-solver derives a generalization from discovery of commonalities among previous and current situations and the successful application of the policies to solve these problems. The derivation of a generalization, however, is flexible enough that past behavior is not incorporated automatically into the current situation, but adapted to meet its special demands. Moreover, if in a new situation the problem-solver performs an action that proves to be inappropriate, discovery of the error that brought about the unintended results could trigger a discrimination process that would help delineate the range of applicability of the generalization from which the initial action had been derived.

Critical to Carbonell's theory on learning by analogy is the concept of "familiar problem space." Invariably, an individual will solve a familiar problem faster and with more self-assurance than he will an unfamiliar one. What makes a present problem space familiar is the memory of similar past problems and their corresponding solutions. At this point, however, it is important to differentiate between two processes: remembering and reasoning. Rumelhart and Abrahamson (1973) propose that the retrieval of specific information stored in the memory involves remembering, while the retrieval of the structure of one or more relationships among concepts is referred to as reasoning. Although Carbonell does not specifically differentiate between remembering and reasoning, it is evident that he is concerned with the latter process when he notes that the best method of computing similarities among episodic memories is by comparing their structures based on a "relative invariance hierarchy" (1983: 151–2).

The first step in analogical reasoning, notes Carbonell, is the retrieval of a structure defining the relationships among one or more concepts. To decide what structure to retrieve from the memory, the decision-maker remembers an experience in which he was fulfilling similar goals. Hence, a comparison of the structures of goals is a crucial component for modeling a reasoning process. Having retrieved a structure that was applicable to the solution of an old situation, the decision-maker must transform the structure to fit the criteria for the new problem. Insofar as the structure was retrieved because the goals addressed in past and present situations are similar, the decision-maker must assess the extent to which the structure must be altered to meet the new goals.

The critical factor in Carbonell's theory of learning by analogy is that the transformation process requires only that present and past problems be structurally similar, rather than identical. A decision-maker, therefore, can learn by simply storing solutions to new problems. Moreover, if one type of problem recurs with frequency, the decision-maker might formulate a generalized plan for dealing with future occurrences of that problem. At this stage, the decision-maker would no longer be engaged in analogical reasoning, for he would not be reasoning from a particular member of a cluster of similar experiences (1983: 152).

The theories proposed by Sternberg and Carbonell approach analogies from significantly different perspectives. Sternberg's theory is static in the sense that although it can describe the process involving the inference, mapping, and application of a hierarchical relationship between four concepts, it cannot explain why a particular structure was selected over another, or how a structure retrieved from a past situation is transformed when applied to a new one. Carbonell's theory, on the other hand, takes the position that learning by analogy is a dynamic process involving the retrieval and transformation of structures from one problem to another. But this theory omits from its framework the different stages in the structure generation process. To develop a rich and differentiated analogical theory of foreign policy, the two processes just described must be incorporated into a single framework.

A THEORETICAL FRAMEWORK OF REASONING AND LEARNING BY ANALOGY

The first phase in the analysis of a foreign policy is to recreate the process by which policy-makers define a problem. Analogy, as the similarity of relations, is a good starting point.[5] In the case of the United States, for instance, let us assume that its leaders believe that a useful measure of a foreign government's ideological predilection is its treatment of US companies in the country it rules. A government that engages in expropriation (e) is described as being dominated or influenced by communists (hgc), while one that grants preferential tax treatments is identified as being anti-communist (hgnc).[6] These relationships can be structured in the following analogical format:

$$e{:}hgc :: ptt{:}hgnc$$

This analogical format does not delineate the full structure of the problem. The next step in the process is to identify the types of inferences, if any, that Washington derives from each relationship.[7] One of Washington's practices since 1945 has been to infer that control of a government by communists enhances Moscow's ability to dominate the affected state and other bordering states. Conversely, to the extent that a government shows signs of supporting a capitalist economic system, the assumption in Washington generally has been that Moscow's capacity to impose its will will be measurably constrained. We can define the two additional concepts as the presence and absence of Soviet control, respectively, and symbolize them as follows: presence of Soviet control = PSC, and absence of Soviet control = ASC. The new relationship can be structured in the following analogical format:

$$hgc{:}PSC :: hgnc{:}ASC$$

The two-pair relationships delineate the boundaries of Washington's potential actions. But actions must be placed in the context of purposes. To minimize the chances that the continued presence of a government that shared Moscow's ideological preferences might provide the latter with opportunities to expand its own power, Washington has often concluded that its only option was to overthrow the weaker party. At the same time, Washington has been adept at supporting governments that favor a capitalist economy. Decision-makers in Washington have assumed in many instances that one of the most effective ways of containing the Soviet Union was by helping capitalist economies to flourish. The two new concepts just introduced can be symbolized as follows: overthrow = o, support = s. Thus,

$$hgc{:}o :: hgnc{:}s$$

The last step in the structuring of the problem requires the determination of how to implement the alternatives selected. Two of Washington's most common practices have been to resort to paramilitary forces to covertly overthrow a perceived communist regime, and to provide economic aid to a government that supports the continued development of a capitalist economy. The selection of the first policy instrument has been driven generally by the need to fulfill two subgoals. On the one hand, the United States was determined to obstruct any attempt by communists to create Marxist regimes in Latin America. On the other hand, Washington did not want to promote the belief among Latin Americans that the United States was an interventionist power unconcerned about violating the sovereign rights of states. The second policy instrument, in turn, has often been used as a means to strengthen the governing capability of regimes friendly to the United States. The two new concepts can be symbolized as follows: covert paramilitary invasion = cpi, economic aid = ea. Thus,

$$\text{o:cpi :: s:ea}$$

The problem just described is represented by four two-pair analogical relationships structured in a hierarchical mode. The domain and range of each pair relationship can be divided into independent pairs in such a way that the pairs defining each domain can be linked in order to structure one case, while the pairs defining each range can be linked in order to structure a diametrically opposite case. Washington's reasoning process prior to the invasion of Guatemala in 1954, for instance, could be described by the first pair relationships linked among themselves in the form of conditions, as follows:

If (hg) does (e),
then (hg) is (hgc).
If (hg) is (hgc)
then the likelihood of (PSC) increases.
To avert (PSC)
then (o),
If (o)
then (cpi).

In 1954, the United States toppled Guatemala's government. This success could have convinced Washington that it was justifiable to store in its memory the structure that defined the relationships among the different concepts relevant to the problem. The composition of the structure defining the problem in 1954 is what Carbonell refers to as the "problem space." It is at this stage that the application of analogical reasoning to the analysis of foreign policy moves away from the consideration of what types of pair relationships are inferred by decision-makers to the comparison of problem structures. Having stored in memory the relationships between different concepts, the decision-maker no longer needs to recreate the same process. Instead, as a new situation develops, he must decide whether the conditions defining it are compatible with the conditions defining the old problem. In addition, the decision-maker must determine whether the respective goals correspond. In 1961, for instance, Washington seems to have retrieved the problem structure it had stored in memory seven years earlier and used it as a guide to attempt to topple a new regime – the Castro government. A definitive answer, however, must await a detailed analysis of Washington's decision-making process at that time.

CONCLUSION

In sum, the comparison of the theory of reasoning and learning by analogy with alternative explanations is conducted in the hope of fulfilling three major theoretical objectives. Since both the strategic and the two economic theories discussed are drawn from the assumption that the foreign policies of the United States can be explained without reference to the cognitions of its decision-makers, it will be feasible to assess whether the understanding gained by relying on cognitive perspectives more than balances the parsimony that results from the application of non-cognitive theories.

In addition, it is critical to develop a better grasp of the strengths and weaknesses of cognitive theories. Since these theories reflect some of the most serious attempts to explain how decisions are affected by cognitive processes, their application to the analysis of US intervention in the Caribbean Basin and Latin America will help identify some of their main theoretical strengths and weaknesses. And finally, if success results from the attempt to ascertain with some degree of confidence the appropriate theoretical utility of the various cognitive theories, it will be possible to speculate whether the theory of reasoning and learning by analogy can stand on its own, or should be integrated as part of a broader construct.

3

Methodological Criteria

INTRODUCTION

Thomas Kuhn writes that the "decision to reject one paradigm is always simultaneously the decision to accept another, and the judgment leading to the decision involves the comparison of both paradigms with nature and with each other" (1970: 77). This study is not designed to reject paradigms. But one of its objectives is to promote an alternative way of studying US foreign policy. The reader's decision as to whether to accept this alternative perspective must be founded on the types of theoretical problems and anomalies it can resolve. To facilitate this decision it is imperative to ensure that the empirical analysis is designed to address the theoretical issues that are at stake. With this concern in mind, this chapter focuses on: (1) how to define intervention; (2) what unit of analysis to use in order to clear the way for the comparison of explanations that range from those that focus on the nature of the threat posed to the United States, to those that concentrate on the beliefs of its decision-makers; (3) how to measure a country's strategic and economic significance to the United States, and that same country's economic relevance to investing US corporations, without being totally hampered by overlapping indices; and (4) what cases to select in order to posit reliable generalizations.

THE CONCEPT OF INTERVENTION

It has been suggested that the more common the word, the more numerous the concepts for which it stands (Sartori, Riggs, and Tuene, 1975: 3). Second to "power," the term "intervention" might very well be one of the most widely employed words in the arena of international affairs. As a concept it has been used, at one time or another, to cover almost the entire spectrum of possible actions of one state toward another.

In 1969, James N. Rosenau wrote:

Notwithstanding the voluminous literature on intervention, there appears to be no agreement whatsoever on the phenomena designated by the term. Even in international law, where the definitional problem is an especially recurrent preoccupation, uniformity of usage has yet to develop. (p. 984)

Richard Little echoes Rosenau's preoccupation when he contends that the term "intervention," like many other terms used frequently, "possesses no accepted technical meaning" (1975: 2). The hope and intent of both scholars was to persuade the intellectual community that in order to address systematically the moral and legal implications of intervention it was first necessary to delineate its conceptual boundaries.

The two most common conceptions of intervention are those posited by Thucydides and Hans Morgenthau. Thucydides' "pull-theory" defines the act of intervention as the response by a party in a bipolar international system to a call for assistance by actors operating in the target state. Thucydides conveyed this idea when he wrote:

in time of war, when each party could always count upon an alliance which would do harm to its opponents and at the same time strengthen its own position, it became a natural thing for anyone who wanted a change of government to call in help from outside. (Quoted in Little, 1975: 3)

Morgenthau's "push-theory," on the other hand, seeks to explain intervention by concentrating on the motives that drive the aggressor to intervene. It proposes that states intervene in the affairs of other states whenever they estimate that the action will serve their own interests and undermine those of the others (Little, 1975: 3).

According to Little, neither explanation is entirely satisfactory. Morgenthau, by emphasizing the utility and efficacy of the state-centric model, can define intervention only in terms of the dyadic interaction between two states. Thucydides, on the other hand, although he seems to provide a link between inter-and intra-state politics, his solution applies only to a bipolar international system in which two international actors are linked to two intra-state actors (1975: 4–5).

Richard Little's solution to the conceptual and theoretical problems that emanate from the analytical constructs proposed by Thucydides and Morgenthau is straightforward. He stipulates on an a priori basis that the triad, rather than the dyad, is the most useful structure for examining intervention in all areas of social activity. The triad can contain four distinct situations in which conflict or cooperation create the stimulus, and the response by the third actor can be impartial or partial. Little concludes that of the four situations the most important in the analysis of international politics is that in which an actor takes sides in a conflict between two other actors. When such a condition is present, three types of situations can be assumed: (i) the three parties have similar powers; (ii) one party is more powerful than the others; and (iii) although initially the focus of the analysis is on the interaction between two parties, one is divided by conflict, thus stimulating intervention on the part of the undivided party (1975: 5–6).

At this juncture Little acknowledges that the tendency in international politics has been to restrict the term "intervention" to the involvement in the domestic affairs of one state by another. Using this idea as a stepping-stone, he concludes that by focusing on the third situation he can integrate the dyadic and the triadic conception of intervention. He then proposes that:

> An interventionary situation exists when an actor responds to an interventionary stimulus. The stimulus emerges when conflict develops between the units in a bifurcated actor, creating a potential for system transformation. Maintaining a relationship with one side of a bifurcated actor constitutes an intervention response, maintaining a relationship with both sides of a bifurcated actor constitutes a nonintervention response. (1975: 8)

Little's approach to the study of intervention is not without flaws, but it is significantly better than the way the concept was characterized by James Rosenau. Intervention, explains Rosenau, has two central characteristics: it is convention-breaking, and it is authority-oriented (Rosenau, 1969: 990). Intervention is convention-breaking in the sense that it begins when conventional modes of behavior are replaced by new modes of action and ends when the conventional modes are restored or the convention-breaking becomes conventional through persistent use; and it is authority-oriented in that the action is designed for the purpose of preserving or changing the structure of political authority in the target state (p. 997).

The fallacies behind Rosenau's characterization of intervention can be captured by considering one of his examples. He proposes that US involvement in Vietnam was not interventionist until just prior to February 7, 1965. Although US efforts to affect the political structure of Vietnam had been carried out by conventional military, economic, and diplomatic means for several years, on that date the United States altered its behavior pattern: it resorted to bombing. Rosenau then adds that when the bombing was halted, intervention could be perceived as having ended, even though massive US presence in Vietnam continued.

The first problem with Rosenau's argument is that it views the relationship from a dyadic perspective. He is correct in stating that the United States did not intervene directly against North Vietnam until it began the bombing, and that direct intervention ended, at least temporarily, when the bombing was halted. But this dyadic perspective disregards the fact that South Vietnam was a major party in the struggle, that it was divided into two conflicting factions, and that each faction was aided by a different foreign actor: North Vietnam in one case and the United States in the other. Another major limitation with Rosenau's approach to intervention is that it does not perceive as interventionist those actions that were originated with the intent of altering another actor's economic structure, ideology, or relationship with a third external party. If Rosenau's standard were to be accepted, one would have to conclude that the United States was not intervening in Cuba's domestic affairs when it pressured the Castro regime not to alter radically the country's domestic economic structure, or when it warned against the dangers of adopting a communist ideology and becoming a major ally of the Soviet Union. Very few analysts, regardless of whether they approve of Washington's actions, would contend that they were not interventionist.

Another analyst who has attempted to delineate the conceptual boundaries of intervention has been Howard Wriggins. According to Wriggins, the actions by an interventional actor can be viewed as a continuum moving from influence to involvement, to intervention, and finally to clandestine intervention (1968: 217). The central element differentiating the two adjacent concepts – involvement and intervention – is that in the former the actor and the recipient of its actions agree on ends and means, while in the latter, activities are not mutually acceptable. The problem with this conceptual differentiation, as explained by Caroline Thomas, is that in the case of a civil war, "intervention by an outside power may be at the request of the existing government. Conversely, recognition by an outside power of the *de facto* control by an insurgent group of a portion of the state may be considered as intervention by the government which formerly claimed sovereign powers over the whole of the state" (Thomas, 1985: 17).

Rosenau's assumption – that the utility of the term as an analytical concept declines as the range of phenomena to which it is attributed widens – is shared by several students of intervention. Some, in an attempt to deal with the problem in a rigorous manner, have suggested alternative definitions of intervention. But in almost every instance, these analysts have excluded actions that are typically perceived as being interventionist. A major exception has been the attempt by R. J. Vincent not necessarily to give intervention a precise set of conceptually rigid boundaries, but to identify its major features. Instead of trying to emulate the commitment by other analysts to come up with a precise definition of intervention, he argues that it is more valuable to identify some of the general conditions that can be attributed to intervention (1974: 3).

According to Vincent, intervention can be broken down into six component parts, namely: actor, target, activity, types, purposes, and context. Historically, intervention has been undertaken by a single state, a group of states acting independently of an international organization, or a group of states acting as representatives of an international organization which has approved the action. Intervention has also been initiated by a revolutionary group within a state which either enjoys or does not enjoy the tacit support of its government. Vincent's identification of the actor that intervenes is not entirely at odds with Little's definition. Although Little does not attempt to account for those instances in which the intervening party is a revolutionary group, his definition of the concept does not exclude them.

"Target" refers to the party against whom the act or acts of intervention are directed. Vincent, borrowing from James Rosenau, proposes that intervention is directed at the "identity of those who make the decisions that are binding for the entire society and/or to the processes through which such decisions are made" (1974: 7). The nature of this definition of "target" does not fully correspond with that presented by Little, but at the same time it does not present an entirely different perspective. Little sought to emphasize the view that the impulse for the intervention by an outside party could come from the government itself or from a competing faction. In other words, an actor can intervene in the domestic affairs of a foreign state either on the side of the government against a rebellious faction or on the side of the rebellious faction against the government. As presented by Vincent, intervention would seem to be directed only against the government. But Vincent is careful not to identify "government" as the sole target; instead he refers to the "authority structure of the state." This distinction is critical in the sense that the "authority structure of the state" is bound to be affected regardless of whether the foreign party intervenes on the side of, or against, the government.

The activity of intervention entails "coercive interference" (Vincent, 1974: 8). Or, as stated by Thomas and Thomas (1956), intervention "is the attempt to compel" (p. 72). This idea originated from the assumption that a fundamental attribute of sovereignty is the omnipotent right of a government to rule within the territorial boundaries of a state. Any attempt to affect a state's sovereign right, therefore, amounts to intervention. The problem with this conception is that it grants the full authority to decide whether an act is interventionist to the party governing the state. But this, as already explained by Little, is not correct, for intervention can entail coercion directed against either the government of the state or parties within the state that oppose the government.

The notion of coercion is central to the analysis of intervention. According to the definition relied on by Vincent, to coerce is to "constrain or restrain by application of superior force or by authority resting on force; to constrain to compliance or obedience by forcible means" (1974: 8–9). This definition is too exclusive. As Vincent acknowledges, the definition confines intervention to activity which uses, or threatens to use, force, and excludes the use of economic instruments. Ultimately, however, the definition of coercion cannot be bounded by the type of instrument used to achieve compliance; instead it must be rooted in the idea that compliance was brought about without regard for the desire or volition of the target. Identifying types of intervention and distinguishing interventions according to their purposes is the task of classification and not of definition. To design a list that encompasses the entire range of types of intervention is a very complex task. This task can be simplified significantly if the focus is narrowed to the identification of the instruments relied on by the United States as it intervened in the affairs of Caribbean and Latin American states.

The clearest form of intervention exists when the troops of a state enter foreign soil against the will of some of its constituents and when the invasion constitutes neither a reprisal nor war. This form of intervention, however, has not been the one most commonly practiced by the United States. Its leaders have long realized that lesser means of coercion can often accomplish the same results as military force but at a lower cost (Graber, 1959: 2).

Generally the United States has relied on three types of intervention: military, economic, and diplomatic. In some instances it has used these means overtly; in other cases it has used them covertly. Moreover, there have been instances in which, rather than actually using one policy instrument or another, the United States simply made it evident that it would be willing to use one of them if the party in question did not acquiesce to the stipulated demand. In other words, the signaling of a threat is also a form of intervention. The types of intervention resorted to by the United States can, in turn, be divided into separate subcategories. Military means of intervention can be divided into four broad subcatrogies: (i) direct combat involvement; (ii) indirect combat involvement; (iii) direct paracombat involvement; and (iv) indirect paracombat involvement (Duner, 1983: 60).[1] Economic means of intervention, in turn, can be divided into two broad subcategories: (i) trade; and (ii) capital (Baldwin, 1985: 41–2). Finally, diplomatic instruments can be arranged according to the context in which they are used. Three diplomatic reference areas can be identified initially: (i) interstate diplomatic means; (ii) international organization diplomatic means; and (iii) interpersonal leadership diplomatic means.

Purposes of intervention, or, for that matter, any other type of international activity, are not always easy to identify. Any attempt to come up with an empirical definition of national interest, for instance, is likely to face the problem of dealing with the fact that decision-makers describe the concept in a broad context, encompassing political, strategic, and economic concerns, and that these concerns often coexist with one another. Cognizant of these problems, Barry Blechman and Stephen Kaplan (1978) have proposed a methodology that is both simple and relevant to the analysis of objectives sought by a party intervening in the affairs of another. Blechman and Kaplan argue that any analyst attempting to ascertain why decision-makers turn to armed forces as an instrument of foreign policy must first decide whether to concentrate part of the investigation on the personal motives of the decision-makers, or on the strategic or operational objectives sought by them. They discard the first two concepts for similar reasons. Motives, they contend, are extremely difficult to determine in any situation, for they may be singular or multiple in number, consciously or unconsciously held, and present- or future-oriented. Moreover, motives may be of a personal nature, may concern the "national interest," or may simply relate to domestic political matters (1978: 59).

Strategic objectives are also very difficult to identify. It is not uncommon, for instance, to argue that the fundamental strategic objective sought by the United States during the Vietnam War was to avoid being perceived as a weak actor. Although such an objective may have been pursued, it is evident that it was not the only one, and it is debatable whether it was the most important one. Further, it is very difficult to formulate a viable operationalization of the concept that will be useful in the elicitation of systematic comparisons.

One viable method proposed for the operationalization of objectives has been designed by analysts who apply multi-attribute utility measurement to the study of decision-making processes. The central idea that made utility measurement practical was the recognition that most outcomes not only are abstract but are composed of numerous attributes. This recognition invited the thought that in order to engage in a rational decision, the decision-maker faced the task of assigning a utility measure separately on each dimension of value for each outcome of concern (Raiffa, 1968, 1969; Keeney and Raiffa, 1976). The set of values that a policy intends to serve can be identified by constructing a value tree, referred to by Keeney and Raiffa (1976) as an "objective hierarchy" (see also von Winterfeldt and Edwards, 1986). At its roots, a value tree has abstract, aggregated values. These abstract values are hierarchically desegregated throughout the tree until a level of specificity is reached, at which point the performance of a policy can be assessed. The level of complexity of the value tree is a function of the issues addressed by the policy.

Although Blechman and Kaplan do not rely on the ideas advanced by analysts using multi-attribute utility measurement in the analysis of decision-making processes, their operationalization of objectives follows a similar rationale. To focus on operation objectives allows for the consideration of objectively determined and empirically verifiable phenomena without endangering the validity of the study's results (1978: 65). In other words, although personal motives and strategic objectives are crucial components of a foreign policy-making process, policy-makers must deal more directly with operational objectives. The success or failure of a foreign policy, and the interests of the state implementing the policy, are affected primarily by the content of the policy's operational objectives (p. 65).

Operational objectives can be differentiated according to the type of behavior one party wants another party to engage in. In the case of the United States, for instance, its operational objectives with respect to Caribbean and Latin American actors can be broadly differentiated according to whether it intervenes in order to affect its target's (i) control of the government; (ii) disposition toward domestic political participation; and/or (iii) actions toward other parties, domestic and/or international.

It goes without saying that these three categories are too general. Specificity can be added by further differentiating each type into additional subcategories. The first category – control of the government – is further divided depending on whether the United States seeks to influence its target's control of the executive (including the armed forces) or its parliamentary body. The United States's attempt to affect its target's disposition toward domestic political participation is assessed in terms of the target's policies with respect to political elections, the press, and/or labor unions. Finally, the third category – the target's actions toward other parties, domestic and/or international – is the broadest of the three operational objectives. This category encompasses the target's military, economic, and diplomatic actions.

The last component of intervention refers to the conditions that define the subsystem in which the action is conducted. According to Vincent, the rate of intervention can vary depending on the distribution of power between the states that delineate a sybsytem, on whether the subsystem is composed of satisfied actors, and on whether in the subsystem there are small states whose internal political authority is under constant challenge (1974: 12–13).

One of the most common problems faced by social scientists is how to control for alternative explanations. Few theorists would dispute that the United States has intervened in the affairs of other states to preserve its power, or to protect its general economic interests or those of specific US corporations investing abroad. But to acknowledge this, without explicating the relationship that exists between the interests being affected and the types of responses generated to protect them, is to say little. Any explanation of US intervention will remain at best only equal to alternative theses until the comparisons are conducted in the context of a common unit of analysis.

THE ANALYSIS OF INTERVENTION AND ITS RATIONALE IN THE CONTEXT OF SCENARIOS

Every foreign policy-making activity involves problem formulation and ordering and selection among alternatives. The appropriate unit of analysis to deal with this process is the "historical narrative" or "scenario."

The scenario is a historical case which consists of a sequence of events interconnected in time. By observing how the interacting parties formulate the problems and how they order and select their respective alternatives, and by systematically comparing the evolutions of these different policies in time, it is possible to identify the patterns that different forms of reasoning and learning assume.

To compare scenarios, it is necessary to identify the sequence of events in terms of generalized components. Each event, in effect, is a package that answers questions at two levels. Questions at one level refer to the interactions between states. At a second level, it assumes that states are not monolithic actors, but rather are composed of individuals and groups capable of imposing differing interpretations on situations. Thus, at the intra-state level, questions refer to the interactions among its principal decision-makers. The questions addressed at the interstate level are:

1 What action was initiated?
2 Who initiated the action?
3 Who were the principal intended targets of the action?
4 What was the extent of the action?
5 When was the action initiated?

The questions addressed at the intra-state level are:

1 What were the alternatives considered?
2 Who were the principal proposers of these alternatives?
3 What objective(s) did each principal proposer believe had to be achieved?
4 How did each proposer rationalize his choice of alternative?

In sum, both sets of questions help fulfill different analytical objectives. For instance, in June 1960 the United States cut the Cuban sugar quota by 95 percent. The record of this event at the interstate level reads as follows:

WHAT	Trade sanction
WHO	United States government
INTENDED TARGET	Cuba
WHEN	June 1960
EXTENT	95 percent reduction in sugar quota

The description of the event is incomplete. To understand the reasoning process in the United States that led to the reduction in the sugar quota, it is necessary to look at the decision-making process. The initial narrative, thus, must be expanded. In June 1960, the White House, beliving that it was necessary to hurt Cuba's economy in order to get rid of Fidel Castro, ordered a 95 percent reduction in the sugar quota. This decision was much harsher than the action proposed by the US ambassador to Cuba, Philip Bonsal. The US ambassador, convinced that the proposed action would strengthen Castro's hand in Cuba and draw him closer to the Soviets, suggested that the United States either warn Cuba that the balance of sugar would be reduced, or simply reduce the quota less drastically. This description tells a richer story. It is built on the assumptions that actions have purposes and that decision-makers in one administration do not always agree as to how goals should be realized. The record of this event at the intra-state level reads as follows:

ALTERNATIVES   Major versus limited reduction in sugar quota
PROPOSERS   White House versus US ambassador to Cuba
OBJECTIVES   Undermine Castro's power
RATIONALIZATION   Major reduction in sugar quota would undermine Castro's power, versus major reduction in sugar quota would strengthen Castro's power and draw him closer to the Soviets.

The described event represents the action of the United States and the process that led to the selection of an alternative at one point in time in the overall scenario structure that defines Washington's interactions with the Castro regime. As presented, the story is static and ahistorical. The side-by-side examination of two distinct but not fully unfolded scenarios should help clarify the context in which cases can be compared (see tables 2 and 3).

Table 2   *Comparison of two not fully unfolded scenarios*[a]

	US–Guatemala 1952–1954	US–Cuba 1959–1960
WHAT	Passage of agrarian reform law and expropriation	Passage of agrarian reform law and expropriation
WHO	Arbenz government	Castro government
TARGET	United Fruit	Oil refineries and other US-controlled companies
WHEN	June 1952–Feb. 1953	July 1959–Oct. 1960
EXTENT	234,000 acres of land owned by United Fruit	Texaco, Esso, Royal Dutch, and agricultural land
PROPOSERS	President Arbenz	Fidel Castro, Raul Castro, Ernesto Guevara
OBJECTIVES	Eradicate dependency on US investors	Eradicate dependency on US investors
RATIONALI-ZATION	Independence could be achieved only by breaking all ties with foreign investors	Independence could be achieved only by breaking all ties with foreign investors

	US–Guatemala 1952–1954	US–Cuba 1959–1960
WHAT	Intervention plans ordered	Intervention plans ordered
WHO	Eisenhower administration	Eisenhower administration
TARGET	Arbenz government	Castro government
EXTENT	President Eisenhower orders CIA to draft plans for paramilitary intervention	President Eisenhower orders CIA to draft plans for paramilitary intervention
ALTERNA-TIVES	1 Draft plans for paramilitary intervention 2 Pressure Central American states to exert economic and political pressure on Guatemala	1 Draft plans for paramilitary intervention 2 Use economic sanctions 3 Do nothing
PROPOSERS	1 Eisenhower, John Foster Dulles, and Allan Dulles 2 C. D. Jackson and Adolf Berle	1 Eisenhower, Richard Bissell, and Richard Nixon 2 C. D. Jackson and Adolf Berle 3 Philip Bonsal
OBJECTIVES	Clear the communists out of Guatemala	Clear the communists out of Cuba
RATIONALI-ZATION	1 Political and economic pressure had failed 2 Paramilitary activity was too risky	1 Political and economic pressure would not be enough to topple Castro regime. Force might prove to be only alternative 2 Paramilitary activity was too risky 3 Economic pressure or military force would only help strengthen Castro regime
WHAT	Paramilitary invasion begins	Paramilitary invasion begins
WHO	Eisenhower administration	Kennedy administration
TARGET	Arbenz government	Castro government
WHEN	June 18, 1954	April 17, 1961
EXTENT	Small number of Guatemalan nationals, financed by CIA enter Guatemala	1,400 Cuban nationals financed by CIA land at Bay of Pigs in Cuba
ALTERNA-TIVES	Launch invasion	Launch invasion
PROPOSERS	Eisenhower and Allan Dulles	Kennedy and Allan Dulles
OBJECTIVES	Eliminate communist influence in Guatemala	Eliminate communist influence in Cuba
RATIONALI-ZATION	Only by overthrowing Arbenz would the US be able to eliminate communism in Guatemala	Only by overthrowing Castro would the US be able to eliminate communism in Cuba

[a]The comparison is incomplete. It excludes many important events that transpired between the dates identified, such as the decision arrived at in June 1960 by Washington to impose a 95 percent reduction in Cuba's sugar quota.

Table 3   *Comparison of partial reasoning processes in two not fully unfolded scenarios*

	US–Guatemala 1952–1954	US–Cuba 1959–1961
	Guatemala–US	Cuba–US
Altern. 1	To achieve full independence from foreign control, Guatemala must expropriate foreign companies	To achieve full independence from foreign control, Cuba must expropriate foreign companies
Policy	Foreign companies expropriated	Foreign companies expropriated
	US–Guatemala	US–Cuba
Assump. 1	If Arbenz government expropriates US companies, then Arbenz government is communist	If Castro government expropriates US companies, then Castro government is communist
Assump. 2	If Arbenz government is communist, then US national interest is threatened	If Castro government is communist, then US national interest is threatened
Altern. 1	To protect US national interest, Arbenz government must be overthrown by a covert paramilitary invasion	To protect US national interest, Castro government must be overthrown by a covert paramilitary invasion
Altern. 2	To protect US national interest, Arbenz government can be pressured to resign by exerting economic and political pressure jointly with American states	To protect US national interest, Castro regime can be undermined by exerting economic and political pressure
Policy	Covert paramilitary intervention initiated	Covert paramilitary intervention initiated

The limited time-reach of the Guatemalan and Cuban scenarios and the simplicity of their preliminary representation make it difficult to grasp fully the implications of this type of analysis. But even with these constraints, it is possible to imagine the types of comparisons that this method of analysis facilitates. With more fully developed scenarios it will be feasible to delineate how decision-makers reasoned, whether they made references to past events, and, if they did, how they structured such events in order to confront the new problem.

The use of the scenario, moreover, facilitates the task of assessing the impact that beliefs have on decision-making. With a few exceptions (for example, Walker, 1977; Hoagland and Walker, 1979; Larson, 1985), most efforts to assess the role of a decision-maker's belief in his decision-making have been somewhat impressionistic and of a tentative nature. This should not be surprising. As noted by Holsti:

> Unlike the analyst who can index his variables with such measures as GNP per capita, arms budgets, trade figures, votes in the UN General Assembly, or public opinion, those interested in the beliefs of decision makers have no yearbook to

which they can turn for comparable evidence, much less quantitative data presented in standard units. (1976: 35)

A thorough analysis of the potential relationship between beliefs and decisions requires detailed data, amassed from documents, public statements made by the decision-makers, open-ended interviews, and inferences made by participant observers. This task is not unsurmountable if the subject involves just a few decision-makers, focusing on the same problem, for a very short period of time.[2] A complete analysis, on the other hand, is almost beyond reach if the focus is on seven US administrations, responding to problems emanating from seven different countries, across a period of almost forty years. Considering these difficulties and the fact that in order to bring to light the role played by analogies under the conditions just identified also demands vast amounts of data, it should not be difficult to appreciate why this study does not attempt to include all the evidence that would be needed to conduct a fully comprehensive analysis of cognitive consistency theory. Instead, this study makes certain that there is sufficient information to describe the dominant beliefs of the foreign policy actors most involved in defining problems and selecting solutions.[3]

One of two techniques is generally used to evaluate the effect that beliefs have on decisional choices: the "congruence" procedure or the "process-tracing" procedure (see Walker, 1977; George, 1979: 105; Larson, 1985). The first procedure relies on a nomothetic-deductive mode of explanation for the purpose of assessing whether congruence exists between the content of certain beliefs and the content of certain decisions. The analyst establishes the decision-maker's beliefs on the basis of data from his earlier life-history and considers whether they are congruent with his policy preferences and decisions. The determination of congruency is arrived at deductively. To show that the inferences derived are justified, the analyst must demonstrate that congruency between beliefs and decisions is genuine, not spurious, and that the decisional output would have been different under a dissimilar set of beliefs (George, 1979: 105–9).

The process-tracing approach requires more information than the congruence procedure with regard to how the actual policy was made. This approach is similar to the one used in historical narrative. Rather than relying on a deductive argument to contend that beliefs affect decisions, the process-tracing procedure seeks to establish the potentially broad influence that beliefs have on foreign policy by outlining their effect on the actor's receptivity to and assessment of incoming information regarding a particular problem, his definition of the problem, his identification and evaluation of alternatives, and his choice of policy and policy instruments (George, 1979: 113). In other words, this approach must also rely on extensive sources to depict the decision-maker's beliefs; but then, rather than by-passing what goes on inside the black-box, it tries to schematize the effect that beliefs have at different stages of the decision-making process.

Because there are not always good data available on information-processing, the analyst must on certain occasions resort to the congruence procedure. The quality of the data on decisions that led to different types of intervention in the

Caribbean and Latin America is mixed. In some cases it will not be difficult to outline the information-processing from the moment US foreign policy-makers concluded that a situation demanded their attention to the instance in which they actually began to implement a foreign policy; in other cases such data will not be as rich. Keeping in mind this variance in the quality of data, this study will rely on the process-tracing procedure whenever the information-processing can be represented, and on the congruence procedure in those instances in which only the beliefs and the final decisions can be described.

MEASURES OF STRATEGIC AND ECONOMIC INTERESTS

How leaders reason may or may not be related to specific interests. If relationships exist, it is critical to ascertain the form that they assume. It is quite common to argue that since the end of the nineteenth century, Washington has sought to protect the hegemonic status of the United States in the Americas (see Kurth, 1984: 4). This argument concurs with Morgenthau's proposition that a powerful actor will react to any attempt to undermine its power status in a region. But as designed, the argument is imprecise and, thus, difficult to apply to specific cases. Developments in Cuba in the 1960s and Chile in the early 1970s, for instance, threatened to alter the status quo. These threats, however, were not equal in intensity. The two countries differ in terms of their geographical proximity to the United States, their individual influence in their own region, and their military and economic strength and interaction with the United States. Differences in conditions, in other words, affect the extent to which a state can threaten another. From this it can be proposed that in order to evaluate the explanatory reach of the strategic-realist perspective when applied to US intervention, it is first necessary to design a way to differentiate between strategic values and their correspondence with threats.

Five dimensions are used to assess a country's strategic value to the United States. The potential ability of an international actor to undermine or strengthen the interests of the United States is the function of geographical distance, military and economic capability, strategic national resources, and control over maritime passages. Stated in propositional form, one could argue that the United States feels more threatened by countries that are close geographically and are powerful from both an economic and a military perspective than by faraway, weak countries (Hybel, 1986: 28). From this it can be inferred that the greater a country's geographic proximity to the United States and the greater its power, the greater its strategic value to the United States. However, in some instances, distant, weak actors can also be strategically valuable. The United States has for years attempted to ensure the adequate supply of strategic raw materials from faraway countries (Maull, 1984: 8). Of the twenty-four major non-fuel minerals consumed by the industrial nations, for instance, the United States is now substantially dependent on imports of twenty-one of them (Jordan and Kilmarx, 1979: 15; Cammarota, Jr, 1984: 30–2). Thus, it can be hypothesized that a country's strategic value to the United States is directly related also to the amount of strategic material (as defined by the US government) it provides to the United States. Finally, as most geopolitical analysts have long recognized, the strategic significance of the maritime passages to which a state has direct access affects such a state's strategic value to another state (Brodie, 1977: 74–118).

The relative relevance of the five factors identified to measure a state's strategic value to the United States is not evident a priori. Theoretically, it is feasible to posit several combinations. However, rather than developing a formula that can be applied systematically to the empirical cases but that can also distort the relative relevance of each dimension, each state's strategic value is measured using each dimension. This way it will be feasible to assess the potential relevance not only of each dimension but also of their aggregated value.

The criticism rendered at the beginning of this section against the methodology generally relied on by the strategic–realist perspective also applies, at least to a degree, to instrumental- and structural-Marxist perspectives. Analysts who rely on a Marxist approach do not always use well-defined concepts, and often test their arguments against cases in which a variety of other factors could have influenced the studied outcome.

As a first step in conducting a more systematic evaluation of the relevance of economic dimensions, it is necessary to differentiate between US economic interests abroad and the interests of US corporations investing abroad. This end can be achieved, in part, by accounting for imports from and exports to foreign states, and private direct investments in or net capital flows to foreign states. The differentiation between trade values and investment values does not facilitate, in and by itself, the task of ascertaining whether the instrumental- or structural-Marxist argument carries greater weight. It is not difficult to envision a situation in which there is a clear correspondence between the general economic interests of the United States and the economic interests of certain US corporations. To postulate a verdict one way or another, it will be necessary to have cases in which measurable variance between the two sets of values existed.

As they stand, the criteria just identified might still fail to eradicate the overlapping of the two arguments. Washington's interventionist behavior has been attributed in some instances to acts designed to protect its economic relationship not with particular states, which could possibly be insignificant, but with the adjacent states (Chomsky, 1972; Krasner, 1978). This argument is rooted in the assumption that one of Washington's central fears is that a state might consciously and overtly reject US economic domination, and that leaders of neighboring states might subsequently assimilate this idea. To address this type of argument, data on the status of the economic relationship between the United States and states adjacent to the intervened party will be considered. If Washington is driven by a commitment to ensure continued regional economic dependability, then it can be hypothesized that this commitment will be a function of the economic significance to the United States of a particular regional structure: the greater its economic significance to the United States, the greater Washington's commitment to act.

THE RATIONALE BEHIND THE SELECTION OF CASES

The United States and its Caribbean and Latin American counterparts are part of a unique subsystem. It is unique, first, in the sense that the United States, since at least the beginning of the twentieth century, has been the dominant force, willing to act when conditions did not satisfy its needs. Second, the United States has found in intervention an acceptable tool against revisionist regimes that burdened the stability of the subsystem. And finally, the absence of legitimate authority among many of the weaker states has often compelled the United States to intervene in an attempt to temper internal political turmoil.

The uniqueness of the subsystem to be investigated in this study bounds the types of propositions that can be derived. The empirical analysis does not focus on cases representing the universe of acts of intervention in the international system. Instead, it focuses on actions that took place within the subsystem defined by the relationships between the United States and Caribbean and Latin American states. Therefore, the propositions derived will be of a "confirmatory mode" only at the subsystem level, and of an "explanatory mode" at the international system level (see Hybel, 1986: 20).

With this qualification in mind, it is now possible to move to the discussion of the rationale behind the selection of the cases. The analysis of US intervention in the Caribbean Basin focuses on five cases:

1   US–Guatemala: 1944–1954
2   US–Cuba: 1953–1961
3   US–Dominican Republic: 1958–1965
4   US–Nicaragua: 1976–1983
5   US–Grenada: 1979–1983

The remaining two cases refer to US intervention in South America's southern cone. They are:

6   US–Peru: 1963–1975
7   US–Chile: 1964–1973

The Caribbean Basin cases are important for various reasons. First, each targeted state had a different military capability, and a different economic value to either the United States or its corporations investing in the region. Second, the military, diplomatic, and economic instruments used by the United States against these states varied significantly. Third, the United States did not always intervene with the intent of achieving the same political objectives. In some cases, it acted to replace unpopular allies with moderate governments; in other cases, to strengthen the power of moderate governments; and in a third set of cases, to overthrow regimes that were believed to be under communist influence. Fourth, different US administrations acted in more than one case, and in some instances, the same case was addressed by more than one administration. And finally, although the leaders of the various US administrations generally shared a common ideology, they did not always share the same beliefs.

The Chile and Peru cases are characterized by different factors. First, the goals sought by the US varied measurably from one target to the other: Washington sought to topple the Allende regime, but tried to induce the Velasco regime to adopt a more conciliatory posture toward the United States. Second, the instruments used to attain these goals were dissimilar in content and intensity. Third, Chile and Peru were led by different types of political regimes; the former was governed by a democratically elected socialist government, while the latter was ruled by a leftist military government placed in power following a military coup.

However, there were also many important similarities between the two countries. To begin with, the economies of Chile and Peru were both very dependent on the United States. The two countries traded heavily with, and received extensive financial loans and foreign aid from, the United States. Critical sectors in their economies were dominated by US investments. Moreover, their military forces had maintained for many years close links with the United States through the purchase of military weapons and the training of military personnel. In addition, both the Allende and Velasco regimes engaged in economic and social policies designed to diminish dependency on the United States. And, finally, although the identities of those occupying the White House changed, the critical decision-makers in both cases were members of Richard Nixon's administration.

CONCLUSION

This study, as already stated, hopes to demonstrate that US intervention in the Caribbean Basin and Latin America can best be explained by relying on a theory of reasoning and learning by analogy. But in the process of promoting an alternative way of analyzing US foreign policy, this study also hopes to build two intellectual bridges.

For years, students of foreign policy have been divided by an artificial, and too often counterproductive, boundary. Some students have sought to upgrade the intellectual status of foreign policy by trying to design "theories" that could address, on a systematic and comparative basis, questions pertinent to the foreign policy field. Others have adopted the position that theories of foreign policy are for the most part irrelevant, for they do not help the foreign policy-makers determine how to react to specific situations. Thus, these students seek to delineate the conditions that might facilitate or obstruct the construction and implementation of a specific policy.

The criticism rendered by the latter group is not entirely unjustified. As Alexander L. George notes, "The importance and difficulty of situational analysis in policymaking is perhaps not well enough understood by many academic scholars engaged in developing theories of international politics" (1980: 243). For too many years, analysts who have claimed that there was an intrinsic need to develop theories of foreign policy have been enamored with one theoretical criterion – parsimony. In the process, they have forgotten that parsimony is too often achieved by sacrificing a significantly more critical criterion – relevance. On the other side of the coin, foreign policy experts do not always keep in mind that the responses of policy-makers and their staffs to specific situations are based on what they consider to be the appropriate theories (George, 1980: 239). The quality of their decisions, thus, will be directly related to the methodology they, or more likely their advisors, relied on to derive them. Thus, analyses designed to expand our theoretical understanding of foreign policy-making are essential to the work of "policy analysts" as well as "theory builders." And this brings us to the second bridge.

The state of the literature on US intervention in the Caribbean and Latin America is rich in content but weak in methodology. The analyst exploring this literature is immediately struck by both the abundance of data and the conflicting arguments. Such an analyst, however, is likely to be startled by the absence of any serious attempt to design an analytical method that would facilitate the task of systematically comparing the data. The systematic comparison of data does not guarantee the creation of a viable theory of US intervention. A theoretical argument will ensue only if the analyst has an idea of what are the possible factors that could contribute to the formulation of a reliable explanation. Such knowledge already exists insofar as it is expressed by the content of the existing literature. But to derive general explanations from such knowledge, it is critical that the analyst rely on rigorous methodological criteria.

4

Guatemala: The Designing of the Future

The United States has made an example of Guatemala in order to demonstrate the ability of the United States to respond to and contain the forces of liberation in Latin America. Guatemala was the first Latin American country after the Second World War that seriously threatened the hegemony of the United States and drove it to intervene openly.
Jonas Bodenheimer, *Guatemala: Plan Piloto Para Continente*

THE RESTATEMENT OF AN OLD QUESTION

The question, "Why did the United States intervene in Guatemala?," is not a mute issue. Although a myriad of articles and books have been published since the day Castillo Armas's US–financed forces entered Guatemala, significant disagreements still remain.

The debate is bounded by four factors: US strategic interests; US economic power; communism; and the private interests of US multinational corporations. The most parsimonious argument is proposed by Cole Blasier, who contends that strategic interests in the US with respect to rivalry with the Soviet Union shaped Washington's decision to intervene in Guatemala (1985: 212, 236). Richard Immerman expands on Blasier's argument by proposing that the United States intervened to halt the spread of the international communist conspiracy, which was posing a direct threat to the interests of the United States in Latin America (1982: 82). Walter LaFeber adds a twist to Immerman's argument. Like Immerman, LaFeber acknowledges that the United States intervened to halt the transformation of Guatemala into a communist state. However, the danger of Guatemalan communism, he argues, was not that it would increase the power of the Soviet Union in Latin America, but that it would challenge the authority of the United States to dictate economic policies in Latin America, thus undermining US economic power (LaFeber, 1983:

119–20). Finally, José Aybar (1978) proposes that ideology was not the reason for intervention; rather, the United States intervened to protect US multinational corporations from the threat of expropriation in Guatemala. He acknowledges that to the degree that there was a threat to the interests of US multinational corporations, there was also a threat to US core interests (p. 294).[1]

In this chapter it is contended that these theories are not competing arguments. It is proposed that in order to capture how the various arguments are related, it is essential to delineate how the Guatemalan problem was defined by US leaders at different times between 1944 and 1954. Based on this breakdown of the decision-making process, it is postulated that ultimately the United States intervened to stop the perceived spread of communism in Guatemala. But it is also noted that the leaders in Washington defined the problem as a communist threat based on inferences derived from actions taken in different instances by the Guatemalan government – specifically, the establishment of political connections with a few communist labor leaders, the filling of some of its offices with individuals affiliated with the communist party, and the implementation of radical agricultural and economic reforms. Moreover, it is argued that these inferences had their roots in lessons derived from past experiences, particularly developments in China prior to and following the communist party's ascencion to power.

The definition of Guatemala as a communist threat did not dictate the choice of covert paramilitary intervention. The leaders of the United States concluded that this would be the most appropriate instrument to eliminate the threat after deciding that diplomatic measures and economic sanctions alone would not be sufficient, that an earlier covert action had been successful in overthrowing the Mossadegh regime in Iran, and that the government of Guatemala could not rely on the support of its military to defend itself.

The analysis of the competing arguments lies not in the discovery of new information but in the decomposition of the general question – why did the US intervene in Guatemala? – into more precise queries, and on the examination of the data in a chronological sequence in order to capture the change in US reactions to Guatemala's policies. The general question can be readdressed by asking:

1   Why did the Truman administration wait more than six years after Guatemala's revolutionary government had come to power to impose economic sanctions?
2   Why did the Truman administration impose economic sanctions against Guatemala gradually rather than swiftly?
3   Why did the Truman administration wait more than seven years after Guatemala's revolutionary government had come to power, to consider toppling the regime by means of covert paramilitary invasion? And why did it subsequently decide against using such means?
4   Why did the Eisenhower administration agree with the previous administration that the government of Guatemala should not remain in power?
5   Why did the Eisenhower administration decide to topple the government of

Guatemala by means of a covert paramilitary invasion organized and financed by the CIA?

Answers to these five queries will help develop a better understanding of how the decision-makers in Washington structured the Guatemalan problem and selected their policy means accordingly. Moreover, an analysis of the way the Guatemalan problem was structured and tackled will serve as the focus for comparison of subsequent instances of US economic, diplomatic, and military intervention in the Caribbean and Latin America.

THE DEFINITION OF THE PROBLEM AND THE SELECTION OF ALTERNATIVES

Two of Washington's central problems since the end of the Second World War have been, first, how to respond to the internal political threats posed to regimes friendly to the United States; and second, how to react to political groups that succeed in overthrowing such regimes. These problems are not endemic to any one region, but they have a distinct quality in the Caribbean Basin and Latin America.

Guatemala was the first country in the Caribbean Basin to confront the United States with these problems as the Second World War was drawing to a close. This Central American country had been ruled since 1931 by one man – José Ubico. Afraid of labor unions and the general concept of democracy, Ubico, supported by wealthy indigenous landowners, the army, and foreign corporations, controlled Guatemala's political, economic, and social systems (Immerman, 1982: 39). His control eventually began to deteriorate. In fact, US Secretary of State Cordell Hull had known since 1940 that Ubico's repressive policies were beginning to incite resentment among his fellow countrymen (1982: 36).[2]

Under ordinary circumstances one might have expected the United States to take certain measures to assuage Guatemala's battling parties. But the first half of the 1940s was not a normal time for the North American actor. With its attention focused on the wars in Europe and Asia, Washington was forced to limit its involvement in the internal affairs of states in the Caribbean Basin. But Washington's aloofness with respect to Guatemala's domestic problems changed to concerns following the demise of the Ubico regime and the termination of the Second World War.

Convinced that his tenure as Guatemala's leader was severely threatened by the downfall of two other Latin American leaders, Carlos Arroyo del Rio of Ecuador and Maximiliano Hernandez Martinez of El Salvador, Ubico decided in May 1944 to suspend constitutional guarantees, arrest opponents, and place his own supporters in high university positions (Blasier, 1985: 29). These measures were not left unanswered. Ubico's opponents called for a general strike and demanded that a democratic structure emphasizing the universal rights of all individuals be instituted. The strike, which occurred between June

23 and June 30, achieved part of its intended objective: on July 1, 1944, Jorge Ubico resigned.

It is not in the nature of dictatorial rulers to remove themselves from the political arena without first attempting to retain some modicum of control over the new political regime. Ubico, cognizant that he could no longer remain in power as Guatemala's chief executive, sought to institutionalize his political vision by designating the creators of the government that was to succeed him. The intent of his design was first felt on July 4, when General Federico Ponce, one of the members selected by Ubico to create a new government, was elected Guatemala's provisional president. Ponce's election did not reflect the will of the people nor of their representatives; members of the Guatemalan National Assembly, under the threat of death, were ordered to elect Ponce over the more popular candidate, Dr Ramón Calderón. The Roosevelt administration, convinced that US interests would be best protected by supporting the status quo, was quick to recognize the newly installed government. On July 8, the US ambassador, Boaz Long, under orders from Secretary of State Cordell Hull, extended full official recognition.

Given General Ponce's pledge to hold early free elections, Washington's initial expectation was that the general's tenure as provisional president would be short-lived. By September of 1944, however, the US Embassy in Guatemala began to wonder whether Ponce would willingly proceed with elections (Immerman, 1982: 42).[3] The concern was well founded; between July and September, General Ponce's new regime began to institute repressive measures that entailed primarily the arrest, and sometimes assassination, of opposition leaders (1982: 41–2).

Once again, the Guatemalan government's actions did not remain unchallenged. For the second time in less than four months, the leaders of Guatemala's middle class and labor unions called for a general strike. The strike was followed by a military *coup d'état*. The United States, realizing that Ponce's days as Guatemala's leader were numbered, helped undermine his ability to fight the coup by refusing to supply bombs for his air force. Washington's assessment was correct. Unwilling to fight under these circumstances, General Ponce resigned on October 21 and was replaced by the Provisional Junta.

Although the US Embassy had provided extensive assistance to promoting a settlement between Guatemala's two battling parties, Washington did not feel entirely comfortable with the new regime. Facing the task of deciding whether to recognize the new provisional government or delay recognition until more information about its leaders was gathered, the State Department found itself slightly divided. The majority of the officials who were engaged in determining what status to confer on Guatemala's new government favored extending full recognition. A small minority, however, led by Assistant Secretary of State Spruille Braden, was concerned about reports that José Arévalo, the most popular member of the Provisional Junta, might have communist connections. Braden recommended that formal recognition be postponed. His advice was not followed, and on November 7, 1944, Washington recognized the Provisional Junta (Immerman, 1982: 86).

In the meantime, political events in Guatemala were moving at a rapid pace. The most obvious development was the election of Arévalo on December 19 to become Guatemala's new president. His election was followed by three signficant occurrences. In February 1945, Guatemala's Provisional Junta nationalized Guatemala Airways – a company controlled by Alfred Denby, a US citizen, and Pan American Airways. This action raised some additional concern among certain US officials, particularly Nelson Rockefeller, who at that time was serving as assistant secretary of state for American republic affairs (Immerman, 1982: 87; Schlesinger and Kinzer, 1983: 32–3).[4] The second important political development was the adoption of a new constitution on March 13. Three factors made this constitution newsworthy. To begin with, it forbade military members to become political candidates. Moreover, the constitution limited presidents to a six-year, non-renewable term. And finally, via thirty-four separate articles, it guaranteed individual rights, including the rights of workers (Schlesinger and Kinzer, 1983: 32–3). The import of these three factors, particularly the last one, would become evident in later years.

The third major event occurred on March 15, 1945, when President-elect Juan José Arévalo took the oath of office. In retrospect, it can be said that Arévalo's inaugural speech signaled quite clearly his intention to free his country from Washington's control. Committed to addressing Guatemala's political and economic ills, Arévalo emphasized the need to promote the concept of freedom and to breathe a socialist spirit into the system (Aybar, 1978: 115). Arévalo's program of "spiritual socialism" was predicated on the assumption that government must create the conditions that will facilitate man's psychological development and moral liberation. The advocacy of these two goals had a pragmatic undertone. The new president was convinced that in order for Guatemala to break its patterns of dependency on the United States it had to reconstruct its overall economy; and he believed that this goal could be attained only by increasing man's economic and spiritual achievements (LaFeber, 1983: 112). Arévalo's program disavowed both Marxism and individualistic capitalism. By viewing man as an economic animal and by prescribing class struggle, he noted, Marxism sought to undermine man's spiritual foundation. On the other hand, individualistic capitalism, with its emphasis on the individual over collective interests, tended to weaken the structure of society (Immerman, 1982: 48).

Washington began to be seriously concerned about the political nature of Guatemala's new government from the moment Arévalo was sworn in as president. Certain State Department officials feared that Arévalo's ideas on the psychology of development and the concept of social integration, developed while he was teaching at the University of Tucumán in Argentina, might be camouflaging a communist heart. Most of them, however, hoped that under Arévalo's leadership Guatemala's political system would veer toward the center. For those sharing this hope, Arévalo was perceived as a "man who does believe sincerely in the United States" (quoted in Immerman, 1982: 86). This perception would not live long.

Arévalo's first actions as Guatemala's new leader did not win him many friends in Washington. Committed to the eradication of dictatorships in Latin

America, he decided that his country could no longer continue to maintain formal diplomatic relationships with oppressive regimes. As a result, he severed diplomatic relations with the Somoza and Trujillo regimes, in Nicaragua and the Dominican Republic respectively. The depth of Arévalo's commitment to the elimination of dictatorial regimes was further reflected by his decision in 1946 to begin to support the Caribbean Legion, a radical Latin American organization created for the purpose of ousting dictatorships, by force if necessary (Schlesinger and Kinzer, 1983: 38).

Arévalo's actions in the domestic environment also began to gather momentum. In late 1945 his government created two new institutions, the Institute for Development of Production and the Bank of Guatemala, for the purpose of diversifying Guatemala's economic base. A year later, in October 1946, the Congress enacted the Social Security Law. This bill guaranteed Guatemalan workers the right to safe working conditions, injury compensation, maternity benefits, basic education, and health care. The enactment of the Social Security Law brought to light the intensive division that was taking root in Arévalo's government. Defense Minister Jacobo Arbenz sided with the president, but Guatemala's upper class and Javier Araña, the chief of the armed forces, both argued that the new law would institute unaffordable expenses and generate social and economic chaos (Schlesinger and Kinzer, 1983: 38–9).

The passage of the Social Security Law was followed by the enactment, in February 1947, of the Labor Code Law. This law, modeled after the US Wagner Act, guaranteed urban workers the right to organize unions, bargain collectively, and strike. It also regulated child and female labor, and provided fixed minimum pay scales. Once again, the law was opposed by Araña and Guatemala's upper class (Immerman, 1982: 76). The most striking characteristic of the passage of the Labor Code Law was not that it was designed to transform the status of Guatemala's working class but that it followed in the wake of a major labor strike against United Fruit.

In 1946, Guatemalan workers had gone on strike against United Fruit to demand salary increases, time-and-a-half overtime pay, and ten vacation days annually. They also demanded that unions be treated like industrial or commercial concerns. United Fruit's reaction was to fire the strikers. This action led the Arévalo government to threaten United Fruit with partial nationalization if it did not rehire the discharged workers. United Fruit responded by acquiescing to the government's demand that the strikers be rehired, but not to the strikers' other claims. Needless to say, United Fruit did not welcome the passage of the Labor Code Law in early 1947. Fearing that the law would severely undermine its economic standing in Guatemala, United Fruit turned to Washington for help. The Truman administration, although concerned that the actions of the regime posed a threat to the interests of US companies, did not act immediately (Immerman, 1982: 88–92).[5]

President Arévalo was aware that some of his actions might trouble the US government. In February 1947 he invited President Truman to visit Guatemala, hoping that top-level discussions would help eliminate some of the tension that was developing in their relationship. Arévalo's assessment was not entirely incorrect. President Truman's first move to signal Washington's displeasure with Guatemala's domestic policies was to reject the invitation, claiming, in a letter to the US ambassador, Edwin Jackson Kyle, that he was too busy (Immerman, 1982: 55, 57; Schlesinger and Kinzer, 1983: 40). This was not an isolated act. In March and May of the same year, the State Department informed the Guatemalan government that it viewed the Labor Code Law as an attempt to discriminate in practice against US companies. Displeasure with Arévalo's policies was far from universal. Not only was there some disagreement among officials at the State Department, but Ambassador Kyle went so far as to suggest that Washington support the newly approved Labor Code Law, arguing that it did not target foreign interests in Guatemala and that it would enhance workers' morale and help improve Guatemala's economy (Mecham, 1961: 281). In sum, although the Arévalo regime was behaving in ways that did not meet the approval of everybody in Washington, there was not a sense among members of the Truman administration that these actions warranted a dramatic change in US foreign policy.

The groundwork for another problem in US–Guatemalan relations was laid in September 1947. Since 1945 the United States and Latin American countries had been considering the formulation of a treaty of reciprocal assistance. Finally, on August 15, 1947, American delegations, headed by their respective foreign ministers, met at Quitandinha, Brazil, in the state of Rio de Janeiro. The conference was convened primarily to formalize, by means of a mutual assistance pact, the obligation of continental solidarity in the face of aggression (Blasier, 1985: 189). For the United States, the signing of and adherence to the Rio Treaty was to become a critical test of a Latin American government's commitment to the inter-American system. On September 2, 1947, the Rio Treaty was signed by all the participating representatives, with one major exception: Guatemala. Arévalo's unwillingness to sign the treaty had nothing to do with the treaty's general political implications. He was willing to accept the treaty so long as a provision stating "Guatemala refuses to recognize British sovereignty over Belize," was accepted by the other signatories. The provision was rejected by the majority, and Arévalo withdrew ratification of the treaty (Immerman, 1982: 93–4). It was a decision that would haunt Guatemala years later.

Relations between Guatemala and the United States reached an impasse throughout the remainder of 1947 and early 1948. The most distinct activity during this time was the constant pressure exerted by United Fruit on the State Department to intervene on its behalf. The United States's reluctance to augment its pressure on Arévalo was in part due to conflicting opinions as to the latter's intention. On May 6, 1948, the first secretary of the US Embassy in Guatemala, Milton K. Wells, sent a secret memorandum to Secretary of State George Marshall arguing that the growing labor movement in Guatemala clearly demonstrated startling communist growth between 1944 and 1947. He added that the Soviet Union had designed a master plan which called for mass strikes with the intent of producing domestic chaos and, as a result, a communist coup (Immerman, 1982: 89).[6] Although it was not evident that the communists were planning a major coup, it was quite clear that some of Guatemala's most influential labor leaders had communist affiliations. For instance, the Confederacion de Trabajadores de Guatemala, led by Víctor Manuel Gutierrez, was a member of the Confederacion de Trabajadores de America Latina, a pro-communist and pro-Soviet labor organization led by a Mexican citizen, Vicente Lombardo Toledano (Blasier, 1985: 57). Within six days of Wells's secret memorandum, however, the CIA released a policy statement contending that the cause of political instability in the region was the contest between democracies and dictatorships. The communists, argued the CIA, "are not a major factor" (CIA, 1948; Immerman, 1982: 96).

US indecisiveness over the nature of the Arévalo regime came to an end in the summer of 1948. In a policy statement dated August 17, the State Department argued that Arévalo's policies encouraged chaotic conditions and that the communists were exploiting these conditions to weaken Guatemala's neighbors and hence dominate the entire hemisphere (Immerman, 1982: 50, 95).[7] This assessment did not fall on deaf ears. Two months after its release, President Truman appointed Richard Patterson as the new US ambassador to Guatemala. Ambassador Patterson's two most important qualifications for the new post were his strong anticommunist sentiments and his ability to deal effectively with the communists as ambassador to Yugoslavia.

It did not take long for Patterson to pressure the Arévalo regime to change its ways. One of his first major acts was to persuade President Truman not to visit Guatemala. Patterson's rationale was that a visit would imply goodwill and support for the policies of the Guatemalan government, while a refusal to visit would evince the opposite. Patterson's most potent action, however, did not come about until the first month of 1949. At a dinner hosted in his honor, Patterson told Arévalo that his job as US ambassador was to protect and promote US interests in Guatemala; and he warned that the relations between both countries would suffer if the host country did not stop persecuting US interests (Immerman, 1982: 99).

Although the Guatemalan presidential elections were not scheduled until November of 1950, by the beginning of 1949 the principal presidential contenders were already campaigning energetically. The two principal candidates were Francisco Javier Araña and Jacobo Arbenz. On July 18, 1949, this political rivalry came to a dramatic end. Araña, who at one point had been impeached for treason by the National Assembly, was assassinated. His death provided Arbenz's adversaries with the excuse to mount a *coup d'état*. The intent behind the coup was to restore the conservative forces to power. But after two days of intensive fighting, the government was able to blunt the attempt. Guatemala's organized labor was the decisive factor in the struggle to keep the Arévalo government in power (Blasier, 1985: 57).

Arévalo's domestic adversity was immediately exploited by the United States. A few days after the coup attempt had run its course, Ambassador Patterson once again accused the Arévalo regime of persecuting, prosecuting, and unmercifully abusing US interests in Guatemala for two years. Patterson did not restrict his actions to diplomatic accusations and political threats. In March 1950 he went so far as to demand that Arévalo dismiss seventeen government officials, all of whom were denounced as being communists. Failure to respond in the requested manner, added Patterson, would lead the United States to deny any further aid. Patterson's demand drew an immediate reaction from the Guatemalan government. On March 24, 1950, Foreign Minister Ismael Gonzalez-Arévalo flew to Washington to demand Patterson's removal. On the following day, Secretary of State Dean Acheson recalled Patterson (Immerman, 1982: 96).

Throughout the remainder of 1950, US officials dealing with Guatemala focused their attention on the possible directions the president-to-be would follow. It was agreed that under Arévalo the communists had obtained influential positions in the government, political parties, and labor organizations. There was, however, some disagreement as to what would happen to the communists once the new president was elected. Based on the expectation that Jacobo Arbenz, the former defense minister, would be elected, two conflicting predictions were made. Edward Miller, the assistant secretary of state for inter-American affairs, and Milton Wells, the first secretary at the US Embassy in Guatemala, argued that Arbenz's military background would help him understand the political realities better than Arévalo did, and that as a consequence he would change Guatemala's pro-Soviet course and veer toward the center. State Department official Tapley Bennett and Ambassador Richard Patterson did not share Miller's and Wells's optimism. They both argued that the Soviet Union had approved Arbenz's candidacy, that all communist-controlled organizations in Guatemala supported him, and that Arbenz was committed to following a communist policy (Immerman, 1982: 106–7).[8] It was in his criticism of Arbenz's role as Guatemala's future president that Bennett made reference to Arévalo's decision not to sign the Rio Treaty. Such an act, he noted, was "a pertinent example of the influence on government thinking by Communist-minded individuals (quoted in Immerman, 1982: 84).

Miller's and Wells's assessment prevailed. It was this view that convinced the State Department in 1950 to continue its existing assistance programs and to set aside as a reserve contingency $850,000 that had been allotted for future use in Guatemala (Immerman, 1982: 110). The same view continued to dominate until early in 1951. In February of that same year, the Truman administration nominated its new ambassador to Guatemala. Convinced that Arbenz, under the guidance of an experienced but moderate and cautious diplomatic hand, could be persuaded to soften the radical policies undertaken by Arévalo, the United States appointed Rudolf Schonfeld. A month after Schonfeld's appointment, Jacobo Arbenz was sworn in as Guatemala's new president. In his inaugural speech the new head of state declared his commitment to using the government to transform his country's predominantly feudal system into a modern, capitalist economy (p. 63).

Washington was not impressed by Arbenz's speech. The deputy assistant secretary of state for inter-American affairs, Thomas Mann, who led the US delegation to Arbenz's presidential inauguration, returned from the trip convinced that the new Guatemalan leaders was indeed a Marxist. Although this view was still not predominant in the halls of the State Department, it began to gain momentum. Tapley Bennett wrote in a special report two-and-a-half months after Arbenz's inauguration that the new president had appointed communists to several strategic government positions, permitted an increase in the volume of communist propaganda, supported labor leaders with communist affiliations, and conducted a foreign policy parallel to that of the Soviet Union (1982: 108, 119–20).[9]

In and of themselves, Mann's and Bennett's assessments might not have been critically important. Both individuals had been inclined for some time to suspect that Guatemala's new leader was soft on communism. The person who seems to have played a critical role in tilting a majority at the State Department toward reconsideration of their perception of Arbenz was Edward Miller, the assistant secretary of state. Miller had argued just prior to Arbenz's election that as president, the former defense minister would move his government toward the center. Impressed by Bennett's analysis and concerned about Arbenz's policies, Miller began to reconsider his own views and requested that the report from the senior advisor to the president be circulated (1982: 108).

It was not long before the State Department decided that it was time to begin exerting pressure on the Arbenz regime. In June of 1951, Thomas Mann recommended the refusal of any type of aid to Guatemala and the slow cut-off of trade between the two countries. His justification for reducing trade quietly was that the policy violated the Non-Intervention Agreement reached by the United States and Latin American countries, and US failure to adhere to it would lead the Latin American countries to side with Guatemala (LaFeber, 1983: 114–15).[10] All aid and technical assistance to Guatemala were cut off immediately; trade between the two countries, however, was reduced very slowly, as planned. In 1951 the United States imported 87.6 percent of all Guatemala's exports; in 1952, 83.3 percent; in 1953, 76.6 percent; and in 1954, 70.8 percent (Aybar, 1978: 320–1). The drop in Guatemala's exports to the United States had no immediate negative effects on the former's economy; in fact, it may have helped reduce Guatemala's dependency on the Colossus of the North. Just as the United States was reducing its imports from Guatemala, Western Europe was increasing them at a comparable rate. The pattern repeated itself with respect to Guatemala's imports from the United States and Western Europe.

In the meantime, Arbenz began to implement his economic vision. Between July 1951 and June 1952 the new regime adopted three economic measures, all of which had immediate repercussions on the financial well-being of United Fruit. On July 2, 1951, Arbenz announced plans to build a new port at Santo Tomás and a highway that would run parallel to the railroad tracks owned by International Railway of Central America, a company controlled by United Fruit. The rationale behind the plan to construct the new highway was that United Fruit charged excessive freight rates, thus undermining Guatemala's developmental attempts. The new highway, it was hoped, would pose a direct challenge to United Fruit's control of Guatemala's transportation network (Blasier, 1985: 153).

In January 1952, the Arbenz government delivered its second major blow to United Fruit. In June of 1949, after several storms had damaged many of the company's farms, the general manager in Guatemala laid off 1,500 employees. An additional 3,000 workers were discharged in September 1951, after a hurricane hit one of United Fruit's plantations on the Pacific Coast. The

Guatemalan government pressured United Fruit to rehire the workers, but the company did not give in. Finally, at the beginning of 1952, Guatemala's Labor Court ordered United Fruit to rehire the dismissed workers and pay them $650,000 in back wages. Failure to comply, added the court, would lead to the confiscation of property. United Fruit eventually relented (Immerman, 1982: 77–8).

Guatemala's third major economic assault was not launched directly against United Fruit, but United Fruit was the company that experienced the greatest effect. On June 17, 1952, Guatemala's National Assembly passed its most radical agrarian reform bill ever. The objective of the law was to develop Guatemala's agricultural sector in order to help subsidize industrial development. This objective was to be achieved by dividing and distributing idle land exceeding 223 acres. This land, in turn, would be redistributed among as many peasants as possible (Aybar, 1978: 171–2; Immerman, 1982: 64–5).

In light of Guatemala's latest economic policies, a few comments are in order regarding Washington's earlier decision. First, the decision to undermine Guatemala's economy was made well before the Arbenz regime's Agrarian Reform Bill was approved by Guatemala's National Assembly. This bill was the result of careful governmental studies begun in 1950, during the Arévalo presidency. During Arévalo's tenure, however, although a number of proposals were under public consideration, no consensus existed on the scope of agrarian reform (Aybar, 1978: 167). It is quite difficult, therefore, to conclude that the State Department's decision to rely on economic means to undermine Arbenz's power was the result of its commitment to protect the private interests of US companies in Guatemala. In 1951, as in 1950, the State Department could not determine which of the competing proposals would prevail, and thus was uncertain about how an agrarian reform bill, if in fact enacted, would affect US private interests. On the other hand, Arbenz's unwillingness to put some distance between his government and communist labor leaders could lead to the conclusion that it was the continued presence of these individuals that finally convinced the State Department that it had to toughen its policies toward Guatemala.

The second point of significance is the State Department's decision to reduce gradually its trade with Guatemala. Although the focus of Washington's concern in 1951 was the alleged spread of communism through the ranks of Guatemala's political system, US leaders were well aware that the boundaries structuring the problem encompassed additional concerns. A possible reaction to the belief that communism was rapidly dominating Guatemala's political agenda would have been to clamp down on trade. In view of Guatemala's economic dependency on the United States, a trade cut-off would have devastated Guatemala's economy. But this action would have also incited the wrath of Latin American states. As explained by Thomas Mann, if it became obvious that the United States was violating the Non-Intervention Agreement, to which it was a party, "other Latin American parties would rally to the support of Guatemala" (quoted in LaFeber, 1983: 115).

Just as economic and political changes were gaining momentum in Guatemala, the decision-making process in Washington was also experiencing critical modifications. In the summer of 1952, Nicaragua's leader, Anastasio Somoza, met with President Truman, Secretary of State Dean Acheson, Under-Secretary of State Robert Lavett, and Truman's military aide, General Harry Vaughn. At the meeting, Somoza proposed a plan that called for the united efforts of Guatemala's neighbors to bring down the Arbenz regime. Truman agreed to explore the viability of the plan and sent one of his aides to Central America to analyze the situation. Following his aide's return, Truman received a report describing Somoza's plan as workable. The president approved the report and sent it for further consideration directly to the CIA director, General Walter Bedell Smith. Preparations began, but in time the plan was aborted by Truman.

Two questions come to mind at this juncture. First, why did President Truman contemplate resorting to covert paramilitary means to overthrow the Arbenz regime, to the point that he ordered that a plan be designed? And second, why did he order that the plan not be executed?

President Truman ordered the drafting of the contingency plan just a few months after Guatemala's domestic policies had acquired a measurably more radical tone. During the previous year the Arbenz regime had announced the creation of a major highway, hoping that it would help undermine United Fruit's monopoly over transportation; its Labor Court had ordered the same US company to rehire its dismissed workers; and, most importantly, it has succeeded in persuading the National Assembly to pass a radical agrarian reform bill. But these developments do not address the issue of why Truman might have initially favored a covert paramilitary invasion over another interventionist policy, such as direct military intervention. The attraction of a covert form of intervention can be attributed to the same desire that led the Truman administration to reduce trade with and economic aid to Guatemala gradually – to avert criticism from Latin American states. This need was not unimportant. Washington was quite concerned that Latin American opposition to US policy in Guatemala could be costly in that it could reduce hemispheric unity in fighting the Cold War.

The decision to order the design of a covert paramilitary plan is not followed automatically by the decision to implement it. Although Truman found Somoza's plan attractive, he seems to have concluded that the Guatemalan military was still supporting President Arbenz and that a defeat could not only embarrass the United States if its complicity were discovered, but could also, in the process, enhance the revolutionary government's support within Guatemala (Immerman, 1982: 119–21).[11]

A few months after Truman aborted the covert paramilitary plan, General Dwight D. Eisenhower became the new president of the United States. His administration wasted little time in signaling its displeasure with developments in Guatemala. On March 25, 1953, the State Department evinced its unwillingness to allow further endangerment to US private interests by submitting a formal complaint to the Arbenz government concerning the nationalization of property owned by United Fruit. At the same time, however, President Eisenhower seems to have concluded that the Guatemalan situation called for a properly structured, dynamic plan. With this goal in mind, he asked State Department official C. D. Jackson to study how the United States could best control Soviet expansion on Central America. Jackson, in turn, solicited the assistance of Adolf Berle.

Within a short period of time, Berle submitted a report containing three alternatives. One – direct US armed intervention against Guatemala – was perceived as being too risky in that it would raise immediate hemispheric complications for the United States. A second alternative – covert intervention led by Nicaragua, with support from Honduras, Costas Rica, and El Salvador – could not be properly assessed for lack of adequate information. As a result, Berle proposed that the United States form a coalition with the countries surrounding Guatemala, with the intent of mounting intense political and economic pressure. Berle estimated that Arbenz would not be able to resist the pressure for more than eighteen months and would be forced either to expel the communists or to resign (Immerman, 1982: 130–1).[12] Jackson and Berle reported the analysis and plan to Thomas Mann, who was still serving at the State Department.

Although aware that his policies were not being well received throughout Central America and in the United States, Arbenz was not willing, at least initially, to compromise. On April 1 his foreign minister, Raul Osegueda, informed the Secretary General of the United Nations of a plan being designed with the intent of destroying "by force the constitutional government" of Guatemala (Aybar, 1978: 224). Ambassador Richard Patterson, former under-secretary of state for inter-American affairs Spruille Braden, Foreign Minister of the Dominican Republic Rafael Leonidas Trujillo, and the president of United Fruit, were the principal figures accused of promoting the invasion. Arbenz followed this action by withdrawing Guatemala from the Organization of Central American States. He charged that the Central American press had joined in a defamatory campaign against Guatemala and that El Salvador was responsible for initiating a secret conspiracy to isolate Guatemala politically and economically (1978: 225). These actions paralleled Arbenz's continued commitment to implementation of Guatemala's newly approved agrarian reform bill. By May 1953, his government had redistributed 740,000 acres.

These acts further aggravated Eisenhower's attitude toward Arbenz. More specifically, they helped dispel any remaining doubts over the wisdom of removing the Guatemalan government. Additional reinforcement concerning the nature of Guatemala's governmental structure came from Eisenhower's brother, Milton, who reported after his July 1953 trip to South America that Guatemala had "succumbed to communist infiltration" (quoted in Immerman, 1982: 133).[13] These developments seem to have convinced Eisenhower that the imposition of diplomatic pressure and economic sanctions were not enough; to topple the Arbenz regime he would have to rely on covert means.

But why was the decision to rely on covert means made in mid-summer 1953?[14] On June 25, 1953, Kermit Roosevelt, a CIA operative, was authorized by President Eisenhower to try to overthrow Prime Minister Mohammed Mossadegh of Iran. The scheme had a simple foundation, objective, and structure. After concluding that under Mossadegh's leadership Iran might be lost to the communists, the CIA and the State Department decided that the best way to alter the outcome was by his overthrow. Since this objective could not be attained by overt means, and since the ability of the United States to engage effectively a large number of its own personnel in a covert activity was limited, it was resolved that the Iranian armed forces and population would have to be mobilized. To engage the participation of these two groups, the CIA sought to foment domestic turmoil in Iran. The means it employed were quite simple. On the one hand, the Eisenhower administration resorted to anti-Mossadegh propaganda, while on the other hand it heightened Iran's economic woes by refusing to make up for the revenues lost from the nationalization of the Anglo-Iranian Oil Company. The intent behind these actions was to create discontent and fear of a communist takeover among the significant majority of Iran's armed forces and population. Thus, when Mossadegh's power was finally challenged, few would be willing to come to his aid (Roosevelt, 1979). Operation Ajax was a major success and provided the framework for the Guatemalan operation (Immerman, 1982: 135).

One of the first steps taken by the Eisenhower administration to ensure that the covert plan would succeed in fulfilling its objective was to appoint a new ambassador to Guatemala. In August 1953, John Peurifoy, who while serving as US ambassador to Greece had been instrumental, with the CIA, in excluding communists from participation in the government, was appointed Guatemala's new ambassador. Peurifoy's central task was to help coordinate the paramilitary attack on the Arbenz government (Immerman, 1982: 136–7; Blasier, 1985: 174). He wasted no time in voicing his dissatisfaction with the Guatemalan regime; on his arrival at his new post on October 29, Peurifoy warned the Guatemalan government that the United States did not approve of the decision to implement agrarian reforms. As already demonstrated by developments in China, added Peurifoy, putting into effect agrarian reforms was a manifestation of a country's commitment to communism (Immerman, 1982: 138).[16]

Arbenz was not blind to the new developments. Aware that his policies were alienating not only other Central American governments and some US private investors, particularly those associated with United Fruit, but also the US government, Arbenz took two steps to abate the threat. On February 9, 1954, he proposed the appointment of a neutral commission to arbitrate Guatemala's dispute with United Fruit. Arbenz was hoping that his proposal would convince Washington that he was a reasonable individual who had no intention of turning Guatemala into a communist state. His commitment to negotiation with Washington, however, did not prevent him from considering that his regime might still have to cope with a paramilitary invasion. Earlier in the year, Arbenz had obtained a letter from a Guatemalan national, Castillo Armas, to Nicaragua's leader, Anastasio Somoza. In the letter, Armas informed Somoza that the United States had finally agreed to permit him to resort to military means to overthrow the Arbenz regime (Blasier, 1985: 161). Aspiring to protect his regime against this eventuality, Arbenz asked the United States to lift its arms embargo against Guatemala (Immerman, 1982: 155).

Arbenz's new awareness came too late; Washington had no intention of deviating from its commitment to purge Guatemala's government. At the Inter-American Conference held in Caracas, Venezuela, throughout March of 1954, Secretary of State John Foster Dulles introduced a proposal titled

"Declaration of Solidarity for the Preservation of the Political Integrity of the American States against International Communism." In an attempt to minimize Latin American opposition, Dulles had to compromise and only emphasized the need to take appropriate action in accordance with existing treaties against any attempt to establish communist domination, without ever mentioning Guatemala or the possibility of military intervention. After extensive debate, the resolution was approved (Immerman, 1982: 144–9).

Pressure by the United States on the Arbenz regime continued to mount. On April 20, 1954, the Eisenhower administration rejected an offer by the Guatemalan government to indemnify United Fruit for the sum of $1,185,000; instead, the US government submitted a bill for $15,854,849. Less than two weeks later, on May 1, the CIA began to broadcast an announcement that Castillo Armas would soon return to liberate Guatemala.

In mid-May the Arbenz regime unwittingly afforded the United States a major political leverage. The US Embassy in Guatemala disclosed the arrival of a ship transporting some 2,000 tons of Czechoslovakian small arms and light artillery pieces. The purchase of these weapons was the direct result of the unwillingness by the Eisenhower administration to lift the arms embargo. In response to this embargo, and concerned that his military would not be able to withstand a CIA-backed paramilitary invasion, Arbenz solicited assistance from the Soviet Union.

The arrival of the weapons generated a political uproar. Congressional leaders called the weapons shipment "part of the master plan of World Communism," and asserted that the weapons "were to be used to sabotage the Panama Canal" (Immerman, 1982: 156). The Eisenhower administration did not allow the opportunity to escape.[17] At the end of May, the president authorized the CIA to put into effect its plan to overthrow Arbenz.

Convinced that an invasion organized and financed by the United States was forthcoming, Arbenz offered on June 1 to visit Eisenhower in Washington to see whether differences between the two leaders could be discussed. As part of his negotiating strategy, Arbenz once again proposed that a third party be chosen to act as an arbitrator in the dispute between the government and United Fruit. Believing that Arbenz was acting from desperation rather than from a fundamental change in policy goals, Ambassador Peurifoy declined the meeting and emphasized, during a conversation with Guatemala's foreign minister, that US concern was not the fate of United Fruit but of communism in Guatemala. The latter point was stressed again by Secretary of State Dulles on June 8 and 10, when he stated that even if the United Fruit matter were settled, the presence of communism in Guatemala would still remain a problem (Immerman, 1982: 165).[18]

On June 18, 1954, Castillo Armas and a small number of paramilitary forces entered Guatemala. The intent of the invasion was not to engage Arbenz's forces in an open battle but to convey the message that Castillo Armas had the backing of the United States and that it would be futile for the Arbenz regime to mount a major defense. The strategy, as in the Iranian case, was based on the assumption that the armed forces and the population would desert Arbenz – not out of anticommunist fervor, but out of fear of a massive military operation

(Immerman, 1982: 166–7). US estimates were correct. Arbenz resigned on June 27, and ten days later Castillo Armas was elected Guatemala's new provisional president.

Was there any particular event at the end of May 1954 that persuaded President Eisenhower it was finally time to approve the CIA's plan to overthrow Arbenz? By then it had become quite evident that economic sanctions and diplomatic pressure were not having the intended effect. Moreover, it had been known for some time that Arbenz's support within Guatemala's military was not as strong as it had been estimated to be a few years earlier, when Truman had contemplated launching a covert paramilitary invasion against the same regime (1982: 162). What finally persuaded Eisenhower that the time was right to launch the invasion, however, seems to have been the discovery that Arbenz was purchasing weapons from the Soviet bloc, and the criticism that surged from the US Congress following this discovery.

REASONING AND LEARNING BY ANALOGY

In chapter 2 it was proposed that the context of a problem was the function of the structure defining the relationship between a set of concepts. It was also noted that the way in which policy-makers structure a problem can be delineated as a form of analogy, i.e., analogy as the pairing of similar relations. Some of the conclusions arrived at in the previous section can be defined in an analogical form.

In early 1945, the foreign policy-makers in Washington were still unplagued by doubts. Happy that Ubico and Ponce had been replaced without the inducement of political chaos, Washington was willing to adopt a "wait and see" posture toward Guatemala's new government. The Truman administration reasoned that Guatemala's new leaders, although committed to instituting reforms, would recognize the tremendous obstacles they had to overcome and as a consequence would moderate their aspirations. This reasoning process can be delineated as follows:

Accept newly formed government in target state dominated by political leaders who are committed to political, social, and economic reforms, and express willingness to help so long as they avoid radical reforms.	Political leaders in newly formed government in target state recognize constraints under which they must work, welcome offer, and express commitment to moderate reforms.
Reject newly formed government in target state dominated by political leaders who are committed to political, economic, and social reforms, and voice opposition to extending any help.	Political leaders in newly formed government in target state criticize response and consider seeking help elsewhere to implement radical reforms.

The first pair is joined by ":" and the whole relation by "::".

But while the US government was initially willing to give Guatemala's new government the benefit of the doubt, it also developed a sense of how to determine when to begin to challenge the new government's policies. Washington inferred that there was a relationship between the extent to which Guatemala's government associated with communists and implemented economic and agricultural reforms, and the degree to which it was controlled by communists. Arévalo's association with communist labor leaders and his decision to carry out moderate economic and agricultural reforms meant in Washington that his government was under communist *influence*. Arbenz's government, on the other hand, was believed to be *dominated* by communists, largely because Arbenz had placed in government a few individuals with communist affiliation, had relied on the political support of communist labor leaders, and had implemented radical economic and agricultural reforms. These relationships can be captured as follows:

Government in target state affiliates with communist labor leaders and implements some moderate economic and agricultural reforms.	Government in target state is : influenced by :: communists.	Government in target state affiliates with communist labor leaders and implements radical economic and agricultural reforms.	Some governmental + positions in target state are held by communists.	Government in target : state is dominated by communists.

It cannot be ascertained with complete certainty which historical event or set of historical events influenced the derivation of the above analogical structure. But the evidence suggests quite strongly that US decision-makers were particularly affected by developments in China prior to and after Mao Zedong's communist party became the country's sole political force. In a book titled *The Yenan Way* published in 1951, Eudocio Racines describes the way the Chinese communists allied themselves with middle-class politicians and ambitious army officers and worked themselves into positions of power within local communities. The results of these developments were the Labor Code, agrarian reform, and strict censorship. Racines's book had an extraordinary effect on policymakers in Washington. For instance, Raymond Leddy, the Department of State officer responsible for Central American and Panamanian affairs, testified, after Arbenz's fall, before the House of Representatives hearing on communist aggression that the "Guatemalan Way" proved to be an improvement for the communists over the "Yenan Way" in the sense that they had used the latter to infer ways in which the situation in Central America could be dealt with more effectively (Immerman, 1982: 104–5).

Leddy's definition of the Guatemalan problem was not unique. As Immerman writes, "after the publication of Racines' book, policymakers began to apply his analysis to conditions in Guatemala" (1982: 105). But the most obvious reference to the China case was made by Ambassador John Peurifoy. The day of his arrival at his new post in October 1953, the US ambassador informed the foreign minister of the host country that the parallels between the

Guatemalan problem and the Chinese problem had portentous implications. He stated, "agrarian reform has been instituted in China . . . and today China is a communist country" (quoted in Immerman, 1982: 138).[19]

The last relationship in the analogical format does not capture fully the international constraints faced by the Truman administration as it was contemplating acting against Guatemala. Aware that the radical cut in economic trade and an overt military intervention would not be well received by Latin American states, the Truman administration chose to decrease gradually US trade with Guatemala and to rely on covert paramilitary means. This decision can be structured as follows:

| High threat in international environment free of constraints. | : | Impose extensive economic sanctions and diplomatic pressure on, and be prepared to rely on overt military intervention against, government in target state. | :: | High threat in international environment bounded by constraints. | : | Impose economic sanctions and diplomatic pressure gradually on, and be prepared to rely on covert paramiliary intervention against, government in target state. |

Three additional developments need to be accounted for in order to structure fully the Guatemalan problem. In 1952, President Truman ordered the CIA to prepare a covert paramilitary plan in order to topple the Arbenz regime. This order was eventually rescinded by the same president. Originally, the design of the covert operation had been based on the assumption that Arbenz would have difficulty persuading the military to help him retaliate against any attempt to bring down the regime. This perception, however, seems to have changed to the belief that Arbenz's support in the Guatemalan military was extensive. The effect on the willingness to rely on covert paramilitary means by the change in perception can be delineated as follows:

| Government in target state dominated by communists is supported by military. | : | Delay the launching of covert paramilitary intervention against government of target state. | :: | Government in target state dominated by communists is not supported by military. | : | Order the launching of covert military intervention against government in target state. |

With the advent of the Eisenhower administration came the belief that economic sanctions and diplomatic pressures would not be enough to topple the Arbenz regime. This was precisely the conclusion arrived at by John Peurifoy after his first meeting with President Arbenz. In his report about the meeting to the Department of State, the US ambassador wrote: "In view of the inadequacy of normal diplomatic procedures in dealing with the situation, there appears no alternative to our taking steps which would tend to make more difficult continuation of [Arbenz's] regime in Guatemala" (quoted in Immerman, 1982: 138).[20] The removal of Prime Minister Mossadegh of Iran seems to have persuaded President Eisenhower that the United States could also rely on covert means to bring down the Guatemalan government. Stated analogically:

Economic sanctions and diplomatic pressure imposed on government in target state dominated by communists failed to undermine their power.	:	Covert intervention used to overthrow another government dominated by communists achieved objective.	:	Order the preparation of plan for covert paramilitary intervention against government in target state dominated by communists.	::
Economic sanctions and diplomatic pressure imposed on government in target state dominated by communists failed to undermine their power.	:	Covert intervention used to overthrow another government dominated by communists failed to achieve objective.	:	Do not order the preparation of plan for covert paramilitary intervention against government in target state dominated by communists.	

Having been ordered to draw plans to overthrow the Arbenz regime, the CIA planners modeled their Guatemalan strategy on many of the ideas that they had relied on in designing the overthrow of Iran's prime minister in 1953. It could be suggested, therefore, that:

Covert paramilitary intervention plan drawn to overthrow another government dominated by communists achieved objective.	:	Draw new covert paramilitary intervention plan to overthrow government in target state dominated by communists according to ideas that had structured earlier plan.	::	Covert paramilitary intervention plan drawn to overthrow another government dominated by communists failed to achieve objective.	:	Do not draw new paramilitary intervention plan to overthrow government in target state dominated by communists according to ideas that had structured earlier plan.

Eisenhower's decision to approve the implementation of the CIA plan can be seen as the result of several interrelated factors. First, there was the recognition that the imposition of economic sanctions and diplomatic pressure had not succeeded in altering the behavior of the Arbenz regime. Second, it was believed that the Guatemalan military seemed less committed to defending the Arbenz regime. And finally, the US Congress had almost unanimously criticized the purchase of Czechoslovakian weapons by the Arbenz regime and demanded that steps be taken against it. Thus:

Economic sanctions and diplomatic pressure imposed on government in target state dominated by communists failed to undermine their power.	:	Government in target state dominated by communists is not fully supported by the military.	:	International criticism of government in target state dominated by communists intensifies.	:	Order the launching of covert paramilitary intervention against government in target state dominated by communists.

The second set of relations is not included in the last analogical structure, in large measure because the reversal of any one single factor could have persuaded the Eisenhower administration not to order the launching of the covert invasion. In other words, the Eisenhower administration could have easily decided to delay the invasion if it had concluded that the diplomatic and economic measures imposed on Guatemala were undermining the power of the Arbenz regime, if it had inferred that the Arbenz regime could still rely on the support of the Guatemalan military, or if it had believed that the majority in the US Congress was not intensely disturbed by the Arbenz regime's purchase of Soviet bloc weapons.

LESSONS FOR THE FUTURE

This chapter's central intent has been to delineate the structure of Washington's reasoning process as it attempted to diagnose the problems posed by Guatemala's policies and to find solutions to them. By focusing on changes in the foreign policy of the United States toward Guatemala between 1944 and 1954, and on the causes of those changes, it was feasible to show that the decisions to intervene and to intervene by stages, beginning with diplomatic and economic pressure and ending with covert paramilitary action, cannot be explained by attributing causes to one factor. In other words, changes in US responses cannot be ascribed just to Washington's commitment to avert communist domination of Guatemala, or just to protecting the economic interests of US companies investing in the country, or just to ensuring that the overall strategic and economic interests of the United States would not be undermined. These concerns did not exist independently of one another. For the United States, communist domination of a central American government was not an acceptable scenario. But to conclude that such a situation was about to become a reality, the foreign policy-makers in Washington had to identify conditions that would justify such an inference. The presence of communists in a few governmental posts, the willingness to maintain close relationships with communist labor leaders, and the implementation of major agricultural and economic reforms were interpreted to mean that Guatemala was becoming a state dominated by communists. Moreover, defining the problem as a communist threat entailed imposing on the data analogical structures derived from an earlier case: China. A similar process was relied on to select policy instruments. In an attempt to decide which instruments would be the most effective, US foreign policy-makers derived inferences of results by structuring relationships between policies and consequences analogically. This process was particularly evident when the CIA concluded that the general plan designed to topple the Mossadegh regime in Iran could be used to bring down the Arbenz regime in Guatemala.

The imposition of an artificial beginning on the analysis of empirical cases limits somewhat the student's ability to determine which past events influenced the leaders in Washington to conceptualize the analogical structures in the context it is believed they did. But, at the same time, this strategy makes it feasible to gauge the relevance of the identified analogical structures to the remaining cases. More specifically, this strategy will help assess in what ways, and the extent to which, both the Eisenhower and Kennedy administrations relied on the same set of analogical pairs to define the problems posed by Fidel Castro's ascension to power in Cuba in 1959, and to decide how to address those problems. Via this strategy it will also be possible to ascertain whether the situation in Cuba was defined as a communist problem and, if it was, whether the definition could be attributed to the political affiliation of key labor and governmental leaders and to the types of agricultural and economic reforms implemented by the new regime. In addition, it will be feasible to establish whether any lessons were inferred from the initial failure to overthrow the Arbenz regime by relying solely on diplomatic and economic instruments. And finally, at a more general level, reference to the analogical structures delineated in this case will facilitate the task of determining whether changes in the way problems are defined and instruments are selected in subsequent cases, if such changes do occur, can be imputed to lessons inferred from the Guatemalan experience.

5

Cuba: The Application of the Wrong Lesson?

We cannot learn that we have made a mistake unless we can make a mistake, and our mistake is almost always in the form of an anology.
                                Robert Oppenheimer, "Analogy in Science"

THE RESTATEMENT OF AN OLD QUESTION

The question, "Why did the United States intervene in Cuba?," poses the same dilemma encountered in the analysis of the Guatemalan case. The debate has been delineated, at least partially, by the same four concepts identified in the previous chapter: US strategic interests, US economic power, communism, and the private interests of US multinational corporations. However, because the policy against the Castro regime ended in failure, numerous analysts have attempted also to explain why President Kennedy agreed to a policy which, in retrospect, was unlikely to bring about the intended result. Four ideas have bounded these explanations: (i) Kennedy's fear of alienating Latin American allies; (ii) Kennedy's concern that the American public would accuse him of being soft on communism; (iii) Kennedy's cognitive process; and (iv) the structure of the Kennedy administration's core decision-making body.

One student of US foreign policy who has argued that the United States intervened in Cuba in order to protect its strategic interests in the Caribbean is Henry Wriston. Wriston maintains that Fidel Castro, after rejecting US domination, needed a substitute sponsor in order to make his new political system viable. As the Soviets were eager to gain a base of operations in the Western hemisphere, adds Wriston, a congruence of interests between Cuba and the Soviet Union emerged. This new alliance strained the Washington–Havana relationship and led the United States to conclude that Castro's displacement by force was the only way to prevent Soviet domination of Cuba (Wriston, 1967: 32).

Wriston's thesis, although explicit in its account of why the Kennedy administration decided to intervene, cannot explain why it engaged so few military resources in its attempt to overthrow the Castro regime when Cuba had long been considered one of the most important allies of the United States in the Caribbean region. Hans Morgenthau seems to have an answer. It is his contention that the decision by the Kennedy administration to overthrow Castro and to rely on clandestine means to do so was the result of trying to advance two competing values. On the one hand, Kennedy was cognizant that US strategic interests in the Caribbean would be severely threatened if the Soviet Union succeeded in establishing military bases in Cuba. On the other hand, Kennedy feared that if the United States intervened overtly, Latin American states would accuse him of violating the hemispheric principle of non-intervention. Kennedy's mistake, concludes Morgenthau, was his failure to rank the interests of the United States rationally. "Had the United States approached the problem of intervening in Cuba in rational fashion, it would have asked itself which was more important: to succeed in the intervention or to prevent a temporary loss of prestige among the uncommitted nations" (1969: 123). For Morgenthau, as for Wriston, the answer was clear: the threat posed to US strategic interests was the critical value, and therefore Kennedy should have intervened with sufficient force to successfully deny Soviet access to Latin America.

Cole Blasier's analysis of these events, although similar to that of both Wriston and Morgenthau, introduces another component. According to Blasier, both Eisenhower and Kennedy believed that the United States had to intervene in Cuba (1976: 203, 208). Blasier also seems to agree with Morgenthau that Kennedy feared the reaction of Latin American states when he notes that the president emphasized the need to ensure that the "full military might of the United States would not be directed against Castro" (p. 202). But for Blasier, the critical component was Kennedy's fear of the American public's reaction if he did not approve the CIA plan. Unwillingness by Kennedy to support an operation approved by the previous administration would have led to the disclosure of the plan by Cuban exiles, and subsequently to the accusation by the American press and public that Kennedy had refused to challenge communist control of Cuba (p. 201).

Certain scholars, particularly those who have advocated a revisionist interpretation of the Cuban episode of 1961, maintain that economic considerations were paramount in the decision by the United States to try to topple the Castro regime. Maurice Zietlin and Robert Scheer assert that Castro's revolutionary practice not only threatened the Cuban oligarchy but also jeopardized US private interests that traditionally had benefited from the status quo. "As the revolutionary government persisted in its evident determination to put through a program that seemed in Cuba's interest, but that would harm the immediate interests of US private investors, relations between the two countries deteriorated" (Zietlin and Scheer, 1963: 126). The violent US reaction to the Cuban revolution, note Zietlin and Scheer, was triggered by the enactment and implementation of the agrarian reform. The United States "became actively concerned with Cuban affairs, when the Agrarian Reform Law was proclaimed and US companies lodged strong complaints with the State Department" (1963: 98). This argument, add Zietlin and Scheer, is further strengthened by an examination of who were the principal Cuban leaders of the counterrevolution supported by the Central Intelligence Agency. The high command of the counterrevolution consisted of individuals who represented conservative forces committed to the return of expropriated properties to their original owners. "The one grouping that proclaimed its intention to retain the nationalization of the utilities and agricultural properties was completely excluded from the attempted putsch" (p. 206).

The effect of Castro's policies on US companies investing in Cuba may not have been Washington's only concern; a broader structural interest might have also been at stake. As one aide in the Kennedy administration put it: "We've been needling President Frondizi in Argentina and Nehru in India every chance we get to let private enterprise have a bigger role in the economy. What do you think they'd say if we undercut them by overthrowing the principle in Cuba?" (Zietlin and Scheer, 1963: 132). Morris Morley's analysis of the US decision to intervene focuses primarily on the structural necessities of the capitalist system to which Zietlin and Scheer alluded. Morley argues that under certain conditions the US government enjoys a degree of autonomy from the capitalist class. The most important condition that permits "discretionary power" to the state occurs when the capitalist class does not act as a unitary actor. This condition existed during the Cuban episode. At the outset of the Cuban revolution, the capitalist class was fragmented. This fragmentation was the result of variance in the economic stakes of US companies, particularly in terms of the relative importance of investments, and also variance in the perceptions regarding the likelihood of reaching a reasonable accommodation with the Castro regime. For example, the Cuban Electric Company, which was one of the firms most severely affected by Castro's nationalization policy, advocated, at least initially, the enforcement by Washington of a policy measurably more severe than that supported by the sugar and plantation owners (Morley, 1983: 72–3).

Morley asserts as a general principle that the "imperial-state," i.e., the United States, would become involved in a conflict "only when the enterprise cannot gain an objective which coincides with the desires of the imperial-state" (1983: 71). The revolt against Batista and the subsequent attempts by the Castro regime to remake the Cuban economy, society, and class structure, were the central factors shaping US responses. Confronted by a fragmented and vacillating capitalist class, the US government took the initiative and defined the policy goals. Thus, "the imperial-state began to interpret specific conflicts between the Castro regime and individual capitalists as reflections of this larger process of state transformation and, in the absence of a coherent American capitalist-class opposition, assumed the initiative by instrumentalizing the corporations in a determined effort to destabilize the Castro regime" (p. 75).

As an illustration of the US government's role in mobilizing a particular fraction of the capitalist class to accommodate to its overall strategy, Morley cites the case of the oil refineries. The confrontation between the Castro regime and the oil companies did not originate from pressures within the capitalist class itself but was promoted by the US government. The action, according to Morley, was not in response to immediate economic conflicts such as nationalization of US-owned properties but was part of a larger executive branch effort to insert itself into, and dictate the outcome of, the class struggle in Cuba (1983: 80).

Additionally, the contention that the United States sought to overthrow the Castro regime solely for the purpose of averting the spread of communism throughout Latin America has not received wide support. Walter LaFeber attributes some degree of relevance to this factor when he notes that one of Allan Dulles's central concerns was that most of the states of Central America were confronted with "the insidious penetration of Cuban communism" (1983: 150). Moreover, as explained by Dean Rusk, many of the Latin American states were having problems responding to the powerful offensive launched by the Sino-Soviet bloc because they already had been penetrated heavily by the communists and Castro-type movements. For the most part, however, this line of argument – that the United States was trying to avert the spread of communism – is combined with the argument that the spread of communism, spearheaded by Cuba, would be harmful to US strategic and economic interests.

One of the truly interesting aspects of the Cuban case is that it has served as a laboratory for those seeking to analyse why US decision-makers activated a plan which was bound to fail. These analysts are not trying to unveil why the United States concluded that the Castro regime posed a threat; their central interest is in understanding why the Kennedy administration made such a terrible policy choice. Lucien Vandenbroucke proposes that the most appropriate method for understanding the Kennedy administration's decision to accept the CIA recommendation to implement "Operation Zapata" is to focus initially on the channels through which, and the context in which, the decision was made. The central players, notes Vandenbroucke, had different standings, values, goals, and power resources. The CIA, because of its resources and goals, had a significant advantage over other players and thus was in a much better position to push for its plan. The plan, however, was not approved as designed, but in fact was replaced by a slightly modified version. This development leads Vandenbroucke to conclude that the choice of the plan was the result of bargaining, with the CIA controlling the way the game was played (1984: 486).

But Vandenbroucke is not entirely satisfied by the depth of his answer. He notes that the governmental politics model cannot explain why the decision-makers persisted in their refusal to assess information that would question the viability of the proposed plan. To fill the gap, he resorts to cognitive theory – specifically, the notion that perceptual distortions are a function of an individual's tendency to disregard information that might challenge an existing assumption. By using this perspective, adds Vandenbroucke, the operatives' dismissal of unfavorable reports on Castro's strength becomes more understandable; the CIA's planners could always find offsetting reports, stressing Castro's weakness, to bolster their beliefs (1984: 488). Compounding these perceptual distortions is the recurrent pattern of wishful thinking. This thought process of wishful thinking was encouraged by Kennedy's very successful past (p. 489; see also Etheredge, 1985: 15–16).

Irving Janis, uncomfortable with relying solely on cognitive theory when dealing with decisions reached by a group, proposes an alternative explanation. He begins by contending that an explanation of the decision to intervene in Cuba must be able to address five major miscalculations on the part of Washington. The miscalculations were that: (i) the United States could easily disassociate itself from the action against Cuba; (ii) Cuba was weak and ineffective; (iii) the members of the invading party would fight even without US contingent support; (iv) the invasion would trigger popular support; and (v) if the invasion failed, insurgent activities would be initiated which would eventually undermine the Castro regime. To address these miscalculations, Janis proposes that it is necessary to assess the dynamics of the group making the decision.

The actions by the decision-making group, notes Janis, reflected the conditions commonly identified with "groupthink." Or, as he put it,

> The failure of Kennedy's inner circle to detect any of the false assumptions behind the Bay of Pigs invasion plan can be at least partially accounted for by the group's tendency to seek concurrence at the expense of seeking information, critical appraisal, and debate. The concurrence-seeking tendency was manifested by shared illusions and other symptoms, all of which helped the members to maintain a sense of group solidarity. Most crucial were the symptoms that contributed to complacent overconfidence in the face of vague uncertainties and explicit warnings that should have alerted the members to the risks to the clandestine military operation – an operation so ill-conceived that among literate people all over the world the name of the invasion site has become the very symbol of perfect failure. (1976: 92–3)

Groupthink was particularly evident on the part of Kennedy's immediate advisors, who resisted any substantive discussion of the plan they proposed by the CIA. Although it is true that Kennedy's advisors were being coaxed by the CIA to reach a quick decision, it was largely because of overconfidence about US superiority *vis-à-vis* Cuba that they foreclosed the detection of warning signals and stressed the selection of compatible information. This illusion of invulnerability prevented the recognition of the disparity in size between Castro's armed forces and the 1,400 strong brigade that would invade Cuba. Furthermore, misgivings about the merits of the CIA plan, held by individuals such as Arthur Schlesinger, either were self-censored or were suppressed by Dean Rusk or Robert Kennedy.

The review of the literature focusing on the Cuban case demonstrates that these analyses are significantly more complex than the studies of the Guatemalan case in at least two respects. To begin with, several analysts recognize that both Eisenhower and Kennedy might have had more than one goal in mind when they decided to intervene against Cuba. Decision-makers, after all, whether in government or in the private world, are rarely driven by the need to fulfill just one objective. Thus, it might not make sense to propose that the

United States acted to protect its security interests rather than the economic well-being of private corporations investing in Cuba. The two interests, in fact, were threatened by Castro's revolution.

Second, critical to the study of the Cuban case has been the attempt by analysts to unravel not only why the United States intervened but also why it intervened via a covertly paramilitary invasion. Needless to say, this interest arose because, in retrospect, the decision was so "irrational" that it was necessary to uncover the rationale behind the choice. Be that as it may, such an analysis adds a dimension that was not present in the Guatemalan case.

It has been said that the "Bay of Pigs affair is perhaps *the* classic case of presumptions unexamined. The affair was marked from first to last by an absence of explicitness even about 'maybes,' let alone about 'if/thens' and 'truths'" (Neustadt and May, 1986: 140). This criticism is, in some measure, justified. The Kennedy administration committed a number of errors that could have been averted had its members been willing to examine developments in Cuba more closely. At the same time, however, studies that fault Kennedy and his associates for the Bay of Pigs fiasco tend to adopt a "narrow focus" approach – that is, they concentrate their investigation on the decision-making process immediately preceding Kennedy's decision to accept the CIA plan, without attempting to discern how such a process might have been structured by decisions arrived at earlier.

Problems in the international arena have a dynamic constitution. As problems develop, decision-makers may or may not admit their presence. If their existence is acknowledged, decision-makers will attempt to define them based on existing information and past experiences. The way international problems are defined, however does not always remain constant. Changes may be the result of new information, of changes in the nature of the problems and/or of changes in leadership. In any case, changes in the definition of problems may prompt decision-makers to alter their objectives, foreign policy instruments, or both.

To bring to light possible relationships between different factors and changes in ways the Cuban problem was defined, one can refer to the five questions addressed in the Guatemalan case. These questions, however, must be preceded by a set of questions that capture the switch in US foreign policy toward Cuba as the Batista regime was experiencing its political demise. Specifically, it is important to ascertain:

1 Why did the Eisenhower administration wait only a few months after Fidel Castro had returned from exile, to begin distancing itself gradually from the Batista regime?
2 Why did the Eisenhower administration wait almost two years after Fidel Castro had returned from exile, to pressure Batista to resign?
3 Why did the Eisenhower administration wait only two days after the new Cuban government was formed, to grant it diplomatic recognition?

The first two questions posed in the Guatemalan case (see chapter 4) asked why the Truman administration waited more than six years to impose economic sanctions on Guatemala and then decided to implement them gradually, rather than swiftly. For the Cuban case, these two questions can be readdressed as follows:

4   Why did the Eisenhower administration wait a little over a year after Cuba's economic revolution had begun, to impose economic sanctions?
5   Why did the Eisenhower administration impose economic sanctions against Cuba swiftly rather than gradually?

The subsequent questions asked in the previous case referred to why the Truman and Eisenhower administrations concluded that Arbenz could not remain as Guatemala's president and why they decided that a covert paramilitary invasion might be the most effective means to topple him. For the Cuban case, these questions could be posed in the following way:

6   Why did President Eisenhower wait a little less than a year after Cuba's economic revolution had begun to order the CIA to draw up a plan to topple the Castro regime?
7   Why did President Kennedy agree with President Eisenhower that the Castro regime could not remain in power?
8   Why did President Kennedy decide to topple the Castro regime by means of a covert paramilitary invasion organized and financed by the CIA?

President Kennedy, however, went a step beyond approving the CIA plan; he, in fact, altered it. It is suggested that it was his decision to change the nature of the plan at the last minute which led to the defeat of the invading forces. For this reason, it is essential to pose one more question:

9   Why did President Kennedy order that Cuba not be struck prior to the landing of the invading forces with as many planes as originally planned and, why did he subsequently cancel the granting of air cover to the invaders?

Answers to these questions serve four purposes. First, they help analysts understand how the decision-makers in Washington structured the Cuban problem at different stages and selected the policy instruments to resolve it. Second, they assist in delineating the general structure of the Cuban scenario, which in turn can be compared to the general structure of the Guatemalan scenario. From this comparison it is feasible to theorize, in a somewhat tentative form, the context in which, and the extent to which, policies in the Cuban case were influenced by the Guatemalan experience. And finally, answers to these questions serve as the focus for the comparison of subsequent cases of political, economic, and military intervention by the United States in the Caribbean and Latin America.

THE DEFINITION OF THE PROBLEM AND THE
SELECTION OF AN ALTERNATIVE

During the first half of the twentieth century, Cuba and the United States had become so intertwined that the Spanish Caribbean island was often referred to as the 51st state of the United States (Starr, 1987: 10). At the beginning of the 1950s, there were no indications that in a short time the relationship would change radically. On March 7, 1952, about a year after Jacob Arbenz had been elected president in Guatemala, the Truman administration signed a major military assistance pact with Cuba. These two events were closely interconnected. Developments in Guatemala had convinced the Truman administration that the Arbenz government could, in the long run, pose a direct threat to US interests in the Caribbean Basin. These interests could be protected, in part, by undermining the ability of the Arbenz regime to govern and by strengthening the military capability of Guatemala's neighbors, including Cuba (Bonachea and San Martin, 1974: 198; Blasier, 1985: 21).

Three days after the agreement was signed, Cuba's president, Carlos Prio Socarras, was overthrown in a bloodless *coup d'état* led by the chief of Cuba's armed forces, General Fulgencio Batista. Batista's justification for preempting the presidential elections scheduled for July of that same year was that President Prio had not been able to maintain peace and order, and that it was doubtful whether a newly elected government would be more successful (Bonsal, 1971: 10; Bonachea and San Martin, 1974: 1).

The Truman administration, concerned that Batista might not be able to hold his new position, waited more than two weeks, until March 27, to recognize the new regime. But once it became evident that no effective resistance to the coup would ensue, Washington extended diplomatic recognition to the new government. In the meantime, Batista had taken some exceptional steps to endear himself to the Truman administration. Cognizant that his own political survival was in part the function of his position on the issue that was dominating the international arena – the Cold War – one of Batista's first foreign policies as Cuba's new leader was to break diplomatic relations with the Soviet Union. In addition, Batista gave private assurances to Washington that US interests in Cuba would be respected (Bonsal, 1971: 11–12; Benjamin, 1989).[1]

The change in government in Cuba in 1952 did not alter Washington's perception of, or attitude toward, the way the Caribbean and Latin American states were ruled. As stated by Milton Eisenhower, the brother of the president who would eventually authorize the invasion of Guatemala, leaders in Washington "unquestionably had become preoccupied with the maintenance of military strength among all nations that would oppose imperialistic Communism, and our overriding purpose in this regard may have made us less critical in our judgments than we might otherwise have been" (Eisenhower, 1963: 257).

The US commitment to the solidification of Batista's domestic political power remained strong and stable until mid-1957. During this period, approximately 70 percent of Cuba's imports came from, and about 66 percent of its exports went to, the United States. US participation in Cuba's telephone and electric services exceeded 90 percent, in public railways service reached 50 percent, and in raw sugar production reached roughly 40 percent. In addition, the Eisenhower administration conferred on the Batista regime $12 million in military assistance and helped train Cuban military forces.

The relationship between the two states reached an all-time high in February 1955. The Guatemalan experience had convinced the Eisenhower administration that US hemispheric dominance could not be taken for granted. Thus, shortly after Arbenz's overthrow, Eisenhower sent Vice President Richard Nixon on a tour designed to shore up US support in the hemisphere. Nixon visited Mexico, Central American republics, and the Caribbean, including Cuba. Upon his return, Vice President Nixon reported that affairs in both Cuba and Guatemala were fine, and that the United States should promote more private investments and more trade in the area. Although not all these governments had been erected on democratic foundations, he added, the United States should accept them as they were, while at the same time recommending that they slowly become more democratic (LaFeber, 1983: 127).[2]

As the United States and Batista were strengthening their diplomatic and economic ties, Cuba's political arena was experiencing a subtle, yet deeply rooted, structural transformation. The major spark of discontent with Cuba's new political regime first flashed on July 26, 1953. On that date, two attacks were launched simultaneously against the Moncada and Bayamo barracks. The leader of the rebel forces, a young Cuban lawyer named Fidel Castro, hoped to incite a major coup in order to overthrow Batista and reinstate a government under the precepts of Cuba's 1940 constitution. Although the attack failed to incite the coup and instead resulted in Castro's capture and imprisonment, discontent with Batista's regime continued to grow throughout Cuba.

In May 1955, Batista released Castro from prison as part of a general amnesty program. Shortly thereafter, Castro went into exile in Mexico to raise funds in order to organize a new revolutionary movement. He returned to Cuba secretly, with men, weapons, and money, on December 2, 1956.

From the moment Castro and his forces landed in Cuba, almost everything imaginable went wrong, to the extent that his forces were at the brink of total destruction.[3] By the middle of January of the following year, however, the rebel forces had gained enough strength to organize a successful attack against a small military post named La Plata. The military value of the attack, as explained by Ernesto Guevara, one of the leaders of the Cuban revolution, was insignificant; instead its import must be viewed from a psychological perspective. The defeat of Batista's soldiers at the La Plata military post helped erase some of the antagonism and differences that had existed between the urban people and the peasants. The city people, who comprised the central group of the guerrilla forces, realized that to continue with the struggle they needed the support of the peasants, support which had to be secured by providing them something they desired greatly – land. The peasants, on the other hand, learned that regardless of how badly the army hurt them, the guerrillas were there to stay and would be willing to provide protection to those who sought it. Castro's forces repeated their success a few months later, on May 27, when they launched a major attack against a well-armed and fairly well-situated garrison at Uvers (Bonachea and Valdez, 1969: 51–2).

In the meantime, decision-makers in Washington were slowly beginning to question the rationale for maintaining a close relationship with Batista. The US Congress, dominated since the 1954 elections by the Democrats, began to pressure the US State Department to become less identified with Batista. This pressure created a small dilemma for the State Department – what to do with its ambassador to Cuba, Arthur Gardner.

By 1957, Ambassador Gardner had managed to acquire the reputation of being not only a committed representative of US private investments in Cuba but, more disturbingly, a strong supporter of the Batista regime and a close friend of its leader. This image bothered the State Department greatly, for it feared that keeping Gardner at his post would convey the impression that the United States supported President Batista (Matthews, 1961: 67–9; Bonsal, 1971: 17). To alter this image, the Eisenhower administration decided in the summer of 1957 to replace Gardner with E. T. Smith.

The appointment of the new US ambassador almost coincided with the release of a major "manifesto" by Castro's revolutionary group. There were two major parts to the July 12, 1957, manifesto. On the political side, Castro proposed the establishment of a democratic government selected via free and impartial elections and backed by a constitution; on the economic side, he called for land grants to tenant farmers working fewer than 170 acres, and indemnification for owners (Bonachea and San Martin, 1974: 144–5). At the same time, Castro sought to widen the distance between Batista and the Eisenhower administration. Between July 1957 and March 1958, the rebel leader made a point of bringing to the attention of the US Congress the fact that US weapons were being used by the Batista regime to fight domestic opposition. This action, noted Castro, challenged US restrictions on supplying such weapons to Batista, restrictions which dictated that they be used only to fight against foreign aggression (1974: 199). The initial reaction by the State Department was to warn the Cuban government that the continued use of US-supplied arms to fight Cuban nationals could result in the suspension of arms sales to Cuba (Blasier, 1971: 46).

During this period, Castro's economic plans for Cuba experienced an interesting twist. The rebel leader was convinced that in order to convert Cuba into an economically independent actor, the state, as one of its first moves, would have to regain control over the power and telephone companies dominated by foreign investors. At the end of 1957, he promised to implement this policy as soon as his struggle against Batista came to a victorious end. Apparently cognizant that his statement might arouse the animosity of the US government and of foreign investors, Castro announced in February 1958 that he had "no plans for the expropriation or nationalization of foreign investments [in Cuba]" (quoted in Blasier, 1971: 45).

By this time an important debate was beginning to gain momentum among mid-level US officials. The central issue dividing some of these decision-makers was how to respond to Cuba's ensuing crisis. In January 1958,

Ambassador Smith publicly noted that the United States would not be able to do business with Castro. The ambassador's strategy was to convince Batista's other opponents not to support Castro. Without their support, argued the ambassador, Castro would never be able to gain power (Blasier, 1978: 48). Smith, however, was also aware that Washington was beginning to have serious doubts about being closely identified with dictatorial regimes. Convinced that US interests would suffer under Castro's rule, Smith sought to preempt the rebel leader. At a meeting held in January 1958, the ambassador persuaded Batista to call for a presidential election to be held in June of that same year. The Cuban constitution dictated that a president could not serve another term – for this reason it was agreed that it would be unwise for Batista to try to disregard this ruling.

The following month, the Pentagon and the State Department began to debate whether it would be wise to ban the sale of weapons to Cuba. The Pentagon, citing Cuba's strategic position, Batista's commitment to fight communism, and the importance of close ties between the United States and Cuban militaries, opposed the embargo. The State Department continued to argue that it would serve the interests of the United States to ban the sale of weapons, for this action would signal Washington's displeasure with Batista's dictatorial regime. The position of the State Department prevailed, and on March 14 the US Congress ordered an arms embargo against Cuba. The embargo was extended for an indefinite period the following month.

At first glance it may seem that Washington was willing to accept Castro as Batista's replacement. This conclusion would be misleading. Although Washington did impose an arms embargo, small quantities of arms continued to flow as a result of bureaucratic procedures. Further, the United States decided to maintain the US military missions in Cuba to help Batista's armed forces. As explained by the director of the Office of Caribbean Affairs at the State Department, William A. Wieland, the military missions had to be kept, for although "governments and administrations change ... hemispheric defense needs present a constant problem the solution of which calls for a cooperative program carried out on a steady, long-range basis" (quoted in Blasier, 1971: 47; Benjamin, 1989). It was this support that made it feasible for Batista to launch a major offensive against Castro and his guerrillas on May 24, 1958.

But the winds of change had begun to gather force. In the spring of 1958, Vice President Richard Nixon traveled to South America. The trip was a major débâcle. The vice president and his entourage were met twice by violent anti-US demonstrations. These demonstrations had a sobering effect on Nixon. Upon his return to Washington in May, he delivered a powerful challenge to well-rooted views. The United States, he argued, could no longer afford to continue embracing dictatorial regimes; instead, it had to warmly support democratic leaders, avoid creating the impression that it was helping protect the privileges of a few, and dedicate itself to raising the standard of living of the masses, thereby removing communism's breeding ground. Nixon's policy recommendation was challenged by Secretary of State John Foster Dulles, who feared that the promotion of democracy would only "bring in more of a dictatorship of the masses" (LaFeber, 1983: 137).[4]

Nixon's idea was not new, nor did it fall on deaf ears. Since 1954, some Latin American leaders had been pressuring the United States to help create and finance a regional development bank. This type of bank, they argued, would help alleviate social and economic inequalities in Latin America. The Eisenhower administration had rejected this idea for several years. Its official rationale was that the correction of social injustices in Latin America was strictly a Latin American problem (Eisenhower, 1963: 205); its private attitude was that such a program would be very expensive (LaFeber, 1983: 127). Considering that balancing the federal budget was a very high priority for Eisenhower, it is easy to understand why the latter consideration carried so much weight. But following Nixon's return from South America, the president sent his brother, Milton, on a fact-finding tour of Central America. Milton Eisenhower's recommendations supported the conclusions arrived at earlier by the vice president, and President Eisenhower was finally willing to listen. As explained by Walter LaFeber, "It is a measure of the crisis the president saw developing that he initiated policy changes even before Fidel Castro came to power in Cuba" (1983: 140). One of the first major changes agreed upon by the Eisenhower administration was the creation of the Inter-American Development Bank (IADB) to supplement the World Bank and Export–Import Bank funds.

In the meantime, the situation in Cuba had continued to deteriorate. In June, Batista, possibly believing that his latest military offensive would stop Castro's guerrillas, decided to postpone the elections. Ambassador Smith, aware that this decision could undermine Batista's image in Washington, persuaded the Cuban leader to delay the elections only until November. By then, Castro's level of anxiety had increased measurably. In July 1958, afraid that the elections and the continued supply of US weapons to the Batista regime would endanger the revolution, Castro's brother, Raul, kidnapped 31 US citizens, hoping to pressure the United States to alter its policy course. Raul Castro immediately made it clear that unless the United States ceased shipping weapons to and training Batista's armed forces, the hostages would not be released (Blasier, 1971: 47).

Washington's reaction to the kidnapping was divided. The Pentagon proposed sending in a military force to free the hostages, while the State Department emphasized the importance of finding a diplomatic solution to the problem. The assistant secretary of state for inter-American affairs, Roy Rubottom, finally succeeded in obtaining the release of the captured Americans through diplomatic channels (Benjamin, 1989).

In retrospect, August turned out to be a very important month for Castro's revolution. By August 7 it had become quite evident that Batista's military offensive against Castro's guerrillas would end in defeat. That same month, the State Department's Bureau of Intelligence and Research produced a document arguing, among other things, that Batista's regime could not last much longer, while Castro's movement was strong, well disciplined, and "lacked any significant ideology" (quoted in Benjamin, 1989).

Between August and the end of 1958, Batista's control over political developments in Cuba deteriorated rapidly. On November 4, his hand-picked successor Dr Rivero Agüero, won a clearly fraudulent presidential election. His victory, rather than reducing opposition, increased it. During that same period, decision-makers in Washington were still struggling with the issue of how to respond to both Batista and Castro. The Commerce and Treasury Departments, because of Batista's stellar record in protecting US economic interests in Cuba, joined the Defense Department in advocating continued US support of the Batista regime (Benjamin, 1989). By November, however, it became clear that the Batista alternative was no longer a viable one. The State Department asked Ambassador Smith to fly back to Washington for a meeting, at which time he was ordered to tell Batista it was unreasonable for him to hope to remain in power until Aguero assumed the official duties of the presidency in February of the following year. Smith was also ordered to inform Batista that the United States would not support the Aguero regime.

Smith returned to Havana but never transmitted the message. Instead, he softened the statement and subsequently proposed to Washington that Batista resign in return for US support of the Aguero presidency. Upset by Smith's independence, the Eisenhower administration called him back to the United States and sent William Pawley to ask Batista to resign in favor of a military junta. On December 9, Batista counteracted by stating that he would leave only if the United States publicly acknowledged that it was the instigator of the pressure. Pawley, knowing very well that the request would not be approved by the State Department, left Cuba without having accomplished his mission (Blasier, 1971: 48).[5] Less than a week later, Ambassador Smith approached Cuba's foreign minister, Gonzalo Guell, and requested that he ask Batista to resign in favor of a "caretaker" government. Smith, although opposed to the policy, made it clear to Guell that the United States could no longer support the Batista regime and that unidentified elements existed that could salvage the situation if they assumed control of the government immediately (Matthews, 1961: 118; Blasier, 1971: 48; Bonachea and San Martin, 1974: 303–6). Once again, the Cuban ruler refused to acquiesce. His main fear was that the United States would include as members of the military junta some individuals over whom he had no control (Blasier, 1971: 48).

By then, time had run out. The Castro-led rebels' actions had gained a critical momentum, and nothing but a major military intervention on the part of the United States would prevent a revolutionary victory. On December 23, the acting secretary of state, Christian Herter, informed President Eisenhower, in a long memornadum, that "the Communists are utilizing the Castro movement to some extent, as would be expected, but there is insufficient evidence on which to base a charge that the rebels are communist-dominated." That same day, Allan Dulles, in a briefing to the National Security Council, stated that "If Castro takes over, they [the Communists] will probably participate in the government." Herter, moreover, added that in view of the strong anti-Batista sentiment in Cuba, "Batista must relinquish power . . . He probably should also leave the country." The acting secretary of state also recommended that the United States use every means short of outright intervention to bring about a political solution that would exclude Castro. Eisenhower, claiming that he had been kept in the dark regarding US opposition to the formation of a Castro government, called a meeting the next day to see whether anything could be done to prevent Castro's victory. At this meeting, the chief of naval operations, Admiral Arleigh Burke, proposed as an alternative the use of military force. Eisenhower rejected Burke's recommendation and ordered that the US government try to find a solution to the Cuban problem that would exclude both Batista and Castro (Ambrose, 1984: 505; Benjamin, 1989).

In the meantime, Batista had also concluded that his options had been narrowed to one – relinquishment of power. His resignation, on the final day of 1958, was followed by the naming of a military junta led by Batista's chief of military operations, General Eulogio Cantillo (Bonachea and San Martin, 1974: 309–11). The demise of the military junta came about swiftly. On January 1, 1959, after having learned that the opposition had established military control over the entire island, General Cantillo and his associates resigned. Two days later, Manuel Urrutia, who had been designated Cuba's new president by Fidel Castro, arrived in Havana.

In sum, 1958 marks the year in which the United States reached the conclusion that its ability to continue maintaining a pro-US status quo in Latin America was being severely undermined by its historical association with dictatorial regimes and by its reluctance to help alleviate social and economic inequalities in the region. This realization did not, however, lead the Eisenhower administration to embrace the likes of Fidel Castro. On the contrary, during the final months of 1958, as it became evident that Batista would not be able to arrest the momentum gained by Castro's revolutionary forces after their battlefield triumph in early August, Washington began hesitantly to attempt to ease the Cuban president out of power in favor of a moderate government. The campaign was driven not by the fear that Castro would become a communist menace, although this concern was already being voiced by some Washington officials, but by the concern that he might pursue an independent path.

Castro's rise to power created a new reality. Initially, the US State Department believed that since the new Cuban regime was politically divided, with the moderates playing an important role, Castro could be persuaded to implement political, social, and economic reforms that would not alter dramatically the role the United States had played in Cuban affairs since the turn of the century. The State Department, however, cognizant of the Guatemalan experience, also concluded that the conciliatory policy should be combined with careful attention to the behavior of the new regime. Specifically, it was decided that the United States had to watch for the presence of communists in the government, increased state control of the economy and the effect this would have on US interests, reduced support for the inter-American system, and movement towards neutrality in the Cold War (Starr and Lowenthal, 1988: 26).

As part of its conciliatory strategy, Washington extended full diplomatic recognition to the new Cuban government on January 7, the same day Fidel Castro marched victoriously for the first time into Havana. In addition, the State Department named Philip Bonsal as the new ambassador to Cuba. Bonsal, who arrived in Havana on February 19, was not a stranger to this type of delicate mission. In his post as US ambassador to Bolivia, Bonsal had played a crucial role in helping implement a monetary stabilization program to avert

Bolivia's economic collapse. The central objective to this program had been to get Bolivia to return to a free market economy, at least in the matter of freedom from price controls, from foreign exchange control, and from import and export controls, despite the socialist orientation of many of Bolivia's political leaders (Bonsal, 1971: 26; Bonachea and San Martin, 1974: 309–11; Blasier, 1985: 139–40).

The steps taken by the State Department paralleled the way Eisenhower and Nixon were viewing the latest developments in Cuba. The president, influenced partly by his general preference for accommodation, believed that communism could be contained in Cuba by supporting moderate political, economic, and social reforms. Nixon, in turn, felt that the radicals, most of whom were known to be members of Castro's 26th of July Movement, would have difficulty consolidating their power and, thus, that a conciliatory US policy toward the new regime would "have a positive political pay-off in Cuba and throughout Latin America" (Starr and Lowenthal, 1988: 28–9).

This attitude and behavior was not out of character for the US government. Washington, hoping to influence the moderate forces, had extended diplomatic recognition to the Arévalo regime in Guatemala in 1945 and had hoped to establish a solid working relationship with Arbenz as soon as he became that country's new president. Moreover, in both instances Washington had initially appointed ambassadors who were known for their ability to work with governments committed to social and economic reforms. In the Cuban case, as in the Guatemalan case, however, this attitude on the part of US leaders would not last long.

Castro's revolutionary government moved swiftly to redesign Cuba's military and political structures. Castro had concluded that the central reason for Arbenz's demise was his failure to secure the allegiance of the Guatemalan armed forces. Determined to avoid this mistake, one of his first acts was to restructure the Cuban armed forces by replacing elements loyal to Batista with a "peasant force" committed to the revolution. Castro's resolve to annul the military threat to his revolution was not limited to the Cuban military. In January, the Cuban government ordered the termination of the US military mission in Cuba (Blasier, 1985: 178; Banjamin, 1989).

In the political arena, changes were equally rapid and substantial. On January 21, the new regime granted all political parties the right to organize and propagandize; in the process, they effectively legalized the Cuban Communist Party. This was followed in early February by a decree authorizing the concentration of executive and legislative powers in the hands of the cabinet, and on February 16 by the announcement that Fidel Castro would become prime minister.

Castro wasted very little time in signaling the direction of his economic policies. On May 13, the Cuban government nationalized the Cuban Telephone Company, a subsidiary of the International Telephone and Telegraph Corporation. The nationalization of the telephone company was intended as a major step toward not only controlling telephone rates but, more importantly, beginning to reduce dependency on the United States (Kenner and Petras, 1969: 11).

The Eisenhower administration's perceptions of these events and of the anti-US pronouncements by the more radical Cuban leaders were mixed. At a meeting held in San Salvador in the first half of April for US ambassadors to the twelve hispanic republics of the Caribbean area, two opposing alternatives were proposed. Ambassador Bonsal, speaking for the majority position, argued that the United States should let things settle. He noted that responses to criticisms of the United States would only help poison the atmosphere and might lead to the accusation of undue interference in Cuban affairs. On the opposite side, the US ambassadors to Mexico, Robert Hill, and to Costa Rica, Whiting Willauer, proposed that the United States alert Latin American leaders to the growing danger of communist intrusion in Cuba. Hill and Willauer's approach was rejected (Bonsal, 1971: 59; Blasier, 1985: 189–90).

Just as the meeting in San Salvador was coming to an end, Washington began to prepare itself to receive Fidel Castro, who had been invited to the United States by the American Society of Newspaper Editors. President Eisenhower, hoping to signal his displeasure with the anti-US rhetoric voiced by many members of the new Cuban government decided not to meet with Castro (Blasier, 1971: 52; Bonsal, 1971: 64). It was left to Vice President Richard Nixon and Secretary of State Christian Herter to measure what type of man the revolutionary leader was.

After a three-hour talk with Castro on Capitol Hill on April 19, Nixon concluded that the visitor had the potential to become a strong leader but was "either incredibly naive about Communism or under Communist discipline" – my guess is the former..." At the same time, Nixon recommended that the United States, because it had no choice but to accept Castro, "try to orient him in the right direction" (Safford, 1980: 425–31). Herter's evaluation of Castro did not differ markedly from Nixon's. The secretary of state suggested that Castro was "a strong personality and a born leader" who should not be underestimated by the United States. While the secretary argued that there was no reason to expect Castro to alter the radical course of the revolution, he also suggested that an understanding attitude on the part of the United States potentially could moderate the future course of the revolution. But Herter was hesitant to propose US support for Castro, arguing that he still was an "enigma." Thus, he proposed a less activist policy than did the vice president, arguing that the United States should continue its "wait and see" policy until the Cuban government undertook concrete actions through which it could be judged more effectively (Declassified Documents Quarterly, 1976).

The State Department's actions during Castro's visit to the United States reflected both Herter's suggestion for the need for a conciliatory US response to the revolution, and Nixon's proposal to try to orient the revolution in the right direction. In a meeting with Cuba's finance minister, Rufo Lopez-Fresquet, Assistant Secretary of State R. Richard Rubottom offered to help Cuba fulfill its economic plans. But under orders from Castro, Lopez-Fresquet declined the offer. Castro had observed that rejection at this stage would evince Cuba's increasing independence and, as a result, generate more attractive offers in the future (Blasier, 1971: 52). It was also during this period that the Cuban government commenced arms negotiations with the United States,

France, and Great Britain. Castro hoped to augment Cuba's self-defense capabilities by spending some $9,000,000 to purchase destroyers and other military equipment (1971: 59).

The first phase in the relationship between the Eisenhower administration and the Castro regime began to take a turn on May 17, 1959. On that date, the Castro regime announced Cuba's most radical agrarian reform law. The intention of the government was to appropriate all rented lands and estates larger than 402 acres and to grant to tenant farmers cultivating fewer than 27 hectares full and free title to their land (Kenner and Petras, 1969: 11–12; Dumont, 1970: 28–9). Promulgation of the law began on June 3.

The United States quickly responded to the new Cuban law. In a measured response, Ambassador Bonsal expressed sympathy with some of the objectives defined in the law and acknowledged Cuba's right to nationalize. But he also called for the prompt, adequate, and effective compensation of those companies affected by the law (Bonsal, 1971: 73). He also warned that the legislation could have "an adverse effect on the plans of private foreign investment in Cuba in many fields other than agriculture" (quoted in Benjamin, 1989). Bonsal's position was not unique. Rubottom, who for some time had been advocating a policy of patience toward the new Cuban government, made it clear to the Cuban ambassador in Washington that the legislation could affect Cuba's status as a privileged supplier of sugar (Benjamin, 1989).

During June and July of 1959, Castro's persona became once again the focus of Washington's attention. Aware that the governments of Haiti, Nicaragua, and the Dominican Republic were not very popular throughout the Americas, Castro sponsored expeditions against them. He seems to have concluded that since few countries would actively support the dictators that governed the targeted states, successful invasions would augment measurably his prestige and power (Bonsal, 1971: 76). At the same time, Castro continued to take extraordinary measures to further consolidate his political authority. In July, convinced that his power was not the result of his position within Cuba's institutional political structure, Castro resigned as prime minister. His charismatic authority became evident immediately. One of his first actions as Cuba's latest former prime minister was to denounce President Urrutia vehemently. The public responded by demanding the resignation of Urrutia, who took little time in obliging (Benjamin, 1989).

The United States did not welcome any of Castro's latest moves. State Department officials who had advocated a policy of moderation were finding it very difficult to justify Castro's agricultural reform law. At the same time, they found it very disturbing that Urrutia, who had been opposed to the growing influence of the communists in Cuba, had been pressured to resign. And finally, although many of these officials questioned the wisdom of the United States in maintaining a close relationship with the leaders of Haiti, Nicaragua, and the Dominican Republic, they had no desire to have these government toppled by forces sponsored by Castro.

The United States's reaction to developments in Cuba was subtle. Ambassador Bonsal met with Foreign Minister Raul Roa in July and August and with Castro in early September. The US ambassador expressed displeasure with a number of policies implemented by the Cuban government, but he also called for greater understanding between the two governments. During this period, but in a different political arena, the Organization of American States, under pressure from the United States, approved a resolution calling for the propagation of democratic ideals throughout the Americas and for the support of non-intervention. The resolution did not make any allegations about any government and did not call for any investigation (Bonsal, 1971: 76–7; Starr and Lowenthal, 1988: 46–7).

At the same time, however, the United States made it clear, in an indirect manner, that it would not sit still while Castro sought to consolidate his power in Cuba and augment his prestige throughout the Caribbean Basin. On October 27, the State Department announced that the arms embargo against Cuba would continue because of Castro's attempts to topple some of the neighboring regimes. In concurrence with this action, the State Department pressured Great Britain not to sell weapons to Cuba (Blasier, 1971: 59; Gonzales, 1972: 18).

These actions reflected Washington's increasing concern with developments in Cuba. In a policy memorandum submitted to President Eisenhower on November 5, Secretary of State Herter noted that:

(a) there is no reasonable basis to found our policy on a hope that Castro will voluntarily adopt policies and attitudes consistent with minimum Washington security requirements and policy interests;

(b) the prolonged continuation of the Castro regime in Cuba in its present form would have serious adverse effects on the United States' position in Latin America and corresponding advantages for international Communism; and

(c) only by the building up within Cuba of a coherent opposition consisting of elements desirous of achieving political and economic progress within a framework of good United States–Cuban relations can the Castro regime be checked or replaced.

In arriving at these conclusions, the Department has in effect applied a series of tests to the Castro regime for the past ten months, meanwhile exercising just restraint in the face of provocations and giving Castro every opportunity to establish Cuban–United States relations on an acceptable basis. He has, instead, on important occasions elected a course inimical to the United States and its interests. Specifically, his deliberate fomenting of anti-American sentiment in Cuba and seeking to do so in other Latin American countries now represents, beyond doubt, the basic policy and orientation of his government. He has veered towards a "neutralist" anti-American foreign policy for Cuba which, if emulated by other Latin American countries, would have serious adverse effects on Free World support of our leadership, especially in the United Nations on such issues as the Chinese representation problem. He has, in fact, given support to Caribbean revolutionary movements designed to bring into power governments modeled on or responsive to his government and by such interventionist activities sought to undermine the Inter-American system. He has tolerated and encouraged the infiltration of Communists and their sympathizers into important positions in key government institutions, the armed forces, and organized labor while, dating back to the meeting of Latin American Communist leaders in Moscow last January, the international Communist apparatus has made clear that it sees in the advance of Castroism the best chance of achieving its immediate objectives. On the economic side, Castro's policies have been drastic and tended increasingly towards statal control of the economic life of Cuba. Not only have our business interests in Cuba been seriously affected, but the United States cannot hope to encourage and support sound economic policies in other Latin American countries and promote necessary private investment in Latin America if it is or appears to be simultaneously cooperating in the Castro program.[7]

Viewed from a comparative perspective, the way in which Washington structured the Cuban problem in 1959 is quite similar to the manner in which it constructed the Guatemalan case in 1951. In the earlier period, Washington had been concerned with the fate of US interests in Guatemala under the Arévalo regime, but never to the extent that it felt a need to undermine the regime's authority. When Arbenz was elected, Washington's initial hope was that his policies would begin to veer to the center. This hope was short-lived, and its death can in great measure be attributed to Washington's firm belief that the Arbenz government was being dominated by communists. Washington's new perception was subsequently reinforced by the passage of Guatemala's most radical agrarian reform law.

The sequence of events in the Cuban case does not correspond precisely with the earlier one, but the dissimilarities are not significant. When Castro came to power, the US State Department hoped not that he would veer toward the center but, more specifically, that he would not deviate too far away from the center. This hope faded with the implementation of the agrarian reform, and it suffered a major blow during the second half of 1959, when it became clear that the Communist Party had succeeded in broadening its popular appeal and attracting recognition by the Castro regime. In other words, in both the Guatemalan and Cuban cases, Washington defined the problem on the basis of how close to the center the governing regimes set their economic and political markers; and it measured these distances, partly, in terms of the content of the countries' respective agrarian reform laws and disposition towards individuals or parties with known communist affiliation.

The Eisenhower administration began the new year by expressing a willingness to observe a policy of non-intervention. On January 26, 1960, President Eisenhower announced that the US would not enact reprisals against Cuba and would respect Cuba's right to undertake a social revolution (Gonzales, 1972: 19). Moreover, the US State Department informed the Castro government that it was willing to negotiate all disputes, including those arising from Cuban nationalization of American property. These announcements came on the heels of a meeting between Eisenhower, Herter, Rubottom, and Bonsal, held a day earlier to discuss how the United States should respond to the most recent developments in Cuba. Exasperated by Castro's behavior, the president considered blockading the island. He dropped this idea when Bonsal and Rubottom noted that any action against Castro by the United States would only reinforce his powers while undermining the capability of the Cuban opposition to overthrow the regime. Moreover, Herter warned that although many Latin American leaders were disappointed with Castro's behavior, they would not tolerate US reprisals against Cuba, economic or otherwise (Baklanoff, 1971: 258–9; Starr and Lowenthal, 1988: 55–6).

The months of February and March, however, confirmed for US officials that they had to work against Castro. On February 4, Soviet Deputy Chairman Anastas Mikoyan arrived in Cuba on an official visit. The Cuban government extended lavish welcoming receptions to the Soviet leader and his entourage. Eisenhower, convinced that the trip indicated closer Cuban–Soviet relations and that it would culminate in some type of agreement, met with CIA director Allan Dulles on that same day to discuss US options. Dulles did not come empty-handed to the meeting. Since December 1959, the Central Intelligence Agency had been working on a plan designed to undermine the Castro regime. Moreover, Dulles had already formed, on January 18, 1960, a special Cuban task force composed mainly of individuals involved in the 1954 covert operation against Arbenz. Dulles's plan involved the sabotaging of sugar refineries in Cuba. Eisenhower, after listening to Dulles's presentation, stated that he did not object to such an undertaking and believed that something like that was timely. However, the president "felt that any program should be more ambitious, and it was probably now the time to move against Castro in a positive and aggressive way which went beyond pure harassment. He asked Mr. Dulles to come back with an enlarged program."[8]

Eisenhower's fear was justified. On February 15, the leaders of the Soviet Union and Castro signed a five-year contract by which Cuba would sell to the USSR 425,000 tons of sugar in 1960 and increase it to one million tons a year from 1961 through 1964. The USSR also promised to supply Cuba with different types of oil at a price 33 percent cheaper than that charged by the United States, and it granted $100,000,000 in credit at $2\frac{1}{2}$ percent interest for twelve years to purchase machinery and materials from the Soviet Union in order to build an oil refinery and a steel mill (Bonachea and Valdez, 1969: 223–4; Blasier, 1971: 60; Bondal, 1971: 131).

During March, the relationship between Cuba and the United States continued to deteriorate. On March 4, a French merchant ship, La Coubre, carrying a cargo of munitions, blew up at a Havana dock (Blasier, 1971: 59). In a speech on the following day, Castro accused the United States of being responsible for the ship's destruction. Four days later, on March 9, Castro's regime took over the management of the Moa Bay Mining Company, a subsidiary of the Freeport Sulphur Company. The takeover was designed to keep the company running, for it had experienced serious financial problems as a result of the chaotic conditions of Cuba's economy (1971: 62).

Eisenhower, who had just returned from a trip to South America, became further convinced that the Castro regime had to be toppled. On March 17, he approved the CIA plan he had received three days earlier (Blasier, 1981: 191). The CIA had drafted a four-part proposal: (i) to create a Cuban government in exile; (ii) to initiate a propaganda campaign against Castro, financed with secret funds; (iii) to build an "intelligence" network in Cuba; and (iv) to develop and train a paramilitary force for future infiltration into Cuba to develop guerrilla operations. These were the same four components that delineated the Guatemalan plan implemented six years earlier (Etheredge, 1985: 3. See also Wyden,

1979: 20–1; Vandenbroucke, 1984: 472–3).

From that day on, the relationship between Washington and Havana became more and more acrimonious. On March 28, Fidel Castro, in a television interview, repudiated Cuba's obligations under the 1947 Rio Treaty. The Cuban leader argued that the treaty was nothing more than a tool of the United States to control the behavior of Latin American states. The US State Department responded by stating that the Cuban denunciation provided additional evidence of Castro's anti-US disposition (Blasier, 1971: 60).

The bickering intensified in tone the following month. On April 19, just about the time the Soviet union and Cuba began to exchange ambassadors for the first time since Batista had discontinued diplomatic relations with Moscow, a shipment of Soviet crude oil arrived at the Caribbean island (1971: 60). One of the main problems created by the buying of Soviet crude oil was that Cuba depended on two US companies, Esso and Texaco, and the Anglo-Dutch company Shell, for the refining of petroleum. Sometime in mid-May, Ernesto Guevara, who had been Cuba's minister of industry, president of the National Bank, and head of the Department of Industrialization of the National Institute of Agrarian Reform since November of the previous year, demanded that the companies refine the petroleum bought from the Soviet Union. Guevara's demand was accompanied by a threat; he informed the oil refineries that only by agreeing to refine Cuban-imported Soviet oil would the companies receive the $50,000,000 Cuba owed them (Bonsal, 1971: 148; Blasier, 1985: 191).

A small debate ensued among officials of the Eisenhower administration as to how to respond to Cuba's ultimatum. Ambassador Bonsal proposed that the companies refine the petroleum as called for by the Cuban government. His rationale was that to act differently would simply make it easier for Castro to take drastic measures against the oil companies, thereby enhancing his own reputation (Bonsal, 1971: 149–50). US Treasury Secretary Robert Anderson disregarded Bonsal's advice and pressured the oil refineries to refuse to give in to Cuba's demand. He believed that such an action would not only signal US displeasure with Castro's domestic and foreign policies but would also help undermine his attempts to accelerate Cuba's economic development (1971: 149–50). On June 7, the oil refineries rejected Guevara's demand.

The Cuban government did not react immediately to the challenge. This did not mean, however, that it had decided to maintain a low profile. On June 10, the Cuban government nationalized four hotels in which US citizens or corporations had interests. The action was driven by the same rationale that had led to the nationalization of the Moa Bay Mining Company in March – to keep the businesses running (Blasier, 1971: 62).

In the meantime, pressure to cut the Cuban sugar quota had been mounting at a rapid pace in the United States. Many arguments were advanced by both the Eisenhower administrstion and Congress to justify this action (Schreiber, 1973: 392; Blasier, 1985: 192–3). After extensive debate in both the House of Representatives and the Senate, the Congress granted the president, at the end of June, discretionary power to alter the Cuban sugar quota. While the US Congress was deciding whether or not the US should act against Cuba on the sugar issue, Guevara was attempting to conclude what to do about the challenge posed by the oil refineries. His decision surfaced on June 29, when he ordered the nationalization of the three oil companies – Texaco, Esso, and Royal Dutch Shell – that had refused to refine Soviet petroleum (Dumont, 1970: 34–5; Schreiber, 1973: 391–2). Within a week of Guevara's order, the United States reciprocated. On July 6, President Eisenhower suspended the balance of Cuba's 1960 sugar export quota (Blasier, 1971: 67; Bonsal, 1971: 151; Schreiber, 1973: 391–2). Determined not to be outdone by the United States, Cuba responded on the following day with the announcement that $800,000,000 out of the $1,100,000,000 invested in Cuba by the United States would be nationalized (Dumont, 1970: 34–5). Castro also stated, on July 8, that the arrival of weapons purchased from the Soviet bloc was imminent (Blasier, 1985: 195).

The intensity of the discord between Havana and Washington became so high that it drew the involvement of Moscow. On July 9, Premier Nikita Khrushchev stated that "speaking figuratively, in case of necessity, Soviet artillery men can support the Cuban people with rocket fire" (Bonsal, 1971: 157). Moscow's challenge did not fare well in the United States. The following day, the Eisenhower administration stated that it would not "permit the establishment of a regime dominated by international communism in the Western Hemisphere" (Schreiber, 1973: 395). A few weeks later, on July 26, Fidel Castro announced that Cuba had received its arms shipment from the Soviet bloc (Blasier, 1971: 69).

Two major events took place during the month of August. On August 6, the Cuban government nationalized twenty-six companies wholly or partially owned by US citizens. The action was designed to accelerate Cuba's economic development and reduce US domination and, more specifically, to compensate for Cuba's loss of the sugar quota (Blasier, 1971: 71). The United States, in the meantime, sought additional international support for its actions against Cuba. At the meeting of the foreign ministers of the American republics held in San José, Costa Rica, a resolution submitted by the Eisenhower administration was approved on August 25 which condemned "intervention or the threat of intervention by an extra-continental power" as well as attempts by the Sino-Soviet powers to exploit the political, economic or social situations of American states for their own ends (Bonsal, 1971: 161–3).

The resolution was approved just a week after Eisenhower had agreed to upgrade the covert plan against the Castro regime. On July 7, a day after suspending the balance of Cuba's 1960 sugar export quota, Eisenhower, during a meeting in which a full range of military options were discussed, rejected the immediate use of overt military force to topple Castro. "If we were to try to accomplish our aims by force," reasoned Eisenhower, "we would see all of [the Latin countries] tending to fall away and some would be Communists within two years ... If the United States does not conduct itself in precisely the right way *vis-à-vis* Cuba, we could lose all of Latin America." But Eisenhower was not ready to sacrifice the use of covert means. At a meeting with Allan Dulles and Richard Bissell held on August 18, Eisenhower, after reviewing the steps the CIA had already taken to implement the plan he had approved in March, approved a $13 million budget for the execution of the remainder of the operation, and authorized the use of US military personnel, but insisted that they not be employed "in a combat status." However, Eisenhower also made it very clear that he would not approve any action without a popular genuine government-in-exile. His warning came after learning from Bissell that the CIA was having difficulty convincing the different Cuban factions to unite (Ambrose, 1984: 583, 584).[9]

During the final months of 1960, the disputes continued. On September 16, the Castro regime ordered the nationalization of US-owned banks. A little over a month later, the Eisenhower administration instructed the ban of all US exports to Cuba except non-subsidized foodstuffs, medicine, and medical supplies. Washington's action, however, did not receive the unanimous approval of US officials. Diplomats at the US Embassy in Cuba argued that the United States ought simply to reduce its exports. Their argument was based on the rationale that any kind of ban would fail so long as other states remained willing to trade with Cuba. Moreover, a full ban would encourage Cuba to solicit aid from the Soviet Union (Blasier, 1971: 71; Bonsal, 1971: 165). Once again, not to be outdone, Cuba responded, on October 24, by nationalizing 166 US companies (Blasier, 1971: 71). Four days later, Secretary of State Herter, convinced that Castro needed a clear signal that US patience was reaching its limit, recalled Ambassador Bonsal. Herter's order was not well received by Bonsal. The US ambassador, hoping to persuade the secretary of state that he should not be recalled, argued that the Cuban government was shaky and disorganized and, therefore, that it would be wise for him to remain in Cuba in case Castro fell (Bonsal, 1971: 167–70).

By late October, the need for greater toughness against communism had been turned into a major political issue by the presidential candidate of the Democratic Party, John F. Kennedy. He charged the Eisenhower administration with insufficient firmness against communism for allowing such a government to come to power in Cuba (Etheredge, 1985: 4). Kennedy's stand was particularly disconcerting to the Republican presidential candidate, Vice President Richard Nixon, who for some time had been trying to convince Eisenhower to eliminate Castro before the election date. Nixon knew about the CIA plans but was unable to breach intelligence to defend himself.[10]

The November elections brought into the international picture a new US president, John F. Kennedy. A few weeks after Kennedy's election, Allan Dulles and Richard Bissell briefed the president-elect on what the CIA had been planning against Castro (Etheredge, 1985: 4–5). In the meantime, Castro had been moving aggressively to compensate for the embargo imposed on Cuban sugar by the United States. In late November, the Soviet Union announced that it had agreed to purchase 2.7 million tons of Cuban sugar for 1961 (Blasier, 1971: 71). On December 16, the Eisenhower administration responded by fixing at zero Cuba's sugar quota for 1961's first quarter (1971: 67). The Soviet Union counteracted three days later by announcing its full commitment to mantaing Cuba's independence against unprovoked aggression (p. 71).

The starting of the new year did not change the nature of the interaction between Havana and Washington. On January 2, 1961, after describing the US

Embassy in Cuba as a center of counterrevolution, subversion, and espionage, the Cuban government demanded that the US personnel be reduced to eleven, the same level maintained by the Cuban Embassy in Washington (Bonsal, 1971: 1975). Castro's accusations were not unfounded. His government had frequently intercepted arms drops and penetrated underground networks (Etheredge, 1985: 4). The Eisenhower administration responded swiftly a day later by breaking all diplomatic relations with Cuba. On January 6, convinced that the United States would launch an invasion against Cuba, Castro ordered the full mobilization of his government's armed forces (Bonsal, 1971: 175).

The same pattern of US actions toward the Castro regime continued after the swearing-in of the new president. On January 28, President Kennedy was briefed, once again, by the CIA on the plan it had designed to topple the Castro regime. The plan, referred to as Operation Trinidad, called for the daylight landing of 1,400 troops at the town of Trinidad, on the southeast coast of Cuba, near the Escombray Mountains. The strategy depended heavily on the extensive use of B-16s to destroy Cuba's air force prior to the landing of the troops, and the bombing and strafing of Cuban troops, barracks, and other military targets during and after the landing of the Cuban exiles. As was the case six years earlier during the operation to topple Arbenz, the CIA strategy was designed to produce not a military defeat but the demoralization of Castro's forces and the political destabilization of his regime (Etheredge, 1985: 5, 12–13).

It was not pure coincidence that the Cuban strategy was so similar to the Guatemalan plan. Allan Dulles served as CIA director in both cases. Richard Bissell, who had been Dulles's special assistant in 1954, had become the chief planner of the new operation. The position of deputy director of the CIA was held by the same person in both cases, General Charles P. Cabell. The propaganda operation, which had played such an important role in unnerving Arbenz in 1954, was being run by the same person in 1961, David Phillips. E. Howard Hunt served in the capacity of chief of political action in both cases, and his boss, Jake Engler, had worked as the CIA station chief in Guatemala City (Etheredge, 1985: 7).

The president and his advisors met on several occasions in February and March to discuss the CIA plan. Kennedy, although favoring extraordinary measures to overthrow Castro, was unhappy about the specifics of the plan. He felt that it was necessary to reduce the exposure of US involvement. With this criterion in mind, the CIA proposed the infiltration of 1,400 men and most of their ammunition and supplies before sunrise. The invasion could take place at any one of three sites. The CIA, however, recommended that the forces be put ashore at the Bay of Pigs. The area was sparsely populated, included an air strip that could be seized, was accessible by only three roads, and was surrounded by the Zapata swamps. The new strategy was named "Operation Zapata" (Etheredge, 1985: 13).

On April 4, Kennedy's advisors held a major meeting to decide whether or not to implement the Zapata plan. Although the paramilitary invasion was finally approved, some opposition arose during the discussion. Three alternatives were discussed by the senior advisors. The first alternative – to approve the paramilitary invasion – received the endorsement, as might be expected, of Allan Dulles and Richard Bissell. The two CIA officials were convinced that a plan that had worked for the United States against Arbenz in 1954 would work a second time. Dulles and Bissell also believed that if the invasion began to fail, President Kennedy would agree to provide full support to the intervening forces. The paramilitary invasion was also supported by two State Department officials, the assistant secretary of state for inter-American affairs, Thomas Mann, and the special assistant to the secretary of state, Adolf Berle. These two individuals were not strangers to US intervention. Mann, it may be recalled, had been among the first State Department officials under the Truman administration to conclude that Arbenz was a Marxist. He had, as a result, recommended the refusal of any type of aid to, and the slow reduction of trade with, Guatemala. Adolf Berle had been one of the first officials in the Eisenhower administration to suggest that the United States form a coalition with countries surrounding Guatemala, and he had recommended that the United States mount intense political and economic pressure in order to force Arbenz to resign or to expel the communists working in the government.

The CIA plan was questioned by two different groups. Presidential advisor Arthur Schlesinger and Senator William Fulbright proposed that the invasion be cancelled and the paramilitary forces disbanded. They both believed that an invasion would be legally and morally reprehensible. The Joint Chiefs of Staff also questioned the wisdom of engaging in a paramilitary mission, but for different reasons. The military leaders found it unreasonable to stage an operation that depended on the erosion of Castro's support while the invasion was taking place. As an alternative, the Joint Chiefs of Staff suggested that the United States launch a major overt military invasion. The two challenges to the covert action were not voiced forcefully, and therefore the CIA was able to have its plan approved (Vandenbroucke, 1984: 483–7; Etheredge, 1985: 41). One day after having approved the plan, Kennedy met privately with Secretary of State Dean Rusk, Secretary of Defense Robert McNamara, and CIA Director Allan Dulles to emphasize his commitment against overt US involvement. Initially, the plan had called for an attack on Castro's air force with sixteen B-26s. Kennedy, afraid that the United States would not be able to camouflage its participation, ordered that the number of planes be reduced to six (Etheredge, 1985: 41).

On April 15, the CIA launched an air strike against Cuba. It sent two B-26s against each of Cuba's main airfields: Camp Libertad outside Havana, Antonio Maceo Airport in Orient Province, and San Antonio de los Banos. On April 16, President Kennedy gave final approval for the invasion. Early the following day, 1,400 Cuban exiles returned to their homeland hoping to topple the regime in power. Their dream came to an abrupt end. Castro, on learning of the invasion, ordered the deployment of 20,000 troops toward the location where the invaders had landed, and an attack by his remaining planes. This order came only a few hours after Kennedy had decided to cancel the air strikes designed to destroy Castro's weakened air force and to protect the invading troops (Etheredge, 1984: 21). Fear of the United States's being portrayed as the aggressor still dominated Kennedy's mind. Within four days of the launching of the attack, the CIA-backed forces were defeated (1985: 18–26).

A superficial comparative analysis of the Cuban and Guatemalan cases could lead one to conclude that the United States resorted to similar measures in both cases. In each instance, decision-makers in Washington sought the diplomatic support of Latin American states, refused to lift an arms embargo, imposed economic sanctions, and designed a covert paramilitary plan, all for the purpose of bringing down the regime that had dared to challenge the North American colossus. This description, although useful, overlooks some important differences.

In the early 1950s, the first step taken by the Truman administration against the Arbenz regime was to impose trade restrictions gradually, rather than suddenly. This action was followed by the consideration, and immediate cancellation, of a covert plan to overthrow Arbenz. The idea of resorting to covert paramilitary means was resurrected shortly after Eisenhower replaced Truman. The selection of these two instruments was followed by the refusal on the part of the US State Department to lift the arms embargo against Guatemala that had existed since the first half of 1940, and by the passage of a resolution by the Organization of American States condemning communist domination or control of any Latin American state.

In the late 1950s and early 1960s, the first policy adopted by the Eisenhower administration against the Castro regime was to continue the arms embargo until the probable future course of the revolutionary government could be ascertained. Shortly afterward, President Eisenhower approved the idea of resorting to covert paramilitary means to destabilize the Castro regime. A brief time later, the US Treasury Department pressured certain US oil refineries not to refine Soviet oil bought by Cuba. In addition, President Eisenhower cut the 1960 quota on Cuban sugar to zero and subsequently ordered the reduction of trade between the two states to a minimum. Thereafter, the foreign ministers of American states agreed, at a meeting held in Costa Rica, to a proposal submitted by Washington censoring intervention or threat of intervention by a extracontinental power. Lastly, the Eisenhower administration recalled its ambassador and ended diplomatic relations with Cuba.

The two most critical differences in the ways in which the United States handled the Guatemalan and Cuban problems are the sequences in which the decisions were made to order the designing of a plan for covert paramilitary action and to impose economic sanctions, and the intensity with which the economic sanctions were implemented. These two variances can be accounted for, in part, by referring to some of the lessons the Eisenhower administration inferred from its Guatemalan experience. To begin with, decision-makers in Washington concluded that it is not always feasible to topple a regime solely with economic pressure but that often it must be paired with a military policy. For this reason, the logical starting point would have been not the imposition of economic sanctions but preparations for a military plan. In addition, these same decision-makers decided that an effective military plan for toppling an anti-US regime would be a covert paramilitary invasion. As argued by some analysts, the ease with which the use of this policy instrument helped topple the Arbenz regime in 1954 convinced President Eisenhower that this type of means could be used to bring about similar results in Cuba (Immerman, 1982; Ambrose, 1984: 556). This kind of rationale seems to have encouraged Eisenhower to suggest in February of 1960 to CIA Director Allan Dulles that his organization design an aggressive plan against Castro "which went beyond pure harassment" (quoted in Benjamin, 1989). However, though Eisenhower had been influenced by the success of the Guatemalan experience, it is important to note that at no time did he recommend that the intelligence agency rely on the same plan it used to overthrow Arbenz to topple Castro.

The third lesson learned from the Guatemalan case refers to the manner in which economic sanctions would be applied. In 1951, when Thomas Mann proposed that the United States reduce its trade with Guatemala gradually, he was hoping not only to undermine Arbenz's ability to govern but also attempting to avert accusations of intervention from other Latin American leaders. Although the latter concern may have been as intense in the Cuban as it was in the Guatemalan case, Eisenhower decided on the basis of Truman's earlier experience, that the application of economic sanctions would be effective only if the administration was willing to risk alienating some of its allies. The Arbenz government, for instance, had had little difficulty in finding trade partners, primarily in Western Europe, as the United States began its gradual imposition of economic sanctions on Guatemala. Eisenhower's willingness to be criticized by some Latin American leaders was reflected in his overt use of the trade relationship between Cuba and the United States as an instrument of coercion.[11]

There was a fourth lesson derived from the Guatemalan case. This lesson, however, rather than simply influencing the decision to resort to covert paramilitary means to overthrow Castro, affected the type of plan the CIA intended to adopt against the Cuban leader. Upon being ordered to design an aggressive and positive plan to topple Castro, the CIA concluded, as it had six years earlier, that the strategy had to be designed to produce not a military defeat but the demobilization and political destabilization of the revolutionary regime. This end, proposed the CIA, would be achieved through extensive propaganda prior to the launching of the invasion, the use of B-26s to destroy Cuba's air force just prior to the actual landing of the troops, and the bombing and strafing of Cuban troops, barracks, and other military targets during and after the landing of the Cuban exiles.

Three questions remain to be addressed regarding the Cuban case. The first and the third look at the problem from the perspective of the Kennedy administration alone, and the second focuses on the difference in behavior between the Eisenhower and Kennedy administrations. The first question – why did President Kennedy agree with his predecessor that the Castro regime could not remain in power? – is the easiest to answer and can be dealt with at two levels: individual and structural.

Addressing the question at an individual level assumes that there might have been something intrinsic in President Kennedy's character that led him to conclude that Castro was such a menace to the United States that his regime had to be destroyed. Although this line of argument is attractive to analysts who are inclined to attribute causality for the foreign policy of states to the central cognitive components of the leaders responsible for the actions of those states, in this case the argument might be afflicted by unnecessary complexity. In 1960 and 1961 there were few decision-makers in Washington who did not agree with Kennedy's assessment. Castro's relationship with Moscow ensured that Kennedy's attitude would be shared almost across the board by principal foreign policy-makers in Washington. Moreover, the US Congress and the American public had been pressing the White House to be more forceful in its dealings with Havana.

The second question that demands close scrutiny is why did President Kennedy, but not President Eisenhower, agree to put into effect the covert paramilitary plan designed by the CIA for the purpose of toppling the Castro regime? At one level, the most obvious reason for Eisenhower not ordering the invasion is that plans were not completed during his tenure. Training of selected leaders to carry out the CIA strategy, approved in March 1960, did not begin until June. Furthermore, the original plan was modified three times – once in November, when it was decided that the original landing point created serious logistical problems; a second time in December; and a third time in January 1961, when it was decided that rather than rely on a 300-man force broken up into small infiltration teams, it would be preferable to engage a larger strike force. Finally, by the end of 1960, the CIA had yet to consolidate a coherent Cuban government in exile (Ambrose, 1981: 311).

Blame for the Bay of Pigs fiasco cannot be lifted from the hands of President Kennedy and his associates. But to acknowledge responsibility is not to say that a different actor under the same circumstances would have acted differently. It is not unusual to believe that a leader could have changed the course of history if only he had said "no" to a proposed policy. It is assumed that in order to say "no" in a credible manner, the negator of the potential action must carefully assess, with the use of reliable information, presumptions of the "if/then" type (Neustadt and May, 1986: 147).

There is nothing wrong with this conclusion, so long as the negator of the proposed action believes that another alternative exists. The critical dilemma faced by the Kennedy administration in 1961 was that no other options besides covert action were believed to be viable. Doing nothing seemed to have been out of the question, for the Washington bureaucracies, the US Congress, and the American public would have questioned immediately Kennedy's ability to lead against any future US adversary. Another alternative, the enforcement of diplomatic and economic pressure, might have served to signal US unwilling-ness to accept passively a challenge to its role as the hegemon of the Caribbean region; but Washington also had learned that economic and diplomatic pressure, in and by themselves, would not alter the structure of Cuba's governing regime. Of all the alternatives, overt military intervention or the implementation of the original CIA plan involving the air support of a covert paramilitary invasion, would have had a better chance of toppling the Castro regime. But at what cost? This consideration brings us to one final question.

Why did President Kennedy order a reduction in the number of planes to be used to strike Cuba before the invasion, and why did he cancel the planned air strikes after the invasion had begun? Hans Morgenthau, as already noted, forwards an illuminating answer. The president, contends Morgenthau, was particularly concerned that the reputation of the United States would suffer extensively if the world learned that the most powerful actor in the Americas had intervened militarily. This concern, adds Morgenthau, blinded Kennedy to the realization that his action was undermining his ability to look after a much more important objective: the strategic interest of the United States.

Morgenthau's analysis is validated by the data. A rational analysis of the Cuban situation in April 1961 would have involved a careful assessment of the effect the reduction in planes and the cancellation of the air strikes during the day of the invasion would have on the overall operation. The CIA, Richard Bissell to be specific, estimated that the operation would not be endangered by the decision to use fewer planes during the air strikes the day before the invasion. From an analytical perspective, thus, the decision could still be seen as the outcome of a rational process. The problem surfaces as one focuses on how the decision to cancel the remaining air strikes was reached. Concerned that the operation was becoming a major news item, Kennedy, after consulting with Secretary of State Dean Rusk and National Security Advisor McGeorge Bundy, and excluding from the process the advice from military experts, ordered the cancellation of the scheduled air strikes. When General Charles Cabell and Richard Bissell learned of this order, however, they informed Rusk that if it were not reversed, the landing would be seriously endangered. Rusk passed this information to the president, but the order was not altered (Etheredge, 1985: 43–4).[12] It was not altered either because Kennedy did not believe that the mission risked failure, or because he did not weigh carefully the extent to which emphasis on protecting the name of the United States would undermine the chances of the invasion's success.

REASONING AND LEARNING BY ANALOGY

The summary in analogical form of the conclusions arrived at in the previous section must begin with the analysis of the policies adopted by the United States toward Cuba during Batista's rule. One of the relationships stipulated with respect to the Guatemalan case referred to the effect the political structure of a foreign government had on Washington's perception of threat. It was contended that conceptual pairings existed between "government of target state *influenced* by Communists" and "low threat," on the one hand; and "government of target state *dominated* by Communists" and "high threat" on the other. From this general relationship it can be inferred that Batista, a leader willing to voice forcefully his anticommunist sentiments, would not have been perceived as a threat by Washington and, moreover, that his eagerness to side with the United States would have been rewarded generously. These two rationales can be captured in the following analogical format:

Government in target state is
dominated by communists who
expropriate foreign property   : High threat :
without adequate compensation,
implement radical agrarian
reforms and establish relations
with Soviet bloc states.

Impose economic sanctions and
diplomatic pressure on, and
prepare to rely on covert   ::
paramilitary intervention
against, government in target
state.

Government in target state is
dominated by anticommunists
who oppose political, economic, : Low threat :
and social reforms.

Extend economic and military
assistance without pressing
government in target state to
engage in political, economic,
and social reforms.

New developments throughout Latin America during the second half of the 1950s, however, convinced the Eisenhower administration that certain dictatorial regimes, even though dominated by anticommunists, could pose a major threat to the interests of the United States. These governments traditionally had opposed political, economic, and social reforms. Many of these governments had been successful in curtailing domestic opposition; however, some officials in Washington became concerned that others might be unable to control the internal turmoil in the future. Thus, although Washington continued to believe that governments dominated by communists were a threat to the United States, it began to revise its image of anticommunist governments that opposed reforms.

Government in target state is
dominated by anticommunists   Low
who oppose political, social, and : threat ::
economic reforms and do not
face strong domestic opposition.

Government in target state is
dominated by anticommunists   High
who oppose political, social, and : threat
economic reforms and face
strong domestic opposition.

The problem faced by the Eisenhower administration in 1958 was how to respond to the pressure being applied to the Batista regime by Castro's guerrillas. At that time, most policy-makers in Washington did not believe that Castro was a communist, but they did fear that he would be very difficult to control. For this reason, they hoped to replace Batista with a moderate government, one that would be willing to continue protecting US interests and at the same time would gradually bring about domestic reforms. To fulfill these objectives, they began to apply political pressure and placed a ban on the sale of weapons to the Batista regime. However, they knew that it would take some time to persuade Batista to relinquish power in favor of a moderate government and for the new regime to consolidate its authority. Therefore, Washington, by guaranteeing that the flow of weapons to Batista would not dry up instantaneously, sought to ensure that Castro would not be able to exploit to his advantage the weakness of the existing regime. Washington's definition of, and response to, the problem can be represented as follows:

Apply gradual ban on sale of weapons and put political pressure on government in target state dominated by anticommunists who oppose reforms and face strong domestic opposition, so that they will relinquish power in favor of a moderate government.	:	Instatement of radical regime preempted.	::	Apply radical ban on sale of weapons and put political pressure on government in target state dominated by anticommunists who oppose reforms and face strong domestic opposition, so that they will relinquish power in favor of a moderate government.	:	Instatement of radical regime not preempted.

The year 1959 marked the dawn of a new era in US–Cuban relations. Washington's initial reaction to Castro's ascension to power differed little from its responses in 1945 when Arévalo became president of Guatemala, or six years later when Arbenz succeeded him. Although in all three instances several decision-makers in Washington were troubled by the prospects of working with leaders whose political orientation deviated measurably from the center, they generally hoped that with proper handling they would be able to mold the policies of those leaders. This objective, it was believed, could be achieved by recognizing the new government and signaling a willingness to support moderate reforms.

Accept newly formed government in target state dominated by political leaders committed to political, social, and economic reforms and express willingness to help so long as they avoid radical reforms.	:	Political leaders in newly formed government in target state recognize constraints under which they must work, welcome offer, and express commitment to moderate reforms.	::	Do not recognize newly formed government in target state dominated by political leaders committed to political, social, and economic reforms, and express unwillingness to extend any type of help.	:	Political leaders in newly formed government in target state criticize reaction, and begin to implement radical reforms.

The attitude reflected in the last analogical structure did not survive long. The change, as in the Guatemalan case, came about when Washington concluded that Cuba was under communist rule. Although the visit to Cuba by Soviet officials in February 1960 was perceived in Washington as a final indication that Castro and his government were determined to establish closer ties with Moscow, the belief that the Cuban government was dominated by communists had begun to take root earlier. As in the Guatemalan case, the analogical relationship can be structured as follows:

Government in target state affiliates with communist labor leaders and implements + radical economic and agricultural reforms.	Some governmental positions in target state are held by communists. :	Government in target state is dominated by communists.

The most striking difference between the Cuban and the Guatemalan cases is the manner in which the US government responded to its belief that the two states were facing the threat of domination by communist regimes. The Guatemalan problem was structured and addressed as follows:

Government in target state is : dominated by communists.	High threat in international environment bounded by constraints. :	Impose economic sanctions and diplomatic pressure gradually on, and be prepared to rely on covert paramilitary intervention against, government in target state.

Three lessons were learned from the Guatemalan case: (i) economic sanctions applied gradually are unlikely to have a noticeable negative effect on the targeted regime; (ii) if a regime is to be toppled, then preparations for military action must begin immediately; (iii) covert paramilitary intervention can be an effective way to topple a regime. These three lessons persuaded the Eisenhower administration that the Cuban case had to be restructured as follows:

Government in target state is dominated by communists.	High threat in an international environment : bounded by constraints.	Prepare to rely on covert paramilitary intervention : against, and impose economic sanctions and diplomatic pressure fully on, government in target state.

Three major issues still need to be structured analogically: (i) the CIA decision to structure the Cuban operation similarly to the Guatemalan plan; (ii) President Eisenhower's decision not to order the launching of a covert paramilitary invasion against Cuba before he left office; and (iii) President Kennedy's decision to approve the launching of a covert paramilitary invasion against Cuba. It is generally agreed that CIA planners modeled the Cuban strategy on many of the ideas they had used to design the plan to overthrow Arbenz in 1954. In analogical form, it could be noted that:

Covert paramilitary intervention plan drawn to overthrow an earlier government dominated by communists failed to achieve objective.	:	Do not draw new covert paramilitary intervention plan to overthrow government in target state dominated by communists according to ideas that had structured earlier plan.	::	Covert paramilitary intervention plan drawn to overthrow an earlier government dominated by communists achieved objective.	:	Draw new covert paramilitary intervention plan to overthrow government in target state dominated by communists according to ideas that had structured earlier plan.

When Eisenhower approved the launching of a covert paramilitary invasion against Guatemala in 1954, he did so not only because he believed that it was imperative that the Arbenz regime be toppled but also, because the plan was ready to be implemented. In January 1961, the plan to overthrow Castro was still in flux; it had just experienced a third major change. Regardless of how much pressure Eisenhower might have faced to topple the Castro regime or how much he might have wanted to be remembered as the president responsible for eradicating communism in Cuba, the risks of implementing a plan that was still going through some major changes were too high. This is particularly true if one takes into consideration that although the extent to which Castro could rely on the political support of Cuba's main political figures was questionable, he had the support of the new military. The analogy can be delineated in a manner similar to the structure designed to explain the rationale behind Eisenhower's decision to proceed with the covert paramilitary invasion of Guatemala in 1954. In order to highlight the differences behind the reasoning processes of the Eisenhower and Kennedy administrations, only those factors that were critical in the final decision will be included in the analogical structure.

Economic sanctions and diplomatic pressure imposed on government in target state dominated by communists fail to undermine their power.	:	Government in target state dominated by communists is supported by the military.	:	Covert paramilitary intervention plan drawn to overthrow government in target state dominated by communists needs additional tuning.	:	Delay the launching of covert paramilitary intervention against government in target state dominated by communists.

The last analogical structure in this chapter deals with Kennedy's decision to approve the covert attack on the Castro regime. To propose, as was done earlier, that Kennedy's freedom to choose was severely constrained by the manner in which similar problems had been structured in the past is not to argue that he could not have selected a different military alternative from that proposed by the CIA. And yet, Kennedy's only realistic alternatives to the CIA plan were an overt, mass invasion of Cuba, involving not only Cuban nationals but also US military forces, or a covert paramilitary invasion involving greater US air support. Since Kennedy shared his predecessors' sentiment that the United States could not afford to be perceived by its Latin American allies as an interventionist power, it is not surprising that he rejected both options and pressured the CIA to rely on covert means with minimum overt US involvement. Moreover, it is essential to keep in mind that the pressure from the US Congress to take a major step against the Castro regime had continued to intensify. There was, however, one critical difference between the way Eisenhower viewed the plan against Castro and the way Kennedy perceived it. Both Eisenhower and Kennedy hoped to minimize the chances that the United States would be accused of instigating the operation against Castro. But Kennedy failed to realize that his last-minute demands that the plan be altered – demands intended to lower the likelihood that the United States would be identified as the instigator of the operation – were in fact endangering the plan's success. Eisenhower under similar circumstances would most likely have demanded a rigorous assessment of the new plan's chances of achieving the objective for which it was designed. Kennedy's delineation of the problem can be structured analogically as follows:

Economic sanctions and diplomatic pressure imposed on government in target state dominated by communists failed to undermine their power.	Domestic criticism of actions by government in target state dominated by communists intensifies.	International environment is bounded by major constraints.	Order the launching of covert paramilitary intervention against government in target state dominated by communists.
	:	:	:

The last two analogical structures capture in a very simple manner the central differences in the reasoning processes of the Eisenhower and Kennedy administrations. The leaders of the two administrations shared the beliefs that the Castro regime posed a threat to the interests of the United States and that past measures to topple the Cuban regime had not been productive. Similarly, they shared the beliefs that: (i) the United States should not be perceived as the power behind any covert operation launched to topple Castro; (ii) the Cuban military supported the new regime; (iii) the US Congress and public were increasingly dissatisfied with the behavior of the Castro regime; and (iv) the plan to overthrow Castro should not be implemented without first ensuring that it would have a good chance of succeeding. But these various beliefs were not shared in the same degree.

Eisenhower did not forget that regardless of how important it was to respond to the demands of the US Congress and public, and at the same time avert international criticism, ultimately both objectives would be best served if he could ensure that the plan to topple the Castro regime was designed to deal effectively with the obstacles likely to be encountered in the process. Kennedy, on the other hand, failed to realize that by responding primarily to the pressures to act against Castro and to ensure that the United States would not be identified as the villain behind the act, he was, in fact, pursuing two conflicting objectives. He failed to focus sufficiently on whether the CIA plan was the right plan to weaken the power of the Castro regime. The paradox in Kennedy's behavior is that ultimately he undermined the two values he sought so intensely to protect: his political reputation and the prestige of the United States. Neither lesson would be overlooked by his immediate successor in the handling of the 1965 Dominican crisis.

THE BURDEN OF ANALOGIES

Reasoning and learning by analogy entails more than borrowing from past experiences. It involves using the past in order to evaluate the context in which concepts are related; it involves ascertaining whether past relationships apply to contemporary problems; and it involves delineating new relationships when existing associations cannot help address new situations.

The Guatemalan experience helped structure the way in which the Eisenhower administration defined the situation in Cuba during the early days of Batista's rule. The Cuban leader, in contrast to Arbenz, sought to promote US economic interests and was willing to voice his opposition to communism. In time, however, the reliability of this standard as a measure of a Latin American leader's worthiness to the United States began to diminish. US foreign policy-makers had more difficulty believing that the increase in political, economic, and social turmoil in many Latin American countries was the result of actions initiated by the communists instead of behavior born of deeply rooted discontent. This new reality began to take form in the minds of the leaders in Washington as they were attempting to give meaning to the challenge posed to the Batista regime by Fidel Castro's guerrilla forces. Thus, as it became more evident that Batista would not be able to survive politically and that Castro might succeed in his drive for power, Washington began to search for a moderate alternative.

Did Washington begin to search for a moderate alternative because it feared that a Castro rulership would open the gates to communism in the Caribbean Basin, would enable the Soviet Union to challenge US hegemony in the region, would undermine the control the United States had over the economic structure of the region, or would pose a direct threat to US companies investing in Cuba? A simple answer is not possible, for these potential realities did not exist independently of one another. At the same time, however, it is evident that the leaders in Washington were not overburdened by the fear that any of these scenarios was a foregone conclusion. This sense of confidence could be attributed, in part, to the belief that although Castro was somewhat an enigma, he was smart enough to realize that it would not be wise to alienate the United States totally. Moreover, Arbenz's failure to free his country from US influence seems to have convinced Washington that Castro would be unable to nurture an independent future for his country also.

Why did the United States decide that it could not tolerate Castro's rulership in Cuba? As in the Guatemalan case, the decision was made after Castro began to staff governmental positions with individuals believed to be communists, to establish close relationships with leftish labor leaders, and to implement his radical agrarian plan. In addition, one must not disregard the fact that President Eisenhower ordered CIA director Allan Dulles to begin designing a plan to replace the Castro regime the same day the Soviet delegation, led by Deputy Chairman Mikoyan, arrived in Cuba.

Castro's actions had an adverse effect on US private interests in Cuba. But the decision by Eisenhower to intervene against Castro was not the result of a commitment on the part of his government to promote the private interests of US corporations investing in Cuba. Both Ambassador Bonsal and Rubottom, the assistant secretary of state for inter-American affairs, had been discouraging US businesses from expecting the State Department to protect their interests. The two US officials believed that the function of the State Department should be limited to ensuring that foreign governments respected international practices toward foreign investments (Starr and Lowenthal, 1988: 40). Washington's commitment had a much deeper rationale. Castro's actions signaled to the US leaders that the Cuban ruler was determined to create a political and economic system that was unacceptable to the United States – a communist system. The task of the US government was to prevent this system from ever becoming a reality in Cuba.

Did the Guatemalan success promote complacency in the approach to the Cuban problem? It is unlikely that it did for Kennedy. He had been in office less than three months, and thus there was no reason for him to know the history behind the Guatemalan experience. The president, for reasons to be considered in chapter 7, chose to place an inordinate amount of weight on trying to ensure that the United States not be perceived as an interventionist actor. But there is little doubt that success in dealing with Arbenz influenced not only the way the members of the Eisenhower administration defined the Cuban problem but also their selection of instruments.

If success begets complacency, which in the Cuban case meant borrowing from the past without carefully ascertaining whether its lessons were relevant to the new problem, what does failure promote? According to Jaime Carbonell, discovery of an error that brought about unintended results triggers a discrimination process that leads to the reassessment of the level of applicability of the analogical structures initially referred to. Stated in the context of the present empirical study, this means two things. First, it signifies that if one accepts the conclusion that the Cuban affair was a costly experience, lessons inferred from it will have transformed the "original problem space." And second, it means that the transformed problem space will be tested against a future, similar problem. More concretely, this means that if a new problem space were designed as a result of the Cuban failure, its principal features will become evident as the empirical analysis focuses on attempts by the United States to deal with the political problems that began to germinate in the Dominican Republic in the late 1950s.

Three lessons from the Cuban experience should have resonated in the minds of the decision-makers in Washington as they tackled the Dominican problem. The first was the belief that the United States must attempt to replace right-wing dictatorial regimes with moderate governments if it hopes to preempt the formation of radical regimes. Second, was the conviction that political stability and economic reforms must be promoted in order to persuade the populus that it is possible to have a viable future without a radical regime. And third was the acceptance that the United States might have to intervene militarily and overtly, and hence be perceived as an interventionist power, if the threat of a "second Cuba" were to increase dramatically.

6

The Dominican Republic: The Future Must Not Resemble the Past

Batista is to Castro as Trujillo is to X. But who would "X" be?
Piero Gleijeses, *The Dominican Crisis*

THE NEW CHALLENGE

In late April 1965, President Lyndon Johnson ordered US forces to invade the Dominican Republic. Students of this event generally agree that rarely does one find in the annals of US relations with Latin America an event that dominated the reasoning process of the leaders in Washington so intensely as the Cuban case controlled the definition of the Dominican problem in 1965. This agreement, however, has not prevented analysts from presenting conflicting explanations as to why President Johnson believed it was imperative for the United States to land its marines on the small Caribbean country (see Lowenthal, 1972: ch. 5).

The simplest and most effective manner in which to consider these various explanations is by delineating the way each responds to the "official line." The most prominent early defender of the "official line" was John Bartlow Martin. According to Martin, the Johnson administration decided to send US Marines to the Dominican Republic only after establishing that the well-being of US citizens living in that country was being threatened. Furthermore, he notes that the decision to engage in a full invasion was made only after learning that the communists were exploiting the situation in order to augment their political control (1966: ch. 27).

Those who have challenged the "official line" have presented a variety of alternative explanations, including both the strategic and economic approaches mentioned previously (see chapter 2). A major representative of the strategic position is Walter LaFeber. LaFeber maintains that the United States was convinced that chaotic conditions in the Dominican Republic presented ripe opportunities for leftists. Johnson, he argues, was determined to ensure that no other communist government be established in the region, so that the Caribbean area and Central America would remain within the United States's sphere of influence (1983: 157–8).

Proponents of the economic approach maintain that the Johnson administration used the "official line" – that the Dominican revolt was being exploited by the international communist movement – as part of a tactic to disguise the efforts by the United States to dominate the Dominican Republic economically and politically. Fred Goff and Michael Locker contend that a government led by Juan Bosch would have posed a direct threat to the economic and financial interests of the United States (1969: 280). Piero Gleijeses arrives at a similar, although more guarded, conclusion when he focuses on the Kennedy administration's decision to allow the Bosch regime to be toppled in 1963. Accordingly to Gleijeses, the Kennedy administration was particularly distressed by Bosch's unwillingness to act forcefully against communists in the Dominican Republic (1978: 96–8). But Gleijeses also maintains that Bosch's cardinal sin was that he "began to reassert the nation's sovereignty" (p. 95). The constitution of April 1963 was designed to bring about an economic transformation, a change that earned Bosch the enmity of US business interests in Santo Domingo. In addition, the constitution led to recognition in the US State Department that its ability to continue influencing the economic policies of the Dominican Republic could no longer be taken for granted. Gleijeses never proposes that the United States was actively involved in toppling Bosch, but he argues that these factors may have persuaded US decision-makers in Washington and Santo Domingo that it would be preferable for them not to go out of their way to avert a coup against Bosch (pp. 95–8).

The strategic and economic arguments are fitted into a single, general framework by Cole Blasier. Blasier states, "The evidence seems conclusive that the prevention of another 'Cuba' was the real explanation from the beginning of the intervention" (1985: 246–9). However, Blasier also notes that it is generally incorrect to assume that the desire by the US government to protect and advance US interests abroad is incompatible with the perception of a communist threat. A communist takeover of the Dominican Republic would have undermined not only the United States's military strategic interests in the Caribbean Basin but also its general economic interests and the financial concerns of US corporations investing in the area (p. 247). Moreover, adds Blasier, it is necessary to acknowledge the importance of two other interrelated factors. First, the psychological climate in the United States during the Cold War, with its strong anticommunist emotionalism, made it almost impossible for Washington to look at the Dominican crisis with a dispassionate perspective. In addition, it is quite evident that President Johnson, still a potential contender for re-election in 1968, was well aware of the domestic political penalties implicit in a "second Cuba" in the Caribbean Basin (p. 248).

Abraham Lowenthal, one of the most respected analysts of the Dominican

Republic, questions most of the arguments just discussed. He proposes that foreign policy be viewed not as the product of a conscious process but as the manifestation of the national attitudes and assumptions of policy-level officials who act as representatives of a broad set of bureaucratic interests, and whose range of effective choices is demarcated by organizational procedures and the need to formulate a compromise agreed to (or on) by the involved parties. At first glance it may seem that Lowenthal is proposing an approach intrinsically different from those discussed thus far. However, a more careful investigation reveals that Lowenthal's analysis does not fall into a completely separate mode.

Lowenthal breaks the analysis of the Dominican crisis into two parts. The first dwells on the tendency of different US organizations to react to the problem in different ways. He attributes this variance to the presence of different organizational interests. In this respect, Lowenthal adds a new dimension. But, as he seeks to explain why the United States finally decided to land its marines in Santo Domingo, he falls back on the type of explanation typical of the other studies: President Johnson intervened to avert a "second Cuba." A second Cuba had to be averted for two broad reasons: "international and domestic political considerations reinforced each other and sustained the US government's determination not to allow a 'second Cuba'" (1972: 153).

Many analysts who have studied the Dominican crisis have also attempted to explain the actions of the United States toward the Dominican Republic prior to 1965 (see Lowenthal, 1972; Gleijeses, 1978). These students share the attitude that without a thorough understanding of the rationale behind such actions, it would be very difficult to comprehend why the Johnson administration ordered the invasion. This chapter adopts a similar perspective. Here it will be demonstrated that the decision to invade the Dominican Republic was not an isolated act but part of a process. Specifically, it will show that the Cuban experience influenced the way the problems posed by developments in the Dominican Republic between 1958 and 1965 were defined, and helped structure the policies resorted to by the United States to resolve these problems.

The definition of problems and selection of instruments for the Dominican case can be divided into three periods. During the late 1950s and first two years of the 1960s, the Batista specter was utilized by Washington to characterize Trujillo as a right-wing dictator whose continued rulership promoted instability in the Dominican Republic, and to justify attempts to replace him with a moderate government in order to avert the birth of a communist regime. Between 1962 and 1965, the failure to handle effectively the Castro regime was referred to in order to promote the argument that it was imperative to create a democratic political system in the Dominican Republic and that that goal could be achieved by responding to the social and economic concerns of the Dominican people. And, finally, in April 1965, the Johnson administration employed the threat of a second Cuba to rationalize the landing of some 22,000 US marines in Santo Domingo.

To address the dilemma faced by the United States with respect to the Trujillo regime, three questions will guide the empirical analysis:

1   Why did the Eisenhower administration wait just over a year after the Cuban revolution had begun, to impose economic and military sanctions and to apply political pressure against the Dominican Republic, when the Trujillo regime had been a close ally of the United States and was not in danger of being toppled?

2   Why did President Eisenhower wait less than one year after his administration had begun to impose economic and military sanctions and to apply political pressure against the Dominican Republic, to approve a CIA plan to topple the Trujillo regime?

3   Why did President Kennedy, although he believed that the Trujillo regime posed a threat to the interests of the United States, order the CIA, just a month after it had failed to topple the Castro regime, to stop the transfer of arms to Dominican nationals plotting to assassinate Trujillo?

A second set of questions focuses on attempts by the Kennedy and Johnson administrations to create a stable political regime in the Dominican Republic. This period, in turn, can be separated into two scenarios: (i) the events from the moment Trujillo was assassinated to the day Juan Bosch was toppled; and (ii) the events from the time of Bosch's political demise to the beginning of April 1965. With regard to the events following Trujillo's assassination, one can ask:

4   Why did the Kennedy administration use economic coercion and the threat of military intervention to pressure the new Dominican government to exile the rest of the Trujillo family?

5   Why did the Kennedy administration place so much emphasis on persuading the Dominican leadership to hold democratic elections and abide by the results?

6   Why did the Kennedy administration initially herald the election of Juan Bosch as the president of the Dominican Republic, but then begin to question whether he was the right type of leader?

7   Why did the Kennedy administration pressure the political right and the military leaders not to mount a *coup d'état* against Juan Bosch?

Following Bosch's demise one can consider:

8   Why did the Kennedy administration suspend diplomatic relations with, and halt all military and economic aid to, the Dominican Republic after Juan Bosch was toppled?

9   Why did the Johnson administration wait less than three months after Bosch had been toppled to renew diplomatic relations with, and resume military and economic aid to, the Dominican Republic?

The final set of questions deals solely with the issue of how the Johnson administration responded to attempts by certain Dominican factions to topple the Reid Cabral regime and reinstate Juan Bosch as president.

10   Why did the Johnson administration refuse to help the Reid Cabral regime

after it came under military attack by a group demanding that Juan Bosch be reinstated as president and the Cabral regime proposed that it be replaced by a military junta?

11 Why did the Johnson administration order the Defense Department to undertake a military intervention in Santo Domingo?

THE DEATH OF A DICTATOR – THE BIRTH OF INSTABILITY

On May 30, 1961, a month and a half after the Bay of Pigs fiasco, and just a few minutes before 10 p.m., two cars carrying several gunmen converged on Rafael Leonidas Trujillo's unescorted automobile and opened fire, killing him. Trujillo's death ended a rule that had begun more than thirty years before, and that had been marked by an unrestrained greed for both political power and economic wealth. Throughout those years, Washington had been willing to accept the Dominican leader's despotic methods so long as he demonstrated a commitment to the protection of US interests (Wiarda, 1975: vol. III, 1437–40).

Rafael Trujillo had been elected president of the Dominican Republic in May 1930, shortly after a *coup d'état* led by Rafael Estrella Ureña had overthrown the government of Horacio Vasquez. Under Trujillo's rule, between 1945 and 1955, the country's national budget increased by more than 1,600 percent; and between 1945 and 1961, capital investment and national production tripled. These achievements were brought about by strict administrative centralization, economic monopoly, extensive exploitation of the population, and the extension of inducements to foreign firms, especially US corporations, to invest in the Dominican Republic (1975: vol. III, 1431–7).

Washington's reluctance to pressure Trujillo to reform the political and economic systems of the Dominican Republic began to decline during the late 1950s. It has been suggested that the turning point in US–Dominican relations came as a result of the death in March 1956 of Jesús de Galindez. A Spaniard who had spent six years in the Dominican Republic, Galindez was kidnapped in New York City, where he had been working on a book highly critical of Trujillo. He was flown to Ciudad Trujillo, and killed (Bell, 1981: 71–2). The widespread attention the Galindez affair received, both in the United States and Europe, pressured the State Department to demand that the Dominican government provide further information about the incident. The importance of this incident, however, has been overstated; for although Trujillo came under intense world-wide scrutiny following Galindez's death, he continued to receive the support and backing of the United States.

In 1958, a minor change took place in the relationship between the two countries. In March of that year, the Eisenhower administration placed a ban on the shipment of weapons to Cuba. This action, as explained in the previous chapter, was initiated to control the criticism launched against the United States for providing weapons to a regime that was using them against its own countrymen. Aware that Trujillo had been funneling weapons to Fulgencio

Batista, officials in Washington decided that no new weapons would be sold to the Dominican Republic until the conflict in Cuba was resolved (Schreiber, 1973: 407).

This decision was made about two months before Vice President Richard Nixon's fateful Latin American trip, which was instrumental in awakening some Washington officials to the resentment that large portions of the Latin American population felt toward the United States. This new awareness, however, did not alter the way the United States dealt with Trujillo. Although the Dominican leader was perceived by some as an embarrassment to the United States, those officials monitoring events in the Dominican Republic felt no sense of urgency.

Washington's reluctance to alter its policy could be attributed to two factors. First, in 1958 Trujillo did not face the level of domestic political opposition experienced by Batista in Cuba. The difference is best explained by Howard Wiarda:

> the oppressive tactics employed by the Trujillo regime against the population and the poverty, misery, hatred, bitterness, and frustration which he bequeathed the Dominican people in a time of rising aspirations provided, as in Batista's Cuba, an especially fertile ground for communist appeals ... Yet, Trujillo had kept the communists under firm control, never allowing them to secure a strong foothold as Batista had done. (1975: vol. III, 1578)

Second, although the Eisenhower administration was not happy with the idea of having to deal with an individual like Castro, many of its members believed, at least initially, that the Cuban leader could be persuaded that it would be in Cuba's interest to maintain good relationships with the United States. With Castro not being perceived as a major, immediate threat, Washington felt no need to pressure Trujillo to modify his country's social, economic, and political structures. Batista's downfall in the final days of 1958 did not alter instantaneously the way in which the United States viewed the Dominican regime, but it had an almost immediate effect on Trujillo's own perceptions. On April 21, 1959, Trujillo placed the Dominican Armed Forces on full alert and declared a state of emergency. The alert was called in response to information which indicated that an attack by Dominican citizens organized in Cuba was forthcoming (United Sates Congress, Senate, Committee on Foreign Relations [CFR], 1965: 4; Diederich, 1978: 28).

The attack did not materialize for some time. Prior to it, however, Trujillo was to suffer condemnation by a major Latin American leader. On June 12, Venezuela's newly elected president, Rómulo Betancourt, who for many years had been critical of Trujillo's government, ended his country's diplomatic relations with the Dominican Republic. Betancourt's action was followed two days later by the invasion Trujillo had been predicting. The invading forces, led by Major Enrique Jimenez Moyar, a Dominican citizen who had fought alongside Fidel Castro in Cuba's Sierra Maestra, attempted to duplicate the Cuban success. The invaders failed, and were captured or killed in a two-week period (Diederich, 1978: 28–9). Immediately following Trujillo's victory, Cuba announced it was ending its diplomatic relations with the Dominican Republic (CFR, 1965: 4).

Opposition to the Trujillo regime continued to mount, not only externally but also within the Dominican Republic. On January 28, 1960, fearing that the strength of the political opposition was getting out of hand, Trujillo ordered the imprisonment of between 1,000 and 2,000 people. International criticism followed almost immediately. On February 5, Venezuelan President Betancourt requested that the Organization of American States investigate charges that the Trujillo regime had undertaken mass arrests (CFR, 1965: 4).

By this time Washington had already decided that Trujillo was becoming a major liability to the United States. On January 14, Eisenhower met with Secretary of State Herter and other members of the National Security Council to discuss, among other things, how to respond to developments in the Dominican Republic. The consensus was to "encourage a moderate, pro-United States leadership among the civilian and dissident elements to take over in the event of the flight, assassination, death or overthrow of Trujillo." But the Eisenhower administration was not just getting ready in case Trujillo lost political control; in fact, Eisenhower and Herter met on several occasions in February to discuss ways they could persuade Trujillo to resign (Ambrose, 1984: 556).[1] During the early stages of these discussions, the State Department approved a trip to Ciudad Trujillo by Senator George Smathers designed to convince the Dominican leader to abdicate in favor of democracy. Smather's message was not unique; it was the product of an immediate US experience. "Communist vultures of the same kind who have overrun Cuba," noted Smathers, would depose Trujillo unless he acted first and instituted a democratic political structure (quoted in Diederich, 1978: 38).

Trujillo, aware that his political destiny was not independent of the United States, agreed to hold elections. On February 9, he announced that municipal elections would be held within one year and nationwide elections in no more than three years. The Eisenhower administration was not impressed by Trujillo's promises. That same month, President Eisenhower ordered the Special Group, a subcommittee of the National Secutiry Council, to consider extending covert aid to Trujillo's enemies.[2] This action was followed by the announcement on February 26 that military aid to the Dominican Republic would be cut in June 1960 (CFR, 1965: 5).

The decision by the Eisenhower administration to pressure Trujillo to alter his country's political structure, and the order by the president himself that the Special Group consider ways to aid those Dominican citizens attempting to oust Trujillo, must be seen not only in the context of the domestic and international pressures the Dominican dictator was experiencing, but also in the context of how the "Cuban dilemma" was being defined in Washington. Although it is evident that by the beginning of 1960 the domestic and international pressures on Trujillo had mounted extensively, equally critical, at least from Washington's perspective, was the fact that the relationship between the United States and Cuba had deteriorated to the point that President Eisenhower found it justifiable to order the CIA to prepare a covert plan to overthrow Fidel Castro. This order was given a few weeks before the National Security Council's Special Group was asked to consider aiding Trujillo's enemies if circumstances required it. Moreover, agreements between the Soviet Union and Cuba that followed the visit of high-level Soviet officials to Cuba in February 1960 must have reminded the Eisenhower administration of the price it might have to pay for supporting a repressive regime.

The Cuban dimension, however, was also very significant in a different sense. Since the middle of 1959, the Eisenhower administration had been trying to persuade the Latin American countries to support the increasing US condemnation of the Castro regime. In early 1960, Betancourt, and President José Figueres of Costa Rica, suggested that Washington could enlist their support against Castro by acting concurrently against Trujillo. In the meantime, the Dominican leader, still convinced that he could appease a dissatisfied US government, announced on April 1 his resignation as leader of the Dominican Party. His action failed to calm Washington.

On April 14, Secretary of State Herter submitted a memorandum to Eisenhower arguing that in view of the recent deterioration of Trujillo's domestic and international position and the possibility that radicals might exploit the situation to bring to power a Castro-type government, the United States should:

(a) Instruct the United States Ambassador in the Dominican Republic to seek – with such intelligence support as he requires – within the next few weeks to make arrangements with appropriate civil and military dissident elements to be prepared to take over the Government. He should be authorized to indicate to them that they should immediately request US recognition, and ask for US military assistance under Article III of the Rio Treaty if unable to maintain themselves against actual or threatened Castro-sponsored invasions or against threatened insurrection incited by pro-Castro or pro-Communist elements inside or outside the country. In the event US military aid is requested, provisional government should simultaneously request assistance from OAS.

(b) Provided step (a) is successful, make appropriate arrangements to persuade Trujillo to leave voluntarily by avoiding any steps or commitments which would identify the US with him or imply that the US condones his past actions.

(c) Be prepared to extend rapidly diplomatic assistance to the new regime.

(d) Be prepared to organize or join in an appropriate OAS action to condemn the Trujillo regime and, if possible, to offer a collective guarantee – including the use of military force – to assure that the will of the Dominican people can be expressed free of outside – i.e. Castro – influence.

(e) Be prepared if necessary to assist unilaterally the new regime militarily, including the landing of US forces at the request of the provisional government should OAS action not be forthcoming immediately.

(f) In the event that there is no request for US military assistance from a provisional government substantially in control of the country nor appropriate action by the

OAS, the United States should then avoid action that would result in the use of US forces against significant resistance within the Dominican Republic or otherwise place the United States in the position of seizing foreign territory by use of force.

President Eisenhower approved the contingency plan a week later (Diederich, 1978: 41).[3]

Trujillo, afraid that he was losing control of the situation, decided to retaliate by going against the individual whom he considered to be the central source of his troubles – President Betancourt. On June 24, 1969, 60 pounds of ammonium nitrate, packed in two suitcases, were detonated in a parked car as Betancourt's automobile passed en route to a military parade. The assassination attempt not only failed but also led to an increase in political pressure against the Trujillo regime. In late June the leaders of Costa Rica and Venezuela warned US Secretary of State Christian Herter that if the United States did not eliminate Trujillo they would invade the Dominican Republic (Diederich, 1978: 41; see also Wiarda, 1968: 154).

Washington was as yet unwilling to rely on extraordinary means to alter the Dominican Republic's political power structure. At the same time, it was aware that Trujillo had to be told in very clear terms that the United States would no longer accept the status quo. In the middle of the summer of 1960, the Eisenhower administration was provided with the perfect opportunity to convey its deep dissatisfaction. The US Congress had authorized President Eisenhower to cut Cuba's sugar quota and to redistribute it among other countries selling sugar to the United States. Under different circumstances, the Dominican Republic would have been the perfect supplier; it was not pure coincidence that the Dominican Republic had been described as "la isla de azucar" (Vicini, 1957). But Eisenhower was well aware that the person who would benefit the most by a decision in favour of the Dominican Republic was Trujillo, as he controlled approximately 65 percent of the sugar industry. For this reason, the president decided not to allocate any portion of Cuba's sugar quota to the republic (Schreiber, 1973: 407–8; Wiarda, 1975: vol. III, 1437).

Pressure on Trujillo continued to mount. On July 1, the Venezuelan government announced its intention to call for an emergency meeting of the Organization of American States to consider charges that Trujillo had been the force behind the attempt to assassinate President Betancourt. Fearing that the United States would finally decide at the meeting to break its ties with his regime unless he signaled his willingness to open the Dominican Republic's political system, Trujillo announced his brother's resignation as the country's president (CFR, 1965: 5; Schreiber, 1973: 409).

The conference of OAS foreign ministers took place in San José, Costa Rica. The Trujillo issue prompted the proposal of two major alternatives. Most Latin American countries favored a break in diplomatic relations and a partial interruption of economic relations with the Dominican Republic. The United States, represented by Herter, opposed these actions on the grounds that toppling Trujillo would not ensure the establishment of a democratic regime and, in fact, could very well augment the likelihood of a communist takeover. As an alternative, the secretary of state proposed that the OAS try to persuade

Trujillo to democratize his regime. But on August 20, the Latin American proposal was approved overwhelmingly (CFR, 1965: 6; Wiarda, 1968: 155–6).

The decision by the OAS made it easier for the Eisenhower administration to increase the pressure on Trujillo. On August 23, President Eisenhower asked Congress to curtail sugar imports from the Dominican Republic. Three days later, he downgraded US diplomatic relationships with the Dominican government by purposely avoiding the appointment of a new US ambassador. In the meantime, some members in the US Congress began to openly challenge Eisenhower's foreign policy toward the Dominican Republic. For instance, Allan Ellender, chairman of the Senate Agriculture Committee, stated, "I wish there were a Trujillo in every country of South and Central America tonight" (quoted in Schreiber, 1973: 408). His challenge and those of other senators and congressmen were strong enough to ensure that Congress would not resolve the sugar issue before it adjourned on September 1. Congress's inaction left standing the law requiring that the United States purchase an additional 322,000 tons of Dominican sugar by the end of 1960 (1973: 408).

On October 27, 1960, Thomas Mann, the assistant secretary of state for inter-American affairs, received a very distressing letter from Henry Dearborn, the US chargé d'affaires in the Dominican Republic. Dearborn, convinced that Trujillo, if allowed to go into exile, would devote his life to preventing the creation of stable governments in the Dominican Republic, proposed to Mann that the Dominican dictator be assassinated. In the meantime, the CIA had not remained inactive. Some three weeks earlier, it had produced a study titled, "Plans for the Dominican Internal Opposition and Dominican Desk for Overthrow of the Trujillo Government." Part of the plan called for the delivery of 300 rifles, ammunition, and an electronic detonating device with remote control features to a place near Ciudad Trujillo. The plan was finally approved by the Special Group on January 12, 1961 (Diederich, 1978: 47–8). But this decision came too late to receive Eisenhower's blessing. Just over a week later, John F. Kennedy was sworn in as the new president of the United States. The Special Group plan was approved following the suspension by the United States and Venezuela of the exportation of petroleum products, trucks, and spare parts (*New York Times*, January 4, 1961).

One of the unusual characteristics of the Eisenhower administration is how differently it handled the problems generated by the Trujillo and Batista regimes. First, the decision to act against Trujillo was made at the highest level of the administration. President Eisenhower, it may be recalled, had not been fully informed of the situation in Cuba until Herter reported to him in late December 1958 that the Cuban leader was about to be toppled, not by his own military but by guerrilla forces, and that Castro might install a government with communists in key posts. This different level of involvement of the president can be explained in the context of the lessons Eisenhower and his advisors had learned from the Cuban experience as well as by their desire to minimize Latin American opposition to US hostility toward the Castro regime. The aftermath of Batista's downfall had led the Eisenhower administration to realize that a threat on the life of a dictatorial regime that had maintained close relationships with the United States could no longer be perceived as a minor problem that could be handled by low-level officials in Washington's foreign policy structure. The costs to the United States of failing to avert Castro's rise to political power dictated that the top US foreign policy-makers in the executive body had to become more cognizant of the potential and actual threats faced by dictatorial regimes in the Caribbean region and had to bear the responsibility of determining responses best suited to cope with such threats.

A second major lesson learned by the Eisenhower administration was that in instances in which friendly dictatorial regimes faced intensive domestic and international opposition, it was not sufficient to apply political pressure on the affected foreign leaders so that they would resign or call for democratic elections. For all practical purposes, the exercise of political pressure was the only means relied on by the Eisenhower administration in its attempt to convince Batista that the creation of a democratically elected government was the only way to avert Castro's rise to power. Although the United States embargoed arms shipments to Cuba in March 1958, the action was designed primarily to placate domestic and international criticism of the US government for supplying weapons to a regime that used them against its own citizens, rather than to pressure the Batista regime to democratize.

The fact that political pressure did not convince Batista to relinquish the reins of government until it was too late was not lost on the Eisenhower administration. As the international and domestic opposition to the Trujillo regime moved to a higher plateau, and as the costs of allowing a Castro-type individual to rule over an area of great strategic and economic importance to the United States became evident, the Eisenhower administration intensified its pressure on Trujillo: it cut off economic and military aid, curtailed the importation of Dominican sugar, downgraded diplomatic relations, and suspended the exportation of certain key commodities. Cognizant that these actions might not convince Trujillo to resign, President Eisenhower ordered that a contingency plan be prepared to help remove the Dominican dictator if the situation warranted it.

These actions, in sum, are much closer to the steps taken by US leaders to try to topple the Castro regime than to their attempts to get Batista to democratize Cuba's political structure. Needless to say, the Eisenhower administration was under intense international pressure to act against Trujillo, and it also recognized that if it wanted the support of other states in its attempt to alienate the Castro regime, it would have to augment its activities against the Dominican leader. But these two conditions do not belittle the fact that the foreign policy-makers in the Eisenhower administration were very much troubled by Trujillo's presence and the domestic opposition his regime was facing. Gleijeses (1978) makes this point very clear:

Despite its own resistance and prejudices, Washington had to acknowledge a new possibility: that these dictators who for so long had seemed the surest guarantors of anti-Communist stability, might instead become Communism's unwitting allies. (p. 34)

Moreover, it is essential to keep in mind that President Eisenhower's request for a contingency plan to remove Trujillo was made before the United States began to apply economic and diplomatic pressure on the Dominican dictator.

If the Eisenhower administration was so convinced that Trujillo's continued rule over the Dominican Republic could undermine US interests in the Caribbean, then why did Eisenhower not order the removal of the Dominican leader before leaving office in January of 1961? Eisenhower's decision falls well within the boundaries of his actions against the Castro regime. He seemed determined to act against the two regimes, but unwilling to take the final steps until he could be convinced that the plans' chances for success were high and that viable governments would be ready to be formed immediately after the two regimes in question were toppled.

Trujillo's fate was not to be changed by the coming to power of John Kennedy. The new president, determined to have an immediate impact on US–Latin American relations, announced on March 13, 1961, the creation of a major financial aid program. Through the Alliance for Progress program, the Kennedy administration pledged some $20,000,000 in aid for a region-wide crash program of development. "Tyrannies," including Cuba and the Dominican Republic, did not qualify as recipients of financial aid (McCall, 1984: 20).

The month of April proved to be disastrous for President Kennedy. The Bay of Pigs fiasco seems to have convinced him that it was imperative that the United States avert being drawn into action against Trujillo without first ensuring that the dictator's demise would not be followed by less desirable events. On May 5, the president ordered that the implementation of the covert plan be delayed until it could be established what type of government would succeed Trujillo. Dearborn, on learning of Kennedy's decision, warned that the plan against Trujillo would most likely be executed even without the backing of the United States, but that if it failed due to the lack of proper support and organization, Washington would be blamed for the setback (Diederich, 1978: 91–3).

Kennedy, believing that if he had questioned the CIA plan against Castro more forcefully he would have averted the embarrassment that followed its execution, took one additional step to ensure that the United States would not be linked in any way to the plan to assassinate Trujillo. On May 29, the US Embassy in Ciudad Trujillo received a cable, approved by Kennedy, ordering that the transfer of arms by the United States to the individuals involved in the assassination plot be cancelled. The cable emphasized that although the United States supported the positions of the dissidents, it could not run the risk of being associated with political assassination (1978: 96). Kennedy's order had very little effect on the execution of the plan. A day after his cable had been received, Trujillo was shot to death.

In sum, the "Cuban" analogy had an unexpected effect on President Kennedy and some of his closest advisors. Although they shared the attitude that Trujillo had to go, they were particularly concerned that the United States might once again be accused of being involved in illegal activities. This concern was intensified by the possibility that the plan to eliminate Trujillo might suffer the same fate experienced by the expedition against Fidel Castro. Moreover, even if the plan succeeded, there was no guarantee that a stable, widely supported government would surface in the Dominican Republic.

Kennedy's concern that Trujillo's death might not be the only step necessary for the creation of a stable Dominican government proved to be justified. On May 31, President Joaquin Balaguer, who had been appointed to the executive office after Trujillo had ordered his brother to resign, sought to avert a military coup by naming Lieutenant General Rafael Trujillo, Jr., the ex-dictator's son, chief of the armed forces. Balaguer's decision and the failure by Trujillo's opponents to form a provisional government were viewed with great concern in Washington. Fearful that domestic unrest would ensue and get out of hand, President Kennedy on June 2 ordered the US Navy to patrol the Caribbean waters in the vicinity of the Dominican Republic. In addition, the president ordered the US Marines to be prepared to land in the Dominican Republic if the political situation became explosive (Lowenthal, 1972: 11).[4]

From the moment Trujillo was assassinated, the Kennedy administration began to pressure the Dominican leaders to start erecting the foundations for a democratic political system. It was very unlikely, however, that this objective would have much chance of being realized as long as members of the Trujillo family remained in the government. Thus, from June to September 1961, the Kennedy administration continued using the economic might of the United States and the threat of military intervention to coerce President Balaguer to oust the rest of the Trujillo family and call for new elections (Slater, 1970: 9; Lowenthal, 1972: 11–12; Schreiber, 1973: 410).

Balaguer was well attuned to Kennedy's messages. On July 11, he permitted the formation of a major opposition group, the National Civic Union, headed by Dr Viriato A. Fiallo. About two months later, Balaguer offered to enter into a political coalition with opposition parties. But Balaguer's most noticeable act came on October 2, in a speech at the United Nations in which he condemned Trujillo, promised personal freedoms, and asked for an end to economic coercion (Schreiber, 1973: 410).

In the meantime, John Bartlow Martin, who had known Kennedy for several years, had returned from a fact-finding mission to the Dominican Republic. He reported to the president that the Dominican Republic "was a sick destroyed nation, to be viewed as one ravaged by a thirty-year war, even one to be occupied and reconstituted." Martin added in his report that the "Trujillo right, not the Communists, was the danger to the Dominican democracy." He then proposed that the United States use military pressure and a high-level negotiator to persuade the provisional Dominican government to expel the Trujillos. Having accomplished this objective, the United States should take steps to promote political freedom, and help the Dominican Republic "borrow money to get the economy moving." On October 5, after meeting with Martin to discuss his report, Kennedy sent his undersecretary of state, George McGee, to the Dominican Republic to negotiate the removal of the remaining members of the Trujillo family. On October 23, Petán and Hector Trujillo left the Dominican Republic (Martin, 1966: 82).

The exit of the two Trujillos did not facilitate the reaching of a compromise among the remaining political leaders on how the Dominican Republic would be governed and by whom. The power vacuum that ensued as a result of the inability of the Dominican leaders to reach an agreement led to political riots and to another attempt by the Trujillo family to regain power. Following the return of Petán and Hector Trujillo to their homeland, the Kennedy administration once again signaled its willingness to intervene militarily to avert domestic chaos. President Kennedy ordered part of the US fleet in the Caribbean to sail near the Dominican Republic. At the same time, the chargé d'affaires, John Hill, warned Balaguer that the United States would not recognize the government or lift economic sanctions so long as the Trujillos remained in the Dominican Republic (Martin, 1966: 82). The firmness of the letter sent by Kennedy finally convinced the Trujillos, including Rafael, that they had to leave.

It is critical to try to decipher the dilemma that the crises in Cuba and the Dominican Republic posed for President Kennedy. He came into office committed to active leadership, yet in one of his first foreign policy challenges, he found his options highly limited by his determination to alter the status quo in Cuba and by the manner in which the Cuban problem had been defined previously by Washington insiders and the US public. This lesson was not lost on the new president. His demand that the United States not be associated with any plan designed to take Trujillo's life was but an extension of his determination to ensure that he would not be blamed for a second fiasco like the Bay of Pigs. And yet, there were two additional, closely interrelated aspects of the Cuban experience that were assimilated by President Kennedy: (i) the notion that regimes that refuse to undertake domestic reforms might be the most dangerous agents of their own destruction; and (ii) the belief that massive intervention against actors determined to block domestic reforms was justified if, in the long run, it would reduce the likelihood of inciting domestic unrest which could be exploited by the communists.

These two aspects of the Cuban experience became evident immediately after Rafael Trujillo's death. His brothers and son, determined to maintain the Trujillo dynasty, acted promptly to ensure that others would not attempt to exploit the new circumstances. But such a move did not stop other Dominican political leaders who were attempting to augment their own power. The resulting internal political struggle led to a power vacuum. In the eyes of the leaders in Washington, this condition provided the communists with a perfect opportunity – the kind of opportunity, in fact, that had been exploited fully by Castro and his associates in Cuba. Thus, to ensure that a situation such as arose in Cuba in 1958 would not repeat itself in the Dominican Republic in 1961, the Kennedy administration was willing to resort to some of its most forceful means of intervention to pressure the Dominican provisional government to expel those who were believed to be communists and those who would most likely prevent the Dominican leadership from breaking the political deadlock – the remaining members of the Trujillo family. In short, as stated by Abraham Lowenthal, the "aim of preventing a 'second Cuba' shaped American policy toward the Dominican Republic at every stage after Trujillo's death in May 1961" (Lowenthal, 1972: 26).

On January 1, 1962, the dawn of a new era in Dominican politics could have been at hand. A council of state was formed, led by Balaguer as president and Rafael Bonnelly as vice president. The Kennedy administration took only five days to recognize the new government and re-establish full diplomatic relations (CFR, 1965: 10). The Dominican public, however, because of Balaguer's past association with the Trujillo dynasty, refused to accept his leadership. The ensuing domestic unrest culminated in a successful January 16 coup, led by the secretary of the Dominican armed forces, Major General Rafael Echavarría. The coup was designed to re-establish order without a substantive change in the character of the Dominican government. But Echavarría's tenure as leader of the Dominican Republic lasted only two days. The United States, convinced that a military ruler would be unacceptable to the Dominican civilian leaders, pressured the Dominican armed forces not to support General Echavarría. Washington's pressure had its intended effect; on January 18, a successful counter-coup removed Echavarría. Bonnelly was sworn in as the new president of the council of state (CFR, 1965: 10; Martin, 1966: 83).

Bonnelly came to power at a critical juncture in the social and economic life of the Dominican Republic. Between 1960 and 1961, the gross national product had plunged by 8 percent, exports had declined by 19 percent, unemployment was estimated at between 33 and 56 percent of the total labor force, and the nation faced a substantial balance of payments problem (Gleijeses, 1978: 68). Aware that Bonnelly and his associates might be toppled unless they began to address some of the most important ills plaguing the Dominican Republic, between January 22 and February 12 the Kennedy administration announced the extension of $25,000,000 in credit, the renewal of military aid, the lifing of all export restrictions to the Dominican Republic, and the renewal of the sugar quota (CFR, 1965: 10). In addition, on March 2, President Kennedy appointed John Bartlow Martin as the new ambassador to the Dominican Republic.

Martin arrived in Santo Domingo with three objectives in mind – "to help keep the Consejo in office, to help hold free elections, and to help get the winner into the Palace alive and on schedule." To achieve these objectives, the new ambassador would have to ensure that the country's military leaders would not feel so threatened by the civilian rulers that they would want to respond with a coup; and would have to convince the competing political parties that they must learn to co-exist (Martin, 1966: 87). In addition, Martin had to persuade the Dominican armed forces that their central military task was not to fight the Cubans – the United States would fight them if necessary – but to become proficient in counter-insurgency in case communist activities began internally (Gleijeses, 1978: 86). The first two tasks proved difficult, and yet, after a countless number of small crises, elections were held.

For President Kennedy and his ambassador, the holding of the elections had an important symbolic value. It signaled that the alternative to a Batista- or Trujillo-like regime need not be a Castro/communist form of government; it could be a democratic regime which would seek to bring about gradual economic and political reforms. The belief that democratic regimes ought to replace dictatorial ones had not been born as a result of the Cuban crisis, but the coming to power of Castro had undoubtedly convinced many leaders in

Washington that unless the United States was willing to live in a sea of communist regimes, it could not remain blind to the need to find a viable alternative to regional dictatorships. The political crisis that ensued in the Dominican Republic during Trujillo's final years as leader and during the year and a half that it took to elect his successor reinforced this attitude. The problem faced by the Kennedy administration now was whether the leader elected by the Dominicans would be able to govern them.

The winner of the Dominican election, Juan Bosch, received 59 percent of the vote, while his principal opponent, Dr Viriato Fiallo, received 30 percent.[5] Bosch's triumph was complete. His party, the Dominican Revolutionary Party, won 22 of 27 seats in the Senate, and 49 out of 74 seats in the Chamber. Two months later, on February 27, 1963, Bosch was sworn in as president of the Dominican Republic. "Few men in our time," wrote Ambassador Martin, "have come to presidential power with a more splendid opportunity, or been confronted by more formidable difficulties, than Juan Bosch" (Martin, 1966: 343). Bosch came to power with the blessings of the presidents of Venezuela, Costa Rica, Honduras, and the United States, but he became the leader of a country on the verge of social, political, and economic chaos. The imbalance in favor of chaos proved to be too powerful; on September 25, 1963, the Bosch regime suffered a fate not uncommon among Latin American regimes – demise at the hands of a military force.

The United States's dilemma with respect to the Dominican Republic during Bosch's tenure was best defined by its ambassador to the small country. According to Ambassador Martin, the United States had to be cognizant of three possibilities with respect to President Bosch: that if he failed to meet the people's expectations he might be overthrown; that he might lose control of his party to the communists; and that he himself might be a communist (1966: 347). Fear that any or all three possibilities might be, or might become, a reality began to surface during the early stages of Bosch's presidency and gained dramatic momentum by September 1963.

One of the first problems faced by Bosch was how to survive in a system in which the left and the right had such conflicting political agendas. After returning from a trip to the United States and Europe, Bosch announced his intention to submit a new constitution. In his announcement Bosch attacked the existing power structure and proposed radical social, economic, and political changes. Bosch's proposal had a divisive effect. The political right joined under the banner known as the Dominican Independent Action, with one purpose: to topple Juan Bosch. The members of this group were mostly businessmen committed to bringing to power an individual more disposed to protecting the interests of the business community. This end, they concluded, would have to be achieved by first establishing that Juan Bosch was linked to the communists (Martin, 1966: 358). The left also wasted very little time in voicing its objections; it soon began to demand greater control over the university and to accuse US companies of exploiting Dominican workers and the republic's natural resources (1966: 346, 357).

Bosch's chances of bringing about some stability did not seem much more promising on the economic front. Bosch had succeeded in persuading some of the Western European leaders to grant his country a $150,000,000 line of credit to finance some of his larger development projects (Gleijeses, 1978: 95). Although Washington did not publicly criticize Bosch's decision, it feared that the high interest rate and repayment schedule would hurt the Dominican economy and would undermine Bosch politically (Martin, 1966: 370). The most crucial economic dilemma faced by Bosch, however, was whether to carry out a radical agrarian reform.

On April 29, 1963, the Dominican Republic adopted a new constitution. It identified the "minifundio" – uneconomical and anti-social conditions – and the "latifundio" – the ownership of excessive amounts of land by individuals or private interests – as the twin evils of Latin America. To deal with these two evils, the constitution affirmed the right of expropriation without sacrificing the right of private ownership. Under Bosch's new consitution, the interests of the property owners would be taken into account when considering indemnification, but the interests of the nation would receive priority over individual interests (Gleijeses, 1978: 87).

Bosch's action did not come as a surprise to the United States. In mid-April, President Bosch had acknowledged to Ambassador Martin that if he hoped to survive politically he would need to institute agrarian reform, small-agricultural credits, a health program, farm-to-market roads, and a hundred waterworks for villages. Martin responded by asking how much time Bosch thought he had and how much money he needed (1966: 414).

Martin's stand was not entirely anomalous. He and Washington seemed to recognize that Bosch would have to introduce agricultural reforms. As stated by Martin in a major speech to the Chamber of Commerce of the Americas, "A better life for the ordinary man was not merely the bar to Castro but the only acceptable road to national independence and individual and human dignity" (1966: 463). And yet, skepticism in Washington about Bosch was on the rise. The Kennedy administration was becoming more and more convinced that Bosch was handing over the government to the communists. This perception traveled beyond the Kennedy administration. Some members of Congress questioned Bosch's ability to counter effectively "the advancing Communist offensive of subversive penetration in the Dominican Republic" (Martin, 1966: 455).

Washington's perception, however, did not seem to conform with the facts. Convinced that Kennedy and his advisors needed a careful assessment of the situation in the Dominican Republic, Martin decided to travel to Washington to present a detailed report. As part of his report, the ambassador informed the leaders in Washington that his political section in the Dominican Republic had concluded after an extensive study that on balance "the total number of Castro/Communists in all branches of governments was surprisingly small" (1966: 457). Martin also proposed that the best way to prevent another Castro in the Caribbean was to help Bosch succeed. To achieve this last end, the Kennedy administration would have to extend a new $15,000,000 Agency for International Development loan, explain Bosch to the press and Congress, encourage United States private investments, and publicly support the Bosch regime. However, since the effect of these measures depended on how well communism could be controlled, Martin also asked for help in training an antisubversive force in the Dominican Republic (1966: 471).

Martin's trip to Washington brought about the commitment he had recommended. Although President Kennedy and Secretary of State Dean Rusk warned Ambassador Martin that land expropriation would create problems in the United States, it was agreed that, for the time being, major attempts to keep Bosch politically alive would have to be made. Martin returned to the Dominican Republic on July 10, hoping that renewed support from the United States would be enough to avert Bosch's downfall. The ambassador's hope did not last long (1966: 471–8).

Bosch's domestic problems continued. After successfully averting a coup by military leaders demanding that the government adopt a stronger anticommunist posture, Bosch announced, on July 22, that he was submitting to Congress a new Confiscation Law. The Chamber of Deputies passed the law within a few days, amid extensive exhortation not to permit the country to become another "Cuba."

From that day on, the situation in the Dominican Republic deteriorated at an accelerated pace. On the domestic front Bosch was being assailed by the Catholic Church and by the political right as being soft on communism. The Kennedy administration also renewed its own pressure. In the middle of August, the State Department informed Ambassador Martin of a firm commitment for 50,000 tons of rice and 10,000 tons of corn under PL-480. The State Department also assured Martin that the Bosch regime would receive a promised $22,000,000 sugar contract. However, Washington made it very clear that unless Bosch improved the quality of his administration and began to take forceful steps against the communists, it was unlikely that new loans would be extended (1966: 504). Martin delivered the message.

By August 23, the US ambassador to the Dominican Republic had become quite discouraged. Domestic unrest led by the business community was providing the military the justification it needed to plot a coup against Bosch. The US State Department ordered Martin on September 17 to communicate to the Dominican political right that Washington was opposed to a *coup d'état*. For the State Department, a failure to avert a coup would signal to the world that the United States did not possess the capability to keep alive those whom it had helped to power.

Time, however, had run out. On September 20, Dominican businessmen called for a "Christian" strike against "international communism." The rumors of a forthcoming military coup increased as each day of the strike continued. On September 25, Martin met with President Bosch and tried to persuade him that a coup could be averted if he called for a special session of Congress to create new laws that would restrict severely the activities of communists in the Dominican Republic. Bosch rejected this suggestion, along with an offer by the ambassador to act as a mediator between the government and the military. Finally, Ambassador Martin asked the Dominican president whether he wanted the US Marines to land in Santo Domingo. The president's response was once again, "No." Bosch's fate was sealed. That same day he was ousted by the military. The United States responded to Bosch's overthrow by suspending diplomatic relations with the Dominican Republic on September 28 and by cutting all military and economic aid on October 4 (CFR, 1965: 12; Martin, 1966: 562–3, 589–98, 601).

The behavior of the Kennedy administration toward the Bosch regime and its immediate successor was, more than anything else, the reflection of an attempt to define the Dominican problem from two somewhat conflicting perspectives. On the one hand, the United States had hoped that the Bosch regime would symbolize the beginning of a new democratic era. "After thirty years the Dominican Republic had returned to the democratic fold, and now it was to be a showcase for the . . . Alliance for Progress" (Slater, 1970: 11). On the other hand, however, foremost in the minds of the US decision-makers in both Washington and San Salvador was the need to monitor very closely the manner in which the Bosch regime dealt with the Dominican communists. Unwillingness on Bosch's part to act decisively against the so-called communist threat quickly soured the Kennedy administration's perception of Bosch. Bosch's astonishing passivity *vis-à-vis* the Dominican communists was a sin that "more than any other alienated American sympathies" (Gleijeses, 1978: 96).

The struggle between these two perspectives came to a final clash in September 1963. Upon learning that the Dominican right, along with the armed forces, was plotting to overthrow Bosch, the Kennedy administration warned that Washington would not tolerate such an act. Washington, however, was not willing to send a more forceful message. As evidence that a *coup d'état* was about to ensue, Ambassador Martin asked the State Department whether the United States would send an aircraft carrier to the Dominican Republic to show support for the faltering Bosch regime. The State Department responded that it would comply only if a communist takeover was perceived as a likely development (Lowenthal, 1972: 29).

It is not certain that Bosch would have been able to remain in power had Washington been more forceful in its warning. But the case can be made that if the Kennedy administration had not defined the Dominican problem so largely within the context of how Bosch dealt with the communists, Washington would have found it easier to furnish the Dominican president with the means necessary to lift his country from the economic chaos in which it had been submerged for so long. It is worth noting, however, that the Kennedy administration showed a much greater willingness to accept radical agrarian reforms from the Bosch regime than had the Eisenhower administration from the Castro regime. In other words, the Kennedy administration was less disposed than its predecessor to use the type of agrarian reforms proposed as a measure of a regime's ideological bent.

Bosch's government was replaced by a civilian triumvirate composed of Emilio de los Santos, a former president of the Electoral College; Manuel Enrique Tavares Espaillat, an industrialist; and Ramón Tapia Espinal, a lawyer. For over a month and a half the United States pressured the Dominican civilian triumvirate to find a way to legitimize its position. Finally, on November 26, the provisional government announced that elections would be held between January 15 and July 15, 1965, beginning at the municipal level and ending with presidential elections. In addition, the triumvirate jailed some prominent leftist leaders, among them, Angel Miolán, one of Juan Bosch's closest associates (Gleijeses, 1978: 108).

The future of the triumvirate was enhanced momentarily by the actions of the 14 of June Political Group (1J4), a poorly organized group of primarily middle-class Dominicans highly influenced by the image of Fidel Castro. Only two days after the November 26 announcement of the election schedule, the 1J4 launched six guerrilla operations in the countryside with the intent of toppling the triumvirate. But these actions actually helped reinforce the triumvirate because of their effect in Washington (Martin, 1966: 595, 627).

Officials in Washington were still attempting to cope with President Kennedy's assassination on November 22. However, it did not take the leader of the new administration, Lyndon Johnson, much time to put his own stamp on US foreign policy toward Latin America. The Johnson administration began to assess the wisdom of recognizing the new triumvirate. On the one hand, there was some degree of displeasure with the fact that the United States had invested its prestige in creating a democratic government in the Dominican Republic, only to see it toppled by the military. On the other hand, the guerrilla operations initiated on November 28 seemed to convince Washington that a communist movement was on the rise.

The debate within the administration as to how to respond came to an end on December 14. On that date, Thomas C. Mann was appointed assistant secretary of state for inter-American affairs, and the new Dominican government was extended diplomatic recognition (Martin, 1978: 91). The occurrence of these two events was not coincidental.

Mann's appointment was a reflection of how the struggle betwen the need to fight communism and the desire to promote democracy had been resolved in Washington. Mann was convinced that Bosch's actions as president had facilitated the return of communism to the Dominican Republic. More importantly, he had derived some distinct "lessons" from the Cuban case. The major mistake of the United States, he believed, had been to be blinded by moral considerations when deciding to cut off aid to Batista. According to Mann, it was critical to recognize that "Latinos" were not ready for democracy, that the threat of communist subversion loomed, and that Latin American armed forces would have to play a decisive role in averting communist expansion. Thus, it was in the interest of the United States to recognize a government that had brought about the downfall of a political leader who had not been successful in controlling the communists (Gleijeses, 1978: 124–5).

In the meantime, the 14 of June Political Group's guerrilla operation disintegrated because of ineffective organization and planning. The last fifteen 1J4 guerrillas, including the group's leader, Manolo Tavárez, surrendered a week after the Johnson administration recognized the new Dominican government. Fearing the worst, the president of the civilian triumvirate, Emilio de los Santos, threatened to resign if Tavárez and his followers were killed by the military. This threat proved to be an insufficient deterrent; de los Santos resigned following the guerrillas' murder. On December 22, Donald Reid Cabral, a prominent Dominican civilian leader who was considered to be "intelligent, understanding, flexible, and Liberal" by several officials in Washington, replaced de los Santos as the president of the triumvirate (Gleijeses, 1978: 114–16).

The year 1964 saw the continuation of the same problems that had plagued the Dominican Republic since Trujillo's death: political division and economic stagnation. Initially, Washington decided that it would treat the Dominican Republic as one of the many Caribbean and Latin American states with economic and political problems and not make it a priority matter. As a result, in February 1964 it appointed William Tapley Bennett, Jr, as ambassador to the Dominican Republic. Bennett was a courtly southern gentleman who was not expected to be an active ambassador. Washington was hoping to soften the criticism from those who in the past had argued that the United States was becoming too involved in the domestic affairs of sovereign states (Lowenthal, 1972: 31). Bennett was also the individual who in 1950 had argued that Guatemalan president-to-be Jacobo Arbenz was a tool of the Soviet Union.

The State Department continued to believe that the image of the United States as a party actively involved in the domestic affairs of Caribbean and Latin American states had to be altered; but it also believed that since the situation in the Dominican Republic was extremely unstable, the United States's only remaining choice was to try to keep the Reid regime alive. With this objective in mind, the US government, between March and June 1964, authorized the release of $885,000 in aid for education and public works. In addition, the IMF extended a $25,000,000 standby credit, and finally, AID granted a $10,000,000 loan and resumed assistance for agrarian reform and agricultural production.

These actions by the United States did not alleviate the economic situation in the Dominican Republic. In April, convinced that it was critical to restore his country's balance of payments, Reid Cabral decided to limit imports by tightening credit. Reid's policy was not well received by a vast majority of the Dominican merchants and labor leaders. Beginning in May, these two groups complained that the austerity program was serving only the interests of the large businesses (Lowenthal, 1972: 39). Their criticism intensified after September 7, when Reid announced that the elections that were scheduled to be held in early 1965 would be delayed until September 1. Although Reid justified the decision by contending that the delay would give his economic policies more time to have a positive effect, most Dominican political leaders were convinced that Reid was trying to buy time in order to be able to run for president (Martin, 1966: 638–9; Lowenthal, 1972: 48).

The end of 1964 was marked by an event which might at first seem fairly unimportant. Juan Bosch, who had been in exile since his overthrow, published a book titled *La Crisis de la Democracia de América en la República Dominicana*. One of his main motivations in writing the book was to emphasize the positive role the Dominican middle class, inside and outside the military, would play in creating a revolution. Bosch had concluded that if he hoped to regain the Dominican presidency he would have to have the support of the middle class and of certain officers in the military. Bosch's plan was not the reflection of a hopeless dream; between December 1964 and April of the following year, his supporters worked to win the backing of a group of individuals in the

Dominican military in order to mount a coup against the Reid regime (Lowenthal, 1972: 51–4; see also Gleijeses, 1978: 145–6). Colonel Fernández Domínguez, Bosch's key military supporter, appointed Lieutenant Colonel Miguel Hernando Ramírez to organize the military plan.

The plan, commonly referred to as the "Enriquillo Plan," was based on five conditions. First, it was hoped that the coup would take the victims by surprise and thus reduce their chance to retaliate as a cohesive group. Second, the attack on the government would have to be launched simultaneously at the center and the periphery. Third, the conspirators did not want a popular revolt, but they did hope to persuade the masses to demonstrate in favor of the movement. Fourth, it was agreed that although the United States would not look favorably on the coup, Washington would not resort to military intervention. Fifth, it was expected that the uncommitted military officers would side with "constitutionalists" as it became obvious that the choice was between Bosch and Reid Cabral, or as it appeared that Bosch would be the strongest contender (Gleijeses, 1978: 153–4).

The "constitutionalist" movement gained significant strength on the first day of February 1965. Since the fall of the Bosch regime, the Dominican political parties had been at odds with one another in their struggle against Reid. However, on that date the Dominican Revolutionary Party and the Christian Socialist Revolutionary Party signed the Pact of Rio Padres, committing their members to the restoration of "constitutionality" (Lowenthal, 1972: 52).

There was no unanimity among US foreign policy-makers on how to address the Dominican problem. Bennett was convinced that when compared with the other two main contenders for the presidency, Joaquín Balaguer and Juan Bosch, Reid Cabral was by far the best candidate. Balaguer had been associated for too long with the Trujillo dynasty, and a regime led by him would only bring about greater political turmoil. Bosch, in turn, had proven to be an erratic figure, incapable of governing. Reid Cabral's continued presence as the leader of the Dominican Republic, however, was in jeopardy. His austerity program had increased unemployment, and as a result his popularity had plummeted. Bennett intervened in favor of Reid in February by praising his economic austerity program, his reorganization of the state-owned sugar corporation, and his firing of corrupt military leaders. But Bennett realized that praise would not be enough to save the Reid regime. Thus, at the beginning of April he asked the State Department to pressure the US Congress to authorize an increase in the purchase of Dominican sugar and recommended that the IMF impose less stringent economic requirements on the Reid regime (Lowenthal, 1972: 44–7).

Some foreign policy-makers at the State Department were not entirely comfortable with Bennett's position. In March, Washington announced that the Dominican Republic and the United States had reached a major aid agreement. The AID project, which was created primarily to reduce unemployment, would entail community development programs, agrarian reform projects, and the construction of access roads. On the issue of whether the Reid regime should continue implementing the austerity program, however, the assistant secretary of state for economic affairs, Anthony M. Solomon, was less willing to compromise. Solomon's position was that only through a strict austerity program would the Dominican Republic be able to restore its economic health. Just about this time, Bennett's position suffered a major blow. The Central Intelligence Agency reported it had learned that only 5 percent of the Dominican electorate supported Reid, while five times as many sided with Bosch, and ten times as many favored Balaguer. The Agency also advised, on April 11 and 12, that it had learned that Juan Bosch's party, the Partido Revolucionario Dominicano, "was plotting with military officers to overthrow the Reid government and set up a military junta under Bosch" (Martin, 1966: 645; Lowenthal, 1972: 47–9).

In the meantime, the situation in the Dominican Republic had been deteriorating rapidly. After learning that several military officers, supporters of Balaguer and Bosch, were instigating a military coup, Reid Cabral order them deported, fired, or decommissioned. One of the individuals affected by this order, Lieutenant Colonel Ramírez, was to be decommissioned. On April 24, however, just as General Marcos Rivera Cuesta was attempting to cancel Ramírez's commission and that of Lieutenant Colonel Pedro Augusto Alvarez Hologuín, Rivera was arrested by pro-Bosch military men. Shortly after this arrest, José-Francisco Peña Gomez, who was one of Bosch's chief representatives in the Dominican Republic, announced on Dominican radio that the Reid regime had fallen and a return to constitutionality was under way (Lowenthal, 1972: 61). He then urged the Dominican people to flood the streets in support of the movement (Gleijeses, 1978: 61).

A detailed analysis of rebel and governmental actions and counteractions that preceded Johnson's decision to order a limited military intervention on April 28, and to escalate the US response to a full military intervention on the following day, is unnecessary. All that is presently required is to try to decipher how key developments in the Dominican Republic were interpreted by US decision-makers in that country, communicated to Washington, and, finally, construed by the central foreign policy-makers in the US capital.

A few hours after the countercoup against the Reid regime was announced, government forces recaptured the radio station and arrested Peña Gomez, along with other prominent figures. The fact that the remainder of the rebel forces did not leave their camps after the announcement, and that the radio station with some of the rebel leaders had been recaptured, led Reid Cabral to conclude that the coup had been contained almost at its birth. Confident of his conclusion, President Reid informed the US Embassy that everything was under control.

The US representatives in the Dominican Republic were surprised by the uprising. Ambassador Bennett was visiting his mother in Georgia; eleven of the thirteen members of the Military Advisory and Assistance Group (MAAG) were attending a conference in Panama; the chief of mission of the International Development Agency in the Dominican Republic, William C. Ide, was in Washington; and Lieutenant Colonel Ralph Heywook, the naval attaché, was in the Dominican Republic, but not in the capital (Lowenthal, 1972: 63; Gleijeses, 1978: 177). The person in charge at the US Embassy was William B. Connett, who had been at his post as chargé d'affaires for only five and a half months. Connett's assessment of the situation was optimistic. After some initial confusion, he concluded that there was little need for the United States to do anything, since the government seemed to have the situation under control. He communicated this assessment to the desk officer at the State Department, who concluded that "the rebellion had not amounted to much" (1972: 65; 1978: 177–8). This assessment would change in less than twenty-four hours.

The rebel forces entered the capital in the early hours of the following day, capturing many of the city's strategic points. Reid Cabral, however, still controlled the presidential palace. From the palace, Reid sought the military support of General Elias Wessin y Wessin, who was the commander of the armed forces training center, and General Juan de los Santos Céspedes, who since January of that same year had been serving as air force chief of staff. The two generals declared their loyalty, but they did not act to help Reid. Mindful of his weak position, the president of the Dominican triumvirate initially asked the US Embassy to intervene on his behalf and pressure his officers to defend the regime; and later, he asked whether the United States would consider intervening militarily (1972: 69; 1978: 179). Connett reported to Washington that he had conversed with Reid, informing the besieged leader that he doubted the United States could do anything more at that time. The State Department had by then also concluded that Reid's tenure was about to end and that he should be replaced by a military junta (1972: 70).

The decision by the United States to sacrifice the Reid Cabral regime might seem, at first glance, something of a paradox. For some time Reid Cabral had been abiding by the type of economic and social philosophy that the new administration in Washington had been promoting. Rather than emphasizing, as President Kennedy had, the need for social change, the Johnson–Mann policy had focused on economic growth and protection of US investments. This emphasis explains, in part, Washington's demand that Reid Cabral continue adhering to a strict austerity program (Martin, 1978: 91–2; LaFeber, 1983: 156–7; Blasier, 1985: 242). In view of Reid Cabral's cooperative behavior, it would be tempting to argue that the United States found it necessary to sacrifice his regime when it realized that the Dominican rebels were being led by Bosch supporters, and that this realization led it to fear the return of a leader who was perceived as being incompetent, as well as a weak adversary of the communists. The problem with this interpretation is that it is based on the assumption that US representatives in Santo Domingo and the foreign policy-makers in Washington had an accurate understanding of the intentions driving the actions of the rebel forces. Such an assumption, however, would be quite incorrect. The main reason the United States proposed that Reid Cabral be replaced by a military junta is that it saw the revolt simply as a rebellion of young officers attempting to get a bigger share of the political power. Since it was not assumed that among these officers there would a group committed to fighting for Bosch's return to the presidency, it was concluded that their largest number would welcome a military junta (Gleijeses, 1978: 179–82).

This assumption proved to be both wrong and costly. Just an hour before noon on April 25, about fifty military leaders entered the presidential palace and arrested Reid Cabral. Some four hours later, a new provisional president – José Rafael Molina Ureña, a Boschist – moved into the presidential palace. The new occupants immediately began to try to negotiate an agreement with a representative of the air force, Colonel Pedro Bartolomé Benoit. Benoit's position was simple – appoint a military junta which would set up elections. The rebels, on the other hand, argued that a constitutional leader already existed and all that was needed was to install him as president of the Dominican Republic. The two parties failed to reach an agreement, and as a result Generals Wessin y Wessin and de los Santos decided to fight the rebels (Lowenthal, 1972: 76; Gleijeses, 1978: 192–3).

The US Embassy, meanwhile, took very little time in deciding which side to support. About 5 p.m. on April 25, Connett sent a telegram informing Washington of the situation. Three important points were made. First, Washington was informed that Wessin y Wessin and the Dominican air force had agreed to fight to stop Bosch's return. Second, the telegram noted that the US representatives in the Dominican Republic had "stressed to the three military leaders, Rivera [Caminero], De los Santos and Wessin, our strong feelings everything possible should be done to prevent a communist takeover" (Gleijeses, 1978: 218). And finally, in the telegram, Connett recommended against a show of force by the United States. In fact, Connett had made it clear to the anti-Bosch Dominican military officers not to expect US military support. Connett, however, did not exclude the possibility of changing his mind if conditions deteriorated (Lowenthal, 1972: 79).

Up to this point, the president of the United States, although aware of the developments, had not been asked to make the Dominican crisis part of his agenda; the problem was perceived to be of limited importance and thus was confined to the State Department and the US Embassy in Santo Domingo. The Dominican crisis was in a state of flux between April 26 and April 28. Initially, it seemed as though the anti-Bosch group would succeed in defeating the rebels. This impression was backed by the fact that after the counterattack had begun, Ureña, Ramírez, and many other constitutionalists had sought asylum at several of the embassies in Santo Domingo. And yet, the defeat of the constitutionalists did not come about as expected. On April 27, they were able to push back General Wessin y Wessin's troops and regain control of large portions of the capital.[6]

The effect of this development was immediately felt by US representatives in the Dominican Republic. Early on April 28, General de los Santos requested that the US Embassy provide fifty walkie-talkie radio sets. Ambassador Bennett, who had just returned from his trip to the United States, asked Washington to approve the request immediately. Washington – to be more specific, Thomas Mann – rejected the petition, arguing that such an action would only increase the visibility of the United States. Mann believed that the delivery of the walkie-talkies would be justified only if the "outcome should actually be in doubt" (Gleijeses, 1978: 253). Convinced that without US assistance the anti-Bosch forces could very well be defeated, Ambassador Bennett sent a cable stating

The issue here now is a fight between Castro-type elements and those who oppose. I do not wish to be over-dramatic but we should be clear as to the situation. If we deny communication equipment and the anti-rebel forces lose for lack of heart, we may well be asking in the near future for landings of marines to protect US citizens and possibly for other purposes. Which would Washington prefer? (Quoted in Gleijeses, 1978: 253)

Bennett's request was immediately approved, apparently by the national security advisor to President Johnson, McGeorge Bundy.

Later that same day, the anti-Bosch group installed a military junta led by Colonel Benoit. Benoit immediately contacted the US Embassy and requested that the US intervene militarily to help the military junta in its fight against the pro-Bosch group. The Boschists, noted Benoit, were heavily influenced by communists (Lowenthal, 1972: 102). Bennett's first reaction was to inform Washington of Benoit's request, but also to question whether the situation justified the involvement of US forces. Some hours later, Benoit repeated his plea. Interestingly, in neither instance did Benoit indicate that US citizens were in danger. Finally, around 5 p.m., Bennett sent a cable to Washington stating:

The country team is unanimous that the time has come to land the marines. American lives are in danger. Proposes marine beachhead at Embajador Hotel. *If Washington wishes, they can be landed for the purpose of protecting evacuation of American citizens.* (Quoted in Gleijeses, 1978: 254)

President Johnson was meeting with Secretary of State Dean Rusk, Secretary of Defense Robert McNamara, Under Secretary of State George Ball, National Security Advisor McGeorge Bundy, and White House aide Bill Moyers to discuss the situation in Vietnam when he received Bennett's cable. The consideration of alternative courses of action by the group was brief. Given the tone of Bennett's cable, the president and his advisors felt "there was nothing to do but react quickly" (Ball, 1982: 328). Thus, with the full support of his advisors, Johnson authorized the landing of 500 US Marines.

The initial public posture adopted by the Johnson administration was that it had to intervene to protect US lives. As explained by the president, "I could not risk the slaughter of American citizens. As their President, it was my duty to protect them with every resource available to me" (Johnson, 1971: 195). In view of the fact that the authorization of the landing of the 500 Marines was accompanied by the proviso that they were not to fire unless fired upon, it could be argued that such a condition would not have been attached had the Johnson administration intervened with the purpose of averting a communist takeover (Lowenthal, 1972: 104–6). It also could be suggested, however, that the Johnson administration acted believing that the introduction of US Marines would be enough to discourage the rebels from continuing with the fight (Gleijeses, 1978: 256).

There are several reasons that make the second argument more plausible than the first. To begin with, as early as April 25, both the US Embassy and the State Department had agreed that the revolt had to be crushed because of, in the words of Chargé d'Affaires Connett, the "Communist advocacy of Bosch's return" (Gleijeses, 1978: 291). Moreover, when McGeorge Bundy finally approved the delivery of fifty walkie-talkies on April 28, it was only after Ambassador Bennett had emphasized, "The issue here now is a fight between Castro-type elements and those who oppose." Finally, it is important to take into account the communication that took place between Mann and Bennett. At 6 p.m., after the decision to intervene had been made in Washington, Thomas Mann telephoned Bennett to relay instructions to Benoit to draw up *another* written request for assistance on the grounds that US lives could no longer be protected. Mann's actions were a "splendid example of hypocrisy" which gave birth to the myth of "humanitarian intervention" to hide "an intervention that was purely political in its aims" (Gleijeses, 1978: 402, n. 87). As an aside, not only did Mann ask Bennett that Benoit use the threat on US lives as the justification for requesting US military assistance; Bennett himself had made the same suggestion in his 5 p.m. cable when he wrote, "If Washington wishes, they [the Marines] can be landed for the purpose of protecting evacuation of American citizens." In other words, Bennett recognized that Washington would find it politically difficult to acknowledge that it was intervening with the intention of ensuring that a particular Dominican faction should not succeed in its struggle for power. An admission of this nature would signal that the United States did not abide by its non-interventionist pledge as a member of the OAS and a signatory of the Rio Treaty.

If there is any disagreement as to why the Johnson administration authorized the deployment of 500 Marines on April 28, such a difference is immediately erased as the question turns to why the same administration decided to augment the number of Marines to more than 20,000 by May 10. When Johnson had first sent in the 500 Marines, he had to decide how best to control the criticism that would begin to mount as soon as it was learned that US Marines had landed on a small Caribbean island. The president took three steps. First, he instructed Rusk and Ball to contact the Latin American ambassadors and the OAS to inform them of the decision and to urge the latter to meet in order to address the issue. Second, Johnson ordered Bill Moyers to contact the congressional leaders for a briefing that evening. And, finally, Rusk, Moyers, and Bundy were also assigned the task of drafting an announcement to be delivered by the president that evening on nationwide television.

However, the deployment of 500 Marines was not sufficient to ensure the constitutionalists' defeat. The United States had expected that the Marine landing would spur the loyalist forces to take to the offensive. Instead, the anti-Bosch group remained largely inactive throughout April 29, thus providing the constitutionalists with the opportunity to regroup. These events dispelled any illusion that it would not be necessary to land additional US forces. The following day, President Johnson authorized the Defense Department to undertake an all-out military intervention in Santo Domingo (Lowenthal, 1972: 110).

On May 2, Johnson made it very clear why the United States had to resort to military force:

> Communist leaders, many of them trained in Cuba, seeing a chance to increase disorder, to gain a foothold, joined the revolution. They took increasing control.

And what began as a popular democratic revolution, committed to democracy and social justice, very shortly moved and was taken over and really seized and placed into the hands of a band of Communist conspirators. (Quoted in Gleijeses, 1978: 258)

On May 5, a cease-fire, negotiated by the OAS five-man peace commission, was signed by representatives of the rebels and of the anti-Bosch group. The cease-fire did not bring about an immediate solution to the Dominican crisis. However, after extensive negotiations between the conflicting parties, with the United States playing a critical role, new elections were finally held on June 1, 1966. Joaquín Balaguer, Trujillo's last puppet president, was elected president of the Dominican Republic with 57 percent of the vote; his major opponent, Juan Bosch, received 39 percent.

That President Johnson ordered the landing of US Marines in Santo Domingo because he and his advisors believed that they would be preventing the rise of another Castro in the Caribbean is, by now, beyond question.[7] Castro's rise to power had led the president to conclude that in order to prevent the establishment of a communist regime in the Caribbean, it was critical that the United States intervene before the movement took root. In addition, the Bay of Pigs incident seems to have underscored his belief that the threat of a communist takeover in an area that was perceived to be central to the security interests of the United States fully justified the overt use of massive force. The presence of such a threat, in other words, outweighed any major concern of being castigated by the international community for intervening militarily in the domestic affairs of a sovereign state.

REASONING AND LEARNING BY ANALOGY

The presentation in analogical form of the arguments elicited in the previous section begins with the consideration of the policies adopted by the United States toward the Trujillo regime. The first major relationship stipulated in both the Guatemalan and Cuban cases referred to how the political structure of each government affected Washington's perception of threat. It was proposed that by the end of the 1950s, US officials were beginning to believe that certain anticommunist regimes, not just communist governments, could undermine the interests of the United States. These were the governments that were opposed to political, social, and economic reforms, and that faced extensive domestic opposition.

In the analogical structure defined in the Cuban case, the relationship addressing the issue just referred to postulated that anticommunist governments that opposed social, economic, and political reforms, but did not face strong domestic opposition, were not perceived as posing an immediate threat to the interests of the United States. This relationship explains very well the initial decision by the Eisenhower administration not to distance itself from the Trujillo regime.

Government in target state is dominated by anticommunists who oppose political, social, and economic reforms, but do not face strong domestic opposition.	: Low threat :	Continue maintaining close relationships with government in target state.

As time went by, however, the Eisenhower administration began to alter its assessment of the threat posed by the Trujillo regime. In 1958, Washington would have preferred not to have to deal with an individual like Fidel Castro as the leader of Cuba primarily because it feared that he would be somewhat difficult to control. At the same time, very few leaders believed that Castro would adopt a clear-cut anti-US program and that he would begin to build close ties with the communists. After one year in power, Fidel Castro's policies persuaded the Eisenhower administration that its initial assumptions were no longer valid. Moreover, this change in perception helped alter the manner in which members of the Eisenhower administration started to define the Trujillo problem. The transformation, still regarding the Dominican Republic, can be depicted analogically as follows:

Government in target state is dominated by anticommunists who oppose political, social, and economic reforms, but do not face strong domestic opposition.	:	No single neighbouring state previously dominated by anticommunists opposed to political, social, and economic reforms is now controlled by a communist government.	:	Low threat	:	Continue maintaining close relationships with government in target state.	::

Government in target state is dominated by anticommunists who oppose political, social, and economic reforms, but do not face strong domestic opposition.	:	Neighboring state previously dominated by anticommunists opposed to political, social, and economic reforms is now controlled by communist government.	:	High threat	:	Pressure government in target state to relinquish power in favor of a moderate, preferably democratic, government.

This change in perception is nicely captured by the types of means used by the Eisenhower administration against Batista in 1958 and Trujillo in 1960. In 1958, the leaders in Washington, by applying political pressure and slowly cutting the transfer of weapons to the Cuban armed forces, tried to persuade Batista to relinquish power in favor of a moderate government. Two years later, the same administration sought the same goal in the Dominican Republic, not only by using the two means just identified, but also by resorting to diplomatic and economic coercion and designing a contingency plan to topple Trujillo.

The change in the use of means can be expressed in the following analogical form:

Impose political pressure on, and ban sale of weapons to, government in target state dominated by anticommunists who oppose political, social, and economic reforms and face significant domestic opposition.	Instatement of government in target state dominated by communists is not : preempted. ::

Impose political and diplomatic pressure and economic sanctions on, ban sale of weapons to, and prepare to rely on covert paramilitary intervention against, government in target state dominated by anticommunists who oppose political, social, and economic reforms but do not face strong domestic opposition.	Instatement of government in target state dominated by communists is : preempted.

In the Guatemalan and Cuban cases it was discovered that although the Truman and Eisenhower administrations had been willing to apply political, diplomatic, and economic pressure on the Arbenz and Castro regimes, respectively, neither had used force to overthrow such regimes. Almost the same process and rationale are repeated with respect to the Dominican Republic case. Although President Eisenhower had ordered the formulation of a contingency plan to overthrow Trujillo, he did not ask that the plan be implemented before he left office. His decision can once again be attributed to the absence of a fully developed paramilitary operation complemented by the presence of a suitable successor regime. Analogically, the relationships adopt the following form:

Ban on sale of weapons, economic sanctions and political and diplomatic, pressure on government in target state dominated by anticommunists failed to persuade it to relinquish power in favor of a moderate, preferably democratic, government.	Covert paramilitary intervention plan drawn to overthrow government in : target state dominated by : anticommunists needs additional tuning.

Suitable successor regime to government in target state dominated by anticommunists not available.	Delay the launching of covert paramilitary intervention against : government in target state dominated by anticommunists.

The Bay of Pigs débâcle had a major effect on the way Kennedy handled the plan to topple Trujillo. Kennedy feared that if the operation against Trujillo succeeded but was then followed by an accelerated deterioration of the domestic situation in the Dominican Republic for lack of a suitable government, and if the United States were identified as the principal instigator of the intervention, the United States would be accused of a "second Bay of Pigs" fiasco. Analogically, Kennedy's reasoning process can be structured as follows:

Ban on sale of weapons, economic sanctions, and political and diplomatic pressure imposed on government in target state dominated by anticommunists failed to persuade them to relinquish power in favour of a moderate, preferably democratic, government.	Covert paramilitary intervention plan drawn : to overthrow government in target state dominated by anticommunists is ready to be implemented.	Suitable successor regime to government in target state dominated by : anticommunists is not available.
Covert paramilitary intervention plan drawn to overthrow a previous government dominated by communists failed to achieve objective.	Cancel implementation of covert paramilitary : intervention against government in target state dominated by anticommunists.	

What is critical about Kennedy's behavior is not that his reasoning process changed from the time he approved the implementation of the operation against Castro, but that he remained concerned that the United States not be identified as the perpetrator. And yet, although Kennedy feared that his administration might suffer from being linked to Trujillo's death, there were circumstances under which he would approve overt massive intervention in the Dominican Republic. From the Cuban case he had learned that anticommunist regimes that refused to undertake reforms might be the most dangerous instigators of their own destruction, and that massive intervention against such regimes would be justified if it served to avert the kind of domestic unrest that could be exploited by communists. Kennedy's decision to use the threat of military intervention to coerce the post-Trujillo regime to expel the domestic actors with the power to incite political division and turmoil can be structured according to the following analogical form:

Do not coerce militarily government in target state dominated by anticommunists who oppose political, economic, and social : reforms.	Instatement of government in target state dominated by communists is not preempted.	::
Coerce militarily government in target state dominated by anticommunists who oppose political, economic, and social : reforms.	Instatement of government in target state dominated by communists is preempted.	

After ensuring that the Trujillo dynasty had been brought to an end, the Kennedy administration faced the task of creating a structure in the Dominican

Republic that would prevent the birth of a "second Cuba." The creation of a stable structure was believed to be dependent on the erection of a democratic political system. For this system to rise, however, the United States would have to help create a more equitable economic structure, persuade the different political factions to abide by the rules of the democratic system and the military to refrain from plotting military coups, and pressure the regime in power to be vigilant against communist infiltration. Reference to the Cuban experience with regard to the type of domestic structure a system had to develop can be described by the following analogical relationship:

Government in target state dominated by anticommunists who oppose political, social, and economic reforms is burdened : by strong domestic discontent.	Target state vulnerable to communist activity and influence. ::
Government in target state dominated by anticommunists who respect democratic values and favor moderate political, social, : and economic reforms is not burdened by strong domestic discontent.	Target state not vulnerable to communist activity and influence.

The two-pair analogical relationship just described guided extensively the actions of the Kennedy administration well up to the time the Bosch regime was toppled in September of 1963. The problem with this relationship was that the first concept in the second set contained the fruits of some major contradictions. Although US foreign policy-makers were earnest in their belief that a democratic structure was a desirable goal, they became less supportive of the existing democratic regime as they began to believe that Bosch was not acting decisively against the communists. This frame of mind can be delineated as follows:

Democratic government in target state that faces major domestic problems does not act forcefully against communists. :	Be less supportive and more critical of democratic government in target state that faces major domestic problems but :: does not act forcefully against communists.
Democratic government in target state that faces major domestic problems acts forcefully against communists. :	Support democratic government in target state that faces major domestic problems but acts forcefully against communists.

The hope of maintaining a democratic system and the need to be vigilant against the communists collided in September 1963, when the Bosch regime was toppled. The initial reaction by the Kennedy administration was to suspend diplomatic relations and cut off all military and economic aid. Both decisions, however, were reversed shortly after Johnson had replaced Kennedy as the new president of the United States and Thomas C. Mann had been appointed Johnson's top advisor on Latin American affairs.

Theodore Draper, in his analysis of US foreign policy toward the Dominican Republic under the Kennedy and Johnson administrations, contends that the referred shift can be attributed to Johnson's ascension to power. According to Draper, Johnson was never as committed as Kennedy had been to social change in Latin America brought about within a democratic constitutional framework. This variance in commitment led US officials under the Johnson administration to place greater emphasis on economic development than on social reform, and to be less concerned about whether the political leadership ruled under a democratic constitutional framework (Draper, 1965: 34).

Draper's argument does not withstand close scrutiny. US officials, even while Kennedy was serving as president, were more interested in keeping the communists out of office than in promoting social and economic changes. Prior to Kennedy's death, and immediately after his administration had voiced its extreme displeasure with Bosch's military overthrow by cutting aid to, and suspending diplomatic relations with, the Dominican Republic, the US State Department pressured the Dominican civilian triumvirate to find a way to legitimize its government. The guerrilla attacks against the Dominican government and the triumvirate's decision that new elections would be held in 1965 provided the Johnson administration with the perfect justification for reestablishing diplomatic, military, and economic relations with the new Dominican government. But this decision was not entirely at odds with the decision Kennedy would have made if still in office for, as Lowenthal notes, Kennedy had decided in early November "to extend recognition to the Triumvirate when suitable agreements were reached on when national elections would be held." He then adds that rumors in December "of flickering attempts to promote a countercoup – together with the Triumvirate's own indication that continued nonrecognition might undermine its position and strengthen the hand of leftist opponents – speeded Johnson's decision to recognize the Dominican regime without further delay" (Lowenthal, 1972: 29–30). This argument can be summed up in analogical form as follows:

Military regime in target state that faces major domestic problems acts forcefully against communists and promises to reestablish the democratic process.	:	Support military regime in target state that faces major domestic problems but acts forcefully against communists and promises to reestablish the democratic process.

The last two analogical structures describe an interesting phenomenon. Beginning with the Eisenhower administration, the United States began to toy with the idea that one of the ways to avert communism was to promote democracy. The Dominican case, however, was interpreted to mean that a democratic government might not always be the most powerful tool for containing the threat of communism, and that when such a threat loomed it was justifiable for the military to mount a *coup d'état*. Equally as important, it brought to the forefront a major dilemma: would the United States have been willing to support a military regime that had toppled a democratic government and had subsequently vowed to launch a major battle against communism, but at the same time had made it evident that it would not promote the creation of a democratic structure until it saw fit? Based on the logic of the evolution of the reasoning process behind the decisions by different US governments, one could justifiably speculate that it would have rendered such support. This is not to say that Washington would not have preferred to learn that the military regime in power intended to resurrect democracy in the country it ruled, nor that Washington would have abstained from pressuring the military regime to change its mind. But if ultimately Washington was faced with the choice between supporting or not supporting a military regime committed to eradicating communism in its country but unwilling to state a time for abdicating control in favor of a democratic government, it would have sided with the first alternative.

There are three more issues that need to be structured in analogical form. In April 1965, the Johnson administration decided to sacrifice the Reid Cabral regime and support the creation of a military junta. The United States arrived at the decision not from fear that the rebel forces were being led by pro-Bosch military officers, but from a belief that the challenge was the result of discontent with the Reid Cabral regime among certain military officers and that such discontent would be eradicated as soon as the regime was replaced by a military junta (Gleijeses, 1978: 179–82). This attitude was, in a sense, a reflection of the belief that military regimes are useful tools for maintaining the status quo and thus should be recognized as the legitimate rulers after they overthrow civilian governments (LaFeber, 1983: 157). In other words,

Rebel forces without links to the military in the target state attack anticommunist government.	:	Pressure military leaders in target state to protect anticommunist government.	::	Rebel forces with links to the military in the target state attack anticommunist government.	:	Advise military leaders in target state to replace anticommunist government with a military junta.

The last two issues that must be presented in the context of analogical reasoning refer to why the Johnson administration decided to undertake a massive overt intervention. Students of this decision almost unanimously agree that President Johnson ordered the US Marines to land in Santo Domingo because he and his advisors feared that the Dominican military would not be able to defeat the pro-Bosch forces. This meant that the United States could very well be faced with a "second Cuba" in the Caribbean region. The cost associated with this scenario was not a price President Johnson was willing to accept.

Directly related to this issue is the question of why President Johnson decided to commit such a large number of US troops in an overt activity. The question also can be addressed from a slightly different perspective: would another president – Kennedy for instance – have acted differently, given the information Johnson had received? According to Cole Blasier, one of the central differences between Kennedy and Johnson is that the former had sponsored Latin American paramilitary forces, while the latter used US forces to intervene directly in the Dominican Republic (Blasier, 1985: 242). This difference, however, still does not justify the contention that Kennedy would have responded differently. Piero Gleijeses, in a very critical analysis of the decision, addresses quite succinctly the dilemma faced by Johnson and the issue of whether Kennedy would have responded differently:

> Johnson had no room for maneuvering. There was obviously no time. "Never a second Cuba" was ... a basic tenet of the Kennedy legacy, one that nobody challenged ... None of those with Johnson when he ordered the landing of the marines dissented. Yet these were "liberals" of the Kennedy vintage: Dean Rusk, Robert McNamara, McGeorge Bundy, George Ball, and Bill Moyers. (1978: 293)

In other words, in view of the information received by Washington and the fact that one "Cuba" in the Caribbean region already existed, it would have been impossible for Johnson and his advisors to have even considered resorting to covert paramilitary means. The use of such means requires time, and time was perceived to be running out. Moreover, it should not be forgotten that in 1961 President Kennedy set an important precedent by ordering the US Navy to patrol the Dominican coast and the Marines to be prepared to land if the conflict that had erupted between Dominican political factions following Trujillo's assassination got out of hand. These two issues can be compressed into a single analogical relationship as follows:

Do not extend military support to military in target state dominated by anticommunists who face military defeat by forces influenced by communists.	Instatement of government in target state dominated by communists is not : preempted.
Extend extensive military support to military in target state dominated by anticommunists who face military defeat by forces influenced by communists.	Instatement of government in target state dominated by communists is : preempted.

FROM COVERT PARAMILITARY INTERVENTION TO DIRECT MILITARY INTERVENTION

Governments learn.[8] What they learn is the function of how well past policies have served critical interests. In 1954, the Eisenhower administration, after having decided that it would not be able to alter Guatemala's domestic political structure by relying solely on diplomatic and economic pressure, ordered the covert invasion of the Central American country with a small paramilitary force. The immediate pay-offs of the intervention were high. Washington succeeded in toppling the unwanted regime and replacing it with one that would have a favorable disposition towards the United States. Moreover, it achieved the objective at a fairly low cost. Washington was able to maintain a relatively low profile during the incident and, thus, was able to silence those who might have wanted to voice the view that the United States did not respect the sovereign rights of Latin American states.

The success in bringing about these two objectives and the means used to achieve them were not overlooked by the decision-makers in Washington. But these lessons were accompanied by two other important inferences. First, US foreign policy-makers realized during their handling of the Guatemalan problem that Washington must be prepared to resort to more drastic means than diplomatic and economic pressure, for the application of these instruments does not impose on the affected party the types of costs necessary to persuade it to alter its behavior if that party finds other trading partners. And second, but subsequent to the Guatemalan case, they decided that the United States could no longer afford to be perceived as a party willing to sacrifice its democratic ideals for the sole purpose of protecting its general interests. Promotion of greater political and economic equality began to be viewed as a means to contain attempts by communists to win over the "hearts and minds" of Latin Americans and, as a result, as a means to protect US hegemony in the region.

These lessons delineated the way the Cuban problem was defined and dealt with in its different stages. But lessons are too often historically conditioned and, as George Kennan notes, they do not always enjoy "universal validity" (1967: 12). Eisenhower's 1954 success was followed by Kennedy's 1961 failure – and a new set of lessons.

The inability to impede Castro's rise to power convinced US decision-makers that they had to intensify their commitment to promote the birth of moderate governments, ones that would be inclined to advance more equitable political and economic systems. This new attitude was reflected in the steps taken by the Eisenhower administration to replace the Trujillo regime with a government composed of moderate leaders, and in the policies carried out by the Kennedy administration immediately after Trujillo was assassinated.

But these measures did not invite success, and the effect of defeat was felt immediately in the form of new lessons. Bosch's fall from power and the inability of his successor to create a more hospitable political and economic environment convinced the leaders in Washington that the Dominican Republic remained an infertile ground for democratic reforms and that attention would have to center on ensuring that communism did not succeed in exploiting this domestic condition. Guided by this belief, and by the vivid memory of the costs accrued in the fateful days of April 1961 by an unwillingness to tarnish the reputation of the United States, the Johnson administration decided almost precisely four years later that it was less costly for the United States to be perceived as an interventionist power than to have to cope with the birth of a "second Cuba" in the Caribbean. In other words, Robert Jervis's dictum that decision-makers "avoid policies that have failed in the immediate past" (1976: 275), captures masterfully why the Johnson administration was so willing to ease its pressure on the post-Bosch regime that it promote democratic reforms, and so determined to ensure that a Castro-type regime would not assume the reins of government in the Dominican Republic.

As was the case with the two earlier instances of US intervention, the Dominican problem cannot be approached from a perspective that focuses solely on the interests that were at stake. The United States intervened because it believed that it had to contain the propagation of communism in the Dominican Republic. This decision, moreover, can be attributed to the belief by the leaders in Washington that important strategic and economic interests would have been undermined if a pro-Bosch regime had been erected in 1965 in the Dominican Republic. But the importance imposed on this small Caribbean nation cannot be fully captured without placing the interests it represented in the context of the interests undermined by the Cuban experience. Even the most unsophisticated comparison of the interests at stake would lead to the conclusion that the United States should have intervened more forcefully in Cuba than in either Guatemala of the Dominican Republic. The defining of the problem posed by developments in Cuba, however, came on the heels of the Guatemalan success, while the defining of the problem posed by developments in the Dominican Republic came on the heels of the Cuban failure.

7

The Interplay between Interests, Beliefs, and Cognitive Processes

INTRODUCTION

This study set out to show that the explanatory reach of the theory of reasoning and learning by analogy, when applied to the Caribbean and Latin America, eclipses the elucidative value of other theories of intervention – strategic, economic, and cognitive. A final verdict on this claim cannot be reached yet, but in view of the nature of the cases considered so far, a preliminary evaluation can be carried out at this stage.

THE STRATEGIC–REALIST PERSPECTIVE

The appraisal of the strategic perspective must begin by accepting the assumption that the world between 1945 and 1983 was divided into two opposing alliance systems – one dominated by Washington, the other by Moscow – and that any attempt by either party to undermine the other's hegemonic control over its own alliances would have provoked reciprocation. A well defined strategic paradigm would also contend that the force used by either party to respond to the threat posed by the other or any of its surrogates would have been in direct proportion to the intensity of the threat.

The Monroe Doctrine, promulgated in 1823, set the central theme behind the strategic perspective as it pertains to the relationship between the United States and Caribbean Basin states: any extra-hemispheric influence in the Americas poses, axiomatically, a threat to the United States's security. It has been argued that three factors in the geopolitical environment affect a state leader's perception of threat. They are: (1) how the capabilities of the various states in the system are distributed; (2) the extent to which the state he leads is involved politically and economically in any one particular geographical area;

and (3) the type of relationship the state he leads has with other states in the system (see Hybel, 1986: 12). Using the first factor as a reference point, it can be contended that the intensity of the threat experienced by US leaders will be proportional to the capability of the Caribbean state attempting to undermine the interests of the United States: the greater the state's capability, the greater the intensity of the threat experienced. Regarding the second factor, the leaders in Washington are bound to assign greater value to threats emanating from Caribbean Basin states in which the United States is heavily involved both politically and economically, than from states in which its involvement is limited. And finally, it is to be expected that US foreign policy-makers will feel more threatened by the anti-US steps taken by Caribbean Basin states that have had tense and mistrustful relationships with the United States than by those that have been supportive of its past policies.

Of these three factors, only the first two need to be accounted for in order to extrapolate whether US policies of intervention are the function of the intensity of threat perceived by US foreign policy-makers. It is unnecessary to focus on the type of relationships the United States had with its target prior to the time it opted for some form of intervention, because such relationships did not vary noticeably from one case to another. In almost every single instance, US leaders ordered intervention in the political, economic, and social affairs of states that for years had maintained close and friendly bonds with the United States. The measures used to objectify the first two factors and to guide the empirical investigation regarding the explanatory import of the strategic paradigm are represented in table 4.

It is not essential to derive a precise, aggregated measure of each state's capability and strategic value to the United States to argue that the US policy of intervention has not been guided by a rational assessment of the threat posed by each state to the United States. Or, to put the argument in the context of one of Karl von Clausewitz's propositions, the United States, in its attempt to defeat its different enemies, did not "proportion [its] efforts to [its adversaries'] power of resistance" (von Clausewitz, 1986: 299).

The threat posed by the Castro regime in Cuba in 1959, 1960, and 1961 to the security interests of the United States was much greater than that posed by Guatemala or the Dominican Republic. Not only was Cuba in a better position to strike or help strike against the United States than either of the other two states, but also its population, armed forces, and economic and strategic raw material capabilities were significantly greater. Based on the strategic paradigm, the most obvious inference would be that the United States should have acted more aggressively against Cuba than against Guatemala or the Dominican Republic. Such a prediction would have been entirely off the mark. The policy instruments used by Washington against Cuba were not much more belligerent than those it used against Guatemala, and were less violent than those it used against the Dominican Republic. Moreover, when the United States did intervene militarily with its own forces, it was against an actor who did not pose a major threat – Juan Bosch in the Dominican Republic. In this case, the United States had no real evidence to prove that Bosch would attempt to form a regime dominated by communists, but it had good reason to believe that if he had attempted it he would have been unable to remain in power for long.

Table 4 Measures of the strategic value to the United States of Guatemala, Cuba, and the Dominican Republic

	Distance between the US and:[a]	Military capability Armed forces[b]	Population[c]	Economic capability[d]	Strategic raw material capability[e]	Access to strategic maritime passages[f]
Guatemala	Approximately 600 miles	7,500 (1954)	3.07 m (1954)	$813 m (1953)	Lead: 6,068 m tn Zinc: 10,190 m tn Silver: 458,480 oz (1953)	3
Cuba	Approximately 90 miles	45,000 (1960)	6.67 m (1958)	$2,569 m (1958)	Copper: 82,563 m tn Iron: 105,057 m tn Chrome: 113,505 m tn Nickel: 22,227 m tn Manganese: 146,026 m tn (1957 exports)	1
Dominican Republic	Approximately 680 miles	19,000 (1965)	3.51 m (1965)	$1,121 m (1965)	Bauxite: 1,138,000 m tn Gold: 271,000 oz Nickel: 79,800 m tn (1963, 1974, 1975)	2

[a] These values represent the closest geographical distances between the United States and the respective Caribbean Basin countries.

[b] See Statistical Abstract of Latin America, 1955–84.

[c] Ibid.

[d] These values represent each country's GNP for the year given, but at a constant 1970 value. See Statistical Abstract of Latin America, 1955–84.

[e] These figures are not very useful for comparative purposes. They might help the reader develop an understanding of some of the principal raw materials extracted in each country. See Statistical Abstract of Latin America, 1955–84; The West Indies and Caribbean Yearbook, 1955–67.

[f] These rankings are very rough estimates representing the capability of the Caribbean Basin states to disrupt the maritime passages in the Caribbean Sea and Panama Canal when compared to one another.

THE MARXIST PERSPECTIVES

The Marxist perspectives do not fare much better than the strategic argument. The premise of one of the Maxist perspectives is that the primary cause of US intervention against revolutionary regimes in the Caribbean Basin has been the tendency of these regimes to expropriate property belonging to US multinational corporations. According to this argument, there is a congruency between the interests of the multinational corporations and those of US governmental officials. This argument has been modified by those who contend that such congruency of interests is unlikely to exist, for it is not unusual for US multinational to have competing interests abroad. For those proposing this challenge, the central intent of the US government is to protect not the separate economic interests of corporations but the overall economic well-being of the United States. From this perspective, US foreign economic control is a necessity, for without it the continued viability of the United States's economy would be at risk.

Regardless of which of the two Marxist arguments one seeks to evaluate, it is logical to infer that the responses by the United States government would be proportional to the economic values at stake. This inference, however, is once again not validated by the empirical analysis.

Table 5   *Measures of the economic value to the United States of Guatemala, Cuba, and the Dominican Republic*

	Imports from the US by:[a]	Exports to the US by:[b]	Total earnings from direct US investments in:[c]	Economic interaction between the US and states adjacent to target state[d]
Guatemala	$51.3 m (1953)	$68.1 m (1953)	$11 m (1950)	$1.48 b (1955)
Cuba	$542.5 m (1958)	$490 m (1958)	$48 m (1958)	$1.23 b (1960)
Dominican Republic	$11 m (1964)	$134.6 m (1964)	$5 m (1960)	$1.46 b (1967)

[a] For Cuba, see *The West Indies and Caribbean Yearbook*, 1955–67; for the remaining countries, see *Statistical Abstract of Latin America*, 1955–84.
[b] Ibid.
[c] See *Statistical Abstract of Latin America*, 1955–84.
[d] Ibid., "Economic transaction between the United States and states adjacent to target state" refers to total exports by the United States to all the states in the Caribbean Basin, excluding the targeted state. States in the Caribbean region include all the states considered in this study plus Haiti, Panama, Mexico, and El Salvador.

If US investors dominated the decision-making process in Washington, then the fact that their earnings in Cuba were greater than in Guatemala and the

Dominican Republic should lead to the prediction that the US government would have acted more forcefully against the first state than against the other two. And yet, in the only instance in which the United States government relied on its own forces, it did so against the state in which total earnings from direct US investments were at their lowest and in which no expropriation of US property had taken place.

The explanatory value of the Marxist perspective is not improved measurably by switching to the assumption that the political leaders in Washington are not prisoners of the foreign interests of US corporations but act freely, committed to protecting the economic well-being of the United States and to ensuring that different international economic subsystems are structured to favor the economic interests of the United States. If the United States government had been concerned by the potential damage any one particular regime could have inflicted on its economic dominance over the Caribbean Basin, then there is no question that it would have acted much more aggressively against Castro in 1961 than it did against the pro-Bosch group in the Dominican Republic in 1965. The leaders in Washington would have had to calculate that failure to avert the desertion of the most important actor in the Caribbean Basin, Cuba, would have a much greater effect on the region than failure to prevent the Dominican Republic from falling into the hands of the communists. In other words, it would have been economically rational for the United States to act with greater force against Cuba than against the Dominican Republic, a country whose economic trade value to the United States was between six and seven times smaller than Cuba's.

To recapitulate, the argument that the responses by different US administrators were proportional to threats posed either to the private interests of US corporations investing abroad or to the structure of the regional economic subsystems which were economically helpful to the United States, are not backed by the evidence. This is not to say that these concerns were never present but that, if they were, they were structured as part of a greater problem.

THE COGNITIVE PERSPECTIVES

The Truman administration and the calculation of intervention in Guatemala

To capture the effects of the cognitive processes of policy-makers in the Truman administration on US policies toward Guatemala it is necessary to focus on two issues. First, it is critical to understand why the US government waited until 1951 to begin the slow and quiet implementation of economic sanctions against Guatemala; and, second, why President Truman reversed in 1952 his original decision to launch a covert paramilitary invasion of the small Central American state.

Throughout the second half of the 1940s, the foreign policy of the Truman administration toward its southern neighbors was guided by two objectives. Its most basic goal was to contain communism. Its fulfillment, however, was never in doubt. In 1948, in its first National Security Council document (NSC 16) devoted exclusively to Latin America, the Truman administration noted that "communism in the Americas is a potential danger, but, with a few possible exceptions, it is not seriously dangerous at the present time" (quoted in Rabe, 1988: 15). Guatemala was perceived, as the possible exception. But the problem of how to supress communism in Guatemala, if and when the need arose, had to be accompanied by a consideration of how such action might conflict with a second critical objective: avoiding censure by Latin American and Caribbean leaders.

In a document drafted in 1949, the State Department proposed that during "recent decades, the US had almost completely succeeded in persuading the other American republics that it has renounced, first, additional territorial ambitions and, second, domination or direct interference in their domestic affairs" (quoted in Wood, 1985: 133). The words in the document were not purely rhetorical. In July, fewer than three months after its first draft had been circulated among State Department officials, Assistant Secretary of State Edward G. Miller, in response to a request by United Fruit that economic sanctions be imposed on Guatemala, stated that it would be impossible to use such an "obvious weapon and emphasized that irrespective of the justice of the case, the result would be 100 percent censure by every other nation in Latin America" (1985: 154).

And yet, in 1951 the Truman administration began to impose economic sanctions on Guatemala in a guarded manner. Was this a "rational" decision – that is, in view of the two goals sought by the Truman administration, was the action chosen by its members justified by new developments in Guatemala? To answer the question, the analysis focuses on the most important beliefs of some of the central US foreign policy-makers and the information they processed as they tried to define the nature of the Guatemalan problem. For present purposes, the analysis of the beliefs of Harry Truman and Thomas Mann will suffice.

Harry Truman did not have an extensive formal education. However, from an early age he developed an avid interest in history and the lessons he could derive from its study. In his *Memoirs*, he writes that he learned as a boy "that history had some extremely valuable lessons to teach" (quoted in Larson, 1985: 128). He also notes in a letter to his daughter Margaret that from the study of Ancient History it was possible to "find out that people did the same things, made the same mistakes, and followed the same trends as we do today" (1985: 129).

His dependency on history would become evident as he sought to give direction to his country's foreign policy. But his attitude toward communism, and his beliefs about how to contain the Soviets, would also influence his actions. Truman harbored great skepticism of all extremist ideologies. He liked to argue that there was not any difference among totalitarian states. "I don't care what you call them – you call them Nazi, Communist, or Fascist, or Franco, or anything else – they are all alike;" they are all "an excuse for dictatorial rule" (quoted in Gaddis, 1982: 66 and 16). This attitude, however, did not prevent him from believing that the United States could achieve normal relations with communist states. By designing a policy that showed "patience and firmness," the United States could eventually show the Soviets that "we are too strong to be beaten and too determined to be frightened," and this realization would convince them to "change their minds and work out with us a fair and equitable settlement" (1982: 8).

Truman's lack of expertise on foreign policy led him to rely extensively on experts, and to support their conclusions (Larson, 1985: 144). This did not mean that he would not evaluate the evidence. As he told Henry Wallace: "I shall always be President and make the final decision in matters of major policy after they give me their facts and recommendations" (quoted in Larson, 1985: 144–5). He was, however, inclined to make fast decisions, without careful analysis of the information or of the consequences that could follow from the selection of any one alternative. In fact, he prided himself on being able to make decisions and live with them whether they proved right or wrong (1985: 145–6). In other words, Truman did not engage in very detailed analysis of the various interests at stake, and did not carefully evaluate whether the information available made it feasible for him to gauge properly different alternatives and their possible implications.

The central aspects of this brief synopsis of Truman's beliefs and information-processing style are his tendencies to rely on the advice of experts and to make snap decisions. His first tendency, thus, makes it necessary that the analysis be now switched to focus on a major expert. It is unlikely that Truman interacted much with Thomas Mann, a rising young star in the State Department who was serving as deputy assistant secretary for inter-American affairs. But his advice was not overlooked by two influential individuals in the Truman administration, Mann's immediate superior, Edward Miller, and one of the president's advisors, Tapley Bennett.

Thomas Mann's policy recommendation regarding Guatemala was rooted in two beliefs. In order for the United States to be able to project its offensive power across oceans, it was essential that it have unobstructed access to Latin American resources. Access to these resources could be impeded if the United States were to allow the development of communist regimes throughout the American hemisphere. Communism, in Mann's words, "was not any economic, doctrinal, or even military matter, it was a political one. This government knew that communists the world over were agents of Soviet imperialism and constituted a mortal threat to our own national interest" (quoted in Immerman, 1982: 82).

Mann, as already noted, returned from the trip to Guatemala in 1951 convinced that its new leader was a communist. In June 1951 he recommended that the United States clamp down quietly on all economic aid to Guatemala from international agencies or bilateral organs such as the Export–Import Bank, and also that the United States cut down on trade. Mann believed that this action would create an internal battle within the Arbenz government, with the communists fighting to return to power. This struggle, in turn, would pressure the conservatives, and especially the army, to "get together and clean their own house" (quoted in LaFeber, 1983: 115).

Mann's policy proposal and the decision by the United States to begin implementing economic sanctions against Guatemala do not reflect, in one important respect, the decision-making process expected by the cognitive paradigm. Mann was fully aware that actions by the United States toward Guatemala could not be guided solely by the need to contain communism. Of great concern to Mann and his associates was ensuring that US actions would not be censured by other Latin American states. As Mann stated, the Non-Intervention Agreement "is a cornerstone of our Latin-American foreign policy. If it became obvious that we were violating this agreement, other Latin American governments would rally to the support of Guatemala" (quoted in LaFeber, 1983: 115).

In short, Mann's decisional behavior does not correspond with the contention forwarded by the cognitive paradigm that the decision-maker, when faced with a situation in which two or more values are affected, will deny their possible interconnection and thus force the mental dissolution of the trade-off relationship between values. But this argument still leaves open two questions. Did Mann use the information available to preserve his expectation that Arbenz was forming a communist regime, or was the information so compelling that no other information could have been derived? Did Mann side-step the detailed analysis of alternatives when he proposed that the quiet imposition of economic sanctions on Guatemala would be the most effective policy, or was this a policy arrived at after careful consideration of its potential consequences and those of other alternatives?

Regarding the first question, there is no doubt that the information available left ample room for competing interpretations. Only four deputies of Arbenz's ruling coalition in the Guatemalan Congress were communists. Arbenz, moreover, did not appoint communists in key departments such as the military and the foreign ministry; nor did he appoint any to his own cabinet (Rabe, 1988: 47). And yet, from that information and from discussions he held with numerous individuals in Guatemala, Mann concluded that communism was becoming a major political force in Guatemala. Why?

According to schema theory, one factor that generally influences an individual's decision to apply one schema instead of another is the schema's cognitive availability, or accessibility, in the human mind (Larson, 1985: 56). Studies have suggested that the more recent, memorable, or easily imagined events have the greatest cognitive availability (1985: 57, n. 72). Common sense also tells us that decisions or events that generate great benefits or great costs generally become more cognitively available than those that engender insignificant benefits or costs.

China was, in 1951, "the cautionary example that frightened policy-makers" (Rubin, 1987: 68). US foreign policy-makers, particularly at the State Department, could not fail to remember how costly it had been to them to assume in 1949, after the communists had virtually routed Chiang Kai-shek and his nationalist forces, that the United States might be able, by recognizing and working with Mao Zedong's government, "to detach it from subservience to Moscow" (Gaddis, 1982: 69). Also in 1951 State Department officials were accepting the contention postulated by Eudocio Racines in *The Yenan Way* that the strategy relied on by the Chinese communists had been to form alliances with the middle class in order to work themselves into positions of power. This assumption, along with the fear of being wrong a second time, was sufficient to convince those in charge of Latin American affairs that the threat of a similar occurrence in Guatemala was real.

Thus, schema theory, at least in this case, seems to be missing the mark when it assumes that a schema has no evaluative component.[1] Mann and other State Department officials relied on a set of categories to define the Guatemalan problem, but these categories were not independent of their beliefs. Their beliefs, rather than being overwhelmed by sensations and information, seem to have unconsciously influenced their decision to focus on the China analogy and to conclude without sufficient evidence that Guatemala was facing the threat of being embraced by communism.

It takes little pondering to recognize that Mann did not carefully analyse the effects his proposed policy or other alternative actions might have. When he concluded that the Guatemalan economy would suffer as a result of the imposition of economic sanctions by the United States, he did so without considering the possibility that this action might reduce Guatemala's dependency on the United States. And this was precisely the effect the action helped bring about. As the United States was working quietly to undermine Guatemala's economy, Arbenz was working vigorously to increase his country's economic interaction with Western Europe.

It is not possible to ascertain conclusively whether the decision to impose economic sanctions on Guatemala was arrived at through a faulty process because of a cognitive need to control uncertainty, an ignorance of how to evaluate systematically policies and their potential consequences, or a natural tendency to respond to problems quickly and economically by reasoning analogically. But an answer can be derived deductively, and by considering a few empirical factors.

The decision to impose economic sanctions quietly was in part a measure designed to control uncertainty. It was a policy that was unlikely to have immediate dramatic effects, and one that could be altered if its consequences became costly to the United States. But it was also a policy reasoned, at least partly, analogically. Mann's proposal to impose economic sanctions was challenged by Edward Martin, of the European desk, who argued that when the same problem arose in 1948 in Italy, the United States extended aid which helped reduce unemployment and, as a result, the influence of the communists. Mann granted Martin's point, but noted that the difference between Italy and Guatemala was that in the latter case the communists would not give up power easily and, moreover, that the Guatemalan army could be relied on more than the Italian army "to clean their own house" (LaFeber, 1983: 115). Mann, in other words, was promoting a policy of limited and controllable risks, on the basis of the notion that communists in Latin America, when pressured, would fight to retain power, and on the idea that the army in that region of the world was a key actor that could be impelled to take over the reins of government whenever the threat of domestic instability became too high. His reasoning was not the byproduct of careful analysis of Guatemala's political, military, and economic conditions, but of his general understanding of Latin American politics and his assumption that his neat categories fitted the Central American country.

The second issue that calls for further examination is President Truman's decision in 1952 not to go ahead with the covert paramilitary invasion of Guatemala that he had ordered the CIA to prepare. At one level, the action exemplifies Truman's willingness to rely extensively on the advice of his experts. When the policy was first proposed to him by Somoza, he sent one of his aides to Central America to explore the plan's viability. Upon being informed that the plan was sound, he ordered the CIA to begin preparations. The plan, however, was never executed. Why? As already noted, doubts still existed among members of the Truman administration as to whether the Guatemalan army would respond to the invasion by siding with the rebel forces or the Arbenz government. But more importantly, Truman changed his mind after being convinced by Dean Acheson and Edward Miller that the reputation of the United States would be tarnished terribly by the revelation that it had been the principal promoter and organizer of the invasion (Rabe, 1988: 49).

In retrospect, therefore, it is evident that although State Department officials feared that Guatemala might become the first Soviet satellite in Latin America, this fear did not outweigh their resolve to avoid angering other Latin American states. It seems quite clear that officials at the State Department never engaged in more than just a superficial estimation of the trade-offs between the two values. In other words, at no time was there an attempt to gauge how badly the reputation of the United States would be affected if its foreign policy leaders launched a covert paramilitary invasion against a country that was not yet governed by communists but was permitting a few of them to occupy political seats near the center of power. Instead, the process was one in which the notion that the "United States could never condone military intervention on the part of an American State against one of its neighbors," dominated the thinking process not just as a "traditional, nearly sacrosanct principle for dealing with Latin American governments," but also as an analogical relationship that structured the conditions for the exclusion of military force as a viable alternative.[2]

No definite answer can be derived from the analysis just conducted as to which psychological perspective posits the most plausible explanation. But a few tentative conclusions can be summarized. Truman's tendency to rely on the advice of the experts that he last saw before he made a decision, helps explain, in some measure, the decision not to resort to military force to overthrow the Arbenz regime. His dependency on experts, however, also justifies the need to understand better *their* cognitive processes.

From a somewhat cursory analysis of Thomas Mann's approach to problem-solving, three general arguments can be postulated. First, based on the analysis of how the Guatemalan problem was defined, it is clear that the structure he and others imposed on the situation was borrowed from an event that had been very costly to the State Department: China, 1949. It was the costliness of the experience that made the schema so visible. Second, based on the study of how the decision to opt for the quiet imposition of economic sanctions was reached, it is evident that value complexity did not prove to be the problem anticipated by the cognitive consistency paradigm. Mann concluded that in order both to contain communism and to avert censure of the United States, economic actions against Guatemala had to be carried out covertly. The fact that this type of process took place, however, does not prove that the analysis of trade-offs was conducted by gauging systematically the different dimensions of the values affected. The third major conclusion, which was derived from the analysis of the decision by State Department officials to recommend against relying on military force to topple the Arbenz regime, is that the methodical appraisal of the trade-offs between two competing values might be obstructed by the tendency to define a problem and select its responses in terms of categories. In other words, opposition to the use of military force against Guatemala was not the result of any careful analysis of potential costs and benefits to the United States. Rather, such opposition resulted from a fear of condemnation if military force were used to influence the domestic affairs of a Latin American state.

The Eisenhower administration and the calculation of intervention in Guatemala, Cuba, and the Dominican Republic

The effects of the cognitive processes of the policy-makers in the Eisenhower administration on US policies toward Guatemala, Cuba, and the Dominican Republic are represented by focusing on three issues. First, it is imperative to explain why President Eisenhower ordered the Central Intelligence Agency to develop a plan designed to overthrow the Arbenz and Castro regimes by covert means. Second, it is necessary to focus on why President Eisenhower authorized the plan's implementation in only one case: Guatemala. And third, it is important to understand what led President Eisenhower to decide that the United States should help subvert the Trujillo regime in the Dominican Republic.

The foreign policy of the Eisenhower administration toward the Caribbean Basin was guided by objectives that superficially resembled those that had dominated the agenda of the previous administration. Like the foreign policy establishment that had applauded his rise to the presidency, Eisenhower believed that communism posed the greatest threat to stability in the international arena, and that the United States had a moral obligation to use its political, military, and economic resources to contain it. As he is reported to have stated in an April 30, 1953, meeting of the National Security Council:

> It is the rooted conviction of the present administration that the Kremlin intends to dominate and control the entire free world. The "peace feelers" put forth by the new Soviet leadership, since Stalin's death, have not altered a full appreciation of the continuous, terrible threat posed to the free world by the USSR. (Challener, 1986: 57)

Eisenhower also believed that any attempt on the part of the United States "to sit at home and ignore the rest of the world" in the face of such a threat would lead to one consequence – "destruction" (quoted in Melanson, 1987: 43). This attitude colored his perception of the Caribbean Basin. After lamenting during a National Security Council meeting held on March 31, 1953, that the United States, due to its commitment "to raising the standards of all peoples," is inhibited from assigning "whatever proportion of national income" it so desires to warlike purposes, Eisenhower emphasized that in the case of Latin America his administration would have to design policies to "secure the allegiance of these republics to our camp in the cold war." Similar views were conveyed in 1954 by Eisenhower's secretary of state, John Foster Dulles, when he stated that "the Communists are trying to extend their form of despotism in the hemisphere," and that his challenge would be to convince Latin Americans that communism was "an international conspiracy, not an indigenous movement" (quoted in Rabe, 1988: 30).

In these statements lies the central difference between the Eisenhower and the Truman administrations in their perceptions of communism in the Caribbean Basin. The Eisenhower administration did not adhere, in 1953, to the attitude held by the Truman administration some years earlier that communism in the region was not yet a serious threat. The former came to power convinced that the menace was real and that political and military leaders in the area had to be persuaded to unite to deal with the problem. Interestingly, this difference points to another major discrepancy in perspective between the two foreign policy-making groups.

For the Truman administration, achieving Latin American solidarity was a necessary condition to containing communism in the Western Hemisphere. For this reason, it placed great value on ensuring that Latin American leaders be given no cause to accuse the United States of intervening in the domestic affairs of Latin American states. Although the Republican party had taken no position on the Good Neighbor policy, the new administration initially supported the non-intervention policy stipulated under the Bogota charter (Wood, 1985: 157). The Eisenhower administration, in a preliminary statement on "United States Objectives and Courses of Action with Respect to Latin America," proposed that hemispheric solidarity should be the key objective in US–Latin American relations. As time went by, however, it began to place less value on solidarity and on the need to avert disapproval. Why?

As already explained, in mid-summer 1953 President Eisenhower ordered the CIA to develop a plan to topple the Arbenz regime covertly. About a year later he approved the implementation of the final steps of the plan. The first decision came a little over a year after the Arbenz regime had had its agrarian reform bill approved by the Guatemalan Congress, and shortly after President Eisenhower's brother had returned from a fact-finding trip to Latin America and informed him that Guatemala "had succumbed to communist infiltration." The second decision was reached two months after the Caracas conference, at which time the State Department understood it "could never convince Latin Americans to boycott or invade Guatemala" (Rabe, 1988: 51), and a few days after Washington had been informed that the Arbenz regime had just received some 2,000 tons of Czechoslovakian small arms and light artillery pieces.

Both decisions reflect many of Eisenhower's unique decision-making attributes and the influence that beliefs have on how problems are categorized; and both decisions challenge, once again, the contention that the assessment of value trade-offs is generally avoided by decision-makers. The last point will be tackled first, for it is the easiest to address and will help set up the conditions for the analysis of the other two arguments.

Notwithstanding that the Eisenhower administration biased its analysis of the Guatemalan problem by its underlying expectations, it did attempt to maintain a balance between its two principal objectives: containment of communism and hemispheric solidarity. Initially, these two objectives were perceived as being part of the same package. Containment of communism would be brought about more effectively via the achievement of hemispheric solidarity. Moreover, it was believed, particularly by John Foster Dulles, that the attainment of the latter objective depended on how successful Washington was at persuading Latin American leaders that communism was an international conspiracy, not an indigenous threat. Success in this last objective, in turn, would have made it possible for the United States to receive approval for its decision to topple the Arbenz regime. But failure ensued, and this was acknowledged after the meeting of members of the OAS in Caracas in 1954.

The turn of events in Venezuela did not persuade the Eisenhower administration that it would have to resign itself to live with the Arbenz regime. Covert intervention, writes Stephen Rabe, "offered convenient solutions to both problems: it would eliminate the Arbenz government and preserve the appearance of nonintervention" (Rabe, 1988: 54). In other words, the Eisenhower administration kept a close watch on its two principal objectives; and it did not lose sight of the fact that it might find itself on a collision course which could be avoided only by selecting a policy that would not overly undermine the value of either goal.

Ultimately, however, the containment of communism took precedence over solidarity. The covert paramilitary invasion was initiated to bring down the Arbenz regime without exposing US involvement. But such an operation involved at least two types of related risks. President Eisenhower had been informed by Allan Dulles that success of the plan was more "dependent upon psychological impact rather than actual military strength" (quoted in Rabe, 1988: 56). This meant that Eisenhower and Dulles recognized that the operation might fail and, as a result, that the world might learn that the United States had been the promoter and organiser of the invasion. Eisenhower was prepared for this eventuality. At the end of May 1954, upon approving NSC 5419/1, "US Policy in the Event of Guatemalan Aggression in Latin America," he also accepted a recommendation by the Joint Chiefs of Staff that the United States be ready to take military action "unilaterally only as a last resort," that is, if and when the OAS could not be persuaded to collaborate (1988: 60). It is not known with certainty whether Eisenhower would have agreed to engage US forces if the covert plan had not succeeded in toppling Arbenz. But there is good reason to assume that he would have. As he told his aide General Andrew Goodpaster, any time you "take the route of violence or support of violence . . .

then you commit yourself to carry it through" (p. 60).

In sum, President Eisenhower seemed willing to risk undermining solidarity, but not the containment of communism in Guatemala. Was this a rational decision, driven by intelligence that informed US leaders in fairly substantial terms that Arbenz was indeed transforming his government into a communist regime; or was it a decision forced by existing preconceptions?

The situation in Guatemala had changed between 1951 and 1954. The most obvious alteration had taken place in the economic arena, following the approval of Arbenz's agrarian reform proposal. In addition, in 1953 Arbenz withdrew Guatemala from the OAS after accusing El Salvador of initiating a secret conspiracy to isolate his country politically and economically. And lastly, a few posts in the Arbenz regime continued to remain under the control of political leaders assumed to have connections with the communist party. But none of this evidence was sufficient to justify the contention that Moscow had targeted Guatemala as part of an international conspiracy – and US leaders knew it. For instance, on May 11, 1954, Secretary of State Dulles admitted that it would be "impossible to produce evidence clearly tying the Guatemalan Government to Moscow; . . . the decision must be a political one and based on the deep conviction that such a tie must exist." In fact, even a year after the invasion had taken place, the Eisenhower administration was still unable to find conclusive evidence linking Guatemalan communists with the Soviet Union (Rabe, 1988: 57).

Substantial evidence for postulating an inference is not a necessary condition if the reasoning process involves structuring the problem analogically. And the China analogy was once again a major focus of the reasoning process of some of Washington's most influential foreign policy-makers. In early 1953, during his Senate confirmation hearing, John Foster Dulles stated that the "conditions in Latin America are somewhat comparable to conditions as they were in China in the mid-thirties when the Communist movement was getting started . . . The time to deal with this rising in South America is now" (Rabe, 1988: 24). The United States, in other words, could not afford in 1954 to wait for additional information that would prove beyond doubt that the communist conspiracy in Guatemala was in progress. The parallels with China were too obvious, and any additional delay could result in the loss of the Central American country.

The fact that a second US administration relied on lessons inferred from the 1949 China fiasco to define and respond to an international problem does not explain why Eisenhower, but not Truman, chose to risk Latin American condemnation. In other words, if the evidence in 1954 regarding the threat posed by the Arbenz government did not differ markedly from that informing US foreign policy-makers in 1951, then why was the decision made to use covert military forces in one case and not in the other? The answers can take at least two directions. The simplest response would be to contend that although the available evidence in 1954 was not conclusive, it pointed with greater clarity than in 1951 that Guatemala was moving both politically and economically toward the left. The critical point is that there is good reason to assume that even with the new intelligence the Truman administration would not have chosen to intervene militarily. For an alternative answer to the question just posed, it will be helpful to focus on a few of the beliefs of Secretary of State Dean Acheson and President Eisenhower.

It may be recalled that in 1951 Acheson persuaded Truman not to go ahead with the plan to topple Arbenz militarily. Acheson's action reflects some of his deeply held beliefs about the nature of politics, relations with allies, and the utility of means for advancing one's interests. According to Acheson, foreign policy in a democratic society must rest on popular knowledge and understanding. "Any course of action must be deeply rooted in popular understanding and popular support – not merely in theory but in fact." Acheson's belief that US leaders should be above reproach was not confined to dealings with the American public. In fact, he was deeply convinced that "what we do affects our friends abroad quite as much as it affects us. They must never have cause to believe that we have disregarded their dangers. They must always know that their problems are in the forefront of our judgments" (quoted in McClellan, 1971: 60).

Acheson's two beliefs were closely intertwined with his beliefs about the relationship between political ends and means. Although he did not presume that foreign policy-makers could be held accountable to the same moral code that governs individual morality, he eschewed the idea that ends justify means. "The means we choose to overcome the obstacles in our path must be consonant with our aims and must accord with our deepest moral sense." The United States, furthermore, ought not to rely on violence "as long as there was the slightest chance that a tolerable future could be found by other means." The use of violence, in other words, could "only make the accomplishment of . . . democracy more difficult" (McClellan, 1971: 73).

Acheson's beliefs corresponded with his recommendation to Truman. A covert invasion of Guatemala would have been not just a deceptive act reflecting a total disregard of the United States for the attitudes and concerns of its Latin American allies; it also would have been an unnecessary act so long as there was still a chance of persuading the Arbenz regime to alter its course via other means. Acheson's dislike for the conduct of covert paramilitary invasions against Latin American states was not tempered by time. On May 3, 1961, following the Bay of Pigs fiasco, he wrote to his former boss, President Truman:

> Why we ever engaged in this asinine Cuban adventure, I cannot imagine. Before I left [the State Department] it was mentioned to me and I told my informants how you and I had turned down similar suggestions for Iran and Guatemala and why I thought that this Cuban idea had been put aside, as it should have been. (Quoted in Wood, 1985: 159)

The decision to rely on covert military means to overthrow Arbenz exhibits the personal imprint of President Eisenhower's beliefs. First, he was not burdened by a tremendous sense of obligation toward US allies. Although he and his secretary of state were committed to maintaining close relations with allies throughout the world, they were both inclined to disregard their allies' interests and to apply pressure on them publicly when it seemed necessary

(Gaddis, 1982: 153). More significantly, however, Eisenhower disagreed with Acheson that ends did not justify means. In 1955, he wrote: "I have come to the conclusion that some of our traditional ideas of international sportsmanship are scarcely applicable in the morass in which the world now flounders." He then added:

> Truth, honor, justice, consideration for others, liberty for all – the problem is how to preserve them, nurture them and keep the peace – if this last is possible – when we are opposed by people who scorn . . . these values. I believe we can do it, but we must not confuse these values with mere procedures, even though these last may have at one time held almost the status of moral concepts. (Quoted in Gaddis, 1982: 159).

This belief tells us a great deal about Eisenhower's possible penchant for covert paramilitary means, but not much about what might have led him on certain instances to postpone or reject its use. To get a clearer picture, it is necessary to focus on how he approached an operational decision. One of Eisenhower's favorite aphorisms was: "Rely on planning, but never trust plans" (Gaddis, 1982: 133). As a decision-maker, Eisenhower acted on the axiom that although uncertainty could never be controlled fully, every effort should be made to minimize it. For this reason, he emphasized that the final decision should be made "at the latest possible time that would still permit its implementation" (1982: 133).

Just as Acheson's beliefs corresponded with his recommendation to Truman that the United States refrain from using covert paramilitary means to overthrow Arbenz, Eisenhower's beliefs corresponded with his decision to follow a directly opposite path. During the Second World War Eisenhower learned that covert means, if used judiciously, could fulfill certain needs quietly, quickly, and cheaply. This fondness for covert activities, however, could have died easily at the war's edge if he had believed that the analysis of procedures ought to be conducted in the context of moral ideals.

The use of covert means can help control risks, but it does not guarantee their elimination. Eisenhower knew this and that is why he decided to approve the implementation of the final stages of the plan designed to topple Arbenz, but to delay the implementation of the plan to bring Castro down. For Eisenhower, Cuba was Guatemala a second time. As in the earlier case, he lacked "all of the hard evidence [of Communist domination] which would be required to convince skeptical Latin American Governments and the public opinion behind them" (Rabe, 1988: 130). The absence of hard intelligence, however, is rarely an impediment to problem definition when the decision-makers have access to analogies. And that Eisenhower had.

Having decided that Castro was moving his revolution toward communism and that a way to bring this process to an end was via a covert paramilitary invasion, President Eisenhower was left with two questions: should I give the order to proceed, and if so, when? These questions were not independent of one another in Eisenhower's mind. On January 3, 1961, during discussions with members of the National Security Council, Eisenhower noted that there were only two reasonable courses of action open to the United States: "(1) supporting Cubans to go in March or (2) abandon the operation" (quoted in Rabe, 1988: 171). For Eisenhower, March was an important month for two reasons. First, he was aware that Castro was improving Cuba's military capability at a very rapid pace. And second, he feared that if the invasion were not launched by March, the Guatemalan government would insist that the Cuban exile forces training in Guatemala be moved elsewhere.

At the same time, however, Eisenhower was determined not to be rushed to approve a badly rationalized operation. In the fall of 1960, for instance, after learning that the CIA was not able to persuade Castro's opponents to work together, Eisenhower warned Allan Dulles and Richard Bissell with the statement: "Boys, if you don't intend to go through with this, let's stop talking about it" (Wyden, 1979: 31). Needless to say, planning for the operation did not stop there. On November 29, after contending that he did not want to leave the newly elected president "in the midst of a developing emergency," he asked: "Are we being sufficiently imaginative and bold, subject to not letting our hand appear?" (quoted in Rabe, 1988: 170). A desire to make sure that the operation continued its logical evolution was further evinced when he informed Kennedy, on January 9, 1961, that planning of the anti-Castro operation was moving along well and that it would be the new president's responsibility to bring it to a successful end. But this desire never blurred his understanding that the operation could not be initiated until the Cubans themselves were properly organized. Equally important, in 1961 he remained firm in his belief, voiced in 1954, that any time you "take the route of violence or support of violence . . . then you commit yourself to carry it through." For Eisenhower, Kennedy's decision not to provide air support to the Cuban invaders reflected "a very dreary account of mismanagement, indecision and timidity at the wrong time" (1988: 173).

The last issue to be addressed in this section – how to explain President Eisenhower's decision to subvert the Trujillo regime in the Dominican Republic via covert means – will require only a scant analysis. Castro's rise to power in 1959 persuaded the Eisenhower administration that the Dominican Republic under Trujillo's leadership could become a potential Cuba. This decision, however, was arrived at without substantial evidence, and analogically. In 1960 the CIA estimated that the Dominican communist party had fewer than 100 members, that opposition to Trujillo lacked a charismatic leader and was scattered and disorganized, and that it was very unlikely that Trujillo could be ousted without outside help. Early in 1958, however, few also estimated that the Batista regime would meet the fate that befell it. The fact that it did, persuaded the Eisenhower administration to view Trujillo through the Batista prism.

Just as he relied on an analogy to define the problem posed by Trujillo's intransigent behavior in the Dominican Republic, Eisenhower dependend on his penchant for covert actions and his belief that they help control risks to act against the Dominican leader. On January 14, 1960, the president agreed that the United States should intervene in the Dominican Republic to prevent the rise to power of a "Castro-type government or one sympathetic to Castro." But he did not implement the decision immediately. His administration first tried to persuade Trujillo to relinquish power in favor of a moderate regime. When this measure failed, Eisenhower acknowledged, in May 1960, that it was time to begin imposing economic pressure, and he approved the use of covert means to aid Trujillo's moderate opponents in their struggle to topple him. Eisenhower, however, was still being cautious. He concurred with his undersecretary of state, Douglas C. Dillon, that the more drastic measures had to be implemented carefully to ensure that Trujillo's ousting would not bring to power "an individual of the Castro type" (Rabe, 1988: 156–7).

From this brief analysis of Eisenhower's beliefs and a comparison of his approach to problem-solving with the one relied on by the Truman administration, a few conclusions can be reached. First, based on the analysis of the definitions of the Guatemalan, Cuban, and Dominican Republic problems, there is little doubt that the structures Eisenhower and his advisors imposed on the situations were borrowed from events that had had major effects on their cognitions. In 1954, the 1949 China syndrome was still alive in the minds of decision-makers. In 1960, as the United States found itself needing to respond to a new reality in Cuba, Washington referred to Guatemala to structure the problem posed by Castro's leadership. And that same year they concluded that if they hoped to avert a second Cuba in the Dominican Republic, they would have to remove Trujillo.

Second, based on the analysis of how the decision to opt for covert paramilitary intervention was reached, it can be concluded once again that the foreign policy-makers had no difficulty recognizing that more than one value would be affected by the policy. Eisenhower favored using covert paramilitary means to topple Arbenz, Castro, and Trujillo, fully aware that the United States might not succeed and, thus, might need to intervene overtly with its own forces in order to avert defeat. He realized that there was a good chance of being censured by Latin American states. But Eisenhower's willingness to take the risk by using surreptitious means cannot be attributed to some type of malfunction in his cognitive process. Rather, it reflects his belief that the interests of one's allies are always subordinate to the interests of one's own country and need, on occasion, to be sacrificed. It also represents his belief that it is often necessary to use unprincipled means in international affairs in the struggle for principled values. And finally, it manifests the conviction that risks can be controlled via the use of clandestine means if the operation is well crafted.

In the last section of the analysis of the handling of Guatemala by the Truman administration, it was argued that the decision to by-pass the use of subversive means was not arrived at systematically through the methodical appraisal of trade-offs between competing values. As part of the argument, it was also contended that the propensity of the Truman administration to focus on intervention and censure from an analogical perspective encumbered the process of gauging the potential utility of relying on military means. A similar case, even with a different intonation, cannot be made about Eisenhower's cognitive process. Eisenhower believed, largely because of his experience during the Second World War, that clandestine means could be an effective tool for disrupting or overthrowing unfriendly and/or unstable political regimes. This belief, however, did not seem to lead him to view the relationship between the concepts in a narrow categorical context. In other words, although Eisenhower believed in the effectiveness of covert means, he was also convinced that certain special conditions had to be met before they could be used competently.

This last point raises a potentially interesting question: does the nature and centrality of a belief affect the constitution of an analogy? Acheson's and Eisenhower's beliefs differed not just in terms of content but also in terms of centrality. For instance, Acheson seemed much more intense about his belief that the Truman administration must respect the concerns of Latin American leaders, than did Eisenhower about his belief that Arbenz and Castro posed a major threat to the United States. Eisenhower, after all, during the Second World War had fought and defeated much more powerful adversaries than the two Latin American leaders. If this distinction in beliefs was significant, it will be worthwhile to consider in the analysis of the remaining decision-makers whether the level of complexity imposed on any given analogical structure is a function of the degree of centrality of the beliefs that help format the analogy.

The Kennedy administration and the calculation of intervention in Cuba and the Dominican Republic

When students of US foreign policy focus on President John F. Kennedy's decision in April 1961 to approve the CIA plan to topple the Castro regime, they usually contend that the action reflects the personality of an aggressive, self-assured individual who was determined to be perceived as a vigorous and strong leader and who was afraid of being humiliated. The argument does not seem particularly persuasive if one recalls that just as President Kennedy was approving the invasion of Cuba he was also demanding that US exposure be kept to a minimum. Its general appeal is further weakened by consideration that just a month after the Bay of Pigs incident, President Kennedy ordered that the United States disassociate itself with attempts by Dominican nationals to bring to an end Trujillo's rulership over the Dominican Republic. But just as these two events seem to bring into question the argument that Kennedy's decisions reflect his aggressive personality and his fear of being humiliated, one is confronted by the need to explain why, in early June 1961, he ordered that the US Marines be prepared to land in the Dominican Republic if the political turmoil brought about by Trujillo's assassination got out of hand. These three decisions pose a theoretical puzzle not only to students who study the relationships between personality and action but also to those who concern themselves with the effects of cognitive processes on US foreign policies.

John F. Kennedy moved into the White House in early 1961 determined to give his administration a distinct identity. This commitment went beyond his desire to develop a unique approach to the formulation of foreign policy. His goal was to introduce a different, more positive way of focusing on international problems. Kennedy's keynote concept was the idea of diversity (Gaddis,

1982: 201). As he stated in 1962, "Some may choose forms and ways that we would not choose for ourselves – but it is not for us that they are choosing. We welcome diversity – the Communists cannot" (quoted in Miroff, 1976: 60).

Attached to this goal was his belief that the United States must not perceive every threat to its interests in ideological terms. In 1961, he emphasized that the American people had to stop perceiving "as Communist inspired every anti-government or anti-American riot, every overthrow of a corrupt regime, or every mass protest against misery and despair" (quoted in Gaddis, 1982: 209). It would be incorrect to try to infer from Kennedy's belief and goal that his administration would not be firmly committed to "containing" communism. In fact, if one were to focus solely on the rhetoric of the new president's speeches, one might be tempted to infer that he was signaling a willingness to be much more aggressive in the Cold War struggle. Diversity for Kennedy did not imply accepting the formation of communist regimes. As he noted in his inaugural address, the United States under his administration would "pay any price, bear any burden, meet any hardship, support any friend, oppose any foes, in order to assure the survival and success of liberty. This much we pledge – and more" (quoted in Ambrose, 1988: 180).

Commitment to diveristy meant, in other words, two things. On the one hand, it signified a willingness to accept that other states might have different political, economic, and social aspirations. On the other hand, since communism, in Kennedy's mind, could not live in a world of diversity, it was imperative that the United States ensure that attempts to undermine heterogeneity were counteracted in the appropriate ways. Or, as expressed by Walt Whitman Rostow, the chairman of the Policy Planning Council at the State Department:

> We look forward to the emergence of strong, assertive nations which, out of their own traditions and aspirations, create their own forms of modern society. We take it as our duty – and our interest – to help maintain the integrity and the independence of this vast modernization process. (Quoted in Miroff, 1976: 64)

Battle against those who feared diversity included engaging in a struggle against the Castro regime. As Kennedy stated a few weeks before the 1960 presidential election, a new administration under his leadership would take several measures to correct the policy mistakes of the Eisenhower years. First, it would "let the Cuban people know our determination that they will someday again be free." Second, it would recognize that the Cuban "exiles and rebels represent the real voice of Cuba and should not be constantly handicapped by our Immigration and Justice Department authorities." Third, it would warn the Castro regime that the United States "did not intend to be pushed around any longer." Fourth, it would inform Nikita Khrushchev that the United States would not tolerate the expansion of the Soviet foothold in the American hemisphere. And fifth, it would help Latin American states strengthen the cause of freedom in order to create an environment "where Communism will be resisted, isolated, and left to die on the vine" (quoted in Walton, 1972: 36–7).

The young president's determination not to tolerate the presence of a communist regime in Cuba, however, did not translate automatically into the creation of a major military operation designed to overthrow the Castro regime. Convinced that the concept of symmetry had to be reintroduced into the foreign policy formulation process, Kennedy contended that it was not sufficient to maintain an effective deterrent strength; in addition, it was critical to ensure that such an instrument would do "what we wish, neither more nor less." Or, as stated by W. W. Rostow, the presence of asymmetry brought about by the heavy reliance on nuclear deterrent by the Eisenhower administration made it

> attractive for Communists to apply limited debilitating pressures upon us in situations where we find it difficult to impose on them an equivalent price for their intrusions. We must seek, therefore, to expand our arsenal of limited overt and covert countermeasures if we are in fact to make crisis-mongering, deeply built into Communist ideology and working habits, an unprofitable occupation. (Quoted in Gaddis, 1982: 214)

This meant that Kennedy was willing to increase economic costs if it brought about greater flexibility which resulted in the minimization of risks without either "escalation or humiliation" (1982: 214).

To minimize risks, to control escalation, and to avoid humiliation were some of Kennedy's most important operational goals. Their value, in fact, is fully captured in the analysis of his decisions to authorize the launching of the invasion of Cuba and to order, first, the reduction in the number of planes to be used prior to the invasion for the purpose of destroying Castro's air force and, second, the cancellation of the air support the CIA had planned to provide to the invading forces.

Kennedy had few, if any, moral doubts about intervening in the domestic affairs of other states. Although he promoted diversity and had once claimed that "it will always be a cardinal tenet of American foreign policy not to intervene in the internal affairs of other nations – and this is particularly true in Latin America", he also made it clear that "should any Latin country be driven by repression into the arms of the communists, our attitude on nonintervention would change overnight" (quoted in Walton, 1972: 35). However, intervention, particularly in Latin America, involved significant risks. In this respect Kennedy's beliefs differed little from those of Eisenhower. Each believed that any time he chose to intervene militarily in the domestic affairs of a Latin American state, he was automatically risking inciting the wrath of its neighbors. But Kennedy's concern regarding the risks that such an action could prompt seem to have been greater than the apprehension voiced by Eisenhower.

Since coming to power, Kennedy had decided that the most effective way to fight communism in Latin America would be by bringing about domestic stability in the different countries of the region. This would require nothing less than altering the internal structures of such societies via economic development, combined with social and political reform (Gaddis, 1982: 225). None of the Latin American leaders should be given reason to conclude that the new administration in Washington would not respect their states' sovereignty.

It is often argued that when Kennedy approved the Cuban operation he was, for all practical purposes, disregarding the advice of those recommending that it not be implemented. This argument is partly correct. As it became evident that the invasion would be given the green light, Kennedy was warned by Arthur Schlesinger that at "one stroke [he] would dissipate all the extraordinary good will which has been rising toward the new administration through the world. It would fix a malevolent image of the new administration in the minds of millions" (quoted in Walton, 1972: 43). Schlesinger's warning was accompanied by the contention by the chairman of the Senate Foreign Relations Committee, Senator William T. Fulbright, that Castro was just "a thorn in the flesh, not a dagger at the heart" (quoted in Etheredge, 1985: 15), and, moreover, that it would be morally reprehensible for the United States not to live up to the tenets of its non-intervention code (Walton, 1972: 43).

Kennedy showed little concern that the invasion would be unprincipled, but he did not want others to reach such a conclusion. It was not mere coincidence, thus, that in mid-April, upon being informed by Richard Bissell that some sixteen planes would be used in the first air strike against Cuba, Kennedy responded: "Well, I don't want it on that scale, I want it minimal" (quoted in Etheredge, 1984: 41). A minimal air attack, in other words, would not impede the implementation of the operation but would, at the same time, minimize the risk of the United States's being identified as the principal intervener.

At first glance it would seem that Kennedy, cognizant of the values at stake, engaged in a trade-off calculation between overthrowing the Castro regime and averting exposure, and concluded that a covert operation with minimal air involvement would be an effective way to fulfill the two objectives. Viewed from a theoretical perspective, this argument would seem to question the explanatory viability of cognitive consistency theories. When the decision-making process is analyzed more carefully, however, it becomes quite evident that the reverse is more the case.

President Kennedy was blind to the significance of two types of information. One of his mistakes was to assume that the operation would remain quiet. This assumption did not correspond with the developing reality. In the Miami Cuban community, for instance, it was common knowledge that an invasion was about to be launched. More extraordinary, however, is the fact that just a day before the air strike was ordered, President Kennedy read a column in the *New York Times* in which the highly respected reporter and columnist James Reston attacked the rumored operation (Etheredge, 1985: 41).

Kennedy's second mistake was in not considering more carefully the possibilities that by reducing the air strike force and cancelling the air support to the invading forces he would be undermining the chances of the operation's success, and that if the invasion failed to fulfill its intended objective he would be augmenting markedly the likelihood of exposure. The Kennedy administration had ample evidence that the Castro regime had strengthened Cuba's military force measurably. The president, for instance, had been informed on March 15 by his national security advisor, McGeorge Bundy, that the "revised landing plan depends strongly upon prompt action against Castro's [airforce] (Etheredge, 1985: 40). Former secretary of state Dean Acheson, moreover, warned the president that "it was not necessary to call in Price Waterhouse [the prominent accounting firm] to discover that fifteen hundred Cubans weren't as good as twenty-five thousand Cubans" (Parmet, 1983: 163). Even the CIA made it clear that although on the basis of past experience – the Guatemalan case to be specific – it expected the invasion to ignite a revolt, in the final analysis it would be impossible to predict whether that would happen (Etheredge, 1985: 50). More importantly, Kennedy was informed by Dean Rusk that Bissell and the CIA's deputy director, General Charles P. Cabell, believed that cancellation of the air strikes during the landings would severely undermine the operation's chance of success (1985: 43).

All in all, therefore, Kennedy was well aware that many of his advisors were convinced that the magnitude of Castro's military force made it imperative that the United States use air power to neutralize the Cuban air force and protect the invading forces. If this information was available, then why did Kennedy agree to carry on with the plan? His admiration for Bissell, and the latter's assurance that during the Guatemalan operation the odds for success had been smaller than the odds in the present situation, could have influenced Kennedy to assume a parallel between both problems and, thus, to conclude that similar results would also follow. The problem with this argument is that although it is valid for the CIA decision-makers, Kennedy could easily have been compelled to reject the analogy by the reactions of individuals who were doubtful about the viability of the plan.

It takes no more than a superficial analysis to acknowledge that attribution theory is not very helpful in explaining Kennedy's decision. The decision did not reflect just a lack of understanding about how to conduct a systematic evaluation of various alternatives and their respective possible consequences; it reflected also the absence of an attempt to conduct even an unsophisticated evaluation. And this brings us once again to cognitive consistency theory.

Part of this theory emphasizes that in conditions of high risk, a decision-maker who has doubts about the availability of additional alternatives will alleviate stress by ignoring information that would point to the risk. As already explained, conditions in 1961 were such that it would have been extremely difficult for Kennedy either to choose a different path to topple Castro or to simply decide that he would accept his regime. These conditions may have compelled him, as Vandenbroucke contends, to disregard "threat cues," hoping that somehow the invasion would not expose the United States's hand (1984: 488).

The Bay of Pigs débâcle left a strong imprint on Kennedy. Mistrustful of CIA claims that Rafael Trujillo could be removed from power without exposing the United States, and concerned that Trujillo's various political opponents had failed to form a united front that would facilitate the creation of a new moderate regime, Kennedy ordered, about a month after the Cuban operation, that US operatives stop working with Dominican nationals to plot the dictator's downfall.

Kennedy's decision reflects, once again, his attempt to achieve a balance between two objectives: the creation of a stable, moderate, Dominican government, and the protection of his administration's and the United States's international image. By this time, however, his analysis of the relationship between these objectives was heavily influenced by his administration's failure to overthrow Castro. Unwilling to absorb the costs of a new failed adventure, Kennedy opted for inaction. His decision for inaction, in other words, came as the result not of an attempt on his part to evaluate the available information, gauge the various possible alternatives, and assess their respective potential risks, but of a belief that he could not afford to trust the experts. His words after the invasion: "How could I have been so stupid to let them go ahead," would not die immediately (quoted in Vandenbroucke, 1984: 491).

But Kennedy also inferred other lessons. The new president had ascended to the pinnacle of US power determined to fight for diversity and against communist attempts to obstruct its development. This belief, however, was not accompanied by a grasp of how difficult such a struggle would be. Cuba alerted Kennedy to the difficulties that would lie ahead. On April 20, as the world was learning that the Castro regime had defended itself victoriously against the American giant, Kennedy told members of the American Society of Newspaper Editors that there were at least three lessons that could be derived from the Cuban experience:

> First, it is clear that the forces of communism are not to be under-estimated, in Cuba or anywhere in the world . . .
> Secondly, it is clear that this nation, in concert with all free nations of this hemisphere, must take an ever closer and more realistic look at the menace of external communist intervention and domination in Cuba . . .
> Thirdly, and finally, it is clearer than ever that we face a relentless struggle in every corner of the globe that goes far beyond the clash of armies or even nuclear weapons . . . they [the armies and nuclear weapons] serve primarily as the shield behind which subversion, infiltration, and a host of other tactics steadily advance, picking off vulnerable areas one by one in situations which do not permit our own armed intervention . . . We intend to profit from this lesson . . . (Quoted in Walton, 1972: 51–3)

And these were the lessons that would persuade Kennedy that overt US armed intervention might at times be justified, even if it generated international criticism. Rafael Trujillo's assassination was received in Washington with both apprehension and optimism. Kennedy feared that moderate Dominican nationals would not be able to rise above their political differences in order to create a united government, and that the presence of discord would be exploited by the leftist radical factions and, possibly, by Castro. The president, however, also hoped that the Dominican Republic could be turned into a case example of a nation that could move successfully "through the difficult transition from tyranny through disorder to constitutional democracy" (Lowenthal, 1972: 11). Kennedy's apprehension and optimism are reflected in his contention that after Trujillo's death the United States faced three possibilities. In "descending order of preference," they were: "A decent democratic regime, a continuation of the Trujillo regime, or a Castro regime. We ought to aim at the first, but we really can't renounce the second until we are sure we can avoid the third" (Ambrose, 1988: 219).

This analysis typified Kennedy's approach to the Dominican Republic. He wanted a democracy, but if the Dominican nationals could not reach an agreement on how the new government would be structured, and if their differences were being effectively manipulated by the communists, then he would settle for the continuation of the Trujillo dynasty until a moderate replacement could be found. Avoiding extensive and intensive domestic turmoil became, thus, the short-term objective. Moreover, the determination to ensure the fulfillment of this objective is reflected in Kennedy's decision to order a US Navy Task Force composed of almost forty ships to patrol the Dominican coast, and in his order that the US Marines be prepared to invade if the situation in Santo Domingo deteriorated too far.

The attempt to place Kennedy's three decisions in some type of theoretical perspective seems to indicate that no single theory can capture the process fully. Although the absence of more detailed information prevents the derivation of a systematic argument, it seems quite reasonable to contend that in none of the three instances was there an attempt to engage in some type of "rational" calculation. For Kennedy, John Lewis Gaddis notes, it was more important to have as his advisors individuals, such as W. W. Rostow, who were capable of rapidly synthesizing complex information, than to have a structure that produced policy papers on every conceivable subject and promoted their lengthy evaluation during formal meetings with the president (Gaddis, 1982: 199–200).

Political synthesizers are likely to come in at least two forms: those who synthesize because they seek cognitive consistency, and those who synthesize as a result of responding to problems analogically. These two groups need not always be composed of different individuals. President Kennedy seems to have been driven in April 1961 to overlook some important information by the fear that if he did not approve the invasion of Cuba he would have difficulty persuading his domestic adversaries that he had the courage to lead. This decision, however, also reflects Kennedy's tendency to structure problems and responses in terms of simple categories. For instance, the implementation of a covert operation with minimal use of airplanes was analyzed solely in the context of how it would minimize US exposure, rather than in terms of how the emphasis on controlling US exposure might undermine the success of the operation and, as a result, Washington's chances of concealing its part in the invasion.

This tendency becomes more evident as the focus is directed to the two decisions that followed on the heels of the Bay of Pigs nightmare. Having paid a very high price for being too trusting of CIA expertise, and fearing that major turmoil would follow Trujillo's removal from power, Kennedy opted for the path of least immediate risk: non-involvement. This decision is in no way contradicted by his order shortly afterward that the US Marines be prepared for armed intervention in Santo Domingo. Both decisions were steered by the fear that unmanageable levels of domestic turmoil might ensue, and that the radical left would be the only faction that would benefit from it. Thus, although Kennedy was to claim in June 1961 that not every overthrow of a corrupt regime was communist-inspired, his failure against Castro persuaded him that communism, with its power and discipline to exploit "the legitimate discontent of yearning," is always searching for fertile new grounds, and that the United

States must always be ready to ensure that the communists not succeed. This sentiment, needless to say, did not reflect the tenets delineated by attribution theory. Had such been the case, Kennedy, although he might still have thought that domestic turmoil entices the communists to act, would at least have tried to determine the communists' chance of gaining politically in the Dominican Republic if extensive violence were to erupt. Such a factor was never taken into consideration by the president, although numerous analysts in Washington had known for quite some time that Trujillo had never really been threatened by the communists. For Kennedy this was not important; what was significant was that he had already paid a major cost and was not willing to repeat the experience.

The Johnson administration and the calculation of intervention in the Dominican Republic

If there was ever a case in which the international actions of a state must be associated with the cognitive process of a president, that case is Lyndon Johnson's decision to intervene militarily in 1965 in the Dominican Republic. Viewed through an historical prism, the decision might not seem particularly unique. Kennedy, after all, had been ready to take a similar step just four years earlier. Thus, in view of the lessons derived from the Cuban experience by Washington's foreign policy elite, there is no reason to think that a president other than Johnson would have defined and responded to the Dominican problem differently. And yet, even with this footnote in mind, it is difficult to disregard the effect Johnson's cognitive process seems to have had on the decision.

Johnson came to the presidency in 1963 recognizing that his talent for international affairs was limited, but determined to ensure that the rest of the world understood his commitment to protect and promote the interests of the United States. The first sentiment was best expressed by his wife when she said that "foreign policy problems do not represent Lyndon's kind of Presidency" (quoted in Goldman, 1969: 378). But Johnson was not about to be intimidated by the international realm, and he had a clear vision of how he would represent his country. In 1964 he observed "what Theodore Roosevelt said back there half a century or more ago is true tonight as it was then: 'Speak softly and carry a big stick' We speak softly, we carry a big stick" (quoted in Dugge, 1982: 133).

Johnson's general approach to politics was in terms of personalities, power, and good works (Kearns, 1976: 195). His philosophy for dealing with international adversaries, especially communists, however, was almost solely in the context of power. By the time he became president, he was convinced that many of the problems faced by the United States had grown out of miscalculations by others of its intentions and will. He often stated that foreigners viewed the United States as "fat and fifty, like the country club set," with no hard-headed understanding of its own interests or willingness to protect and promote them (quoted in Goldman, 1969: 379). Or, as stated by one of Johnson's associates:

> He thinks relations turn on fundamentals, on what you do and the motives you show by doing, on whether other nations think you have a tough-minded view of

your own self-interest. He believed that the persistent misunderstandings of America make it necessary for the United States, more than any other country, to communicate its purposes and its awareness of its self-interest loud and clear and over and over again by deeds rather than words. (Goldman, 1969: 382)

Deeds, rather than words, Johnson was convinced, were the only way the United States would succeed in protecting itself against communist encroachment. For Johnson, this meant two things: spending the money necessary to fight communism, and resorting to military force whenever the threat of a communist takeover arose. His rationale for these policies was very simple. As he stated in July 1964, "We can afford to spend whatever is needed to keep this country safe and to keep our freedom secure. And we shall do just that" (quoted in Gaddis, 1982). Money, however, had to be accompanied by resolution. In 1947, he told members of the House of Representatives:

Whether a communist or fascist or simply a pistol-packing racketeer, the one thing a bully understands is force and the one thing he fears is courage . . . human experience teaches me that if I let a bully of my community make me travel the back streets to avoid a fight, I merely postpone the evil day. Soon he will chase me out of the house. (Quoted in Kearns, 1976: 95)

Two historical events were recorded deep in Lyndon Johnson's cognition: the Second World War and Castro's rise to power. Regarding the first event, he noted:

From the experience of World War II, I learned that war comes about by two things – by a lust for power on the part of a few evil leaders and by a weakness on the part of the people whose love for peace too often displays a lack of courage that serves as an open invitation to all the aggressors of the world. (Quoted in Kearns, 1976: 95)

From the Cuban experience, Johnson drew a different lesson, revealed by his statement that "any man who permitted a second Cuban state in this hemisphere would be impeached and ought to be" (quoted in Goldman, 1969: 381).

And this brings us to Johnson's decision to invade the Dominican Republic overtly and with US Marines. For the president, the issue was not whether the rebel forces attempting to bring Juan Bosch back to power included a few or many communists or communist sympathizers. For Johnson, the issue was that so long as there were some fighters who were communists or communist sympathizers, there was always the possibility that they might take over the revolution (Goldman, 1969: 395). Defining the problem as a communist threat, however, need not lead automatically to the decision to quell it with the direct use of US military power. In the case of Johnson, it almost did.

In their dealings with Latin American states, past presidents had tried to minimize criticism of US actions. Johnson, convinced that it was critical for the United States to act decisively in order to protect its interests, "did not worry long over the opinion of other nations" (Goldman, 1969: 382). This attitude applied specifically to the Organization of American States, an institution which, in his words, "couldn't piss out of a boot if the instructions were written on the heel" (1969: 382). Moreover, the decision to rely on overt military force against the Dominican rebels would, in the words of Eric Goldman, "make clear to everyone that he would brook no further Castroism" (p. 395).

To give a theoretical content to Johnson's decision to intervene militarily in the Dominican Republic is not very difficult. The decision did not follow an attempt to ascertain the extent to which the rebel forces posed a communist threat. In view of the Cuban experience, the presence of a few communists or communist sympathizers was the sole justification needed to view the situation as a communist threat. The decision to resort to military force, however, was reached with the realization that it would have repercussions beyond its effect on the rebel forces. It was acknowledged that the action might initially instigate international criticism. But there was a willingness to absorb some criticism, for it was believed that this would be outweighed by the lesson some of the same censurers would infer from the action: that the United States is an international actor that knows its interests and has the capability and willingness to protect them. Furthermore, the Johnson administration tried to control the extent and intensity of international censure by turning what initially was a US invasion into an OAS operation.

In sum, Johnson's actions do not reflect those of an individual whose cognitive process engages in a semi-scientific analysis of a situation, or who is burdened by the need to maintain consistency. He was a leader who "like so many people who do not read history, was peculiarly a creature of it, and prisoner of one particular interpretation of it" (Goldman, 1969: 380). As a prisoner of history, thus, he defined situations in terms of categories. Three categories dominated Johnson's cognitive process as he focused on the Dominican problem in 1965. His basic category was that a rebellion could become a communist revolution if some members of the rebel forces were communist or communist sympathizers and the United States failed to respond forcefully to the event. Related to this category was the notion that failure by the United States to move forcefully against the Dominican rebels would signal a lack of resoluteness which could, in turn, act as a catalyst for other revolutions throughout the entire international arena. Finally, because of the Cuban experience, Johnson simply concluded that the fall of the Dominican Republic into the hands of the communists would translate into his own political demise.

CONCLUSION

The requirement for cognitive consistency did not drive the actions of US policy-makers as they attempted to respond to the Guatemalan, Cuban, and Dominican problems. The only exception to this argument is President Kennedy, as he was confronted by the need to decide whether or not to move covertly against Castro. For the most part, decision-makers consciously disregarded data that would question the validity of viewing the targeted government as communist regimes or regimes that were paving the way for a communist takeover. Eisenhower knew in 1954 and 1961 that he did not have sufficient information to prove that Arbenz and Castro had become Moscow's new puppets in the Americas; and Johnson was aware that not all of Bosch's supporters were communists or communist sympathizers. But none of this was relevant, for history had taught them how to categorize the conditions that led to the birth of communist regimes.

It is also quite evident that few of the US policy-makers had any difficulty realizing that a problem is rarely bounded by non-competing values and that the formulation of a policy must account for the contradictory effects it might have on them. But this awareness did not always lead them to opt for a policy that would achieve a perfect balance between competing values. Values do not exist independently of beliefs; and how much of one value the various decision-makers were willing to sacrifice in order to promote another value was the function of their respective beliefs. Acheson feared communism and was convinced that the United States should respond to the threat; but he also believed that the use of deceptive measures could undermine his country's moral presence. He was willing to use surreptitious means, but only as a measure of last resort. Eisenhower, on the other hand, was less burdened by the moral implications of relying on deceit to achieve ends that would serve the interests of the United States.

And finally, there is the issue of how policies were chosen. If a decision-maker's rationality had to be established on the basis of his willingness to evaluate the consequences that might flow from the implementation of a variety of policies, there is little doubt that Eisenhower would top the list. Notwithstanding Eisenhower's somewhat anomalous predilection for careful analysis, however, it is safe to suggest that the policy-makers' past experiences, or their reading of history, time and again burdened their selection processes. Eisenhower in 1954 was not immune to the CIA's earlier success in Iran; nor was he safe from being influenced by his failure to preempt Castro's rise to power as he decided that Trujillo had to be eased out of power. Kennedy, in turn, could not help recalling the Bay of Pigs failure as he ordered the CIA not to extend any additional help to those Dominican nationals plotting Trujillo's demise. And last, as Johnson contemplated whether to intervene militarily against the rebels forces in the Dominican Republic, he was determined not to relive Kennedy's April 1961 experience. In other words, the force of history in the context of analogical schemes, time and again bounded the US leaders' respective evaluative processes.

8

Peru and Chile: Does the Past
Have More Than One Pattern?

I don't see why we should have to stand by and let a country go Communist due to the irresponsibility of its own people.
Statement by Henry Kissinger, June 1970, two months before Chilean presidential elections

The main concerns [of Peru's military regime] were agrarian reform, to begin to expropriate the International Petroleum Company, and to ensure that communism did not become an important force in Peru.
Cynthia McClintock, "Velasco, Officers, and Citizens"

TWO DIFFERENT RESPONSES

On September 11, 1973, Salvador Allende's Chilean government, the first democratically elected Latin American socialist regime, was toppled by its own military. But the Chilean armed forces were not the only party responsible for this event; the US government, under the leadership of Richard Nixon, worked for approximately three years to destabilize the Allende government. North of Chile, in Peru, a different scenario had unfolded by 1973. After years of pressuring that country's military government to modify some of its policies which were harming US economic interests in Peru, the Nixon administration approved, within a period of five months, a new economic loan, new credits, and a new military aid program to the Peruvian military regime (Werlich, 1978: 338).

Explanations vary as to why the Nixon administration reacted so differently to these two governments, both of which had been committed since their conceptions to bringing about radical changes in the social and economic structures of their respective states. According to Cole Blasier, the difference in behavior can be attributed to two factors. First, and most importantly, the social and economic revolution in Peru was instigated by the military. Unlike Allende, "Peru's rulers could count on the loyal support of the armed forces and allowed little or no organized political opposition. With far less political involvement in Peru under Belaunde than in Chile under Frei, the United States had far less capacity to interfere in Peru's domestic affairs than in Chile's" (Blasier, 1985: 269). And second, although the changes sought by Peru's military regime were extensive, they were never as radical as those intended by the Allende regime. Moreover, while Peru also established relationships with Cuba and the Soviet Union, they were never as close as those instituted by Chile (1985: 268–9).

James Petras and Morris Morley present a somewhat different argument. Their basic contention is that the Nixon administration had been very dissatisfied with some of the policies adopted by the Peruvian military government with respect to fishing rights and investments by US companies in Peru. The existence of a socialist government in Chile, however, forced the Nixon administration to come to terms with Peruvian nationalism.

> The United States preferred to accept limited nationalizations that contributed to stabilizing a regime supportive of a mixed economy than risk radicalizing the situation in Peru through confrontation tactics. Beginning in early 1971, the United States realized that the nationalist measures in Chile could strengthen political forces in Peru which were pressuring for a more rapid and thorough transformation. (Petras and Morley, 1975: 76)

This chapter demonstrates that neither explanation properly accounts for the variance in US behavior. More specifically, these explanations cannot help account for the following developments: throughout part of 1968, all of 1969, and the first eight months of 1970, the Peruvian government took steps that repeatedly undermined the interests of US private investors in Peru; but the US government, still unaware that a socialist regime would be placed in power by the Chilean populus, never applied the political, diplomatic, and economic pressure on Lima's leader that it did on the government in Santiago from the moment it became evident that it would be led by Salvador Allende. In addition, these arguments cannot help explain why the Nixon administration committed itself to thwarting Salvador Allende's rise to power before the Chilean political leader had had the opportunity to implement his economic program. In other words, if the United States was driven to act more harshly against the Chilean government than against the Peruvian government because the former engaged in more radical economic and social reforms than the latter, then how does one explain the US government's determination to undermine the ability of the Allende government to rule even before it came to power?

As an alternative thesis, this chapter proposes that the differences in the responses of the Nixon administration to political, economic, and social changes in Chile and Peru can be attributed to its tendency to delineate the two problems by relying on the same ideological prism used by previous administrations. The Chilean problem was defined within the same ideological context that earlier US administrations had relied on during the Guatemalan dilemma in 1954, the Cuban situation in 1960, and the Dominican crisis in 1965. The Peruvian case, on the other hand, represented a situation in which the US government found itself wavering; should it define the problem as one bounded by the militaristic structure of the government in power, or should it define it by the radical policies it implemented? This wavering, however, was anchored to one critical belief – that the military regime was committed to ensuring that communism would never become a viable political force in Peru.

The analyses of the three cases already presented were conducted separately and were followed, whenever appropriate, by a discussion of the context in which US decision-makers referred to previous cases in their approach to the problem under consideration. This strategy is somewhat modified in the examination of the Peruvian and Chilean cases. These cases are so intertwined in terms of (i) the changes their respective governments sought to bring about, (ii) the time frame in which these attempts came to life, (iii) their strategic and economic values to the United States, and (iv) the administration in Washington that had to respond to the problems as they arose, that it is preferable to study both as part of one large scenario. The scenario for this chapter is broken into a set of events, linked together chronologically, that describe the actions and reactions of Chile and Peru on the one hand and the United States on the other. This chronological linkage can best be appreciated by referring to the following questions:

1 Why did the Kennedy administration grant diplomatic recognition to the same Peruvian military regime it had refused to recognize and to which it had suspended all economic and military aid less than a month earlier for its role in toppling Peru's civilian government?

2 Why did the Kennedy administration support the suspension of constitutional rights by Peru's military regime?

3 Why did the Johnson administration order a slowdown on its loan commitment to Peru in response to President Fernando Belaunde Terry's request to the Peruvian Congress for the authority to resolve the International Petroleum Company (IPC) issue as he saw fit?

4 Why did the Johnson administration covertly channel millions of dollars to help finance the presidential campaign of the Chilean Christian Democratic Party's candidate, Eduardo Frei?

5 Why did the Johnson administration provide economic and military aid to Chile, even after the Frei regime had begun to engage in the nationalization of the copper industry and in agrarian reforms?

6 Why did the Johnson administration withdraw its earlier slowdown order and begin making new loan commitments to Peru?

7 Why did the Johnson administration reduce economic aid to Peru, just after the Belaunde regime had announced it would purchase several Mirage II jets aircraft from France?

8 Why did the Johnson administration recognize the military regime that had just toppled the Belaunde regime, and why did it fail to act against the new regime for expropriating IPC?

9   Why did the Nixon administration refuse to apply strong sanctions against Peru although its military regime took measures that adversely affected US economic interests in that country?

10 Why did the Nixon administration covertly channel some $400,000 to help finance the operation against the Popular Unity Program presidential candidate, Salvador Allende?

11 Why did President Nixon, after learning that Allende had received the largest percentage of popular votes in the Chilean presidential election, order the US government to use extreme measures, including inciting a military coup, to prevent Allende from becoming Chile's new president?

12 Why did President Nixon, following Allende's presidential inauguration but before his regime began to take measures that would adversely affect US economic interests in Chile, order the US government to apply strong sanctions against the Chilean economy?

13 Why did the Nixon administration provide loans to the Chilean military to purchase military equipment while it continued to apply strong sanctions against the Chilean economy?

14 Why did the Nixon administration, three years after Allende had become president, seek to ensure that State Department and CIA officials in Chile avoid contact with the Chilean military, although its leaders were suspected of plotting a coup against the Allende regime?

15 Why did the Nixon administration start to approve new loans to Peru although its military regime was still taking measures that adversely affected US economic interests in Peru?

16 Why did the Nixon administration finally decide to reach a settlement with the Peruvian military regime concerning the expropriation of US private interests in Peru?

THE BIRTH AND UNFOLDING OF TWO DISTINCT PROBLEMS

The most striking contrast between Peru and Chile in the 1960s was the behavior of their respective military leaders toward their constitutional governments. At the dawn of 1962, Peru found itself in the midst of a major presidential campaign. The three principal candidates were Victor Raul Haya de la Torre, leader of the American Popular Revolutionary Alliance; Manuel Odria, leader of the National Union Odriista; and Fernando Belaunde Terry, leader of the Action Popular. By the end of May, as it became evident that Haya de la Torre had a very good chance of receiving a plurality of the popular vote, the Peruvian military warned that the will to commit fraud was so potent that intervention to correct the problem might become necessary (Payne, 1968: 44; Ingram, 1974: 22). The military leadership, afraid that a political victory by the American Popular Revolutionary Alliance might lead to reduction of the military's power, made it clear that the establishment of such a government would not be allowed.

In spite of the threat, Haya de la Torre received the highest number of votes, approximately 557,000, in the June 10 presidential election. But since this total did not equal the one-third popular support required by the constitution to win the election, it was left to the Peruvian Congress to decide who would be the next president.[1]

In early July, the military leaders informed the incumbent president, Manuel Prado, that they would not accept Haya de la Torre. About a week later, on July 13, Fernando Belaunde, who had received some 544,000 votes, demanded that the elections be annulled and suggested that the military intervene if his demand was not met (Payne, 1968: 46). On July 18, after Peru's National Election Jury Committee rejected Belaunde's demand, the expected coup took place and the elections were annulled. On the same day, a military junta led by Generals Ricardo Perez Godoy, Nicolas Lindley Lopez, and Pedro Vargas Prada, and Vice-Admiral Francisco Torres Matos, was formed (Payne, 1968: 47; Ingram, 1974: 105).

The Kennedy administration's reaction to the military coup was swift. Having warned in mid-July that the United States would sever all formal ties with Peru and suspend military and financial aid if a military coup were initiated, the Kennedy administration carried out its threat that same month. Washington, however, was willing to compromise. On July 28, just a few days after having announced that new elections would be held in June of the following year, the Peruvian military junta announced the restoration of constitutional rights (Werlich, 1978: 276). In the following month, Washington recognized the new Peruvian government by announcing the appointment of John Wesley Jones as its new ambassador to Peru (Goodsell, 1972: 247).

The policy reversal by the Kennedy administration was not out of character. Since becoming president in 1961, John F. Kennedy had been emphasizing that the most effective way to stop the rise of "second Cubas" throughout Latin America was by bringing about economic and social development via democratic means. But if Kennedy was determined to push for the creation and solidification of democratic regimes, he was not willing to risk the creation of communist regimes. Toward military regimes which demonstrated, at least publicly, a disposition to give democracy another chance, Kennedy reasoned that it was preferable to reinstitute relations and economic assistance than to help produce a chaotic environment which could in time have undesirable repercussions on US interests (see chapter 6).

The new Peruvian junta wasted very little time in signaling that its plans went beyond protecting the status quo. The first hint came in August, when it ordered the expropriation of all unused land and its distribution to landless peasants or those whose plots were insufficient for their needs (Strasma, 1972: 178; Werlich, 1978: 277). Two months later, the military government created the National Planning Institute to analyze the steps Peru needed to take to bring about economic and social change (Villanueva, 1963: 115–24).

Just as these steps were being taken, Peruvian peasants, led by Hugo Blanco, began an intensive campaign to demand major changes in Peru's agricultural laws. Many of Blanco's proposals had their origins in the new agricultural structure being implemented by the Castro regime in Cuba (Villanueva, 1963: 161–6). These demands elicited an immediate response from the Peruvian military. Claiming that an externally financed guerrilla movement was on the rise, Peru's military junta began in December an intense anti-guerrilla campaign. This campaign was followed by the suspension of all constitutional rights on January 5, 1963 (1963: 68–9, 166–73). The Kennedy administration, contending that it had known for some time that a guerrilla movement supported by Cuba and the Soviet Union was attempting to topple Peru's military junta, immediately supported the suspension of constitutional rights (pp. 183–4). This decision by the US government was in tune with its earlier rationale that it was preferable to absorb the costs of supporting the implementation of undemocratic measures – measures that in time could be revoked – than the costs associated with the radicalization and intensification of domestic unrest. The Kennedy administration reasoned that under the latter scenario it would be more difficult to control the expansion of communism.

Within ten days of extending its support, however, the United States found itself once again at odds with Peru. On January 16, 1963, General Perez Godoy announced that his government was considering expropriation of the La Brea y Pariñas oil complex under the control of the International Petroleum Company (IPC). The US Senate immediately warned that expropriation of US property without proper payment would lead the US to enforce the Hickenlooper Amendment (see below, pp. 178–9) (1963: 46–7). Certain Peruvian military officers, afraid that their reputations would be damaged by Godoy's attempts to embark on economic reform, ousted the General on March 3. A month later, a spokesman for the military junta announced that the Peruvian military leaders were in no position to ensure that the La Brea y Pariñas issue would be addressed before the new elections (p. 113). Finally, on June 9, new elections were held, as promised. Fernando Belaunde Terry, the candidate favored by the military, received a plurality of the Peruvian vote and well over the one-third popular support required to become president without Congressional involvement.

Belaunde's election marked the beginning of a major attempt to bring about significant social and economic changes in Peru. Immediately after being inaugurated on July 28, the new Peruvian president received Teodoro Moscoso, the coordinator for the Alliance for Progress, who had flown to Lima to offer economic aid. In his conversation with Belaunde, Moscoso made it clear that the United States would provide aid to Peru regardless of the outcome of the dispute with IPC, so long as no outright confiscation without compensation took place (Pinelo, 1973: 112).

The International Petroleum Company, a wholly owned subsidiary of the Standard Oil Company (New Jersey), had been a bone of contention in Peruvian politics since at least 1922. In that year Standard Oil succeeded in pressuring the Peruvian government to grant the company a special tax status for fifty years that would reduce dramatically its tax burden. In addition, the company prevailed in maintaining a unique ownership of subsoil rights in Peru. IPC's ownership of the mineral deposits beneath its Peruvian properties was unprecedented in Latin America. Throughout the region, subsoil mineral deposits are considered to be owned by the nation, regardless of who owns the surface property, and are under the custody of the state, not the property holders (Einhorn, 1974: 12–13).

By the late 1950s and early 1960s, the tension between IPC on the one hand, and the Peruvian government and public on the other, had increased noticeably. The company, hoping to maintain its business in Peru, sought to reach a compromise by proposing to trade its ownership of the property for concession status. The Peruvian government and the public rejected the appeal, but no major steps were taken against the company. In his inaugural speech Belaunde promised to solve the IPC issue, and negotiations were begun immediately (Pinelo, 1973: 110).

President Belaunde concluded by October 28 that he could adopt a hard posture in the negotiations with IPC. He asked the Peruvian Congress for the authority to impose his own solution on IPC or to transfer La Brea y Pariñas – an area controlled by IPC since 1914 – to the state-owned oil company Empresa Petrolera Fiscal. Belaunde's solution, one which had been submitted to IPC some eleven days earlier, included the exchange of IPC's property rights for a twenty-year operation contract, the payment of $50 million debt throughout a five-year period, and a very high tax rate which, according to the company, would have exceeded 100 percent of the profits (Pinelo, 1978: 110).

Belaunde's proposal was not well received by either the United States government or the company. On October 30, the president of IPC, M. M. Brisco, accused the Belaunde administration of wanting to engage in "economic confiscation." The following day the US State Department expressed disillusionment with Belaunde's proposal and announced that US aid would be suspended if expropriation without compensation were adopted as policy. Finally, on November 7, Peru's National Federation of Petroleum Workers threatened the Belaunde government with indefinite strike if IPC were nationalized (Pinelo, 1973: 113–15, 117).

President Belaunde, realizing the formidable obstacle he was facing, announced that he would prefer reaching an agreement with IPC whereby the company would continue operating Le Brea y Pariñas. Around this time, however, a major change in leadership was taking place in Washington. Following Kennedy's assassination, his successor, Lyndon Johnson, appointed Thomas C. Mann as the new assistant secretary of state for inter-American affairs. Mann wasted very little time in intensifying the pressure on the Belaunde regime. At the beginning of 1964, the State Department ordered a slowdown on loan commitments to Peru (Pinelo, 1973: 118–19).

The decision by the US State Department to pressure President Belaunde to be more attuned to US private interests in Peru was not an anomaly. The rebellion that had surfaced in late 1961, and that had been linked to communist activities elsewhere in the continent, had been successfully suppressed by the military. This success enabled the US government to respond forcefully whenever it believed that US private interests in Peru were not being cared for properly. The ascension of Thomas Mann to the role of assistant secretary of state for inter-American affairs signaled that the protection of the interests of US corporations would assume a leading value so long as the task did not debilitate the preservation of US security interests.

The US message was not misread by the Peruvian government. In April 1964, IPC and the Belaunde regime began a new round of negotiations. By the end of July the two parties had reached a tentative agreement whereby IPC would cede its property rights over Le Brea y Pariñas in exchange for a release from all back taxes claims. As payment for operating the oil fields, the company would receive 20 percent of petroleum sales. Belaunde, concerned that the Peruvian Congress would challenge the terms of the agreement, delayed submission for ratification. When he did, on December 30, he deleted the principle of exchange of property rights for an operation contract and did not grant IPC a clear release from back taxes claims (Pinelo, 1973: 122–3). IPC reacted immediately by rejecting the proposal submitted to the Peruvian Congress.

The end of 1964 marks the beginning of the rapid deterioration of Peru's economy. A cut-off of US loans and the reluctance of the Peruvian Congress to vote new taxes abetted the rate of inflation, which in turn brought about an increase in opposition to the government (Goodsell, 1974: 128).

In the meantime, a very different scenario was unfolding in Chile. On September 4, 1964, Eduardo Frei, a Christian Democrat, became Chile's new president. Frei's election was welcomed by the United States. Since the 1840s, some twenty years after independence from Spain, Chile had served as the symbol of democracy in Latin America. Elected presidents shared authority with a strong legislature and an independent judiciary (Valenzuela and Kaufman, 1984: 179). Toward the end of the conservative presidency of Jorge Alessandri (1958–1964), however, the Johnson administration became increasingly concerned over a possible move to the left in the 1964 national elections (Petras and Morley, 1975: 20).

The two principal presidential candidates in 1964 were Frei and Salvador Allende, the leader of the leftist coalition, the Popular Action Front (FRAP). While at this time there was no danger of the leftists' winning the election, the declining domestic economic situation created the possibility that the left might be able to deny the Christian Democrats a solid majority. Part of the problem lay in the fact that US development assistance to Chile – as well as to other developing countries – was made dependent on whether the country achieved "several narrowly defined fiscal and monetary goals aimed at stabilizing domestic prices and effecting exchange reform" (Petras and Morley, 1975: 23). The result of this policy was that neither development nor stabilization took place. Inflation for 1963 and 1964 was significant, while the rate of economic growth declined. Afraid that the left might exploit these economic issues, the Johnson administration appropriated some $4 million to be used to support Frei's presidential candidacy and allocated a $15 million loan for commodity imports and a $40 million general economic development grant. The rationale for these decisions can be traced to the 1963 report of the Presidential Committee to Strengthen the Security of the Free World, chaired by General Lucius D. Clay. As noted by the Clay Committee:

We live in a world in which poverty, sickness, instability, and turmoil are rife and where a relentless Communist imperialism manipulates the misery to subvert men and nations from freedom's cause. A foreign aid program is one instrument among many which we and other developed countries adequately can afford and vigorously must use in the defense and advancement of free world interests. (Quoted in Schoultz, 1981: 140)

For the Johnson administration, Frei and his political party promised the electorate a social revolution without "Marxist" undertones. Rather than resorting to class struggle to achieve structural reforms that would help resolve Chile's long-standing economic and social problems, the Christian Democrats were advocating a program designed to attain the same ends by establishing a harmonious relationship between workers and capitalists. It was for this reason that the United States saw Frei as a "model 'Alliance for Progress' candidate" (Roxborough, O'Brien, and Roddick, 1977: 42).

Following Frei's election, and with massive support from the Johnson administration, the Christian Democrats began to embark on significant reforms. One of Frei's earliest successes was his handling of the copper mines issue. During the 1964 presidential election, Allende's political party proposed that the copper, nitrate, and iron mines, along with the utilities, insurance companies, and private banks, be taken over by the government and integrated into a national system. Frei, on the other hand, argued that it would be possible "to give concrete expression to the association of the interests of [foreign] investors and those of the Chilean national community" by the purchase by the Chilean state of majority ownership of the mines (Sigmund, 1977: 30, 33). Within a month of taking office, Frei reached an agreement in principle with Kennecott whereby the state would purchase 51 percent of the company, with the proceeds reinvested in the expansion of the production capacity of the Chilean copper industry. Cerro Corporation agreed to a 30 percent arrangement for its Rio Blanco mine, while Anaconda, although refusing to Chileanize its El Salvador and Chuquicamata mines, agreed to a 25 percent arrangement for its Exótica mine (1977: 36–7).

During this time, the Frei regime also submitted an agrarian reform bill to the Chilean Senate on November 22. The document contained 167 articles and formed the strongest agrarian reform proposal ever presented to Chile's democratic legislature. It was erected on the idea of achieving economic growth by expanding family-type, intermediate-size agricultural holdings and creating cooperative agricultural communities to jointly work the land (1977: 48).

The United States was highly supportive of both the Chileanization program and the agrarian reform bill. From the US perspective, the Chileanization program was a far cry from the nationalization program proposed by Allende. The foreign companies were properly compensated for the acquisition of their interests and were asked to continue managing the operations. The agricultural reform, in turn, was in many ways as radical as the program proposed by the Chilean left, but the process of redistribution was never presented in the Marxist context of "collectivization" but in the Christian theological context of "cooperatives."

These differences were critical to the United States government. Besides the fact that US private interests in Chile were not being undermined by the reforms, the reforms themselves lacked a communist tone. Viewed from a slightly different perspective, the social and economic reforms being implemented by the Christian Democrats invalidated the need to institute the reforms preached by the communists. It is not surprising, therefore, that Charles Dungan, who had been appointed US ambassador to Chile at the beginning of 1965 with orders to actively help the Christian Democrats consolidate political power, voiced strong support for their economic reforms (Sigmund, 1977: 40).

Frei's successes in 1965 were more than matched by his triumphs during the following year. His government succeeded in reducing inflation, increasing production, redistributing income, and expanding education. Below the surface, however, the winds of discord were beginning to gather strength. By May of 1967, the inflation rate had climbed again, production was down by 5 percent from the previous year, and the price of copper, which was vital to Chilean foreign exchange, had dropped somewhat (1977: 41).

Failure by the Frei government to prevent the downfall of Chile's economy, and its unwillingness to introduce more radical reforms, gave rise to domestic opposition. On July 15, leftist members of the Chilean Christian Democrats voiced their disapproval of Frei's economic policies and demanded that the party recognize the state as the fundamental dynamic element in economic change. At just about the same time, the Movement of the Revolutionary Left staged dynamite attacks on four US installations. Similar attacks were launched in March of the following year against the Chilean and North American Cultural Institute, the US Consulate, the Christian Democrat Party's main office, and the office of the newspaper *El Mercurio*. These attacks, along with an increase in strikes and public disturbances, led to speculation that the Chilean military was considering a coup (Sigmund, 1977: 66–70).

Speculation about military intervention had also gained force in Peru's capital, Lima, where the problems faced by Belaunde were not entirely different from those confronting Frei. By December 1965, the Peruvian economy was virtually at a standstill, and communist guerrilla movements had sprung up in the mountains. The Johnson administration conceded that the aid cut-off was not forcing the Belaunde government to reach a compromise with IPC (Goodwin, 1969: 60). In February 1966, the Johnson administration withdrew its previous slowdown order. This change in policy was accompanied by a change in personnel at the State Department; in March, Thomas Mann left the department and was replaced as assistant secretary of state for inter-American affairs by Lincoln Gordon (Goodsell, 1974: 128). That same month, Walt Rostow visited Belaunde in Lima to inform him that if IPC were not confiscated the Johnson administration would begin to reinstate financial aid to Peru. Belaunde, surprised by Rostow's offer, informed him that he had never intended to take over the company. Aid from the United States was immediately resumed (Goodwin, 1969: 60).

The decision by the United States government to soften its pressure on the Belaunde regime did not reflect a change in attitude on the part of the Johnson administration. The administration realized that a decision by the United States to respond to Peru's economic needs would not necessarily persuade the Belaunde regime to be more compromising with regard to IPC and might, in the process, facilitate attempts by the communist guerrillas to undermine Peru's political status quo. In other words, while in 1964 there was little fear in the Johnson administration that the inposition of economic sanctions on Peru would undermine the security interests of the United States, such fear was much more visible in early 1966.

The relationship between Peru and the United States remained relatively stable until mid-1967. By then, however, Belaunde's general political position had been seriously weakened by the continuing deterioration of the Peruvian economy and by his failure to solve the Le Brea y Pariñas problem. As if that were not enough, in 1967 the Johnson administration decided to reduce US economic aid to Peru by approximately $60 million. The decision was made in response to Peru's decision to purchase military aircraft from France. In late 1966, the Peruvian air force attempted to purchase Northrop Aviation's F-5s to replace its F-80s. When the United States rejected the request, Peru immediately contracted with the French for the purchase of several Mirage II jet aircraft. Convinced that it was critical to demonstrate to Peru and other developing countries that the United States was unwilling to allow the purchase of sophisticated weapons when so many economic ills still remained uncured, the Johnson administration in June 1967 ordered a reduction in aid to Peru (Ingram, 1974: 51–2). In addition, Washington feared that the presence of supersonic planes in Peru could alter the regional military balance of power (Goodwin, 1969: 65).

Washington's decision to cut US economic aid to Peru might seem, at first glance, a major contradiction of the policy implemented in early 1966. If in fact the Johnson administration was concerned about the effect the growth of Peru's economic ills would have on the country's guerrilla activities, then why would it implement in 1967 a policy that would, at minimum, help perpetuate such ills? An important element to take into consideration, although it is doubtful that it was the sole cause, was the fact that by late 1965 the Peruvian military had succeeded in putting down the young dissidents of the communist and Aprista parties that had taken up arms in the Andes earlier that year. In early 1966, when the Johnson administration had decided to renew some loans to Peru, many US foreign policy-makers still feared that a new guerrilla uprising might ensue. By 1967, however, it had become quite evident that the guerrilla activities in the Andes had been fully controlled (Klaiber, 1977: 170–1). As stated by John Child (1980), "While Guerrilla movements (and especially urban ones) would continue to be a threat to specific Latin American countries, from 1967 on, there was no overriding fear of the easy triumph of guerrillas in the Hemisphere" (pp. 178–9). By 1967, therefore, it was perfectly rational for the Johnson administration to adopt a tough stand against the Belaunde regime. The dissipation of fear about a communist-led uprising made it once again feasible for Washington to place greater emphasis on other issues.

The economic situation in Peru continued to deteriorate at a rapid pace, until finally in mid-1968 President Belaunde found it necessary to ask the Peruvian Senate to grant him the authority to set up new taxes in order to finance the unbalanced budget (Ingram, 1974: 57). Initially, the Senate refused. However, with the cut in economic aid and the continued deterioration of the economy, the Peruvian senators finally concluded that failure to adopt some drastic measures could lead the country into political and economic chaos, which in turn could incite the military to step in. Therefore, at the end of June, the Peruvian Senate gave Belaunde sixty-day emergency powers to enact an economic program to balance the budget and curb inflation.

This decision was soon followed by an agreement that had the potential to pull Belaunde out of the troubled waters in which he had been swimming for quite some time. On July 25, IPC agreed to surrender the company's mineral rights and production facilities in return for a debt quitclaim and agreeable refining, marketing, and exploration concessions (Goodsell, 1974: 129). On August 12, the Belaunde government and IPC signed the agreement which came to be known as the "Act of Talara."

After members of the Peruvian military, the Senate, and the former director of Empresa Petrolera Fiscal, Carlos Loret de Mola, had engaged in intensive debate regarding the content of the agreement, Peru's Joint Armed Forces Command announced in mid-September that it found the agreement unacceptable. Its rejection was based on the government's authorization of IPC to expand one of its oil refineries, and on the cancellation of the nation's back taxes claim (Goodwin, 1969: 88). A few weeks later, on October 3, Peru's Joint Armed Forces Command ordered military tanks to surround the residency of the Peruvian president and place him under arrest. That same day, General Juan Velasco Alvarado, who had been serving as the chief of Joint Armed Forces Command, was sworn in as Peru's new president (Philip, 1978: 89; Werlich, 1978: 297).

The military came to power convinced that it was imperative to address immediately Peru's social and economic ills. The guerrilla movements of 1965 led many military officers to believe that Peru needed industrialization combined with agrarian reform (North, 1983: 249–50). To bring about these changes, greater control of economic activities and resources would have to be placed in the hands of national actors (Guasti, 1983: 181). And yet, at that time few observers, including those in the Johnson administration, believed that the Velasco regime would launch any major reforms. As stated by Cynthia McClintock, "The Velasco regime was of course a military government, and few Latin American regimes had advanced significant reforms benefiting the popular class" (1983: 275).

The Velasco regime immediately took aggressive steps to address Peru's economic ills. On October 9, the government expropriated the entire oil complex of Talara and La Brea y Pariñas fields, both owned by IPC. The Johnson administration was very cautious in its reponse. On October 25, it recognized the new military government and signaled that it would not use the Hickenlooper Amendment against Peru for expropriating IPC (Goodsell, 1972: 250). The amendment had been passed by the US Congress in 1962 as a provision to the Foreign Assistance Pact. It stipulated the suspension of foreign aid to any government which expropriated US property and did not take appropriate steps to make equitable and speedy compensation within a period of six months.[2]

The decisions by the Johnson administration, first to suspend diplomatic relations and then to grant recognition, parallel previous responses under similar circumstances, but with one major variance. The US government had suspended and then reestablished, diplomatic relations with Peru and the Dominican Republic in the early 1960s when their respective military leaders had mounted coups against their countries constitutional governments. In each case, however, the leaders of the coups had promised to hold new elections before the US government agreed to rescind its previous decision. In 1968 the Peruvian leaders never made such a commitment. In fact, they made it clear that the changes they hoped to achieve could be carried out only during the course of a long period of military government (Philip, 1978: 77).[3]

Another factor that persuaded the Johnson administration not to retaliate against the measures taken by the Velasco regime is that it found itself in 1968 at a transition point. The administration in power had no desire either to make a stand on a thorny issue or to create a political environment that would be very difficult for the incoming administration to address effectively. As explained by Einhorn:

> The focus of the outgoing administration was not on the critical issues since they would not have to face the deadline ... In the meantime, the career officers in State took several conscious, though not publicized steps, to insure later flexibility. (1974: 38)

Not everybody in the Johnson administration, however, was willing to be flexible. Cognizant that the Peruvian government had six months to decide how it intended to compensate IPC for the expropriation, Secretary of the Treasury Henry Fowler presented his views against preferential treatment toward Peru by proposing that for the time being a new loan not be approved. He felt that he could not ask the US Congress for new appropriations so long as Peru refused to state how it planned to compensate IPC (Einhorn, 1974: 38).

The Velasco regime was not intimidated by Washington's response. On December 3 and 11, its minister of finance, General Angel Valdivia Marriberón, accused the Johnson administration of increasing its "futile pressures against Peru" (Goodsell, 1972: 250). More significantly, in early February 1969, the Velasco regime announced that IPC owed Peru $690 million in back taxes and that it was initiating diplomatic relations with the Soviet Union and Eastern European states (Philip, 1978: 91 and 93).

The presence of a new administration in Washington was reflected almost immediately in its public response to the IPC issue. Shortly after Nixon's presidential inaugural, his administration threatened to cut $25 million in aid and $65 million in sugar quota if the Peruvian government did not grant proper compensation to the company for the expropriated property. Determined not to be intimidated by the new decision-makers, the Velasco regime responded on February 14 by overpowering two US tuna boats fishing near Peru's coast. The action was initiated to signal Peru's right to regulate commercial fishing in its 200-mile zone (Goodsell, 1974: 132). The United States responded by suspending the sale of weapons to the Velasco regime. The decision, however, was not announced until April 3 (1974: 134). Moreover, the Nixon administration, convinced that it would be preferable to resolve its differences with the Velasco regime in a non-confrontational manner, began a round of quiet and intensive negotiations with some OAS members in an attempt to enlist their participation as mediators (Einhorn, 1974: 40).

Throughout the rest of 1969, the two parties kept sending each other mixed signals. Overall, however, it would be fair to contend that the Nixon administration seemed more disposed to compromise than did the Peruvian leadership. On February 24, Foreign Minister Edgardo Mercado Jarrín intensified the tone of the dispute by warning the United States that if it were to cut its loans and aid, his government would respond by moving against the more than $600 million worth of US investments in Peru (Ingram, 1974: 64–5; Philip, 1978: 94). The Nixon administration responded by stating publicly that if Peru did not properly compensate IPC, the US government would "take appropriate action with regard to the sugar quota, and also with regard to aid programs" (Goodsell, 1972: 251).

And yet, the Nixon administration still believed that a negotiated settlement could be reached. On March 11, President Nixon appointed John Irwin II as his personal representative with the rank of ambassador, to try to negotiate an agreement with the Peruvian government regarding IPC. In addition, six days later the US Department of Agriculture announced that it would grant a bonus sugar quota to Peru if the dispute with IPC were to be settled before April 9. This date was very important for the Nixon administration; it marked the point at which it would have to begin enforcing the Hickenlooper Amendment (Einhorn, 1974: 44–5).

The Velasco regime did not take the bait, but it sought at the same time to weaken the legal rationale the US government could rely on for implementing the amendment. On March 22, it offered IPC $71 million in compensation in exchange for an agreement from the company to pay the $690 million debt for alleged illegal debts (Einhorn, 1974: 46). Velasco's offer provided the Nixon administration with the justification it needed to avoid invoking sanctions. Contending that the negotiations that were going on between IPC, the government of Peru, and the Nixon administration constituted appropriate steps within the meaning of the Hickenlooper Amendment, Secretary of State William Rogers announced on April 7 that the imposition of sanctions would be deferred pending the outcome of the process (1974: 48).

The Velasco regime was still unwilling to show any signs that it wanted to compromise. Between April 15 and May 19, the Peruvian government accused the Nixon administration of economic oppression; announced the nationalization of the Peruvian telephone company, which was owned by International Telephone and Telegraph; seized another US fishing boat; assessed an additional $54 million on IPC for a total debt of $774 million; cancelled Nelson Rockefeller's scheduled visit to Peru; and expelled the US military mission in Peru (Einhorn, 1974: 55; Goodsell, 1974: 150). In addition, on June 24, it promulgated an agrarian reform law which was to become by 1975 the most radical in Latin America, with the exception of the program implemented by Castro in Cuba (Philip, 1978: 118–19; McClintock, 1983: 275).

The Nixon administration, hoping to control the tension that had been gaining momentum since the beginning of the year, announced on July 3 that it would lift its ban on arms sales to Peru. The announcement had the intended effect. The Velasco regime responded to the latest gesture by the United States by declaring that Nelson Rockefeller would be welcome to visit Peru (Einhorn, 1974: 56–7; Ingram, 1974: 66). These latest actions, however, did not stop the Peruvian government from expropriating at the end of August the remainder of IPC's property (Ingram, 1974: 67). The Nixon administration, rather than reacting aggressively, decided that it needed in Lima a representative who would seek to establish a more favorable working relationship with the military regime than that formed by the presiding US ambassador, John Wesley Jones. In late August, Jones was replaced by Taylor Blecher (Einhorn, 1974: 75).

By the end of 1969 there were still many bridges for Peru and the United States to cross before they could negotiate a peaceful settlement. In retrospect, an issue can be made of the fact that throughout 1969 the Nixon administration discarded the application of strong sanctions against Peru, even though its military regime had expropriated IPC, refused to permit US boats to fish within Peru's 200-mile zone, threatened to confiscate more than $600 million worth of US investments, demanded that IPC pay Peru an enormous sum of money for an alleged debt, announced the nationalization of ITT's Peruvian telephone company, promulgated a radical agrarian reform law, and accused the US government of engaging in economic oppression. The behavior by the Nixon administration did not resemble that of past US governments which generally had not shied away from using their political and economic might when they felt that the interests of the United States or of US corporations were being threatened.

In searching for a rationalization for the discrepancy in US behavior, three factors need to be considered. First, the Nixon administration had just been inaugurated and was hoping to avoid a major confrontation with Latin America while it engaged in a policy review of the area. Second, Latin America, and Peru in particular, was not a priority issue for the new administration in Washington. From the beginning, President Nixon and his top foreign policy advisors immersed themselves in the search for a solution to a problem that had been dominating the international arena since 1964 – Vietnam. The value attached to finding a solution to US involvement in South-East Asia resulted in a clear division of labor; the key foreign policy players delegated a significant number of responsibilities not linked to the central issue to lower-ranking officials. This distribution of responsibility would be modified, as already demonstrated by the Cuban and Dominican Republic cases, only when the problems at hand gained crisis dimensions. And third, notwithstanding the fact that IPC had been affected by the actions of Peru's military government, there were still many other companies that were in good standing with the regime and whose interests could be greatly damaged if a political and economic crisis were to ensue between the United States and Peru (Einhorn, 1974: 42–4).

Although all the factors identified were quite important in bounding the response designed by the Nixon administration, they leave the story somewhat untold. A clearer picture of the dilemma faced by the Nixon administration can be developed by addressing the following hypothetical question: What is the likelihood that the United States would have responded as it did if the Peruvian government had been composed of civilians instead of high-ranking military officers? Under such a condition, the most likely response by the US government would have been to define the problem in terms of a communist threat and then to select the measures that would effectively counteract it. However, even though the policies by the Velasco regime reflected a break in the way previous Peruvian military governments had ruled, they were in fact being designed by military officers who only a few years earlier had participated in the crushing of major peasant movements and who had been trained at military schools with anticommunist principles. It was this difference that led the Nixon administration to adopt a more conciliatory posture.[4]

As the decade approached its end, a new problem began to loom on the Nixon administration's political horizon. By March of 1968, President Frei of Chile had concluded that the best way to manage the domestic opposition that had been mounting steadily against his regime, and to avert a coup, was to appoint a military officer to his government. That same month he named General Turio Marambio as Chile's new defense minister (Sigmund, 1977: 67). The appointment may have helped to soothe the military momentarily, but it did not help to calm Chile's civilian population. As the inflation rate continued to grow, accelerated by a prolonged drought, and as taxes continued to ascend to pay for expensive social reforms, the Chilean population increasingly expressed its political preferences along ideological lines. This amplification in polarization was particularly evident in the congressional elections of March 1969.

Chile's political elite perceived the 1969 election as a major opportunity for the political parties to promote the qualities of their respective leaders in preparation for the presidential election scheduled for September 4 of the following year. The biggest loser in the March election turned out to be the Christian Democrats, who lost about 30 percent of the votes they had received in the 1965 congressional elections, dropping from 42.3 of the total vote to 29.8 percent. The National Party, a new party launched in March 1966 in a desperate attempt to stop the total disintegration of the right, received approximately 20 percent of the vote. And finally, the Socialist Party, which had concistently opposed the Frei administration, received about 12.3 percent of the total popular vote. The remainder of the votes were cast among smaller parties distributed along the left–right ideological spectrum (Alexander, 1978: 66–77).

The 1969 election results set the pattern for the proceeding 17 months. There was, however, a change that was to have a dramatic effect on the outcome of the presidential electoral process. On January 20, 1970, Chile's left, composed of the Socialists, Communists, Radicals, and Social Democrats, created the Popular Unity Program, led by Salvador Allende (Sigmund, 1977: 103).

Enter the Nixon administration. One of the most striking aspects of the behavior of the Nixon administration toward Chile in 1970 is its seeming indifference to the fact that Chile was getting ready to hold a presidential election. In 1964, as already noted, the Johnson administration had funneled some $4 million to help Frei get elected president of Chile. But in 1970, the Forty Committee of the National Security Council, the body responsible for monitoring covert activities overseas, authorized in March and June a total of only $425,000 to be used covertly during Chile's presidential campaign. In addition to being unwilling to appropriate large sums of money, the Nixon administration decided against using the funds to support the candidacy of a specific Chilean leader. Instead, the funds would be wielded to finance a propaganda campaign against the left and the Christian Democrats. This decision was not supported by CIA director Richard Helms, who contended that it was wrong to think that one could "beat somebody with nobody" (Davis, 1985: 5). More importantly, the action constituted a direct repudiation of the desires of the US business community in Chile which for some time had been attempting to persuade the State Department that Jorge Alessandri was the most appealing candidate. The State Department, however, refused to back a political leader who was perceived as old and insufficiently progressive (Sigmund, 1977: 103; Falcoff, 1984: 73–5).

The resistance by the State Department to become involved in Chile's electoral process took a new form in August. By then it became clear that no single candidate would win the minimum number of popular votes required to avoid the election of the new president by the Chilean Congress. Cognizant of this possibility, the US ambassador to Chile, Edward Korry, requested $500,000 to influence the congressional vote. Ambassador Korry hoped that with the money he could persuade the Chilean Congress to vote against Allende, even if the latter were to receive the largest number of votes in the popular election (Sigmund, 1977: 103). Once again, the State Department was able to dictate that the United States abstain from further involvement in Chile's elections.

According to Mark Falcoff (1984), it is difficult to explain why "a Republican administration would remain so impervious to corporate appeals on matters Chilean" (p. 74). Falcoff is correct in noting that the behavior of the Nixon administration was somewhat paradoxical. But he is addressing the problem from the wrong perspective. It is not unusual for a Republican administration to be unwilling to rise to the defense of private US corporations investing abroad. A more arresting issue is why Nixon, who had had first-hand experiences with covert actions against the Mossadegh regime in Iran in 1953, the Arbenz regime in Guatemala in 1954, and the Castro regime in Cuba in 1960, would be so reluctant to take more drastic measures in 1970 to avert the establishment of a leftist regime in Chile.

In discussing US behavior toward Peru in 1969, one of the points made was that the principal US foreign policy-makers were channeling their energies into the Vietnam crisis. The same international crisis continued to dominate Nixon's foreign policy agenda in 1970 (Kissinger, 1979: 659). This answer, however, is inappropriate for two reasons. First, it disregards the simple fact that the National Security Council, under Henry Kissinger's directorship, had addressed the Chilean situation during the months prior to the presidential elections; and second, it does not explain why the State Department was so disinclined to become actively engaged in ensuring that Allende would be denied Chile's presidency. According to Henry Kissinger, the State Department argued that it was incorrect to grant covert support to political parties that for so long had played such an important role in efforts by the United States to promote democracy in Chile, and that it was preferable to risk an Allende presidency rather than to support Alessandri's candidacy (1979: 663). Kissinger's answer is disingenuous. Regardless of how the State Department felt toward Alessandri, it is doubtful that its Latin American Bureau, fully aware that Allende was the leader of an alliance that included political parties representing Chile's radical left, would knowingly risk the formation of a second communist regime in Latin America.

There are two good reasons why the State Department was initially opposed to channeling vast amounts of money into Chile prior to the September 1970 elections. CIA evaluations of US involvement in the 1964 elections concluded that Eduardo Frei would most likely have been elected president even without financial help from the Johnson administration (Falcoff, 1984: 72). Needless to say, this information would have been of no use in 1970 had it been established that Allende had a very good chance of winning the presidential election. But that was not the case. On the basis of a series of polls carried out by the CIA, the US embassy in Chile predicted that Alessandri would win approximately 40 percent of the popular vote (Petras and Morley, 1975: 29). It could be counter-argued that even though the State Department believed that Allende had little chance of winning the presidential election, it would have wanted to play it safe by mounting a more sophisticated covert campaign to obstruct Allende's election as it did in 1964. The benefits to the United States from such an operation, however, were greatly dependent on whether the plan could actually be implemented covertly. But, as demonstrated by ongoing investigations in Chile regarding the legality of the elections, the United States, specifically the CIA and ITT, was being accused of seeking to affect the electoral results by providing funds to Chilean political organizations opposed to the creation of an Allende regime (Sigmund, 1977: 103–4).

In the final analysis, however, Henry Kissinger could have persuaded President Nixon to disregard the State Department's argument if he had found it unacceptable. Kissinger had been following events in Chile for some time. For instance, during a secret meeting on June 27, 1970, the national security advisor voiced his concern about developments in Chile by stating that he did not "see why we need to stand by and watch a country go Communist due to the irresponsibility of its own people." But his fear could not have been very intense, for if it had been it is unlikely that he would have been convinced by the contention that the United States could not afford to be perceived as an international actor meddling in the constitutional affairs of another state.

In sum, the decision by the Nixon administration not to mount an aggressive operation to help elect a pro-US president cannot be attributed to the propensity of key foreign policy figures in Washington to allocate a disproportionate amount of their enegies to the Vietnam crisis. Henry Kissinger, Nixon's principal foreign policy architect, accepted the assessment by State Department officials that further involvement in Chile was unwarranted and, thus, that there was no need to risk tarnishing the reputation of the US government.

The absence of involvement by top US officials and their unwillingness to adopt drastic measures came to a dramatic end on September 4, 1970. The day before, 36.2 percent of the Chilean people cast their ballot in favor of Salvador Allende. Alessandri, with 34.9 percent, was a very close second. President Nixon, furious about the US failure to avert such an event, immediately insisted on doing "something, anything that would reverse the previous neglect" (Kissinger, 1979: 670–1).

On September 6, the CIA produced an intelligence memorandum stating that Allende's victory would create considerable psychological, political, and economic costs to the United States, but would not alter significantly the regional balance of power. In addition, on September 8, the CIA reported that the Chilean military was unable and unwilling to seize power, and that the United States lacked the means to motivate or instigate a coup. This conclusion was supported by Ambassador Korry, who noted that opportunities for coordinated action between the US government and the Chilean military to avert Allende's ascension to power were non-existent. By this time, however, the top leaders in the Nixon administration had formed a very different opinion. On September 14, the Forty Committee authorized the initiation of a massive anti-Allende campaign involving propaganda and economic pressure. In addition, a contingency fund of $250,000 was approved to be used to support any plan President Frei might have to stop Allende from becoming Chile's new president. On the following day, President Nixon informed CIA director Richard Helms that $10 million had been authorized to instigate an anti-Allende military coup. The tone of Nixon's instructions are captured in the handwritten notes taken by CIA director Helms:

> One in 10 chance perhaps, but save Chile!
> Worth spending
> Not concerned risks involved
> No involvement of embassy
> $10,000,000 available, more if necessary
> Full time job – best men we have
> Game plan
> Make the economy scream
> 48 hours for plan of action.

Helms was also ordered not to inform Ambassador Korry, the State Department, or the Forty Committee of the decision (Sigmund, 1977: 113–15; Davis, 1985: 7–8).

Helms and Ambassador Korry wasted very little time in beginning to implement their respective assignments. On September 16, Helms set up a meeting at the CIA where he related his understanding of the president's instructions and ordered David Atlee Phillips to take charge of a covert operation. The operation called for militant rightists and renegade military officers to stage mutinies and riots, and for the kidnapping of loyal constitutionalist generals. Both actions were designed to provoke the Chilean military to execute a coup.

Phillips was no stranger to this type of operation. It was he who, in 1954, set up the clandestine radio station to orchestrate with disinformation propaganda the overthrow of the Arbenz regime. Seven years later he attempted to relive his earlier success by managing the covert propaganda for the Bay of Pigs operation. And in 1965 he helped facilitate the ascension to power of a moderate leader in the Dominican Republic following the landing of US forces (Freed and Landis, 1980: 38–50; Davis, 1985: 7–11).

Just as Helms was ordering his subordinates to begin implementing Nixon's clandestine operation, Ambassador Korry was visiting President Frei to warn him that "not a nut or bolt will be allowed to reach Chile under Allende . . . We shall do all in our power to condemn Chile and Chileans to utmost deprivation and poverty." Within a week after communicating the warning, however, Korry, began to suspect that the plan he had been ordered to implement was not the only live operation. Thus, on September 25 he sent a cable to Washington stating: "I am convinced that we cannot provoke a military coup and that we should not run any risks simply to have another Bay of Pigs" (quoted in Sigmund, 1977: 114 and 115).

None of the measures initiated by the Nixon administration succeeded. On October 24, the Chilean Congress followed its traditional pattern and elected the candidate with the largest number of popular votes. Ten days later, Salvador Allende was inaugurated president of Chile.

President Nixon's decision to engage every conceivable resource, with the exception of direct US military intervention, to avert Allende's ascension to Chile's presidency, was indicative of a perception that had been in existence for quite some time. For Nixon, Allende's rise to power was a "second Castro" ten years later. Remembering his own early inclination to assume that Castro could be persuaded not to verge too far to the left after the Cuban leader had toppled the Batista regime, and how the failure by the Eisenhower administration to effectively obstruct the creation of a communist regime in Cuba might have helped John F. Kennedy win the 1960 presidential election, Nixon decided not to commit the same error a second time. As a result, the new president resorted to the threat of economic sanctions and ordered immediate preparations for a military coup.[5] These two measures, however, came into place too late and could not thwart Allende's rise to power.

Having failed in its first objective, the Nixon administration wasted no time in deciding what its second goal would be and how it would attain it. On November 9, 1970, Henry Kissinger issued National Security Decision Memorandum (NSDM) 93, establishing the policy the United States would pursue. In the memorandum, Kissinger ordered that the United States appear to maintain the type of posture expected by the OAS. But at the same time he directed that no new financing, assistance, or government guarantees of private investments be initiated and that existing assistance be reduced or ended. In addition, the CIA ordered its agents in Santiago to rebuild their contacts and remain close to the Chilean military officers in order to monitor internal armed forces development (Davis, 1985: 21–3, 314).

The steps taken by the Nixon administration were analogous to the measures adopted by the United States in 1953 and 1960 against the governments of Guatemala and Cuba, respectively. But also, by 1970, some important lessons had been inferred from previous actions. In 1960, the Eisenhower administration had waited until the Castro regime had enacted economic and foreign policies that were contrary to the interests of the United States before it chose to impose economic sanctions. In 1970, the Nixon administration did not wait for the Allende regime to launch its radical economic program. Allende's ideological predilection was perceived to be the same as Castro's, and thus no new evidence was needed to conclude that the new Chilean leader would seek to modify radically Chilean's political and economic structures. Developments in Chile in 1970, moreover, were viewed as posing a greater threat than the turn of events in Cuba some ten years earlier. Henry Kissinger expresses this attitude by contending that as

> a continental country, a militant Chile had a capacity to undermine other nations and support radical insurgency that was far greater than Cuba's, and Cuba has managed to do damage enough. If Chile had followed the Cuban pattern, Communist ideology would in time have been supported by Soviet forces and Soviet arms in the southern cone of the South American continent. (1982: 376)

Another important variance between the measures adopted in 1970 and the steps taken in 1959–60, and in this also in 1954, was the decision by the Nixon administration not to consider mounting a covert paramilitary invasion of Chile. Unlike the situation in Guatemala, and in Cuba until 1959, civilian control of the military in Chile had been the rule more than the exception (Nunn, 1978: 218). This difference was not overlooked by the Nixon administration. During its early attempt to thwart Allende's rise to power, the Nixon administration worked hard at trying to persuade the Chilean military to prevent Allende from becoming president.[6] Although during this time Nixon and Kissinger misread the willingness on the part of the Chilean military to intervene against Allende, their Latin America advisors were fully aware that Allende's rise to power could be prevented only by an internal military action. In other words, they recognized that the structure of Chile's military precluded the launching of an attack from the outside. Equally important is the fact that upon having been informed by Ambassador Korry that attempts to provoke a military coup would not succeed at that time, Nixon and Kissinger decided to accept the ambassador's assessment and to create the economic and political conditions in Chile that would make it justifiable for its military to intervene.

Like the Nixon administration, which wasted no time in acting against the Allende regime, the new Chilean government disclosed its intention to pursue its radical goals early in its tenure. On November 12, upon arguing that the 1964 OAS resolution urging all hemispheric nations to sever their relations with Cuba did not have any juridical or moral basis, the Allende government reestablished diplomatic relations with Chile (United States Congress, House,

1975: 375). Although the US State Department deplored Chile's action, Allende did not lose his nerve. Eight days later, his government took over two companies, one controlled by Northern Indiana Company and the other by Ralston Purina. Allende followed these takeovers by proposing on December 30 the nationalization of banks, the primary foreign targets being National Bank of New York, Bank of America, and Bank of London and South America (1975: 375).

The Allende regime did not alter its tempo with the beginning of the new year. On January 5, 1971, Chile joined Cuba as the only Latin American countries ot have extended diplomatic recognition to the People's Republic of China. In the domestic arena, Jacques Chanchol, Chile's minister of agriculture, who in the 1960s as a Christian Democrat had been very critical of President Frei's policies and had advocated the active involvement of the state in the economic development of Chile, announced that since Allende's inauguration more than 260 farms had been expropriated (Sigmund, 1977: 62 and 139).

By this time, Henry Kissinger had decided that it was imperative for the United States to have a decision-making body that would focus specifically on economic issues that cut across military and diplomatic commitments abroad. At Kissinger's recommendation, President Nixon established the Council on International Economic Policy (Petras and Morley, 1975: 82–3). Also in January, the Forty Committee approved the appropriation of $1.24 million to purchase time on radio stations and space in newspapers supporting anti-Allende candidates for the April municipal elections (Davis, 1985: 21).

Around this period the relationship between the United States and Chile experienced an unusual twist. On February 25, 1971, Pedro Vuskovic, Chile's economic minister, traveled to Washington to request that the United States continue investing in Chile. The US State Department responded by warning Vuskovic that the implementation of Allende's expropriation formula would seriously affect US–Chile relations and possibly cause economic chaos in Chile (Petras and Morley, 1975: 41 and 109). Vuskovic's trip to Washington had come on the heels of a $20 million trade agreement between Santiago and Havana, an agreement that had not pleased Washington (United States Congress, House, 1975: 375). Two days after Vuskovic had met with US foreign policy-makers, the US Defense Department announced that it would cancel the US aircraft carrier *Enterprise*'s scheduled visit to Chile. The decision, made by Kissinger and the State Department, had been opposed by the officials of the Defense Department on the grounds that the United States needed to maintain good military relations with Chile in case its military decided to launch a coup against Allende. The Defense Department finally succeeded in persuading Kissinger that its justification for maintaing good relations with the Chilean military was valid, and on March 19, four high-ranking US Air Force officers arrived in Santiago to attend the Chilean Air Force's 41st anniversary (1975: 375; Petras and Morley, 1975: 42).

Salvador Allende, aware that he could not afford to alienate totally the United States, stressed on March 23 that he wanted the "very best" relations with the United States, that Chile was an authentic democracy, and that he would never provide a military base to any foreign power that could pose a threat to the United States (United States Congress, House, 1975: 375). This statement was followed by an announcement on April 16 by Clodomiro Almeyda, Chile's foreign minister, that Secretary of State William P. Rogers had been invited to visit Chile (p. 376).

The fact that Allende hoped his country could maintain a cordial relationship with the United States did not mean he was less committed to the idea of dramatically altering Chile's economic structure. On April 22, on a visit to the Soviet Union, Foreign Minister Almeyda signed a technical, cultural, and trade agreement with the Soviets and was promised a $50 million credit line. A month later, the Allende government announced that it would purchase a $24.5 million share of the Anglo-Lautoro Nitrate Company and a $19.6 million share of its subsidiary, the Chilean Mining and Chemical Company. In addition, the Chilean government placed the Ford Motor Company, which had reported that it would close its plant in Chile, under state control (1975: 376–7).

The Nixon administration, unhappy with the direction Chile's economic policy had followed, found itself confronting a small dilemma. The Chilean military had requested credit from the United States to purchase military equipment. The US government could have used the opportunity to signal its displeasure with the Allende government. But instead, recognizing that the United States needed to maintain good relations with the Chilean military in case the latter mounted a coup against Allende, the State Department announced on June 30 that it had approved $5 million in credit to Chile to purchase military equipment (Davis, 1985: 28).

The rationale for this decision had its real genesis in 1962. In 1958, Secretary of Defense Neil McElroy attempted to modify the rationale for extending military assistance to Latin American states. He proposed that the primary purpose for providing military aid should be "the maintenance of internal security" with "preparation for defense against any incursion from offshore" assuming a very modest role. This modification was initially opposed by the US Senate. By 1962, however, the Cuban revolution and the US failure to suppress it had managed to legitimize the use of military aid for counterinsurgency purposes. The Defense Department made it clear that since "the principal threat faced in Latin America is Communist subversion and indirect attack, the primary emphasis of the military assistance program was changed from hemispheric defense to internal security in FY 1962 . . ." Moreover, in 1965, Secretary of Defense Robert McNamara stated that it would be unwise to cut military aid to Latin American military leaders, for it "would greatly reduce United States influence on significant elements of host governments" (quoted in Schoultz, 1981: 219 and 221).

From the month of July on, the relationship between Allende and the Nixon administration deteriorated at an accelerated pace. On July 15, President Allende signed a constitutional amendment permitting the nationalization of the copper industry, including the Anaconda, Kennecott, and Cerro mines. The US government wasted little time in responding. The Export–Import Bank had received a $21 million loan application from Chile to purchase three Boeing jets. The State Department was convinced that delaying the loan application would not greatly affect ongoing negotiations in Chile. Treasury Secretary John Connally, however, determined to let Latin American states know that the United States was going to get tough on expropriations, pushed for a postponement on a decision on the loan application. The postponement was announced on August 11. Connally, moreover, who was the principal US decision-maker responsible for coordinating all forms of US participation in the multilateral development banks, wasted little time in implementing Nixon's policy of economic hostility toward the Allende regime. The total amount of multilateral development bank loans authorized to Chile for 1970 was approximately $22 million; the year after, it was cut to almost half; and in 1972 and 1973 it was reduced to zero. Equally as significant is the fact that in 1974, with a military regime in power, the World Bank and the Inter-American Development Bank increased their total lending to Chile to $110.8 million (Sigmund, 1977: 152–3; Schoultz, 1981: 283).

In September, the Allende regime made two announcements that would displease the Nixon administration. On September 28, the Chilean government revealed that $774 million in excess profits would be deducted from compensation owed to Kennecott, Anaconda, and Cerro. The following day, it announced that it would assume responsibility for the operation of the Chilean Telephone Company, 70 percent of which was controlled by ITT. Moreover, on October 11, the Allende regime disclosed that after calculating the copper mines' book value and deducting the assigned "excess values," it had decided that Anaconda owed Chile $68 million, Kennecott owed $310 million, and Chile owed Cerro $18 million (Sigmund, 1977: 154–5).

By this time, the United States had decided that it would have to take additional steps to undermine the Allende regime. Sometime in September, the Forty Committee had approved $700,000 to support the anti-Allende newspaper, *El Mercurio* (Davis, 1985: 21). On October 13, Secretary of State Rogers warned that Chile's decision to confiscate property owned by Anaconda and Kennecott would "jeopardize flows of private funds and erode the base of support for foreign assistance" (Sigmund, 1977: 155). That same day, Nathaniel Davis, a Foreign Service career diplomat who had specialized in Eastern Europe, Latin America, and communism, assumed his post as the new US ambassador to Chile (Davis, 1985: 29).

The actions emanating from the United States were the result of an ongoing debate within the Nixon administration. In the summer of 1971, the Nixon administration produced a memorandum that delineated how US analysts should consider cases of expropriation. It stipulated that analysts should consider when it would be appropriate to end all "forms of bilateral assistance and economic aid, commodity credit shipments and credits of the Export–Import Bank of the United States to countries that had confiscated US property" (Chadwin, 1972: 150–1). Kissinger had played a central role in the study, but as the analysis came to involve economic matters more than politics, he asked Peter G. Peterson, who was serving as director of the Council on International Economic Policy (CIEP), to take over as the top White House representative on the project.

The first drafts of the official statement were prepared by the deputy assistant secretary of state for international finance and development, Sidney Weintraub, and by John Hennessey, an assistant to John Connally at the Treasury Department. On October 8, however, the responsibility for handling investment and expropriation problems was placed in the hands of the CIEP. William J. Mazzocco, who was serving on the CIEP staff as a representative for the Agency for International Development, began to work on the document that would guide future US responses to expropriation. Mazzocco used the Weintraub and Hennessey drafts to delineate a new version, modifying the harsh language of the Treasury draft and emphasizing the theme that private investment flows were larger and more important to less-developed countries than was the flow of public funds. State and Treasury finally agreed on the content of the strategy, but State insisted that it not be made public (Einhorn, 1974: 95–6, 106–9). The agreement was reached only a few days before the Allende regime announced its "negative compensation" with respect to Anaconda and Kennecott, an announcement which elicited a threatening response from Secretary of State Rogers.

Rogers's response had little or no effect on the subsequent actions by the Allende regime. On October 19, the Chilean government proposed the expropriation of 150 domestic firms that were considered key players in Chile's economy. On November 10, Fidel Castro arrived in Chile for a trip that initially had been planned to last ten days but was then extended to three weeks. Castro's arrival coincided with a major attempt by Allende to bring about constitutional reforms. He submitted to the Chilean Congress a bill to replace the existing bicameral system with a unicameral legislature, change the Supreme Court's power, and broaden the power of the executive (United States Congress, House, 1975: 375; Davis, 1985: 2).

By this time, some of the leaders in Washington were beginning to worry that their representatives in Chile might be considering taking covert steps to bring down the Allende regime. Convinced that the Chilean military would not act until it believed that the situation called for intervention, the CIA in Washington ordered its agents in Santiago to "report" history, not "make it" (Davis, 1985: 314–15). Less than month later, Ambassador Davis, believing that some officials in Washington were under the impression that Allende was about to be toppled, sent a telegram warning that such an impression was unwarranted. Davis acknowledged that discontent had been mounting, but he also noted that Chile was not yet on the brink of a showdown and that it was therefore most unlikely that the military would act (1985: 63).

Davis's assessment was accurate. On November 27, the Chamber of Deputies Constitutional Committee rejected Allende's proposed constitutional reform. Four days later, 5,000 women, organized by the Christian Democrats, conducted what is now commonly referred to as the "March of the Empty Pots" to protest Castro's visit and food shortages (United States Congress, House, 1975: 380). These actions, however, were not sufficient to incite the military to take up arms against the government.

In early January 1972, the Allende government accepted the $50 million credit offered by the Soviet Union the preceding year. In the meantime, the Nixon administration made it very clear in its annual report to Congress that before deciding on any new investment or aid, the US government and private sources would carefully consider whether Chile was meeting its international obligations (1975: 380–8).

The following month, the Chilean government suffered two major setbacks. Chile's economic minister, Pedro Vuskovic, was forced to announce the end of a basic foodstuffs subsidy and an increase in prices above the 1971 cost-of-living wage increases. These measures were the result of an increase in the government's budget deficit from 13 percent in 1970 to 40 percent in 1971, and an expansion of the money supply of 116 percent in 1971 (Davis, 1985: 82–3). In addition, on February 19, the Chilean Congress approved by a 100–33 vote a constitutional amendment proposed by the Christian Democrats to prohibit any expropriation without congressional authorization, retroactive to October of the previous year (1985: 58–61). The anti-government constitutional amentment on expropriation, however, was vetoed two months later by President Allende.

In the month of April, at a meeting held in Paris to decide whether to allow the Allende regime to defer payments on its debts, the United States changed its overt tactics, at least temporarily. The previous month, the Nixon administration had vigorously supported the passage of the Gonzalez amendment by the US Congress. The amendment required the president to ask the US directors in the many multilateral aid institutions to vote against loans to countries which, among other things, nationalized or expropriated US properties without arranging for satisfactory compensation (Petras and Morley, 1975: 101–2; Schoultz, 1981: 280–1). While preparing for the Paris meeting, Kissinger and representatives of the Treasury Department had urged that the debt be rescheduled only if Chile agreed to pay "just" compensation for nationalized properties. Ambassador Davis and his colleagues at the Inter-American Bureau at the State Department argued that such a stand would serve only to help Allende build a Chilean consensus against the "foreign enemy" and would irrevocably bind Chile to the Soviet camp. Kissinger and the Treasury Department finally abandoned their stance, and Chile was allowed to defer payment for three years on 70 percent of its debts, giving the country almost $200 million in relief from creditors. Unknown to the Inter-American Bureau, however, was the fact that Connally had already ordered the cut of additional aid to Chile through multilateral development banks (Schoultz, 1981: 274; Davis, 1985: 75–8).

In May, the US government once again had the opportunity to reverse its course of action. – and yet, it chose to follow its dual policy. On the twelfth of the month, the Allende regime submitted to the Chilean Congress a constitutional amendment to expropriate Chitelco, ITT's Chilean telephone company. The amendment asserted that Chitelco's ownership was worth only $24 million, as compared to the $153 million countered by ITT, and that compensation would be paid only after retroactively deducting "excessive profits" (Davis, 1985: 68–71). That same month, however, the Nixon administration approved a $10 million loan to the Chilean military to purchase C-130 aircraft, tanks and trucks (1985: 96).

The second half of 1972 proved to be a major political headache to the Allende regime. Hoping to control inflation and to increase capital investment, the Chilean government announced on July 24 that it would invest $760 million, much of it provided by communist states, in industrial and farm production. The announcement had little effect on the Chilean population. During the week of August 12–18, the Allende government had to declare a state of emergency in the province of Santiago following a one-day strike by most of the capital's 150,000 shopkeepers, who were protesting inflation, shortages, and government restrictions. Less than two months later, after the Confederation of Truck Owners had initiated a national strike, the Chilean government was forced to declare a state of emergency across most of Chile's twenty-five provinces. The intensity of the domestic discontent forced the Allende regime to name military officers as ministers of mining, interior, and public works and transportation, and to pledge to keep the trucking industry in the private sector (United States Congress, House, 1975: 385). Allende's problems were compounded by the fact that after requesting a half-billion-dollar loan from the Soviet Union during a visit to Moscow, the Soviets responded by granting Chile only $30 million to $50 million in short-to-medium-term credit, and only $180 million in longer-term credit (Davis, 1985: 129–30).

In the meantime, the Nixon administration, recognizing that Allende's problems were mounting at an accelerated pace without the United States's having to take any additional repressive measures, chose on December 20 not to stop a $42.8 million International Monetary Fund grant to Chile (Sigmund, 1974: 329–30). The decision was based, once again, on the assumption that any overt attempt by the United States to exert its influence to undermine Chile's economy would only help the Allende regime form a united front against the external enemy and push it closer to the Soviet Union.

By the end of 1972, it had become evident to the Nixon administration that its sanctions against the Allende regime were having the desired effect. The US government, however, had not been imposing these sanctions indiscriminately. First, it made sure that the Chilean military remained the single most important institution in Chile capable of preventing the Allende regime from turning the country into a communist-dominated state. This policy was acknowledged surreptitiously by Secretary of State William Rogers when he stated that "it is quite interesting that we are still providing some military assistance to Chile, for the reasons we think it would be better not to have a complete break with them" (Petras and Morley, 1975: 126–7).

In addition to realizing that the US government could not afford to sever its ties with the Chilean military, the Nixon administration was convinced that it had to be careful not to provide Allende with the means to unify his country by making the United States the party responsible for Chile's economic and political ills. It believed that one of the central tactical mistakes committed by the Eisenhower administration in its attempts to weaken Castro's control over Cuba was to implement its economic sanctions too overtly. This mode of implementation enabled the leaders of the Cuban revolution to use it as a symbol behind which they could solidify popular support in their struggle against the United States. Between 1970 and 1973, however, the Nixon administration sought to ensure not only that its economic sanctions would be implemented as covertly as possible but also that at times certain loans to Chile would not be obstructed. As stipulated by NSDM 93, the United States had to continue maintaining a correct outward posture toward Chile "to avoid giving Allende an easy foreign target that would help him rally support, both domestic and international" (Davis, 1985: 22).

While the relationship between the Allende regime and the Nixon administration deteriorated at a steady pace from the moment Allende and his associates came to power, the relationship that evolved during that period between Chile's northern neighbor and the United States was measurably more complex. In January of 1970, the Velasco regime in Peru nationalized the auto industry, composed of thirteen plants producing 16,000 vehicles a year; required that at least 75 percent of the capital held by banks be controlled by Peruvians; and expropriated W. R. Grace's two sugar haciendas, Paramonga and Cartavio (Goodsell, 1974: 134–5; Ingram, 1974: 76). These actions were followed by legislation amplifying state control over the economy's mining sector and setting new industry investment regulations. The codes encouraged formation of mixed private–state ventures, with the government holding at least one-quarter of the stocks (Werlich, 1978: 317–18).

The opportunity to renew the cooperative relations between the United States and Peru was afforded by a tragic event. On May 31, 1970, a massive earthquake struck Peru. The Nixon administration immediately used the occasion to signal its desire to improve relations with Peru by announcing a $10 million AID grant and establishing a coordinating group for US assistance efforts (Einhorn, 1974: 76). On July 27, the Inter-American Development Bank granted Peru a loan for $35 million. During this time, the World Bank also extended a loan for $30 million.

These actions, however, did not reduce the commitment of Peru's military regime to alter its country's economic nature. In July, the Velasco government approved a law that gave the government extensive control over the fishing industry. Two months later, in September, it passed an industrial law whereby foreign investments would slowly revert back to the state and the state would acquire control over all basic industries (Philip, 1978: 12 3–4; Werlich, 1978: 316–17).

The Peruvian policies of the Nixon administration began to take a more precise form in 1971. Although at one level the US government was not yet willing to impose its full economic might against Peru, it began to focus its efforts on developing a tougher general stand against regimes that engaged in the extensive expropriation of US companies without providing proper compensation. And yet, as it was developing this strategy, the Nixon administration worked hard to ensure that domestic interests would not undermine its freedom to use sanctions at its own discretion.

On May 5, 1971, the Inter-American Development Bank approved a loan requested by the Peruvian government to build a major highway. The loan was granted with a major proviso: Washington warned that if Peru did not alter its expropriation policy, the US Congress would most likely oppose new loans to the country (Einhorn, 1974: 79–80). The Peruvian press was very critical of the warning. But as the debate in the US Congress over how the United States should respond to the expropriation of US interests began to take form, the Velasco regime started to heed the warning.

On April 20, 1971, W. R. Grace formally requested to the House Agriculture Committee that the United States use its economic resources to pressure the Velasco regime to accommodate the demands being made by the company with respect to its investments in Peru. W. R. Grace demanded that the US Congress amend the Sugar Act so that proceeds from the sugar quota of any country that expropriated US-owned sugar-producing properties would be cut $15 per ton. These proceeds would be used, in turn, to pay the owners of the confiscated property. Some congressmen, in the mood to apply more severe pressure on Peru than W. R. Grace had proposed, enlarged the coverage of the expropriation to include any business. The US Senate, in turn, sought tighter restrictions by stipulating that any country that engaged in expropriation would have its quota automatically terminated following Tariff Commission proceedings (Ingram, 1974: 135–6).

The Nixon administration was unwilling to accept such rigid constraints. Thus, after Nixon threatened a veto if the Senate expropriation language were kept, the US Congress wrote into the Sugar Act new sanctions against states that expropriated US businesses, but left to the president the decision to invoke the measures. The new sanctions were written into law on October 14, 1971. A month later, W. R. Grace and the Velasco regime reached a major agreement whereby the government would buy the company's industrial properties over a ten-year period, with the company maintaining managerial control for at least seven years (Goodsell, 1974: 137–8).

In January 1972, the Nixon administration finally made public its new anti-expropriation policy. The statement, delivered by the president on January 27, contained ideas from both the State and Treasury Departments, but it was much less accommodating than the diplomats had hoped it would be. It warned governments contemplating expropriation that:

> when a country expropriates a significant US interest without making reasonable provision for such compensation to US citizens, we will presume that the United States will not extend new bilateral economic benefits to the expropriating country unless and until it is determined that the country is taking reasonable steps to provide adequate compensation or that there are major factors affecting US interests which require continuance of all or part of these benefits. In the face of the expropriatory circumstances just described, we will presume that the United States Government will withhold its support from loans under consideration in multilateral development banks. Humanitarian assistance will, of course, continue to receive special consideration under such circumstances. (Quoted in Lang, 1985: 18)

To ensure that the rhetoric of Nixon's speech would carry some weight, the Treasury Department secretary was granted the authority to use his influence with the World Bank to induce it to apply economic policies favored by the United States and to persuade other institutions to do likewise (Einhorn, 1974: 112–13; Lipson, 1985: 217).

These steps did not persuade the Velasco regime to adopt a more compromising posture. In fact, in July, the Peruvian government initiated diplomatic relations with Cuba after having failed to end Cuba's ostracism from the OAS (Werlich, 1978: 336). But when faced with a decline in the fishing industry because of a dissipation of the anchovie population, the Peruvian minister of fisheries requested US assistance. The Nixon administration saw this request as an opportunity to convey its unhappiness with the Velasco regime's unwillingness to grant US fishing boats unlimited access to Peru's waters and refused to help (Ingram, 1974: 89). The message, once again, did not have much effect on the behavior of the Peruvian government. In fact, in January of the following year, the Peruvian navy seized more than twenty California-based boats fishing within 200 miles of Peru's coast. The Nixon administration responded immediately by warning the Velasco regime that it was placing the arms sale to Peru under review (Werlich, 1978: 338).

This acrimonious US attitude did not last very long, however. In February 1973, General Velasco fell ill and was temporarily replaced by Prime Minister Mercado Jarrín. One of the first international acts of Peru's new leader was to welcome a Soviet military mission which had flown to Lima for the purpose of selling to the Peruvian military a large order of Soviet tanks and other weapons (Philip, 1978: 135–7; Werlich, 1978: 338).

It took the Nixon administration very little time to conclude that refusal to grant new loans until after Peru had properly compensated expropriated US companies could lead Lima to seek financial assistance elsewhere, such as the Soviet Union. In April and May, the Nixon administration agreed to a $30 million Inter-American Development Bank loan to Peru; in June, the World Bank, with full approval from the US government, authorized a $470 million credit for Peru; and in August, the Nixon administration authorized a $15 million military aid program for Peru (Werlich, 1978: 338).

The Peruvian government did not remain unaffected for long by Washington's gestures. The same month that the military aid program had been approved, Velasco, who had resumed his duties as head of the Peruvian government, agreed to hold new negotiations with the Nixon administration to solve the various investment disputes involving US companies (Werlich, 1978: 338). The United States, determined not to let the opportunity escape, accepted the offer and named James Greene, senior vice president with Manufacturers Hanover Trust Company, to act as special envoy to Peru (1978: 98).

The negotiations between representatives of the two countries would continue well into February of the following year. But by December 1973, there was a clear sense that the Nixon administration had no intention of using its tremendous resources to pressure an agreement. The State Department, with extensive backing from the Council of the Americas, AID, and several members of the House Foreign Affairs Committee and Senate Foreign Relations Committee, began to lobby for the repeal of an amendment that demanded automatic aid sanctions against governments that expropriated US property (Lipson, 1985: 218–19).

An agreement between the Nixon administration and the Velasco government was finalized on February 14, 1974. The Peruvian government agreed to pay $76 million directly to the US government, which would then distribute the money among US corporations. In addition, the Velasco regime agreed to pay a total of $74 million directly to Cerro, W. R. Grace, Star-Kist, Goldkist, and Cargill (Ingram, 1974: 95–6).

Chile's scenario in 1973 presents a dramatic contrast to that of Peru. President Allende began 1973 in a defiant mood, but one that would last only a short time. On February 5, in preparation for the March congressional elections, Allende's party, the Popular Unity Front, issued a radical campaign platform calling for the creation of a unicameral "people's assembly" and the writing of a new constitution, and a warning that Chilean socialism was inevitable (US Congress, House, 1975: 387). On this platform, the Popular Unity Front received 43.3 percent of the vote – 7 percent more than in the 1970 presidential election.

These new developments were not overlooked by other important actors in Chilean politics – the military and the US government. In the last month of 1972, just prior to Allende's visit to the United Nations, Ambassador Davis had sent an important cable to Washington. In his assessment of the situation in Chile, Davis had noted that what was most significant was the

> growing conviction in opposition parties, private sector and others that opposition is possible . . . Even more important is the increasing realization that opposition is necessary. What government is doing is beyond transactionalism. [Allende's] objectives are increasingly seen as incompatible and as going beyond what can be accepted. If opposition interests are to be protected, confrontation may not be avoidable. (Quoted in Freed and Landis, 1980: 74–5)

Davis's message prompted an almost immediate US response. In early 1973 the Forty Committee approved additional funding to finance anti-Allende campaigns by *El Mercurio*. In addition, on March 22, the Nixon administration demanded that Chile pay $700 million in nationalized US assets as a condition for renegotiating its US debt of $1.7 billion (Petras and Morley, 1975: 134; US Congress, House, 1975: 388; Davis, 1985: 104–6). Equally critical, the result of the elections proved to General Augusto Pinochet and other Chilean military leaders that a constitutional solution was impossible and that unless the military intervened, "the economic chaos in the country would leave Chile defenseless against hostile assault, and the growth and arming of leftist paramilitary groups" (Davis, 1985: 164–5).

Popular unrest and intrigue continued to mount during the months of May and June. On May 5 and 10, the Allende regime had to declare states of emergency in Santiago and O'Higgins provinces, respectively (US Congress, House, 1975: 388). Shortly afterward, in the week between June 15 and 21, copper miners, physicians, teachers, and students rioted to protest the Chilean government's handling of the copper strike. As these disturbances continued, the Chilean military began to plan a coup. Members of the Chilean army met on May 28, and members of the Chilean air force got together in early June, each to coordinate its set of tasks for the day the coup would be launched (Davis, 1985: 185). In the meantime, Washington's intelligence proved to be well attuned to what was to come. Five days before Chile's top-ranking army officers met to discuss the coup, the CIA headquarters in Washington ordered its agents in Chile to avoid the coup plotters and plotting. By then it had become quite evident that a coup was likely even without US involvement, and the CIA decided that salvaging its reputation was preferable to knowing when the coup would take place (1985: 348–9).

Preparations for the coup were derailed temporarily on June 29 when a right-wing political group named *Patria y Libertad*, led by Colonel Roberto Souper, seized control of downtown Santiago and attacked the presidential palace and the defense ministry. President Allende responded by calling on his supporters to converge on the center of the city and take over the industries and firms. Later in the day, however, Interior Minister General Carlos Prats persuaded the rebels to surrender (1985: 171–4).

The significance of the failed military coup was not missed by Allende. Aware that his government might be brought down unless tensions were moderated, he worked hard throughout July to forge compromises. On July 2, his government ended the 76-day copper miners' strike by increasing their wages from $96 a month to $128, and four weeks later he accepted demands by the Christian Democrats to eliminate private paramilitary groups, define the limits of state and private property, and accept constitutional reforms (US Congress, House, 1975: 390–1). But these compromises were not enough to contain dissatisfaction. On August 1, a dozen private business and professional associations, including lawyers, doctors and builders, formed an anti-government organization for the purpose of bringing down the Allende regime. The following day, more than 110,000 bus and taxi owners went on strike to protest Allende's announced concessions to the Christian Democrats regarding the constitutional amendments limiting state takeovers of industry. Some ten days later, saboteurs blew up an electric power pylon during a television address by Allende, cutting off power to Santiago. These types of events continued well into September, prompting the US government and the Chilean military to consider how to respond (1975: 391).

The US government continued its low profile. On August 20, the Forty Committee approved a $1 million grant for political parties and private sector groups opposing the Allende regime. The funds would not be transferred, however, unless the State Department and Ambassador Davis agreed that it would be in the interest of the United States to have the money used for the designed purpose. Both Davis and the State Department rejected the plan by contending that it would be preferable to allow the Chilean military to decide when and how to initiate the coup. This position was reaffirmed on September 8 at a meeting in Washington between Secretary of State Kissinger and Ambassador Davis (Davis, 1985: 357). But this low profile did not leave the United States unprepared for the coming coup. On the contrary, the CIA was well aware of the approximate time the coup would be launched (1985: 359; Kissinger, 1982: 404).

By the time Davis and Kissinger had finished assessing the Chilean situation, the political stage for a Chilean military coup had almost been set. On August 22, Chile's military Council of Generals voted to accuse the interior minister,

General Carlos Prats, of compromising to Marxism. That same day, the Chamber of Deputies, by an eighty-one to forty-five vote, agreed to censure the Allende government and to urge the military officers in the cabinet to help bring to an end the domestic turmoil (Sigmund, 1977: 231–3; Davis, 1985: 196–9). President Allende, afraid that a military coup might rob him of his presidency, sought to control the dissent by appointing four new military officers to his cabinet (1977: 234; 1985: 201). But by then it was too late. On September 9, just a day after Kissinger and Davis had agreed that a military coup in Chile was likely, representatives of the Chilean army, air force, and navy met to settle on a date the government would be removed. In a final show of defiance, Carlos Altamarina, the secretary general of the Socialist Party, called on the Chilean people to retaliate against coup plotters rather than compromise. His challenge did not produce the desired effect. Two days later, President Salvador Allende lay dead in the grounds of Chile's presidential palace, and a four-man military junta assumed power. On September 13, General Augusto Pinochet became Chile's new president. The Nixon administration, wishing to avert the impression that the United States had been in any way involved in the coup, delayed recognition of the new government until September 28. The absence of concern regarding the composition of the new government made the delay affordable (US Congress, House, 1975: 395; Davis, 1985: chs 10, 11).

Much of the content of this chapter can be neatly summarized by contending that the Nixon administration perceived the Allende regime as the carrier of an ideological flame which, if allowed to grow, could damage the ability of the United States to protect its interests. This perception was not new; it was the product of experience, as was the rationale behind the measures taken to ensure Allende's downfall. In the Cuban case, the US government had been willing to experiment and had allowed the Castro regime to establish itself. The experiment proved to be costly; it demonstrated to US foreign policy-makers that civilian regimes committed to radical reforms might help pave the road to communism. The same mistake would not be permitted in Chile. In addition, in this case the United States had an advantage it did not possess in the Cuban case – the military. When Castro came to power in 1959, his first political move was to replace the old military with one that would serve the interests of the revolution. Allende lacked this advantage, and the Nixon administration knew it and exploited it.

The Velasco regime, on the other hand, posed a dilemma. Traditionally, military regimes in Latin America had been perceived as perpetuators of the status quo. In the early 1960s, the military was trained and strengthened by the US government to combat revolutionary moves. The military played this role either as an institution controlled by a civilian government or as the governing body of the state. Although the latter form of governmental arrangement was not always welcomed by the United States, it was well received in instances in which the civilian rulers had not been successful at moderating the spread of communism. This attitude became quite evident in 1963, when the US government accepted Bosch's overthrow by the Dominican military as a step necessary to arrest the spread of communism.

Another attitude typical of the US government was the viewing of military coups as means to resolve disagreements between different factions within the ruling elite. This was the way the Johnson administration initially defined the challenge posed to the Reid Cabral regime in the Dominican Republic in 1965, and the way it viewed the Peruvian military coup of 1968. When the Velasco regime took over the reins of government in Peru, Washington's first reaction was to define the event as another instance in which the military imposed its will not for the purpose of bringing to life a new social and economic reality but with the intent of protecting its own political power. Although the Peruvian military obviously had no intention of sacrificing the latter goal, it did, however, also adhere to the belief that its political future was tightly linked to its ability to introduce social and economic changes.

The Nixon administration was slow at grasping this new reality. In the early years, the foreign policy-makers in Washington conveyed their dissatisfaction with many of the measures implemented by the Velasco regime, particularly those that undermined US private interests, but at no time did they seek to cripple fully the Peruvian government's ability to rule. Washington held back the use of its economic might not so much because Peru's economic policies were less radical than Chile's but principally because they were being imposed by a regime that had clearly demonstrated its commitment to containing communism. This point was never missed by the Velasco regime, which was very careful to remind officials of the Nixon administration that many of the reforms being implemented in Peru were the same ones as had been recommended by the Alliance for Progress as a recourse against revolution (McClintock, 1983: 286).

An issue that still requires some analysis is the way the Nixon administration linked the Chilean case to the Cuban scenario during the final days of the Allende regime. According to Secretary of State Kissinger, at his last meeting with Davis in Washington before Allende was toppled, the ambassador told him that it was quite unlikely that Chile would become a Cuban-type situation (Kissinger, 1972: 1244–5). Davis doubts that he ever made such a statement, for at that time he was convinced that the "danger was considerable" (Davis, 1985: 357). The problem with Kissinger's and Davis's references is that neither states specifically what the implications of a "Cuban-type situation" were. The analogy can have two distinct meanings. The first analogy can refer to the Eisenhower administration's failure to thwart Castro's rise to power as the Cuban revolutionary leader was battling the Batista regime. The second analogy can refer to the Bay of Pigs débâcle, which resulted in the utter humiliation of the Kennedy administration, both for being involved in an attempt to topple a foreign government and for failing in its attempt. There is a very good chance that both Davis and Kissinger were referring to the second-type analogy – the Bay of Pigs fiasco – but that the ambassador was concerned with the first element of the analogy – an attempt to topple a foreign government – while the secretary of state was focusing on its second element – failing.

By September of 1973 it had become quite clear that the Chilean military was planning to topple the Allende regime. As explained by ex-CIA Latin American operations chief David A. Phillips, the element vital to any coup endeavor was Chilean army participation. Between late August and early September, the United States had learned that the Chilean army would be one of the conspirators. The involvement of this branch of the armed forces more or less guaranteed that the coup would be successful (Phillips, 1977: 246). There is good reason to assume that Kissinger was referring to this aspect of the second-type analogy. For quite some time, the secretary of state had been emphasizing that it was critical to ensure that Allende not be permitted to replicate Castro's success. With this concern in mind, Kissinger would have been focusing on whether or not the Chilean military would prevail in its attempts. Moreover, since Kissinger knew that the Chilean armed forces were planning to act in unison, it is not surprising, regardless of whether he heard Davis correctly, that he would have estimated that the chances of the Chilean military's achieving its objective were quite good and that a Cuban-type situation would thus be averted.

Ambassador Davis, on the other hand, although interested in the fate of the coup, seems to have been focusing on trying to minimize the chances that the United States would be linked to the coup. He had voiced this concern earlier in 1973 and had repeatedly warned his staff not to associate with members of Chile's military. His main fear was that if the United States were to be associated with the overthrow, its reputation throughout Latin America would be undermined. In Davis's own eyes, his concern paid off. As he notes:

> The "cool and correct" US public stance toward Chile was consciously designed to avoid giving Allende a foreign target which would help him rally domestic loyalties and mobilize international support. US policy was largely successful in this regard. In contrast to what happened in Cuba, the United States did not become the great Satan in the eyes of the Chilean people. (1985: 399)

In sum, throughout the handling of the Peruvian and Chilean cases, the US government resorted consistently to various types of analogies, depending on the circumstances. Past experiences had taught US leaders that military coups in Latin America were, in a sense, a way of life, and that it was in the interest of the United States to recognize military governments led by officers who had demonstrated a commitment to battling communism. At the same time, however, these same US leaders had rarely been confronted by situations in which military officers known for their staunch anticommunist stand became identified with policies that sought to transform radically their society's economic structure. The dilemma that resulted from having experience with one form of behavior but not with the other contributed in part to the Nixon administration's unwillingness to act forcefully against Peru's military regime.

The Chilean case never became a definitional problem. Failure by the United States government to act more aggressively against Allende's presidential candidacy did not result from a willingness to permit the formation of a leftist government in the southern region of Latin America. Rather, it was the result of misreading the electoral predilection of the Chilean voters and wanting to minimize possible accusations that the United States did not respect the sovereign rights of foreign states. As it became evident that Chile's new president was going to be a political leader with an ideological bent unacceptable to the United States, the Nixon administration quickly designed a response that was deeply structured in lessons learned from past experiences. Determined to ensure that Allende would not become a second Castro, the Nixon administration committed itself to full application of the economic might of the United States. This strategy had its roots in earlier actions by the United States against Guatemala, Cuba, and the Dominican Republic. But the Chilean case posed a problem different from the earlier ones. The US government was fully cognizant that it could not depend on a covert paramilitary invasion to topple the Allende regime. This constraint, however, did not prevent the decision-makers in Washington from creating conditions that would incite a military coup.

The United States had faced a similar problem in 1964 with the Brazilian government of João Goulart. Goulart's regime had been sliding to the left for some time, and Brazil had become "ripe for political developments which might be antithetical to [US] interests" (quoted in Schoultz, 1981: 1973). The Johnson administration, aware that it needed to create conditions that would instigate the Brazilian military to act against Goulart, began to funnel funds to the American Institute for Free Labor Development for the purpose of disrupting Brazil's economy. As explained by William C. Doherty, Jr,[7] one of the many individuals involved in helping undermine Brazil's economy,

What happened in Brazil on April 1 [1964], did not just happen – it was planned – and planned months in advance. Many of the trade union leaders – some of whom were actually trained in our institute – were involved in the revolution, and in the overthrow of the Goulart regime. (Quoted in Freed and Landis, 1980: 74–5)

The plan, moreover, involved providing assistance to the Brazilian military to oust Goulart. This decision was taken on the basis of recognition by decision-makers in Washington that the United States had developed in Brazil the most institutionalized Military Assistance Advisory Group. Established during the Second World War, the Joint Brazilian United States Military Commission was created for the purpose of providing the United States with "daily contact with Brazilian counterparts at all levels from action officer to Cabinet minister," to assist in "achieving US policy objectives . . ." (quoted in Schoultz, 1981: 239).[8]

Goulart's predicament in 1964 was also Allende's in 1973; and the United States knew it. Aware that Allende's chances of averting a military coup were largely a function of his regime's ability to minimize economic, political, and social disruption, the United States took measures to stir turmoil and tried to maintain a close association with the Chilean military. Through all this time, the Nixon administration was also very careful to avert the costs incurred by the Kennedy and Johnson administrations in their dealings with Cuba and the Dominican Republic. From these cases the Nixon administration learned that the reputation of the United States could be damaged not only for engaging in an operation that results in a major fiasco but also for failing to conceal the absence of respect for the sovereignty of a foreign state. With this last concern in mind, several members of the Nixon administration took numerous steps to minimize the chances that either the State Department or the CIA would be identified as a party actively involved in plotting and implementing Allende's overthrow.

REASONING AND LEARNING BY ANALOGY

A comparative depiction in analogical form of the central arguments formulated so far must begin with analyses of the way the Kennedy administration responded to the Peruvian military coup of 1962 and of the policies implemented by the newly formed military regime prior to the 1963 rescheduled presidential elections. During this period, the US government followed a pattern already described in the Dominican case. The first response by the Kennedy administration was to suspend diplomatic relations with, and economic assistance to, Peru. These two decisions were reversed within a short period of time. Finally, in early 1963, the Kennedy administration supported the suspension of constitutional rights invoked by Peru's military regime.

In the study of the Dominican case, it was argued that the Johnson administration's decision to recognize the military junta that had helped topple Juan Bosch could not be attributed to Johnson's tendency to be less preoccupied than Kennedy with establishing democracies in Latin America. As an alternative, it was proposed that the decision by the US government to support a military regime was the function primarily of the military rulers' commitment to fight communism and to reestablish democracy. The Peruvian case strongly supports this general argument. The Kennedy administration extended diplomatic recognition to Peru's new military regime after acknowledging that its members had proven their anticommunist fiber and made it clear that they intended to hold new presidential elections. As in the Dominican case, this argument can be depicted analogically as follows:

Military regime in target state that faces major domestic problems acts forcefully against communists and promises to reestablish the democratic process.	:	Support military regime in target state that faces major domestic problems, acts forcefully against communists, and promises to reestablish the democratic process.

The suspension of constitutional rights in Latin America has been fairly common. Although the US government has generally disapproved of these actions, it has accepted them on certain occasions. The critical factor for the US government has been whether the suspension came as a result of a communist threat. In early 1963, the Kennedy administration believed that such a threat was on the rise in Peru. Analogically, it can be proposed that:

Communist activities in target state increase.	:	Military regime in target state suspends constitutional rights.	:	Support suspension of constitutional rights in target state.	::
Communist activities in target state are not evident.	:	Military regime in target state suspends constitutional rights.	:	Oppose suspension of constitutional rights in target state.	

By 1964, the situation in Peru had changed measurably. Following the election of Belaunde as president of Peru, the new civilian government began to signal that it was ready to take some major steps against IPC. The US government, fully aware that a communist threat was no longer in evidence, quickly communicated its determination to protect IPC by ordering a slowdown on loan commitments to Peru. The way the US government defined the problem when the Belaunde regime began to move against IPC differs very little from the way it defined the problem when Peru's military regime suspended constitutional rights.

| Communist activities in target state are not evident. | : | Government in target state proposes to expropriate foreign interests. | : | Suspend economic assistance to government in target state. | :: |
| Communist activities in target state increase. | : | Government in target state proposes to expropriate foreign interests. | : | Continue economic assistance to government in target state. | |

The thinking process of the US government continued to follow the same pattern until early 1966, when it decided to relax its suspension of economic assistance. Two factors convinced the Johnson administration that it was justifiable to alter its policy. First, it recognized that the slowdown in US economic assistance had not forced the Belaunde regime to be more compromising. Second, it feared that the slowdown in US economic assistance would continue to undermine Peru's economy, which could then fuel the communist subversion that had resurfaced in 1965. Stated in analogical form:

| Government in target state that seeks to expropriate foreign interests has not been drawn to compromise by suspension of economic assistance. | : | Communist activities in target state increase. | : | Relax suspension of economic assistance to government in target state. | :: |
| Government in target state that seeks to expropriate foreign interests has not been drawn to compromise by suspension of economic assistance. | : | Communist activities in target state are not evident. | : | Continue suspension of economic assistance to government in target state. | |

The comparative quality of this study can be greatly enhanced by turning at this point to the description in analogical form of the way the Chilean problem was being defined during the 1960s. The first issue that needs to be structured refers to the question of why the United States was so committed to covertly helping Eduardo Frei in his 1964 bid for the Chilean presidency. This decision by the Johnson administration was the result of a fear that the left in Chile, although still incapable of gaining the presidency, might gain measurable popular support (if unchecked). In addition, the Johnson administration felt comfortable with the economic reforms advocated by Frei and was convinced that his program was the best antidote to the changes urged by Castro-type political leaders. In analogical form, the thinking process of the Johnson administration was structured as follows:

Presidential candidate in target state committed to major economic reforms espouses strong anticommunist ideology. :	Power of the left in target state likely to increase if moderates do not receive external help. :	Extend extensive covert financial support to target state presidential candidate who is committed to major economic reforms and espouses strong anticommunist ideology.	::
Presidential candidate in target state committed to major economic reforms, espouses strong anticommunist ideology. :	Power of the left in target state unlikely to increase even if moderates do not receive external help. :	Do not extend extensive covert financial support to any presidential candidate in target state, including one who is committed to major economic reforms and espouses strong anticommunist ideology.	

The results of Chile's presidential elections shocked the Nixon administration and immediately led its leader to apply the lessons from his experience as vice president during the Eisenhower administration. Some time after Castro's ascension to power, Nixon recognized that it did not pay to wait until a leftist Latin American leader assumed the reins of government to decide whether such an individual would be sympathetic to US concerns. Castro's success ensured that Nixon's administration would not gamble a second time. Thus,

Do not impose covert sanctions on leftist political leader attempting to gain control of political system in target state. :	Leftist political leader gains control of political system in target state and begins to pave the ground for the creation of a communist regime. ::	Impose covert sanctions on leftist political leader attempting to gain control of political system in target state. :	Leftist political leader has smaller chance of gaining control of political system in target state and of being able to pave the ground for the creation of a communist regime.

During this time, however, the Nixon administration also concluded that if the measures against a regime were administered overtly, as they had been against Castro, the affected party could use them to help rally domestic loyalties against the foreign aggressor.

| Impose overt economic sanctions on government in target state suspected of being dominated by communists only after they have implemented major political, social, and economic reforms. | : Political leaders of government in target state succeed in creating a communist regime. | :: Impose covert economic sanctions on government in target state suspected of being dominated by communists immediately after they have gained power. | : Political leaders of government in target state fail to create a communist regime. |

Covert paramilitary intervention can be an effective policy instrument in instances in which the military in the targeted state is politically connected to various domestic factions and has difficulty in developing a united front. Most Latin American states have politicalized militaries, that is, military institutions that have assumed the responsibility for defining and delegating political authority (see Horowitz, 1967: 148). Not all politicalized militaries, however, have the same type of relationship with the different sectors of society. In some states the military is closely identified with certain classes; in other states the military acts as a stabilizer in the contest between factions. Moreover, not every military institution is capable of maintaining its own internal unity, irrespective of whether it acts as a promoter of special interests or stability.

These factors seem to have affected the decisions by different US governments on whether to intervene militarily. The military in Guatemala during Arévalo's and Arbenz's presidencies was neither a unified actor nor one that sought to put itself above class interests. During Arévalo's tenure as president, the Guatemalan military mounted several coups in attempts to protect various interests. This reality was not overlooked by members of the Eisenhower administration. As noted by Immerman (1982), during the early stages of the invasion, the United States targeted its propaganda activities toward "the wealthier group of urban Guatemalans, many of whom comprised Arbenz's officer corps. If this segment of the population continued to support the government, [the operation] was doomed to failure" (p. 164).

This lesson was overlooked by the Kennedy administration when it focused on the Castro regime. In 1961 the new US administration failed to recognize that upon coming to power Fidel Castro had replaced Batista's dependent, and somewhat divided, military with a united militia deeply committed to the survival of the new regime. Castro, unlike Arbenz, had risen to power by relying on an irregular militia, and once in power he dismantled the existing Cuban army and created his own loyal fighting force (Immerman, 1982: 196).

The military conditions in the Dominican Republic differed measurably from those faced by the United States in Cuba. Following Trujillo's assassination in 1961, the Dominican military was so entrenched in protecting specific interests that it was not able to form a united front committed to the vision that its principal function would be to minimize disharmony between competing factions. As Lowenthal notes, since Trujillo's death various military cliques suppressed opposition, prevented governments from executing specific policies, overthrew regimes, and established others (1972: 34). It was the existence of this type of domestic political environment that helped persuade the Johnson administration that relying on direct military intervention by the United States would be a viable option. The Dominican military, in other words, was in no position to challenge Washington's decision to assume the role of principal guarantor of the Dominican Republic's sovereignty.

These conditions, however, did not dominate Brazil's political and military environment in 1964 not Chile's between 1970 and 1973. Brazil's military was not a newcomer when it came to staging coups. It had chosen this path in 1945, 1954, 1955, and 1961 (Stepan, 1971: 56). But these coups were never designed for the purpose of protecting class interests. Although the largest number of military officers came from middle-class backgrounds, they did not see themselves as representatives of any class group. For some years, in fact, they had been critical of traditional elites for adhering to narrow and personal interests that often conflicted with broader national concerns (1971: 42). As stated by Juracy Magalhães, the foreign minister in the military-dominated government of 1964–6, the armed forces "exercise in practice a form of moderating power whenever there is manifested a strong and legitimate movement of public opinion. The armed forces intervene in the political scene supporting that manifestation and acting as instruments of transformation" (quoted in Stepan, 1971: 43). It is this vision that convinced Washington that the Brazilian military would not tolerate excessive external involvement. In other words, the leaders in Washington rationalized that any attempt on their part to become involved with some type of covert paramilitary operation or with direct military intervention would have elicited immediate opposition on the part of the Brazilian military for fear that such an action would debilitate its institutional power and, thus, undermine its ability to continue acting as an effective moderator.

If the Brazilian military in 1964 was an elite institution determined not to relinquish its role as the final arbiter of how much domestic disharmony was tolerable, the same applies to the Chilean military. For years it had been an institution proud of its commitment not to impose dramatic changes on the constitution of civilian governments and of its independence from social factions. It was the failure to recognize this attitude that led the Nixon administration to pressure unsuccessfully Chile's military to obstruct Allende's rise to power after the presidential elections in September 1970. But from this mistake the Nixon administration learned that it would be unnecessary and futile to promote an interventionist policy that relied on some type of external military action financed and organized by the United States. These arguments, thus, can be structured in analogical form as follows:

| Armed forces in target state have a tendency to intervene for the purpose of protecting very narrow class interests. | : | Government in target state dominated by communists. | : | Contemplate resorting to covert paramilitary invasion to topple government in target state dominated by communists. | :: |

| Armed forces in target state have a well-rooted tradition to intervene only for the purpose of protecting domestic stability. | : | Government in target state dominated by communists. | : | Promote domestic instability in target state dominated by communists and urge its military leaders to mount *coup d'état* against the government. | |

The depiction in analogical form of the arguments presented regarding the Peruvian case was interrupted after structuring the rationale behind the decision by the Johnson administration to relax its suspension of economic aid. Because the United States kept imposing and relaxing economic sanctions, it would be very tempting to infer that the policies of the US government were inconsistent. On closer inspection, however, it is feasible to contend that they were not.

For the most part, the US government sought to signal its displeasure with the Peruvian government whenever the policies of the latter seemed to infringe on the interests of the former or on those of US private citizens, or whenever Peru followed a political path that was perceived as unacceptable. This pattern of behavior was altered on those occasions when the US government feared that Peru's political environment was being threatened by the rise in anti-government activities by communist guerrillas. This was the principal rationale behind the Johnson administration's decision to relax the imposition of economic sanctions against Peru in early 1966. In the middle of 1967, however, Washington once again decided to act against Peru, when its government purchased jet fighters from France. The ensuing aid reduction was in large measure made possible by the fact that by that time the Peruvian military had, for all practical purposes, obliterated any guerrilla threat to the government. The analogical form last presented with respect to the Peruvian case can thus be generalized as follows:

| Government in target state is dominated by anticommunists who implement unacceptable policies. | : | Communist activities in target state increase. | : | Relax suspension of economic assistance to government in target state. | :: |

| Government in target state is dominated by anticommunists who implement unacceptable policies. | : | Communist activities in target state are not evident. | : | Continue suspension of economic assistance to government in target state. | |

In 1968 the Johnson administration was faced with an event that at first glance did not seem to differ dramatically from previous experiences. Following the overthrow of the Belaunde regime by the Peruvian military, Washington responded in typical fashion. Its first move was to suspend diplomatic relations with, and economic assistance to, Peru, followed by the recognition of the military junta and the renewal of some economic aid. Although an analysis of previous responses would have helped predict the type and sequence of steps the US government took in 1968, a critical difference had become evident. In the past, US governments had been willing to recognize military governments only after the latter had made it clear that they intended to revive the democratic process. This message was never conveyed by the Peruvian military in 1968. To the contrary, it stated quite specifically not only that it intended to rule for an extensive period of time, but also that it was committed to the implementation of reforms. This commitment became evident just a few days after the coup, when the military leaders began to expropriate property owned by IPC.

As has been stated on numerous occasions, the critical question to address when comparing the Chilean and Peruvian cases is why the Nixon administration responded so differently to developments in each country. The rationale can be stated succinctly in analogical form as follows:

Newly formed government in target state is dominated by civilian leaders who are committed to radical political, social, and economic reforms.	Civilian leaders in newly formed government in : target state attempt to create a communist government.	High threat : ::

Newly formed government in target state is dominated by regular military officers who are committed to radical political, social, and economic reforms.	Regular military officers in newly formed : government in target state do not attempt to create a communist government.	Low threat :

One of the critical aspects of the reasoning process of the US government is that it seems to have been guided by the belief that the heavy imposition of economic sanctions on Peru would lead its military to adopt a harsher posture against the United States and possibly become more dependent on help from the Soviet Union, but that against Chile the same policy would make it more difficult for the government to create a communist regime. The contrast between the two inferences can be described analogically as follows:

Impose limited and narrow economic sanctions on newly formed government in target state dominated by civilian leaders who are committed to major social and economic reforms.	: Civilian leaders of government in target state create a communist regime.	:: Impose widespread economic sanctions on newly formed government in target state dominated by civilian leaders who are committed to major political, economic, and, social reforms.	: Civilian leaders of government in target state fail to create a communist regime.
Impose widespread economic sanctions on newly formed government in target state dominated by military leaders who are committed to major social and economic reforms.	: Military leaders of government in target state seek assistance and establish better relations with communist bloc countries.	:: Impose limited and narrow economic sanctions on newly formed government in target state dominated by military leaders who are committed to major social and economic reforms.	: Military leaders of government in target state seek compromise with the initiator of limited sanctions.

THE INTERPLAY BETWEEN INTERESTS, BELIEFS, AND COGNITIVE PROCESSES

The strategic and economic perspectives

The analysis of US responses to development in Chile and Peru balances nicely the study of US actions toward Guatemala, Cuba, and the Dominican Republic. By focusing on the policies of the United States toward Chile and Peru, it is possible to show, once again, how inadequate are the strategic and economic explanations. But at the same time, the analysis helps demonstrate that Washington's perception of Chile's strategic and economic importance did not correspond with the often-held view that US interests in west coast South America are less important to the United States than are those in the Caribbean Basin.

Refutation of the strategic argument is not a particularly difficult analytical task. As shown by table 6, Chile and Peru resembled one another in terms of their overall strategic value to the United States. Their military capabilities were almost equal, and so were their economic capabilities. Moreover, each possessed raw materials of significant strategic value. Based on this near parity and the fact that Peru, under the Velasco regime, was not considered to be at risk of falling into the hands of the communists, it might be tempting to propose that the strategic paradigm explains quite well the discrepancy in US policies toward Chile and Peru. This argument is quite justified so long as the other cases considered earlier are excluded from the comparison. It is unquestionable

Table 6 *Measures of the strategic value to the United States of Peru and Chile*

| | Distance between the US and.[a] | Military capability | | Economic capability[d] | Strategic raw material capability[e] | Access to strategic maritime passages[f] |
		Armed forces[b]	Population[c]			
Peru	Approximately 1,800 miles	75,000 (1973)	14.71 m (1973)	$7,279 m (1973)	Lead: 162,900 m tn Zinc: 291,000 m tn Silver: 1,073 m tn Gold: 2,865 kg Manganese: 2,800 m tn Petro.: 3,613,000 m tn (1969)	1
Chile	Approximately 3,100 miles	75,000 (1973)	9.9 m (1973)	$8,251 m (1973)	Coal: 1,558,000 m tn Zinc: 1,500 m tn Gold: 1,827 kg Copper: 669,100 m tn Manganese: 9,900 m tn Petro.: 1,740 m tn (1969)	1

[a] These values represent the closest geographical distance between the United States and Peru and Chile respectively.

[b] See *Statistical Abstract of Latin America*, 1955–84.

[c] Ibid.

[d] These values represent Peru's and Chile's GNP for the year given, but at a constant 1970 value. See *Statistical Abstract of Latin America*, 1955–84.

[e] These figures are not very useful for comparative purposes. They might help the reader develop an understanding of some of the principal raw materials extracted in each country. See *Statistical Abstract of Latin America*, 1955–84.

[f] These rankings are very rough estimates representing the capability of Peru and Chile to disrupt the maritime passages in the southern part of the Pacific Ocean and the Panama Canal when compared to one another.

that Chile, because of its geographical location, is less likely to pose a direct strategic threat to the United States than do Guatemala, Cuba, or the Dominican Republic. But this factor is measurably outweighed by the facts that Chile's population in 1973 was larger than the respective populations of Guatemala, Cuba, or the Dominican Republic in the early 1960s; that the combined military capability of the three Caribbean Basin states was smaller than Chile's; and that the combined economic capability of Guatemala, Cuba, and the Dominican Republic was half that of Chile. Also, it is critical to keep in mind that Henry Kissinger believed that Salvador Allende's rise to power in Chile posed a much greater threat to US interests than did Fidel Castro's political success in Cuba. Kissinger's justification for his belief was not influenced by the variance in military capabilities between Chile and Cuba. For the national security advisor, the critical factor was that Chile was a "continental country" and as such could be a much more effective springboard for Soviet military activity. In sum, the variances in capabilities fail once again to correspond with the variances in responses to threats.

The economic explanations do not fare much better. The economies of Chile and Peru in the early 1970s were significantly more important to the United States and some of its multinational corporations than were the economies of the three Caribbean states. Total earnings from direct US investments, for instance, favored the two more southern states by more than a two-to-one ratio. Imports from the United States was the only measure that made the three Caribbean Basin states more important to the northern actor than their two southern counterparts, but this discrepancy is attributable almost entirely to Cuba's imports.

The weight of the challenge posed to the economic explanations increases markedly as the analysis becomes more focused. Specifically, if the Nixon administration acted in response to the economic and international policies implemented by Chile and Peru, it would have acted differently. In the case of Chile, the Nixon administration would have waited to see how the Allende regime would act before imposing economic sanctions on it. And yet, the Nixon administration did not wait. In the Peruvian case, on the other hand, the first response by the US government to the expropriation of IPC by the newly formed military regime was to try to mitigate any fears that it would apply the Hickenlooper Amendment. Moreover, although the Nixon administration eventually imposed economic sanctions against Peru, they were never levied as extensively as they had been against Chile, and on more than one occasion they were relaxed to see whether the Peruvian military regime could be drawn to the negotiating tables. This last tactic was never used with the Allende regime. In fact, on those few occasions when the Allende regime proposed getting together with representatives of the US government to see whether they could narrow some of their differences, the Nixon administration objected to the holding of such meetings. Moreover, in the case of Chile, virtually all the US corporations investing there refrained from seeking political support from Washington and were resigned to leaving the country following Allende's election. The two exceptions were Anaconda and ITT. Anaconda approached the Nixon administration to seek compensation from the United States for its property expropriated by the Allende regime, but at no time did it propose that Chile's economy be destabilized, for it feared that such action would undermine its ability to acquire compensation. The only company that actively sought to persuade the Nixon administration to take a hard line against Chile was ITT (Krasner, 1978: 302–5).

ITT's role in the Chilean case was important. In July, August, and October 1970, ITT approached the Nixon administration with the offer to provide funds to be used in Chile to either influence the electoral process or pressure the Chilean Congress to act against Allende. The Nixon administration did act against Allende, as ITT had hoped, but its decision to intervene took place before compensation of expropriated US property became an issue. This argument would carry little weight if it were assumed that the Nixon administration knew in advance that Allende would authorize very low payments for nationalized US property. But if that is the case, then why did the Johnson administration not act more aggressively against the Velasco regime in Peru immediately after it was formed on October 3, 1968? This regime came to power by means of a military coup, in reaction to an agreement signed between President Fernando Belaunde Terry and the International Petroleum Company (IPC) whereby IPC ceded its subsoil rights in exchange for Peru's cancellation of $144 million owed by IPC in back taxes (Krasner, 1978: 236–7). Six days after the coup, the Velasco regime seized part of IPC's property and imposed much stricter conditions on the company; and yet, the US government, although determined to protect IPC's interests, never sought to undermine Peru's economy to the degree that it attempted to hurt Chile's.

To summarize, it is one thing to contend that the US government, if asked, will actively represent the threatened interests of US corporations investing abroad, and another thing to argue that it will seek to topple the regimes that pose such threats. Neither the Johnson nor the Nixon administration was driven by the perception that threats to US private economic investments abroad had to be answered with a commitment to bring down those who initiated them.

Table 7   *Measures of the economic value to the United States of Peru and Chile*

	Imports from the US by:[a]	Exports to the US by:[b]	Total earnings from direct US investments in:[c]	Economic interaction between the US and states adjacent to target state[d]
Peru	$199.06 m (1970)	$344.62 m (1970)	$74 m (1970)	$2.96 b (1970)
Chile	$343.58 m (1970)	$177.17 m (1970)	$76 m (1970)	$2.10 b (1970)

[a] See *Statistical Abstract of Latin America*, 1955–84.
[b] Ibid.
[c] Ibid.
[d] Ibid. "Economic transactions between the United States and states adjacent to the target state" refers to total exports by the United States to all the states bordering with Peru and Chile, respectively.

The cognitive perspectives

Conflicting reactions are bound to be generated by an analysis of the effects of Richard Nixon's beliefs on the international behavior of the United States during his tenure as president. Here was an individual who during his earlier political years had smeared Dean Acheson as the "Red Dean" and accused Harry Truman of a "defense of Communism in high places" (Morris, 1977: 61), but who as president brought about better relations with both the Soviet Union and the People's Republic of China. Further bewilderment is bound to surface as one considers Nixon's emphatic demand in 1970 that Salvador Allende, a leftist reformer, not be permitted to become Chile's new president, and compares it with his decision to reach a negotiated settlement with Peru, after its government, led by General Juan Velasco, had seized property owned by US corporations and undertaken substantial economic and social reforms. These assumed contradictions, however, all but disappear as the analyst defines in greater detail the different properties of the beliefs that guided the actions of the principal foreign policy-makers in the Nixon administration.

Richard Nixon moved into the White House in 1969 determined to leave his imprint in the realm of foreign affairs. Unlike Truman and Johnson, he had extensive background in international affairs and looked forward to using this knowledge to change the course of US diplomacy. To achieve this objective, Nixon concluded that foreign policy would have to be run from the White House by an individual able to impose a systematic structure on the decision-making process (Kissinger, 1979: 11).[9] This individual would be Henry Kissinger. The relationship between the two men was complex, and often contradictory. But there seemed to be very little difference in their approaches to foreign policy. As Roger Morris notes, "I'll never know where one ended and the other began" (1977: 3). Their similarities in perspectives and approaches, make it feasible to focus on them not as separate entities, but as a unit.

The formation of the Nixon–Kissinger foreign policy partnership brought two new elements into the national security equation. The first new element was Nixon's combination of strong anticommunist ideology and political pragmatism. The second was Kissinger's conviction that in order to give US foreign policy a "ballast of restraint and assurance of continuity," it was imperative to arrive at a clear conception of its "fundamental national interests" (quoted in Gaddis, 1982: 275). Past administrations, Kissinger believed, had approached the foreign policy-making process by segmenting problems into constituent elements, with little emphasis or concern for their interreltationship. Past fascination with technical issues had obscured the relationships between intentions and consequences (Gaddis, 1982: 276).

Nixon's and Kissinger's perspectives on how to best address the threat of communism also reflected an attempt to break with the past. They concurred with their predecessors that the most important feature of Soviet foreign policy was its communist ideology. Communism, argues Kissinger, "is a doctrine of history, and also a motivating force" (1979: 116). Confident of the flow of history, the Soviets are never inclined to stake everything on a single throw of the dice; instead, they "promote the attrition of adversaries by gradual increments" (p. 118). Faced with this reality, the central responsibility of the United States would be "to foreclose Soviet opportunities . . ." In other words, the chief task of the Nixon–Kissinger apparatus would be "to define the limits of Soviet aims" (p. 119).

The international environment of 1969, however, differed markedly from that which came into existence at the end of the Second World War. To begin with, although the Soviet Union still had its weaknesses, it had gained extensively in industrial, technological, and military power. Or, in Kissinger's words, Soviet foreign policy was "now rooted in real power" rather than in a "rhetorical manifestation of a universalist doctrine" (quoted in Gaddis, 1982: 286). But at the same time, the evidence of Sino-Soviet antagonism had led Nixon to announce that "international Communist unity had been shattered" (1982: 284).

The impact of these beliefs was neither that the United States could finally afford to displace the threat of communism from its main foreign policy agenda, or that it would have to respond to every communist challenge. By contending that it was up to the United States to define the limits of Soviet aims, Kissinger was calling for a strategy that would "relate the desirable to the possible" (quoted in Hoffmann, 1980: 36). This meant, on the one hand, that since it was not possible to depose the communist regimes that ruled over the Soviet Union, China, and Eastern Europe, the United States would have to accept their existence as part of the new status quo. On the other hand, it signified that the United States could not afford to tolerate the creation of new Marxist regimes. Neither Kissinger nor Nixon argued that the adoption of a communist structure by a new regime would actually alter the international balance of power. Kissinger made this clear when he noted that "while a decisive advantage is hard to calculate, the appearance of inferiority – whatever its actual significance – can have serious political consequences" (quoted in Gaddis, 1982: 288). Nixon conveyed a similar attitude, but with a different focus when he stated:

If, when the chips are down, the world's most powerful nation, the United States of America, acts like a pitiful, helpless giant, the forces of totalitarianism and anarchy will threaten free nations and free institutions throughout the world. (Gaddis, 1982: 288)

How and when the United States should pursue its foreign policy goals, and how it should control risks, were issues of great interest to the Nixon–Kissinger team. Negotiations, according to Kissinger, are the most effective means of establishing a common notion of legitimacy and of reducing risks (Walker, 1977: 138–9). However, whenever a common notion of legitimacy is absent, the tendency will be for the most powerful party to resort to force (1977: 140). Force need not always be employed overtly; covert action could often be used as an effective way of reducing costs (Hoffmann, 1980: 47). Covert operations, writes Kissinger

have their philosophical and practical difficulties and especially in America. Our

national temperament and tradition are unsuited to them ... we face an unprecedented problem. We live in an age of ideological confrontation; through every phase of coexistence the Soviet leaders have insisted that it did not imply any lessening of the ideological struggle ...
In these circumstances it was neither morally nor politically unjustified for the United States to support those internal political forces seeking to maintain a democratic counterweight to radical dominance. (1979: 658–9)

The effects these ideas and beliefs had on the foreign policies of the United States toward Chile and Peru are not difficult to translate. For Kissinger, Allende's electoral success in Chile in 1970 meant "a challenge to our national interest. We did not find it easy to reconcile ourselves to a second Communist state in the Western Hemisphere. We were persuaded that it would soon be inciting anti-American policies, attacking hemisphere solidarity, making common cause with Cuba, and sooner or later establishing close relations with the Soviet Union" (1979: 654). For Nixon, the Chilean crisis assumed a special dimension. As Kissinger writes,

Nixon was beside himself. For over a decade he had lambasted Democratic administrations for permitting the establishment of Communist power over Cuba. And now what he perceived – not wrongly – as another Cuba had come into being during his own Administration without his having been given the opportunity to make a decision. This explains the virulence of his reaction and his insistence on doing something, *anything* that would reverse the previous neglect. (1979: 671)

The Jekyll and Hyde nature of the Nixon–Kissinger approach to foreign policy is captured in its full dimension as the focus of the analysis concentrates on US responses to the policies of the Velasco regime in Peru. As Kissinger notes, neither he nor Nixon ever considered the nationalization of US property as the critical issue. Before Allende came to power, notes Kissinger,

Ambassador Korry had cooperated in what amounted to the negotiated nationalization of the Anaconda Company. And with Peru, that same year, the Nixon Administration stretched our legislation almost to the breaking point to reach an equitable settlement of the nationalization of the International Petroleum Company's mining operations without having too restrictive legislation. We repeatedly sought pretexts to postpone application of the Hickenlooper Amendment . . ., so as to maintain friendly relations with an important country – even though Peru was governed by a left-wing military junta that was aggressively nationalistic and leaning toward the more radical elements of the Third World . . . The challenge to our policy and interests posed by Allende was fundamentally different. He was not just nationalizing property; he avowed his dedication to totalitarian Marxism–Leninism. (1979: 657)

Beliefs, in short, never escaped the decision-making process of the Nixon administration as it sought to define and respond to the challenges posed by Peru and Chile.

Although attribution theory does not challenge the proposition that individuals often ignore or misinterpret relevant information, it contends that this generally happens "not because they are emotionally committed to particular values, but because they have succumbed to common error in handling information" (Larson, 1985: 41). This argument does not seem to stand firm when applied to Nixon and Kissinger. Regarding Chile, Kissinger confirms that "Nixon was beside himself . . .;" he could not tolerate the United States and his administration being burdened by a second Cuba. This is not the description of a decision-maker who might not know that the best way to test the validity of a proposition is to try to falsify it; instead, it is the portrayal of an individual who believed that the United States had incurred a heavy price for failing to respond to a communist threat in its hemisphere, and who was unwilling to repeat the same mistake. In other words, it was the cost of the Cuban experience that gave the Cuban analogy so much centrality in Nixon's mind.

The tendency to define problems in the context of categories also surfaces in the Peruvian case. The Velasco regime was not perceived as a potential communist threat, for although it implemented many radical policies, its members were military officers. Based on this contention, however, it could also be argued that this form of reasoning reflects the type of behavior expected by attribution theory. Any quasi-systematic analysis that tries to isolate a particular trait of character among Latin American military governments is bound to note that they have generally been vociferous opponents of communism.

The convergence of attribution theory and schema theory on a similar prediction is not unusual. This, however, does not imply that each posits an equally valid explanation. To differentiate between the two theories, one must pose the following question: was the decision by Nixon and Kissinger to negotiate with the Velasco regime arrived at after gauging how often negotiations had brought about the desired effect when compared to other policies, how much of the wanted effect negotiations had caused in past instances, and how often negotiations had accomplished the intended result on other actors; or was it reached after the problem had been structured in terms of categories?

The question almost begs the answer. Washington officials are not particularly known for trying to formulate policies on the basis of the comparison of the effects that various policies have on different actors across disparate conditions. However, Nixon, with his extensive experience in the international realm, and Kissinger, with much of his academic life dedicated to the analysis of diplomacy and the effective use of power, seemed to come out of a different mold. But did they?

Linkage politics, although not universally praised, has often been described as Nixon's and Kissinger's most original theoretical contribution to the practice of foreign affairs. Linkage, for Nixon and Kissinger, was "synonymous with an overall strategic and geopolitical view" (Gaddis, 1982: 294). It was based on the assumptions that, however diffused and multidimensional power had become, its various elements affected one another, and the existence of these interrelationships should be used in order to promote the interests of the United States and to temper the actions of its adversaries. As Stanley Hoffmann notes, linkage politics was certainly theoretical (1980: 46). But in order to be effective, it had to be applied with a tremendous amount of sophistication. It would simply not do to assume that since issues were interrelated, manipulation on one issue would have an effect on a different one. Rather, the rational use of linkage politics calls for the careful differentiation of the conditions under which various forms and levels of power will be effective in modifying the behavior of different actors regarding a variety of issues and interests. In other words, it expects, at minimum, the type of reasoning process stipulated by attribution theory.

No judgment will be rendered here about how ably linkage politics was used throughout the tenure of the Nixon–Kissinger team. Nor will an attempt be made to argue that linkage politics was the strategy driving the actions of the Nixon administration *vis-à-vis* Peru. But aspects of such a strategy surfaced in numerous instances. Overall, the Nixon administration relied on both positive and negative reinforcements to persuade the Velasco regime to reach an equitable settlement of the nationalization of the IPC and other US-owned companies, to alter its commercial fishing policies, and to modify some of the policies of its military. These attempts at behavior modification, however, were not the result of a quasi-systematic analysis. Instead, they reflected the attitude that since members of the Velasco regime were military officers who in the past had fought communism virulently, the United States could not afford to be too forceful with its demands. The problem, and the responses that were generated to address it, in other words, were consistently placed in the context of a broad category: so long as the United States showed restraint in its demands, the Velasco government, being a military regime, could be relied on to prevent any attempts to create a communist infrastructure, even if many of its policies reflected a leftist bent.

Thus, although the Nixon administration came to power claiming that it would "judge other countries, including Communist countries . . . on the basis of their actions and not on the basis of their domestic ideology," that interests would be carefully differentiated and ranked, and that it would heedfully rationalize the use of power, its actions toward Chile and Peru were colored by ideology and analogy. Whether to support or attack a political regime became a function of that regime's degree of opposition to the political values nurtured by communism. In turn, intolerance of communist regimes in the Americas was, in part, a function of history; it was based on the costs accrued as a result of the Cuban experience.

Cuba, however, was not the only analogy US foreign policy-makers had in mind. If another Castro could not be permitted to come to power in Latin America, the question that still remained was how the United States would accomplish this goal. The policy instruments used by the United States against Cuba in 1961 and the Dominican Republic in 1965 could not be put to use against Chile in 1973. The Chilean military would not tolerate usurpation of its domestic political role by either an overt military of covert paramilitary invasion directed by a foreign power. Cognizant of this constraint, the Nixon administration recognized that Chile's military in 1973 resembled in no small measure Brazil's 1964 armed forces; both were political institutions proud of their independence and of their roles as the chief guardians of domestic stability. This attitude on the part of the two Latin American military forces forced Washington to accept the fact that if it wanted the Goulart and the Allende regimes toppled, it would have to play a central role in instigating domestic political, social, and economic turmoil in both Brazil and Chile. Such turmoil, reasoned the leaders in Washington, would compel the Brazilian and Chilean militaries to bring alternative forms of government to power in their respective countries. In sum, for the United States, Brazil was to Chile what Guatemala had been to Cuba, in each instance the leaders in Washington retrieved the structure that defined the problem space in the first country in order to delineate and grapple with the problem that erupted in the second. The critical difference between the two sets of pair cases is that only the problem space transposed among the first set of pair cases proved to be effective.

How long an analogical structure dominates the analytical process of an institution is a function both of the costs prompted by the event which was responsible for that structure's creation, and of time. Kennedy's failure to topple the Castro regime was to haunt the president's immediate successors, but by 1977, as Central America began to dominate the attention of US foreign policy-makers, more than sixteen years had transpired since the United States had been forced to acknowledge that Castro would remain as a thorn in its side for some time. And with time, a new president moved into the White House – one who brought with him a group of advisors who rejected the notion that the best way to avert a second thorn in the United States's side was by preempting with forceful measures any attempt by Latin American leaders with communist affiliations to create a new political regime.

9

Nicaragua and Grenada: The Past Has Only One Future

The Sandinistas had a mask. Our job was to glue it; to ensure they could not take off their mask...
Viron Vaky, former assistant secretary of state for inter-American affairs

Grenada in 1983 was a replay of Santo Domingo in 1965, another intervention widely remembered in Washington as a success
Eldon Kenworthy, "Grenada as Theater"

THE SEARCH FOR A RELIABLE PAST

On October 25, 1983, US troops landed on the small island of Grenada in what the president of the United States termed a "rescue operation." Contingency military forces from other small eastern Caribbean states, as well as Jamaica, followed shortly afterwards. The joint military intervention brought to an end what was already a "failed revolution" (Croes, 1985: 1). This event, however, reflected only a minuscule picture within the overall situation in the Caribbean Basin in 1983. This year was also marked by the Reagan administration's failure to topple the Sandinista government that had dominated Nicaragua's political arena since 1979.

The comparison of these two cases is important to this study for two reasons. The first, and possibly most obvious, reason is that the contrast should help differentiate more systematically and with greater precision how decision-makers within the Carter and Reagan administrations structured and addressed the Nicaragua and Grenada problems. And second, since the task designated at the beginning of this study's empirical section was to delineate the manner in which the United States' policy of intervention toward the Caribbean and Latin America was reasoned and implemented through a period that covered almost forty years, the analysis of these two cases symbolize, clearly in a somewhat artificial way, the culmination of a problem set.

The comparison of the two cases will proceed in a manner similar to the analysis of events in Peru and Chile in the previous chapter. However, a word of caution must be voiced at this juncture. One of the truly fascinating aspects of the Grenadian case is that the invasion led to the capture and disclosure of important documents depicting the nature of Grenada's ruling party, the New Jewel Movement (NJM), and many of its foreign policies. For the student focusing on revolutionary regimes, these documents are highly valuable. The student of US foreign policy, however, must work under fairly disadvantageous conditions. The event is quite recent, and information regarding the Reagan administration's decision-making process is limited. The analysis of the Grenada case, therefore, will lack the wealth of information so typical of the earlier cases, and the resulting conclusions will be somewhat tentative.

The limited literature that exists on US actions toward Grenada has for the most part attributed very little value to the contention, so common in the previous studies, that the leaders in Washington resorted to military intervention to defend US business interests. The debate generally centers on whether the United States acted for strategic reasons, symbolic reasons, or both.

The most forceful proponent of the strategic rationale has been Robert Pastor, an individual who was deeply involved in helping to formulate the foreign policy of the United States toward Grenada under the Carter administration. According to Pastor, the decision by the Reagan administration to act forcefully against Grenada was the result of one central fear – that its leaders would establish a close alliance with the Soviet Union and Cuba. The Reagan administration approached Grenada "as a small object of a larger East–West struggle" (Pastor, 1985: 59). Pastor's conclusion is backed by Lars Schoultz's analysis, which proposes that US officials perceived in Grenada a "Latin American government exhibiting an independent foreign policy that included linkages to one of our adversaries, Cuba. The Cuban agreement to help construct an airport was perceived not as a Cuban agreement to help construct an airport but as a challenge to US security" (Schoultz, 1987: 245). Stephan J. Andriole, in an analysis that attempts to reconstruct the decision-making process that was implemented at the highest level of the US government just prior to the invasion, agrees with Pastor and Schoultz that one of the central objectives sought by the Reagan administration was the removal of a regime that posed a direct threat to the security interests of the United States. But he also adds that this objective was integrated with two additional ends: protection of the lives of US nationals in Grenada, and replacement of the existing regime with a democratic government (Andriole, 1985: 82).

A slightly different interpretation of the strategic argument contends that the United States intervened against Grenada with the hope of projecting a new image. According to Dov S. Zakheim, the election of Ronald Reagan marked the beginning of a new era for the United States – an era committed to emerging from the psychological cocoon spun by Vietnam. The failure of the United States in Vietnam had given birth to a syndrome characterized by an inward-looking mentality, a fatalistic belief that the ability of the United States to influence world events was limited, a *mea culpa* attitude regarding the world's troubles, an acceptance of the notion that the United States was a reactionary power, and a suspicion of the modernization programs of the US military (Zakheim, 1986: 179). Developments in Grenada gave President Reagan the opportunity to show the world that the United States was no longer a victim of the Vietnam syndrome but a country determined to resume its role as a world power and "stand up to those who threaten American interests" (1986: 180).

One of the critical aspects of the contention that the Reagan administration's central objective in intervening was to eradicate the Vietnam syndrome is that the argument has been posited both by supporters and critics of the intervention decision. For Zakheim the decision was fully justified; it signaled to the Soviet Union that the United States was no longer willing to sit back and witness the expansion of both the capabilities and uses of Soviet military power. Analysts who have not been sympathetic to the policies of the Reagan administration have argued that Grenada provided the United States with the first good opportunity to reverse the Vietnam syndrome, not because Grenada was being created as a major new Soviet military bastion in the Caribbean – it was not – but because the invasion would not be too costly and could decisively take off the map a regime with links to the Soviet Union (Biersteker, 1983: 13–14, 16).

The literature regarding US foreign policy toward Nicaragua is significantly richer than that regarding Grenada. Students of the US–Nicaragua case can be divided into two groups: those who maintain that the rationale behind US actions remained constant through different periods and regimes in power in Nicaragua, and those who argue that different rationales dominated the decision-making process in Washington, depending on the circumstances and the characteristics of the administration in power.

Foreign-policy analysts who maintain that the United States's actions were always driven by the same set of objectives typically adopt the posture that the rationale had a very well-defined strategic–economic theme. For instance, according to James Petras and Morris Morley, although some shifts in strategy became evident as soon as the Reagan administration replaced the Carter administration, the transition was accompanied by a remarkable degree of continuity (1983: 210). The fundamental foreign policy of the United States toward Nicaragua under both administrations was to sustain US economic and strategic interests and prevent the success of the revolutionary struggle. The convergence of interests of the decision-makers in Washington, US investors abroad, and the ruling class in Nicaragua "led to a historic compromise in which successive US administrations sacrificed democratic rights in exchange for capitalistic economic opportunity and US strategic interests" (1983: 191). Marlene Dixon, in an analysis that focuses solely on the foreign policy of the Reagan administration toward the Sandinista regime, also concludes that the actions are the result of a desire to protect the economic needs of the United States. "The present government of the United States does not concern itself for an instant with 'human rights' or 'pluralistic democratic societies' or 'economic progress and social justice' ... It cares only that capitalist ('free') governments be subservient to the Reagan perception of 'national interest'" (1985: 114).

The most ingenuous argument that attributes an economic rationale to US actions was posited by Susanne Jonas. According to Jonas, the US ruling class has always been driven by the need to protect US power – that is, economic power. Generally, when such power was threatened, the ruling class would react by resorting to some form of intervention. The Sandinista victory over the Somoza regime in 1979, however, forced a reappraisal in Washington. For the first time in almost forty years, an administration in Washington favored extending economic aid to a regime dominated by political leaders whose ideological bent was believed to be near the radical left. Why? According to Jonas, this action did not indicate that the US government was altering its goal; it only reflected the fact that the Carter administration was being pressured to help Nicaragua by a consortium of US banks which had just negotiated a refinancing of $600 million of Nicaragua's debt (1983: 95). There were two reasons, she argues, why the banks and their political representatives wanted Nicaragua to receive economic aid. First, they wanted Nicaragua to set a precedent of not defaulting, and of paying its debts at commercial rates. This precedent was to be used in negotiations with other countries such as Bolivia, Brazil, and Jamaica. And second, there was a major political strategy behind the policy. Because only $3.5 million existed in Nicaragua's international reserves, whatever reserves could be accumulated through international aid would have to be used for paying off the loans to the international banks, rather than for reconstruction of Nicaragua's economy. This meant that the Sandinista government would be forced to impose austerity upon the Nicaraguan people which in turn would breed discontent like that experienced some years earlier in Chile. The end result of this involved process could be a "Chile-style counterrevolution" (Jonas, 1983: 96–7).

For the most part, students of US foreign policy toward Nicaragua either refuse to acknowledge the relevance of the arguments postulated by the likes of Jonas, Dixon, and Petras and Morley, or they simply contend that they are "nothing more than the manipulation of past events (or pseudo events) in the service of some current agenda" (Falcoff, 1984: 45). For these analysts, the dynamics of Nicaraguan politics and the responses by the United States are so complex that they cannot be encapsulated by sweeping indictments (1984: 46). This study shares such an attitude and will argue, as in the previous cases, that in order to capture the complexity not only of the Nicaraguan problem but also of the Grenadian case, it is necessary to discover how decision-makers perceived and responded to the domestic political battles that ensued in both countries.

The assumption that perceptions guide the formation of policies lies at the core of Lars Schoultz's analysis of the foreign policies of the Carter and Reagan administrations toward Nicaragua. According to Schoultz, the foreign policies of the United States under the Carter and Reagan administrations were reflections of their respective decision-makers' beliefs about the causes of instability. Early in the 1950s, foreign policy-makers in general agreed that communist adventurism was the main cause of instability in Latin America. This belief persisted in Washington at least until 1989. However, in the interim period, some other explanations for the causes of instability in Latin America have also gained substantial backing. In the 1960s, many officials in Washington proposed that poverty was the main culprit, while others argued that instability was not singularly caused but was brought about by both communism and poverty. An important derivation from the multicausal relationship argument was the contention that the proposition that communism instigated instability was no longer critical; instead, it was sufficient to recognize that communists were quite adept at exploiting the instability brought about by poverty (Schoultz, 1987: 19–20).

The Nicaraguan case enabled the Carter administration to advocate a unique perception. Schoultz notes that although Carter's principal foreign policy advisors differed measurably in their perceptions as to the causes of instability, they tried hard to underplay the role of the Sandinistas and their association with the Castro regime. As an alternative, they stressed that in the new Nicaraguan government there were political leaders seeking profound socio-political change who were also committed to promoting individual rights and democratic procedures. This perception, continues Schoultz, came to a dramatic end when Ronald Reagan became president. Almost overnight, Nicaragua became a casebook example of communist adventurism (1987: 13–49).

The most attractive aspect of Schoultz's argument is its attempt to explain the variances in US actions in terms of conflicting perceptions as to the causes of instability. Schoultz's study, however, is slightly weakened by its failure to assess systematically whether the theory is useful for explaining changes in behavior within the same administration. More specifically, his study never addresses the difficulties faced by the Carter administration as it tried to decide at different times what policy to adopt toward the Somoza regime.[1] For instance, according to Schoultz (1987), in "September 1978, the Carter administration acknowledged that the Somozas had to go, and it stopped the military assistance pipeline" (p. 41). From this statement, one could infer that the Carter administration had finally decided to apply great pressure on Somoza to resign because his continued presence was perceived as being the principal cause of instability in Nicaragua. The problem with this argument is that it does not accurately reflect the dilemma faced by the Carter administration regarding the extent to which the United States should have pressured Somoza to resign. In other words, Schoultz is correct in arguing that the Carter administration had finally decided that Somoza ought to go, but at that time there was no consensus as to what role the United States should play in order to get the Nicaraguan dictator to resign. In fact, the consensus in the Carter administration that the United States should exert political, economic, and military pressure on Somoza did not surface until June 1979. Consensus on the causes of instability, in other words, will not always guarantee consensus on response.

William LeoGrande has attempted to capture the evolutionary process of Carter's foreign policy toward Nicaragua. For LeoGrande, the foreign policy of the Carter administration went through three stages. In the first stage it sought to control instability in Nicaragua by trying to persuade Somoza to implement social, political, and economic reforms. When this policy failed, the Carter administration became convinced that it could preempt the Sandinistas by forming a post-Somoza regime composed of moderates. Finally, when this policy also failed, the Carter administration sought to persuade the Sandinistas to share power with the moderates. LeoGrande attributes these actions to the tendency by the Carter administration to be six months behind schedule regarding which policy was still a viable one. Moreover, he proposes that the source of these misperceptions was the fear of another Cuba and the inclination to believe that the Sandinistas were determined to create one (1983: 89–90).

This present study's construction of the Nicaraguan scenario will bear LeoGrande's argument that the foreign policy of the Carter administration went through three major stages. However, it will also demonstrate that the source of what LeoGrande refers to as "misperceptions" was not always the fear of another Cuba and of the formation of a regime committed to creating one. Specifically, the detailed delineation of the Nicaraguan scenario will show, first, that the Cuban analogy did not begin to influence the officials in Washington until late 1978 to early 1979; second, that during this time other analogies were used by certain officials to counteract the Cuban analogy; and third, that following the demise of the Somoza dynasty, the Carter administration decided to attempt to "co-opt" the new Nicaraguan government into pursuing a moderate path largely because it believed that the hostile policies of the United States toward the early Castro regime had only provided its leaders with a sound rationale for radicalization.

This last point is quite important, for it is similar to the ones presented by Cole Blasier and Robert Pastor. Blasier depicts the Carter administration as an organization caught in a quandary. On the one hand, its members hoped to promote human rights; on the other hand, they feared to back unequivocally the Sandinistas. By temporizing, the Carter administration failed to achieve what it really wanted – the establishment of a moderate regime in Nicaragua. And yet, when the Sandinistas came to power, the Carter administration decided to take a gamble. Hoping to avert the further radicalization of the new regime, US foreign policy-makers rationalized that the most effective strategy for fulfilling this objective would be to engage in a policy of accommodation. This rationale, adds Blasier, was derived analogically. Foreign policy-makers at the State Department in 1979 were determined to ensure that the United States not commit the same mistakes made in 1959 and 1960, when major economic sanctions were imposed against the Castro regime. The negative effect brought about by those sanctions persuaded many US officials that it was important not to narrow Nicaragua's choices, driving its leaders to establish close ties with Cuba and the Soviet Union (Blasier, 1985: 291).

Not even the most superficial perusal of the literature on US intervention against Nicaragua could fail to consider what is likely to become one of the most detailed and intellectually stimulating analyses of the foreign policies of the United States toward Nicaragua under the Carter and Reagan administrations, Robert Pastor's *Condemned to Repetition*. Pastor's book is an intellectual rarity. Students of foreign policy are quite dependent on practitioners who, upon having completed their governmental tour of duty, decide to share their experiences as public officials. The readers of these accounts almost always gain new insights into historical events. But too often these works are dampened by the writers' need to absolve themselves of blame for actions with costly outcomes. This need is not ingrained in Pastor's book. Having served under an administration – the Carter administration – that has been accused of losing Nicaragua to the communists, Pastor is particularly careful to ensure that his analysis does not become a self-serving attempt to exonerate himself or other US officials of miscalculations and ineffective policies.

Pastor agrees with LeoGrande that the foreign policies of the United States toward Nicaragua under the Carter administration went through several stages, and he agrees with Blasier that the "United States had not 'pushed' Castro to the left, but that the tough response to Castro's decision to gain control of Cuba's politics and economy had accelerated its revolution and hardened its anti-Yankee posture" (Pastor, 1987a: 192). But Pastor adds a broad range of new insights. For instance, he notes that Carter and his two most important foreign policy advisors, Cyrus Vance and Zbigniew Brzezinski, rarely had time to keep a close watch on developments in Nicaragua: most of the critical decisions were made by lower-ranking officials who too often disagreed with one another. Pastor also explains that although analogical reasoning generally dominated the decision-making process, the involved parties did not always share a common perspective on what cases to assess to derive analogies. In addition, Pastor captures a reality that is too often overlooked by many analysts: decision-makers do not always agree on what lessons to derive from past cases. He contends that members of the Carter administration were often at odds with one another, largely because of their failure to agree on what lessons to infer from the same event. Discrepancy in interpretations within the same adminis-tration regarding the significance of a particular occurrence can lead to immobility or to the formulation of incongruous foreign policies. But the implication can be measurably different when the same phenomenon disting-uishes one administration from another. The relevance of this variance is placed by Pastor in its proper context when he quotes President Ronald Reagan's assertion that "the Caribbean is rapidly becoming a Communist lake in what should be an American pond and the United States resembles a giant, afraid to move." Pastor then contends that Carter and Reagan learned different lessons from the Cuban revolution:

> Whereas Carter believed that the best way to prevent Nicaragua from becoming another Cuba was to avoid confronting the new revolutionary regime, Reagan had learned the opposite lesson. Reagan felt that the United States must not give Nicaragua time to consolidate its revolution. The time to confront a radical regime was the beginning. (1987a: 231)

Robert Pastor's words reach deep into this study's interrelated theoretical objectives. His statement helps strengthen the contention that to understand foreign policy-making it is imperative to move beyond the reaches of strategic and economic interests, and to focus, instead, on how leaders define and respond to problems. Moreover, the contention, having been postulated by an individual with first-hand experience in foreign policy-making, further prom-otes this study's basic axiom: international problems, and foreign policies designed to address them, are structured analogically.

In sum, the conclusions reached in this chapter regarding the Nicaraguan case do not differ markedly from those advanced by Pastor. However, the present analysis is more precise than Pastor's in linking analogies to past cases and presenting them as general representations of a historical process that extends beyond the Cuban case. In addition, as already explained, one of this chapter's central objectives is to present a comparative perspective between US responses to Nicaragua and its responses to Grenada. The analysis of the two cases is guided by the following questions:

1 Why did the Carter administration initially decide to pressure the Somoza regime to promote human rights in Nicaragua?

2 Why was the Carter administration initially unwilling to pressure Somoza to resign, even though it believed that his continued rule was the overwhelming obstacle to the creation of a center-oriented government capable of successfully counteracting the Sandinistas' drive for power in Nicaragua?

3 Why did the Carter administration, some six weeks after the Gairy regime had been toppled in Grenada, choose not to pursue a policy of co-optation toward the new leaders, the Bishop regime?

4 Why did the Carter administration, after it became obvious that the Sandinistas would succeed in their drive for power, choose not to intervene militarily but instead choose to try to persuade Sandinista leaders to integrate members of Nicaragua's political center into their future government? And why did it attempt to persuade the Sandinistas to avoid dismantling fully the National Guard?

5 Why did the Carter administration wait only a few weeks after the Somoza regime had been toppled in Nicaragua, to pursue a policy of co-optation toward the new leaders, the Sandinista regime?

6 Why did the Carter administration continue to adhere to a policy of co-optation toward the Sandinista regime, even though its leaders had repeatedly expressed hostility toward the United States and a determination to establish closer relationships with Cuba and the Soviet Union?

7 Why did the Reagan administration, as soon as it came to power, begin to apply economic, political, and military pressure against the Bishop regime in Grenada and the Sandinista regime in Nicaragua?

8 Why did the Reagan administration, a few days after Maurice Bishop had been assassinated and his regime replaced by a military council, launch a full military invasion against Grenada?

9 Why did the Reagan administration decide not to launch a full military invasion against Nicaragua to topple the Sandinista regime, even though Nicaragua's potential capability to threaten the security and economic interests of the United States was much greater than Grenada's?

TALES OF TWO REGIMES

By the end of 1976, Nicaragua, which had been ruled by the Somoza family for some forty years, found itself facing an uncertain future. This situation was not unfamiliar to the people of Nicaragua; throughout the nineteenth century sharp economic and political cleavages had resulted in repeated armed clashes. Most notorious was the intervention in the 1850s by Central American conservatives who were attempting to oust William Walker, an American filibusterer who had been invited to Nicaragua by the liberals to fight the landed elite.

The ousting of this interloper was followed by some forty years of rule by the landed elite. During this time, Nicaragua developed its coffee industry and began to create government and public service infrastructures. The relative tranquility, however, would once again be threatened by the winds of change as the nineteenth century came to an end. The seeds of the new future were planted by José Santos Zelaya, a liberal elected as Nicaragua's new president in 1893 (Booth, 1984: 47).

After almost ten years of rule, during which time he accelerated Nicaragua's political and economic development, Zelaya dared to challenge North America's awakening giant. In 1903, following the decision by the United States to build a transisthmian canal through Panama rather than through Nicaragua, President Zelaya proposed to Germany and Japan that they build a waterway in his country. Washington, unhappy with Zelaya's decision, began to search for a public excuse to destroy his power. The opportunity came in 1909, when the conservatives, led by Emiliano Chamorro and Juan Estrada, started a revolution. The United States, under William Taft's administration, supported the revolution, claiming that Zelaya's continued rule was keeping "Central America in tension and turmoil" (LaFeber, 1983: 47). The conservative forces gained control of the government by mid-1910.

Elation in Washington was short-lived. After failing to keep Juan Estrada in power, the United States was unable to avert a revolution against his successor, Adolfo Díaz, who had transferred to New York bankers the ownership of Nicaragua's National Bank and 51 percent of its railroads in order to obtain a $10 million loan. President Taft ordered 2,600 US Marines to intervene in the revolution.

The United States's intervention ensured Díaz five years of rule. US military presence, however, continued until the early 1930s. But US military and economic presence did not bring tranquility. In 1927, the liberals, backed by Mexico and led by General Augusto César Sandino, launched a revolt that lasted some six years. Washington, realizing that its image had been badly tarnished by its tendency to intervene militarily whenever its will in the Caribbean Basin was challenged, and recognizing that its military presence in Nicaragua had become too costly, withdrew its troops in 1933.

This action did not signify that Washington was surrendering control; it merely reflected a change in tactics. Prior to bringing its troops home, Washington had helped form the Nicaraguan National Guard, under the leadership of Anastasio Somoza García. Both actions proved to be far-reaching.

First, hostilities came to an end almost immediately; second, Sandino, whose central goal had been to expel the United States and help end hostilities, was assassinated in 1934; and finally, Somoza took over the reins of government in 1936, with the full support of Nicaragua's upper class. This last action proved to be the beginning of the Somoza dynasty.

Somoza Garcia ruled until he was assassinated in 1956. His oldest son, Luis, replaced him in the presidential palace in 1957, while Anastasio, Jr ("Tachito"), controlled the National Guard. In 1963, René Schick became president after Luis had decided that it would be politically wise to obey the constitutional requirement that the office not be occupied by the same person for more than one term. The move was merely a symbolic gesture. Tachito remained commander of the National Guard, and the Somoza family continued to dominate the economic and political arenas. Ownership of land and industry became further concentrated during the 1960s, with the Somozas sitting at the top. Moreover, the political arena was fully dominated by the Liberal National- ist Party, which remained under the control of one Somoza or another.

Political and economic repression did not go unopposed. Between 1959 and 1961, a wave of armed challenges to the Somoza government broke out. The National Guard had little difficulty in crushing the rebellion, but it could not destroy the commitment of some of the rebels to end the Somoza rule. In 1961, veteran leftists from a variety of backgrounds formed the National Sandinista Liberation Front (FSLN).

The threat posed by this new organization remained low. In 1964 the Central Intelligence Agency concluded that the FSLN did not create "a serious threat to the government" (LaFeber, 1983: 163). But the challenge was not tied ideologically just to the left. Although the sounds of strain in the right had remained almost inaudible during the early 1960s, in 1966 they gained momentum. By then economic progress had virtually come to a halt, the balance of payments had worsened, and unemployment had increased. Elec- tions were scheduled for 1966, and the opposition united behind the candidacy of the conservative leader Fernando Agüero. With editorial support from the newspaper *La Prensa*, owned by Pedro Joaquín Chamorro, Agüero promised land reforms and a more equitable political and social structure.

Agüero and Chamorro were too weak to defeat Tachito and the support he received from the United States. But this new victory did not reduce the opposition; it merely subdued its sound until a new opportunity arose. The opportunity came in the form of a natural disaster. In December 1972, a major earthquake hit Managua, killing some 10,000 people and destroying homes, commercial businesses, and small industries. The United States responded immediately by sending $32 million for reconstruction. But this rescue operation did not bring about the hoped-for recovery. Mismanagement and corruption, along with the increase in the price of energy which resulted from the 1973 OPEC oil embargo, provoked popular mobilization. In addition, in 1974 the Somoza regime began to face something it assumed had been successfully suppressed: hostile armed opposition.

Although the guerrilla activities by the FSLN had not been a match for Somoza's National Guard, on occasion they were quite effective in capturing world attention. On December 27, 1974, for instance, the FSLN, led by Juan José Quezada, occupied the home of José-María Castillo Quandt during a cocktail party that he was giving in honor of the US ambassador, Turner B. Shelton. After overpowering the guests and their guards, the commando group demanded, among other things, the release of all political prisoners, $5 million, and the immediate and complete publication of a communique. Somoza acquiesced to the Sandinistas' demands in spite of opposition from hardliners within the National Guard.

By 1976, however, it had become quite evident that the greatest threat to the Somoza regime was not the Sandinista guerrilla activities. As reported by the US Defense Intelligence Agency, "at this time, no insurgent group poses a serious threat to the existing government" (Schoultz, 1987: 39). Rather, the ability of the Somoza regime to govern was being undermined principally by Nicaragua's political moderates, who in unison with the Catholic Church had been active in drawing attention to the human rights violations committed by the government and in calling for the creation of a political system that would promote "freedom, justice, and equality" (Diederich, 1981: 125).

As events were unfolding in Nicaragua's domestic political arena, a new group of leaders arrived in Washington. The most remarkable characteristic of this new administration was the commitment of its leader to making human rights a pivotal focus of his foreign policy. In his inaugural address in January 1977, President Jimmy Carter introduced into the realm of international affairs a dimension rarely voiced by his predecessors when he stated, "Our moral sense dictates a clear-cut preference for those societies who share with us an abiding respect for individual human rights" (*Vital Speeches*, 1977: 258). For President Carter, the promotion of human rights had to lie at the core of US foreign policy, not just because it was the moral thing to do but also because it was a policy strategy that would effectively further the interests of the United States. As he wrote some years later, "Our country has been strongest and most effective when morality and a commitment to freedom and democracy had been the most clearly emphasized in foreign policy" (Carter, 1982: 142).

Carter's perception was shared by several of his political appointees to the State Department. Many of these officials believed that right-wing regimes, because of their need to rely on brute force to remain in power, tended to mobilize and radicalize their domestic adversaries. Continued support of these regimes would, in the long run, pose a security threat to the United States, for they eventually would collapse and the populace would recall with bitterness that the United States had sided with the tyrants (Moreno, 1987: 228; Pastor, 1987a: 50). Patricia Derian, who was appointed to the State Department's Human Rights Bureau, expressed this viewpoint very clearly[2] when she observed that:

> One of our obligations as a government is to have a long range view of what our obligations are, and what our foreign policy interests are. In such an equation you cannot discount human rights, for if you're aiming for peace and stability, strong democracies make for stable government and strong democracies tend not to make war. Since one of the long-term interests of the United States, from

administration to administration, is a stable and peaceful world, it follows that it is not in our long-term interests to be on the side of dictators. (Quoted in Moreno, 1987: 228–9)

Derian's attitude was not unique among the political appointees to the State Department's Latin American Bureau. Many of them were quite convinced that "traditional right-wing regimes could no longer sustain themselves and the US must accommodate and ally itself with these forces of global change" (Moreno, 1987: 229).[3]

As the Carter administration came to office with its declared policy of respect for human rights, expectations for a change in US foreign policy *vis-à-vis* Nicaragua were heightened almost immediately. On March 24, 1977, the assistant secretary of state for security assistance, Lucy Benson, testified before the Senate Foreign Relations Committee that a cut in military aid to the Nicaraguan government would not pose a risk to the security interests of the United States. Less than a month later, Charles Bray, deputy assistant secretary of state for inter-American affairs, pledged to a congressional subcommittee that the Carter administration would not sign a security aid pact with the Somoza regime unless it improved the human rights situation in Nicaragua.

Charles Bray's pledge, however, did not carry much weight. On July 28, Somoza was stricken with a heart attack while taking a shower at his mistress's villa. The Carter administration helped arrange for his treatment at the Miami Heart Institute in Florida. While Somoza was undergoing treatment in Miami, the new US ambassador to Nicaragua, Mauricio Solaun, arrived in Managua. Solaun quickly made contacts with Nicaraguans across most of the political and economic spectrum. The new ambassador, however, had not arrived with orders to help bring to an end the Somoza dynasty. To begin with, Carter's assistant secretary of state for inter-American affairs, Terrence Todman, was opposed to the idea of putting pressure on the Somoza regime. His central concern was that the United States be very careful, because controlling the consequences that ensue from the application of political pressure is not always possible. As he would state a few months later: "We must avoid assuming that we can deal with one issue [human rights] in isolation without considering the consequences for other aspects of our relationship" (quoted in Muravchik, 1986: 37). In addition, the feeling among certain US officials in Washington was that it might be feasible to create a center-oriented political system, so long as it included members of Somoza's National Liberal Party. The intent, in other words, was to create a 'somocista system' without Somoza (Christian, 1985: 44).

More importantly, the Carter administration had other concerns in mind. President Carter was determined to bring the Panama Canal issue to a successful conclusion, and he recognized that in order to achieve this objective he would have to acquiesce to some of the demands made by Somoza's staunchest allies in Congress. Thus, on September 19, a few months after the House of Representatives and the Senate had voted against not signing a security aid pact with the Somoza regime, President Carter approved a $2.5 million arms credit to Nicaragua. This action did not signal that his administration was willing to extend *carte blanche* to the Somoza regime, but that it had adopted a "wait and see" approach regarding economic assistance in order to assess the seriousness of Somoza's commitment to open up Nicaragua's political system (*New York Times*, October 30, 1977).

October 1977 proved to be of great importance to several political groups opposing the Somoza regime. On the thirteenth, the Terceristas, one of the three factions of the FSLN, launched three small-scale military offensives against military posts in San Carlos, Masaya, and Ocotal (Pastor, 1987a: 57). In some ways the value of the attack resembled that of the Castro forces' successful operation against the La Plata military post in early January 1957. As explained by Ernesto Guevara, the defeat of Batista's soldiers had helped erase some of the differences and antagonisms that had existed between the urban people and the peasants, and had drawn attention to the role the guerrilla forces were playing in challenging the Batista regime. The 1977 attack, as explained by Humberto Ortega, brought the war from the mountains to the cities; it established the popular component of the insurrection. This was not the only parallel between the two guerrilla movements. Just as Fidel Castro had announced in his July 2, 1957, manifesto that the intent of the revolution was to form a democratic government, the Sandinistas voiced their commitment to hold "the first free elections in Nicaragua's history" (quoted in Diederich, 1981: 147). In addition, the Sandinistas, by stating that "no money or weapons from the Castro regime" had been received since 1970, sought to dispel any lingering fears that the Cubans might back their revolution (Pastor, 1987a: 57).

A few days after the guerrilla attacks, a group of twelve prominent Nicaraguans met in Costa Rica to issue *El Documento de Los Doce*. The document praised the political maturity of the Sandinistas and made it very clear that any political solution to the existing problem would have to include active involvement of the Sandinistas (Diederich, 1981: 148). Most members of the group were unaware that its formation had been the brainchild of the Terceristas and that it had been created to persuade the Nicaraguan moderates to take the Sandinistas seriously (Pastor, 1987a: 58).

In sum, although by the end of 1977 the situation in Nicaragua was beginning to crystallize, the Carter administration remained reluctant to act more decisively against the Nicaraguan dictator. The reason must be partly attributed to the unwillingness by top foreign policy officials to consider Nicaragua important enough for their extended attention (Vaky, 1987; see also Christian, 1985: 44). But there was another important factor. By the end of 1977, officials at the State Department were still divided over how to respond to Somoza's intransigent behavior. Assistant Secretary of State Todman, convinced that Somoza had the resources to survive the domestic turmoil he faced, argued that the United States should not attempt to undermine his power. Officials in the Human Rights Bureau, on the other hand, favored a strict implementation of Carter's human rights policy by increasing policial, economic, and military pressure on Somoza (Christian, 1985: 45). Part of the reason the division in the State Department had created immobility was that President Carter had not formulated a foreign policy specifically designed to address the

Nicaraguan problem; instead, he had created "human rights policies that applied to Nicaragua" (Pastor, 1987a: 52).

A question that requires consideration at this juncture is: why did Carter and his top foreign policy advisors choose not to spend more of their working hours analyzing and responding to the Nicaraguan problem? To address this question it will be helpful to compare the way the Carter administration viewed the situation in Nicaragua with the way the Eisenhower and Kennedy administrations responded to threats posed to dictatorial regimes. There is little question that the success of the Cuban revolution in 1959 had persuaded members of the Eisenhower and Kennedy administrations that unless they acted decisively against right-wing dictators, these dictators would experience a fate similar to Batista's; Castro's role would be repeated by some yet-unknown revolutionaries; and the strategic interests of the United States would suffer.

This inferential process was not conducted in the second half of the 1970s for two interrelated reasons. First, few members of the Carter administration feared in 1977 that Somoza might be toppled by a revolution of the left. And second, Carter assumed the office of the presidency convinced that the United States had to alter its tendency to react to every challenge to its interests as an action propelled by the Soviet Union. This perception was directly related to how he viewed US relations with dictatorial regimes. As he stated during his commencement address in 1977 at the University of Notre Dame: "Being confident of our own future, we are now free of that inordinate fear of communism which once led us to embrace any dictator who joined us in that fear" (quoted in Schoultz, 1987: 138).

Carter's statement reflects two facts. On the one hand, it indicates that he was not ignorant of actions by past administrations toward dictatorial regimes, regardless of how undifferentiated his perception might have been. On the other hand, it shows how the new president wanted to revise the way in which problems were defined. Eisenhower, Kennedy, and Nixon had each concluded that by siding with dictatorial regimes, Washington had been providing communists with the justification they needed to ferment further antagonism against the United States. For Carter, however, the world was much more complex. It was a world in which hostility against the United States often surfaced without communist influence and without the ability or desire of the Soviet Union or one of its close allies to affect its outcome (Muravchik, 1986: 53–7; Schoultz, 1987: 137–9).

Somoza suffered a substantial political setback on January 10, 1978. For US officials it was a day that moved Nicaragua "a little closer to the front burner" (Vaky, 1987). On that morning, Pedro Joaquín Chamorro, the editor of the opposition newspaper *La Prensa* and one of the foremost leaders of the moderate opposition to the Somoza regime, was assassinated in Managua. Chamorro's death was followed by an outbreak of spontaneous demonstrations and general strikes, all aimed at weakening the Somoza regime (Diederich, 1981: 155; Christian, 1985: 46–7). Nicaraguan businessmen approached Ambassador Solaun and requested that he pressure Somoza to resign. Further, should the Nicaraguan dictator refuse, they wanted Solaun to ask the National

Guard to mount a *coup d'état* (Diederich, 1981: 165). Knowing that he lacked the authority to fulfill such a request, Solaun refused. Instead, Washington responded by condemning Chamorro's assassination and asking Somoza to initiate negotiations with his adversaries. This decision fell short of the Bureau of Inter-American Affairs's suggestion that the United States act as a direct mediator between Somoza and his Nicaraguan political adversaries (Pastor, 1987a: 63).

The Carter administration's decision to limit its involvement did not signify an unwillingness to exert pressure on Somoza to enter into a dialogue with his opponents. Determined to signal its displeasure with the state of Nicaragua's domestic affairs, on February 10 the Carter administration suspended military aid to the Somoza regime (*New York Times*, February 11, 1978). This action was followed by a statement designed to indicate to Somoza that the United States would respond positively to political improvements in Nicaragua. While assessing the situation in Nicaragua for a February 16, 1978, hearing before the House Subcommittee on International Organizations, Deputy Assistant Secretary of State Sally Shelton stated that "although problems remain, it is our opinion that marked progress [in human rights] has been manifested since early 1977" (*New York Times*, June 27, 1978). Somoza responded quickly to Washington's stick and carrot strategy; on February 27 he announced that he would step aside in 1981, after the presidential elections in late 1980 (Christian, 1985: 50–1).

On March 28 President Carter, accompanied by Secretary of State Cyrus Vance and National Security Advisor Zbigniew Brzezinski, arrived in Caracas for an official visit with Venezuela's president, Carlos Andreas Perez. The Venezuelan president, angered by the death of his friend Chamorro, pressured Carter to intervene more forcefully against Somoza. Perez made it clear that he advocated the immediate departure of Somoza and the establishment of a government that represented all the major political factions in the country, including Somoza's National Liberal Party. Perez kept referring to the Cuban analogy by noting that the threat posed to Somoza by the Sandinistas was very similar to the threat Castro had posed to Batista (Pastor, 1987a: 64). Perez's request for more direct intervention by the United States was rejected by Carter. The president did not believe it was appropriate for the United States to help topple Somoza (1987a: 65). From Brzezinski's perspective, Nicaragua had yet to become an important issue for the United States, for it did not have a significant effect on the fate of East–West relations (Vaky, 1987).

In early April 1978 a major change took place in the Latin American foreign policy-making structure of the Carter administration. Deputy Secretary of State Warren Christopher, unhappy with a speech given by Todman in February that was indirectly critical of Carter's human rights policy, appointed Todman as the new US ambassador to Spain. Christopher then filled the position of assistant secretary of state for inter-American affairs with Viron Vaky, who at that time was serving as US ambassador to Venezuela (Muravchik, 1986: 37–8). The change in personnel was not felt immediately, but it would have asignificant effect by the end of 1978.

By May 1978, one of Somoza's friends in the US Congress, Representative

Charles Wilson, threatened to use his influence in the House Appropriations Committee to hold the entire Foreign Assistance Bill hostage unless the aid embargo on Nicaragua was released. The Carter administration responded by releasing a $12 million package in economic aid, but it decided to withhold further military aid (*Washington Post*, May 16, 1978). Somoza, realizing that he could not gamble away the respite his regime had just received, announced on June 19 a series of liberalizations which included amnesty for political prisoners, a promise to reestablish the electoral system, and an invitation to the Human Rights Commission of the Organization of American States and Amnesty International to conduct on-the-spot investigations in Nicaragua.

In late June 1978, the Carter administration took a somewhat unorthodox step in its dealings with the Somoza regime. Believing that one way to press a political leader to engage in additional reforms is to praise him for his past accomplishments, President Carter asked Brzezinski to draft a letter to Somoza congratulating him on his latest reforms in Nicaragua and encouraging him to continue the process. Brzezinski transferred the responsibility to the NSC Latin American affairs specialist, Robert Pastor. Pastor wrote the letter, which was then reviewed by the Latin American and the Human Rights bureaus at the State Department and by Secretary of State Vance. The two bureaus suggested that the letter not be sent. Patricia Derian, for instance, was convinced that the letter "would be used for propaganda purposes and it would be interpreted by Somoza and by other observers as ringing support" (quoted in Moreno, 1987: 247). However, lacking strong representation at the top, the two bureaus were overruled by Vance.[4]

It is not difficult to explain why President Carter might have believed that the letter was a good idea. The president, as noted by Viron Vaky, "did not understand dictators. He did not know that the last thing dictators will give up willingly is power" (Vaky, 1987). The problem lies in explaining why Vance, a seasoned diplomat, did not point out to the president that the letter would provide Somoza with an extraordinary opportunity to advance his own cause. One reason could be that the secretary of state had already found himself at odds with Carter and Brzezinski on too many occasions and was not convinced that the Nicaraguan issue was important enough to justify his making a strong stand (Vaky, 1987).

This decision proved to be an embarrassment. Somoza, realizing that he had just been given a great opportunity to draw criticism away from his policies, used it during a meeting with President Perez of Venezuela to claim that he enjoyed the support of the president of the United States. It was not long before the contents of the letter reached the American press (Pastor, 1987a: 69).[5]

Somoza's troubles, however, continued to mount. As part of his latest reforms, the members of Los Doce were allowed to return to Nicaragua. At the end of July, shortly after their arrival, the Los Doce group joined forces with the opposition political parties and two labor unions to form the Broad Opposition Front (FAO). On August 21, after overcoming internal disagreements, the FAO announced a sixteen-point program calling for, among other things, Somoza's resignation, the establishment of a government of national unity, the scheduling of elections for December 1981, and the reorganization of the

National Guard and the judicial system (Christian, 1985: 59–60). In the meantime, the three members of the FSLN – the Terceristas, the Tendencia Proletaria, and the GPP (Guerra Popular Prolongada) – afraid of losing out to the growing momentum and power of the non-violent opposition, agreed to unite with the Nicaraguan Socialist Party to form the United People's Movement. The agreement was reached with the recognition that important ideological and strategic differences still remained (Diederich, 1981: 168). The FSLN commitment to capture the limelight was taken a step further on August 22 when Eden Pastora, leading twenty-four members of the Tercerista group, seized the National Palace and took 1,500 captives, including most of the members of the Nicaraguan Congress. Two days later the Somoza regime released fifty political prisoners, made a payment of half a million dollars, published an FSLN communique, and gave safe passage out of Nicaragua to the guerrillas and the released political prisoners (Christian, 1985: 64–5).

The attack on the National Palace ignited a major response on the part of Viron Vaky. On August 29, the assistant secretary of state for inter-American affairs called for an inter-agency meeting to address Nicaragua's political crisis. At the meeting, Vaky insisted that the situation in Nicaragua was getting out of hand; he argued that the United States must pressure Somoza to resign, then assemble a coalition government to replace him. Vaky was convinced that the political problem was not that Nicaragua lacked a political center – such a center existed – but that there was no consensus among the members of the center as to what would be the most appropriate alternative to Somoza. The role of the United States would be to shape a consensus (Vaky, 1987). Failure by the United States to take the initiative, warned Vaky, "would lead to a repetition of the Cuban crisis of 1957–58" (Pastor, 1987a: 79). Pastor and the director of policy planning at the State Department, Anthony Lake, shared Vaky's concern but rejected his recommendation. They were using a different set of lenses to look at history. Their central contention was that many of the current problems faced by the United States stemmed from past willingness to intervene in the domestic affairs of Latin American states (1987a: 79). Finally, at another meeting held on September 4, Vaky gave in and agreed reluctantly to support a mediation effort led by Costa Rica and other Central American states.

September brought a series of FSLN-organized, small-scale attacks on National Guard garrisons in several cities. Five cities fell temporarily under Sandinista control. During the following three weeks, the National Guard launched major offensives to regain control. Washington, shocked by the bloodshed, called for "discussions for a peaceful and [a] democratic solution" (LeoGrande, 1979: 67). More importantly, the ensuing violence pressured the Carter administration to call for another meeting, to be held on September 12. After reviewing some of the alternatives available to the United States, Warren Christopher suggested that only two alternatives made sense: (i) call for mediation with Central America states at the lead, or (ii) call for mediation with the United States at the lead. Christopher, still believing that the United States should try very hard not to be seen as an actor attempting to impose its will on weaker parties, sided with the first alternative. Vaky, on the other hand, was convinced that, much as Central American leaders might want to assume responsibility for the mediation efforts, they lacked the power to guide the negotiating parties. Vaky used this rationale to propose that the second alternative be chosen. Vaky once again was overruled, and the first option was approved. In addition, it was agreed that Ambassador William Jorden be sent to several countries in the area to persuade their leaders to participate in or support the mediation efforts. These latest efforts were to no avail. Finally, President Carter, although still unwilling to compromise his belief that "the age of US unilateralism was past," agreed that his administration should become involved as an active party in the mediation efforts.

Jorden met with Somoza on September 23, and made it clear to the Nicaraguan leader that unless he accepted the mediation unconditionally, his relations with the United States would suffer a great setback (Pastor, 1987a: 91). Somoza accepted the mediation terms two days later. The United States, Guatemala, and the Dominican Republic became the mediators. The mediating team met in Guatemala during the first week of October to delineate a strategy. Prior to this time – between September 23 and 29, to be specific – Ambassador Jorden had tried to persuade Somoza to resign. But at no time did Jorden pressure Somoza to relinquish power. The ambassador emphasized that if it was the Sandinistas who were posing the greatest threat, it would not be difficult to control them. The problem was that general discontent could easily result in domestic chaos which could be exploited by Castro and the communists (Christian, 1985: 71). Somoza was not willing to retire yet.

The negotiations began in earnest on October 6, 1978. On that day the international team and representatives of the FAO agreed that the latter would not meet face-to-face with Somoza. It was believed that if such meetings were held, the deep animosity between Somoza and the FAO would prevent an agreement. The FAO was represented by Alfonso Robelo, a wealthy cooking oil manufacturer who was a moderate and an anticommunist; Rafael Cordova Rivas, a lawyer and a long-time critic of Somoza; and Sergio Ramírez Mercado, a university professor and a member of Los Doce. Ramírez was also the unofficial representative of the Tercerista faction (Diederich, 1981: 207).

William Bowdler, the head of the US delegation, took the initiative by submitting a plan. He proposed the creation of an interim government that would be composed of members of Somoza's National Liberal Party and the FAO. This government, with the aid of the National Guard, would prepare Nicaragua for elections in 1981. On October 25, the FAO, minus the representative of Los Doce, submitted its negotiating position, which was a near replica of the proposal submitted by Bowdler. The FAO called for Somoza to resign and leave power to a government of national unity composed of a council of state and a three-man junta. A constitutional assembly would lay a plan for elections to be held in December 1981; the National Guard would be reorganized but not disbanded; and Somoza's National Liberal Party would be allowed to participate in the next elections. Sergio Ramírez, the Los Doce representative, rejected the proposal and withdrew from the negotiations. For Ramírez, allowing the National Guard to remain as part of the post-Somoza era and the National Liberal Party to participate in the forthcoming elections indicated that the United States and the FAO had no intention of destroying

Somoza's political structure (*Washington Post*, November 14, 1978; Diederich, 1981: 208–9; Christian, 1985).

As the mediators presented Somoza with the FAO proposal, in a parallel move the Carter administration pressured the IMF to postpone the release of a $20 million line of credit (Christian, 1985: 74). Somoza, however, would not acquiesce without a struggle. On November 6 he announced that he planned to serve his term until it expired in 1981, but he proposed a plebiscite designed to measure each of the political parties' relative popularity. The winner of the plebiscite would then be asked to become part of the Somoza regime (1985: 74–5). Reactions to Somoza's plebiscite were heard immediately. US Congressmen John Murphy and Charles Wilson flew to Managua on November 17 to express their support for Somoza (Diederich, 1981: 213). The FAO, on the other hand, called Somoza's proposal "completely absurd," and indicated that it would withdraw from the negotiating process by November 21 unless a more serious response was formulated (Christian, 1985: 75).

The US government found itself divided again over how to deal with Somoza. Bowdler, who had returned to Washington on November 21, and Assistant Secretary of State Vaky argued that the United States should force Somoza out of office and immediately assist the moderates before further polarization occurred. The two US officials believed that with the right amount of pressure Somoza would agree to leave. Otherwise, the moderate opposition would continue to erode and the Sandinistas' influence and popularity would grow. Robert Pastor agreed with Bowdler's and Vaky's premise, but not with the alternative they proposed. He thought that it was time for the United States to pull out of the business of toppling governments, regardless of the circumstances. This view was shared by several of his colleagues at the White House. As Pastor noted:

> We felt that the US should not intervene militarily or even politically in the sense of promoting the overthrow of Somoza. The Carter Administration constrained itself by its belief that it was inappropriate for the US in the future, in part because it's been so usual in the past, to overthrow governments. On the other hand, we felt assistance, whether economic or military, whether bilateral or multilateral, were appropriate instruments to influence developments. (Quoted in Moreno, 1987: 244)

As an alternative, Pastor proposed that the United States adhere to the idea of a plebiscite; but rather than voting on the popularity of the parties, Nicaraguans would vote on whether they wanted Somoza to remain in power. If the people supported Somoza, then the National Liberal Party's program of reform would be put into action; if, on the other hand, the vote went against Somoza, he would resign and the FAO plan would be put into effect. Carter, along with Vance and Christopher, sided with Pastor, and on November 12 the mediating team issued the counterproposal. After some hesitation the FAO accepted the plan under the condition that Somoza leave the country during the plebiscite. The FAO also announced that "since there was nothing more to talk about," it was walking out of the talks (Diederich, 1981: 214; Christian, 1985: 77–8).

On November 28 the mediating team resubmitted the "Washington plan" to Somoza and the FAO and gave both parties seventy-two hours to make a decision. Otherwise, the team would consider its mission failed and would return home. The FAO reiterated its latest position. Two days later, Somoza announced that he accepted the revised version of the plebiscite; but he added that if he lost, rather than hand over the government to the FAO, he would call for a constitutional convention. In addition, he made it very clear that he would not leave the country during the period the plebiscite was held (1981: 220; 1985: 78).

Between the time Somoza announced his acceptance of the revised version of the plebiscite and December 20, the negotiations remained at an impasse. During this period, Congressman Charles Wilson threatened to link support to the Somoza regime to ratification of the Panama Canal treaty and accused the Carter administration of encouraging communism in Central America (Diederich, 1981: 225). For his part, Somoza granted amnesty to all civilian and military persons convicted of political actions since March 1967 and announced an end to martial law.

While the FAO, Somoza, and the mediating team were battling at the negotiating tables, the Sandinistas concluded that if they hoped to succeed in the struggle for power, they would have to consolidate their forces and strategies. On December 9, the leaders of the three factions of the Sandinista Front announced that they had agreed to merge their forces, both politically and militarily. It is widely believed that Fidel Castro made military assistance conditional on the unification of the three groups (Diederich, 1981: 221; Christian, 1985: 82; Pastor, 1987a: 109).

Agreement among the Sandinistas was not counteracted by agreement between Somoza and the FAO. On December 20 the mediating team submitted another proposal, stipulating that if Somoza won the plebiscite he would reorganize the government as he saw fit, while the FAO would remain in "peaceful opposition." On the other hand, if the Nicaraguan president lost, he would leave the country and be replaced by an interim president elected by the Congress. New elections would then be held on May 1, two weeks after the passage of constitutional reforms (Christian, 1985: 81). The Carter administration, in the meantime, was still unwilling to coerce Somoza. The day after the revised proposal was submitted, Lieutenant General Dennis McAuliffe, commander of the US Southern Command in Panama, flew to Managua to try to convince Somoza to be more cooperative with the mediating team. McAuliffe went so far as to tell Somoza that peace would not come to Nicaragua until he had removed himself "from the presidency and the scene" (quoted in Christian, 1985: 82). At no time, however, did McAuliffe threaten Somoza with retaliation if he chose to reject this advice.

Somoza was not intimidated. He rejected the mediating team's new proposal and on December 27 submitted to William Bowdler his own new counterproposal. One of the issues that the FAO and Somoza had been debating was the monitoring of the plebiscite. The FAO, convinced that it would not be enough to have outside observers monitoring the referendum to ensure impartiality, demanded that outsiders actively supervise the process. Somoza, in his new counterproposal, discarded the idea and instead proposed full national supervision. Moreover, rather than have an interim government appointed by the Congress replace him if he lost, Somoza proposed the creation of a constitutional assembly (Christian, 1985: 83).

The mediating team met once again with Somoza on January 12, 1979, and proposed that the plebiscite be controlled by Somoza but supervised by an international team. For the first time, the Carter administration went beyond acting as a mediator and advisor. After the meeting, the State Department said that Ambassador Bowdler had warned Somoza that if he did not accept the new proposal, the United States would have to reassess its relations with Nicaragua (Pastor, 1987a: 114). By now Somoza was immune to this type of threat. The Nicaraguan dictator was convinced that the pressure was coming not from the United States, where he believed he had extensive support, but from the Carter administration. He ignored the warning and rejected the mediating team's latest proposal.

The negotiating team, convinced that Somoza had no intention of compromising, concluded that it was time to bring its efforts to an end. Bowdler, still believing that unless a compromise was reached the violence in Nicaragua would affect "the peace and tranquility of the whole of Central America," returned to Washington for consultation (Christian, 1985: 83). Christopher convened a meeting on January 26 to decide what steps to take next. A consensus to impose sanctions against Somoza surfaced almost immediately. The debate then switched to whether the sanctions should be military and political only or should also involve economic sanctions. The participants all agreed that, for the time being, economic sanctions ought to be excluded (Pastor, 1987a: 116). On February 8, the State Department announced that the United States was withdrawing its military mission and all Peace Corp volunteers from Nicaragua, that it would stop considering new AID projects, and that it would reduce its diplomatic staff in Managua.

The failure of the mediation efforts signaled the end of a distinct phase in the conflict in Nicaragua. Many of Nicaragua's political moderates concluded that there was no room for a peaceful settlement and that they now must either join the Sandinista forces or reconcile with the Somoza regime. These same individuals concluded that the United States was at fault for not having exerted pressure on Somoza. Needless to say, the Sandinistas were the central beneficiaries of the failure to mediate an agreement between the FAO and Somoza. Cognizant of this new reality, the three FSLN factions announced in Havana in mid-March 1979 the creation of a nine-man directorate made up of the three top men from the Terceristas, the Proletariats, and the Guerra Popular Prolongada (Christian, 1985: 89). A few weeks later, on April 7, the Sandinistas launched a major guerrilla offensive by moving into Esteli, near the Honduran border, and into the towns of Ocotal, El Sauce, Condega, León, and Chinandega (1985: 93).

It is not uncommon for students who have focused on the Carter administration's handling of the Somoza regime in 1978 to argue that US officials were unable to design the right policies partly because their analyses were guided by inaccurate perceptions and attitudes. Since it is rarely feasible to ascertain objectively what types of perceptions and attitudes ought to guide the designing of a particular policy, it is more useful to suggest that part of the Carter administration's problem was that its analysts were divided by two competing outlooks regarding what historical lessons ought to be applied to the problem at hand. Many of those who accompanied Carter to Washington shared his belief that it was morally unsound for the United States to intervene in the domestic affairs of other states and that these actions had undermined its reputation. Vietnam was in the minds of many of these analysts. Brzezinski, who had very little use for the Vietnam analogy, writes that since the pre-inaugural day, State Department officials "focused on such peripheral issues as relations with Vietnam" (1988: 197). And he adds that he "could never quite understand [this] from a policy standpoint, but [it] perhaps may be better explained by the psychologically searing impact of the Vietnam war tragedy" (p. 228). But it was President Carter who finally captured the significance of Vietnam to him and some of his foreign policy advisors when he stated:

> For too many years we've been willing to adopt the flawed and erroneous principles and tactics of our adversaries, sometimes abandoning our own values for theirs. We've fought fire with fire, never thinking that fire is better quenched with water. This approach failed, with Vietnam the best example of its intellectual and moral poverty. (Quoted in Schoultz, 1987: 138)

This view was challenged by US officials who believed that under certain circumstances it was imperative for the United States to intervene. Viron Vaky, for instance, recognized that the United States could ill afford to act unilaterally and to use its raw military power to effect a change in Nicaragua's leadership. But his extensive involvement in Latin American affairs had taught him that at times the only way the United States could preempt the ascension to power of a radical regime was by removing the existing government and replacing it with a more moderate leadership. He believed that although Latin American leaders would much rather solve their problems without US involvement, these same leaders were realistic enough to recognize that in some instances Washington was the only actor with sufficient power and authority to take the lead in pressuring an unpopular leader to relinquish his authority, and the only actor strong enough to bring together a coalition of moderates to assume the reins of government. For Vaky, the critical point was to ensure that the United States not be perceived as acting unilaterally (Vaky, 1987).

These two conflicting views dominated much of the debate in 1978 about how the Carter administration should respond to Nicaragua's evolving domestic crisis. But this was not the sole reason the Carter administration found itself facing a major crisis in Nicaragua in 1979. For much of 1978, the principal officials responsible for the foreign policies of the United States continued to pay little attention to developments in Nicaragua. Carter, Brzezinski, and Vance had, for the most part, focused their energies on convincing the US Congress to ratify the Panama Canal Treaty and on creating the negotiating structure that would eventually culminate in the Camp David agreement. These officials, moreover, were drawn to other important matters well into the middle of 1979, when they traveled to Vienna for a summit meeting with Soviet president

Leonid Brezhnev, and then to Japan for a summit meeting with the leaders of the industrialized democracies (Pastor, 1987a: 137).

Just as the Carter administration was beginning to deal with the idea that it might not be able to solve the problems in Nicaragua in a way that would serve the interests of the United States, a new problem arose on the Caribbean horizon. On March 13, 1979, President Carter learned that the government of Grenada had just been toppled by an armed attack involving forty members of the People's Revolutionary Party. The attack was led by Hudson Austin, a leader of the New Jewel Movement.

Grenada's political arena had been dominated since 1951 – the year Great Britain introduced universal suffrage to the island – by one individual: Eric Gairy. A crude and charismatic leader, Gairy began his political career by championing the rights of Grenada's rural workers (Pearson, 1987: 4). As his power increased, Gairy followed two parallel paths. Determined to gain Grenada's independence from Great Britain, he sought to alleviate British concerns by supporting the idea of gradual decolonization. At the same time, he tried to suppress domestic opposition by using the police powers of his regime. Gairy's despotic behavior, however, did not go unopposed.

In 1973, three small political groups, critical of Gairy's regime and aware that independently they would not be able to forestall his continuing abuse of state patronage, formed the New Jewel Movement. The New Jewel Movement, although uncompromisingly socialist in its early days, had not been a Marxist movement (Thorndike, 1985: 43). But as it became more and more evident that a more structured organization would be needed to combat Gairy, the NJM began to affirm its Marxist nature. In the middle of 1974, the leaders of the New Jewel Movement confirmed that it was strictly a vanguard party, reduced the size of the party's Political Bureau by excluding those whose commitment was believed to be questionable, and began to establish village-based support groups (1985: 49). This commitment to organization paid off in the December 7, 1976, elections, when the New Jewel Movement, in coalition with two other parties, captured six of the fifteen seats in the Legislative Assembly (Pastor, 1985: 10).

The elections in Grenada took place just as Carter and his foreign policy advisors were deeply involved in delineating a new international course for the United States. The administration-in-waiting concluded that the Caribbean region should be approached with a North–South rather than an East–West focus. One of the first steps taken by the Carter administration to promote economic development in the Caribbean was to help create the Caribbean Group for Cooperation in Economic Development. The group, chaired by the World Bank and composed of thirty-one nations and fifteen international institutions, sought to move away from the past practice of providing assistance to each small nation on a bilateral basis, which many believed exacerbated the region's dependence. Instead, the group promoted regional projects (Pastor, 1985: 11–12).

The Carter administration plan did not alter Grenada's domestic political battles, which reached a climax on March 13, 1979. Eric Gairy had left the previous day, ostensibly to attend a United Nations Conference on the

International Year of the Child in New York. Gairy's main purpose, however, was to try to persuade the UN's secretary general to authorize a UN investigation of UFOs (Thorndike, 1985: 54). His departure precipitated a warning from NJM informants that he had ordered the arrest of the party's leadership. The NJM decided to preempt Gairy by launching a coup against his regime. The overthrow of the Gairy regime was completed in twelve hours, and it ended with the proclamation of Maurice Bishop as Grenada's new prime minister and Bernard Coard as minister of finance (Pearson, 1987: 6).

The coup surprised the Carter administration. The first reaction by the US State Department was to defer to the British, who had maintained some degree of control over the island until 1974. Bishop and his associates immediately recognized that their action could have some costly repercussions. To minimize the damage, they began to reassure leaders outside the island of their moderate and constitutional intentions (Pastor, 1985: 14). US Ambassador Frank Ortiz, for instance, was assured by Bishop that "US lives and property would be protected, that good relations with the United States were a basic aim of his government, and that there would be prompt and free elections of a legally constituted government" (quoted in Pastor, 1985: 14–15). Based on this meeting, Ortiz initially counseled that the United States adopt a policy of accommodation and refrain from any type of sanctions, which at that stage would be counterproductive, possibly forcing the NJM into the arms of the Cubans (Sandford and Vigilante, 1984: 51).

On March 15 a subcommittee of the National Security Council of the Carter administration met to discuss the latest developments in Grenada. The State Department advocated that the United States support Great Britain and the eastern Caribbean states in their attempts to pressure the new Grenadian regime to hold early and free elections, as it had promised. Although this policy finally received the unanimous support of all the individuals attending the meeting, the Pentagon representatives voiced the need for the United States to keep a close watch on the revolutionaries, in view of their known pro-Cuban sympathies (Pastor, 1985: 16; Thorndike, 1985: 57).

On March 22, the Carter administration finally recognized the new Grenadian government, with the warning that it expected the new regime to adhere to its word that it would reestablish constitutional norms promptly. The following day, Ambassador Ortiz arrived in Grenada to inform its leaders of the interest of the United States in maintaining cooperative relations and to describe the various aid programs channeled to Grenada through the Caribbean Development Bank. Ortiz also informed the Grenadian leaders that the US State Department would be happy to increase the number of Peace Corps volunteers on the island and could disburse grants of $5,000 for community-related projects (Pastor, 1985: 19–20).

The Bishop regime, however, was committed to setting its own agenda. On March 25, Bishop announced the suspension of the constitution and the retention of emergency arrest powers for the People's Revolutionary Army. Moreover, by the end of March he had transferred most of the military and police powers to members of the party (1985: 21). The Carter administration viewed these developments with great concern, particularly once it learned that several Cuban arms shipments had arrived in Grenada during the first nine days in April (1985: 21–2).

In an attempt to reverse the perceived leftward movement of the Bishop regime, the State Department sent Ambassador Ortiz to meet with the Grenadian leader. Although many issues were covered during the meeting, the central message delivered by the US ambassador was that the United States "would view with displeasure any tendency on the part of Grenada to develop closer ties with Cuba" (1985: 24). The message was not well received by Bishop. On April 13, in his first major speech to the country, the prime minister rejected the warning from the Carter administration by stating: "If the government of Cuba is willing to offer us assistance we would be more than happy to receive it . . . No country has the right to tell us what to do or how to run the country, or who to be friendly with" (1985: 26). The speech was followed by the announcement that Grenada had established diplomatic relations with Cuba.

The immediate effect of Bishop's speech was to bring together the NSC and the State Department to discuss the options President Carter should consider. Although some members within the Carter administration believed that the Bishop government could still be co-opted and that this objective could be brought about by extending more aid to the regime, the largest number rejected this view. The general perception was that the new Grenadian leaders had no interest in being co-opted. Moreover, it was felt that to provide bilateral aid to a radical regime could undermine democracy in the region and invite other governments to be more confrontational with the United States in the belief that such a strategy would result in the extension of more aid. These individuals proposed that the United States continue providing regional aid in an attempt to stimulate other governments in the area to pressure Grenada to implement moderate policies (Pastor, 1985: 31–2). President Carter approved the "regional strategy" at a meeting on April 27.

At first glance, this decision by the Carter administration might seem out of character. Since their early days in Washington, Carter and several of his advisors had maintained that the foreign policy of the United States toward the developing world would be driven by the idea that instability was brought about by widespread poverty, rather than by the notion that the forces of communism under the tutelage of the Soviet Union and Cuba were behind every major attempt to instigate revolutionary change. Although this idea was deeply infused in the consciousness of numerous members of the Carter administration, they understood the dangers of accepting or adopting a belief as an all-encompassing strategy. For those who advocated a regional strategy over a co-optation strategy, it was critical to differentiate between a new government that was composed entirely of officials committed to revolutionary change, and a new government whose ranks were filled by a mixture of moderate and radical leaders. Co-optation, it was believed, had a chance of succeeding only in the latter form of government. Moderate leaders would be skeptical about seeking sweeping transformations and would be more disposed to listen to advice from the United States. Clearly, there were no guarantees that in a mixed government the moderates would prevail over the radicals; but the luxury of uncertainty did not even exist in a regime that had excluded moderates from its leadership. Attempts to co-opt a radical regime would only result in the degradation in status of the party pursuing the policy, and might inspire other governments to adopt a like strategy.

The pressure on the foreign policy-making capacity of the Carter administration did not abate after the dust had settled on the Grenada case. For a while, officials were not overly concerned with the latest offensive drive by the Sandinistas. In late April, for instance, the defense attaché at the US Embassy in Nicaragua, Colonel James L. McCoy, sent a report to Washington in which he noted that it was unlikely that the Somoza regime would be able to survive much longer. He based his assessment not on the belief that the Sandinistas had the power to defeat Somoza but on the recognition that the Nicaraguan leader was being repudiated by almost all political factions (Christian, 1985: 94). Moreover, on May 2 the Central Intelligence Agency prepared a secret intelligence assessment in which it pointed out that two Cuban diplomats had informed Panamanian officials that "Cuba no longer believed that the FSLN would be able to topple Somoza before his term expires in 1982" (quoted in Pastor, 1987a: 130).[6]

In the meantime, political turmoil in Nicaragua continued to mount. FAO leaders, along with other opposition members, had been attempting to organize a general strike. On April 30, Somoza ordered the arrest of many of these leaders. Deputy Secretary of State Warren Christopher responded immediately with a major protest (Diederich, 1981: 244). In addition, in a speech delivered on May 18 at a Miami university, Patricia Derian reiterated the unhappiness of the Carter administration with the Somoza regime and its behavior throughout the mediation efforts. Derian added that after the collapse of the OAS efforts, the US had thoroughly reassessed its relationship with the current Nicaraguan regime. Two days later, President José Lopez Portillo of Mexico broke diplomatic relations with Nicaragua and urged Carter to follow the same path (Diederich, 1981: 247; Christian, 1985: 97). On the domestic front, Somoza had to cope with the beginning of another Sandinista offensive; on May 26, Humberto Ortega, commander of the Sandinista forces, called from somewhere in Costa Rica for the mobilization of all Sandinistas. Three days later, the guerrillas launched their final offensive (1981: 247; 1985: 97; Pastor, 1987a: 131–3).

The Sandinista offensive posed a dilemma for the Carter administration. The US mediation efforts had convinced most of its officials that unless the United States applied a great deal of pressure, Somoza would not relinquish control. At the same time, some officials were beginning to recognize that it might be too late to preempt the Sandinistas with a moderate government. The presence of this perception might help explain why the Carter administration supported Nicaragua's application for a $65.6 million loan from the IMF, why it pressured several Latin American leaders not to follow Mexico's lead of breaking relations with Nicaragua, and why it urged General Omar Torrijos not to allow Panama to act as an intermediary for the transportation of weapons to the Sandinista forces in Costa Rica (Christian, 1985: 95 and 99; Pastor, 1987a: 131–3).

By this time Somoza and some of his US supporters were growing desperate. On June 6 the Nicaraguan dictator imposed a ninety-day state-of-seige, giving the National Guard authority to arrest persons without warrants. That same day, Congressman John Murphy, who was the head of the House Merchant Marine and Fisheries Committee, sought to link a vote on remaining legislation on the Panama Canal Treaty to Panama's role as an intermediary in the transportation of weapons to Sandinistas based in Costa Rica (Diederich, 1981: 250–1).

A few days later, on June 11, during a meeting chaired by Warren Christopher, US decision-makers speculated that the war was at a stand-off but that Somoza would have to relinquish power before his term came to an end. By then, Brzezinski seems to have concluded that the situation in Nicaragua was critical enough for him to become more actively involved in the search for a solution. He proposed a plan whereby the United States would: (i) issue a statement calling for self-determination in Nicaragua and an end to violence; (ii) begin to explore the creation of an inter-American peace force that would move into Nicaragua immediately upon Somoza's departure; and (iii) issue clear warnings to bring the flow of arms to both sides to an end (Pastor, 1987a: 134–5). The recommendation was approved on the following day by Carter, and steps were immediately taken to seek support for the plan and advice from Latin American leaders (p. 136).

Three carefully choreographed events took place on June 17. First, a 400-man force led by Edén Pastora moved into Nicaragua to join with forces that had crossed at the end of May. In the eyes of the Sandinistas, this coordinated move was to become their "final" offensive. Second, the Sandinistas announced the creation of a provisional government to replace Somoza. The five members, some of whom were chosen to win international support, were Violeta Barrios de Chamorro, Alfonso Robelo, Daniel Ortega, Sergio Ramírez, and Moises Hassan Morales. And third, the five members of the Andean Pact – Venezuela, Colombia, Ecuador, Peru, and Bolivia – released a statement calling for the "installment of a truly representative, democratic regime" in Nicaragua and recognition of the Sandinistas as "legitimate combatants" (Diederich, 1981: 263; Christian, 1985: 101; Pastor, 1987a: 138).

These developments spurred the United States to action. On June 18, the US ambassador to Nicaragua, Lawrence Pezzullo, approached Somoza's cousin, Luis Pallais, to inform him that the United States wanted Somoza to resign in a "statesmanlike" manner after helping to arrange for a national reconstruction government that would include members from the Nationalist Liberal Party, the Conservatives, the FAO, and the FSLN (Christian, 1985: 101–2). That same day, the State Department proposed a meeting of OAS foreign ministers to address the Nicaraguan crisis. US officials began to discuss immediately the type of plan Secretary of State Vance should submit for discussion to the other foreign ministers.

Brzezinski, however, became impatient with Vance and Vaky for assuming that "some middle-of-the-road regime would somehow or other miraculously emerge in the wake of Somoza" (quoted in Moreno, 1987: 257). Brzezinski's challenge was not out of character. In 1970, in his book *Between Two Ages*,

Brzezinski had argued that the emergence of North–South issues, along with declining importance of the West–East competition, had made the continued assumption of global US hegemony in Latin America obsolete. Some years later, he advised the newly elected president, Jimmy Carter, that he saw the need not for a new anticommunist coalition but for a

> broad architectural process for an unstable world organized almost entirely on the principle of national sovereignty and yet increasingly interdependent socially and economically. In that process of widening cooperation, our relationship will have to involve varying degrees of intimacy: 1) with our closest friends in the industrial world; 2) with the emerging states; 3) with states with which we compete militarily and ideologically . . . (1983: 53–4)

And yet, once in office, the new national security advisor almost immediately began to voice "concern over Soviet expansion in the Third World," and "to disregard the importance of changes in the political, economic and social developments of the countries making up the Third World" (Moreno, 1987: 180–1). As explained by Roger Hansen, an advisor to the NSC:

> Here you have a classic example of a guy who comes into office saying we are paying too much attention to East–West issues and we must start focusing on North–South relations, who within nine months is either unable to do so or doesn't care to do so. In my mind, that raises the question about how much he really understood or cared about what we call North–South relations. The answers seem to be that he was a closet cold warrior from the very onset. (Quoted in Moreno, 1987: 181–2)

Thus, the cold warrior spirit resurfaced once again when Brzezinski argued that Vance, during his speech to the OAS, should propose the formation of an OAS force that would move into Nicaragua as soon as Somoza left the country. Vance and Vaky, believing that Latin American leaders would perceive the idea as a breakdown in the principle against intervention and reject it, tried to exclude from the speech the passage referring to the peace-keeping force. Brzezinski won the bureaucratic battle when Carter sided with him, but he lost the war. Vance delivered the speech as ordered; and as predicted by Vaky, the foreign ministers from Latin America defeated the proposal on June 23 (Vaky, 1987).

In Nicaragua, in the meantime, Somoza, upon learning of the new US proposal, expressed his willingness to resign. He informed the United States that although he resented the ultimatum, he would leave if an orderly transition under OAS auspices were organized, if he and his family would not be extradited from exile, and if they received US visas (Christian, 1985: 102). Somoza's troubles were immediately compounded by the killing in cold blood by a National Guard patrol of ABC newsman Bill Stuart, on June 20. The incident drew mass international protest, with President Carter referring to the killing as "an act of barbarism that all civilized people condemn." In addition, US senators and congressmen signed a declaration labeling Somoza "the Idi Amin of Latin America" (Diederich, 1981: 271).

The significance of the latest developments in Nicaragua was not overlooked by Brzezinski. Possibly recognizing that the Latin American leaders would not accept the idea of forming a multinational peace-keeping force, he sought to persuade Carter, Secretary of Defense Harold Brown, Vice President Walter Mondale, Vance, and one of Carter's closest advisors, Hamilton Jorden, that it was imperative, for domestic and international reasons, that the United States seriously consider intervening unilaterally. Carter rejected the idea (Pastor, 1987a: 147–8).

Time was running out, and the United States was still debating what path to follow. Aware of this reality, Carter asked Brzezinski to convene a new meeting. At a meeting held on June 25, three alternatives were discussed. The White House believed that it was critical for the United States to "establish a second pillar of power that would be independent of Somoza and could then negotiate with the Sandinista Junta" (Pastor, 1987a: 151). Some State Department officials, led by Vaky, were convinced that the only remaining realistic alternative was to accept the fact that the Sandinista Junta held the upper hand and try to persuade its leaders to broaden and moderate the composition of the future government (1987a: 137; Vaky, 1987). Christopher proposed a compromise to pursue both strategies at the same time, and a consensus soon formed to adopt this option.

On June 27, Ambassador Bowdler met with three members of the Nicaraguan provisional government and tried to persuade them to broaden the government's political base. He suggested that pro-Somoza leaders be included in the new government, with the Sandinistas still playing the central role. While Bowdler was meeting with representatives of the provisional government, Ambassador Pezzullo was trying to persuade the ranking officers of the National Guard that their only chance of survival in the post-civil war era was by helping expedite Somoza's departure (Christian, 1985: 104, 106).

The Sandinistas did not give in to the pressure. On July 8, they publicly condemned the request by the Carter administration that pro-Somoza representatives be included in the new government. Father Miguel D'Escoto, who would play a critical role in designing Nicaragua's foreign policy under the new regime, stated that "the only way to characterize this is blackmail" (Diederich, 1981: 296).

The Carter administration realized that its choices had been narrowed measurably. At a meeting held in early July, Brzezinski conceded that the United States had no choice but to give up the idea of creating a separate pole of power and concentrate on trying to influence the junta to broaden its political representation. It was also decided that a major effort should be made to persuade the junta not to fully dismantle the National Guard. Success with regard to the second negotiating point was assigned great value, for it was reasoned that the existence of a force that included members of the National Guard would help balance the Soviet and Cuban-trained forces that were part of the Sandinista army (Christian, 1985: 107).

On July 11 the junta members, during negotiations with Bowdler, refused to expand the junta but agreed to incorporate members of the National Guard into a new Nicaraguan army. The National Guard, in turn, assented to an immediate cease-fire and a return to the barracks upon Somoza's departure (Diederich, 1981: 304; Christian, 1985: 109). The following day, the junta wrote a letter to the OAS informing the organization of its decision "to convoke the Nicaraguans to the first free elections they will have in this century, so that they can elect their municipal officials and a constituent assembly, and, later, the supreme authorities of the country" (quoted in Christian, 1985: 110). Two days later the junta announced its plan to create an eighteen-person cabinet and released the names of twelve of its future members. The following day, Bowdler informed the junta that the composition of the cabinet was acceptable to the United States. On July 17, Somoza, after having named Colonel Federico Mejía director of the National Guard and chief of staff, resigned and left the country. The president of Nicaragua's Chamber of Deputies, Francisco Urcuyo, was immediately sworn in as provisional president.

The US plan to try to integrate the National Guard with the Sandinista forces began to come apart almost immediately after Somoza's resignation. Convinced that the Carter administration would not support them the moment the Sandinistas occupied Managua, members of the National Guard began to board planes to Honduras and other Latin American states. Thus, by the time the Sandinista junta and other top leaders drove into Managua on July 20, very few National Guard commanders still remained in Nicaragua.

When a problem is burdened by uncertainty, and significant differences exist about which path to take, policy choice results from the intellectual representation by the more powerful decision-makers of the critical lessons derived from history. During most of 1978, the Carter administration was divided into two camps. One camp, represented by US officials such as Warren Christopher and Robert Pastor, was determined to promote President Carter's human rights views. Moreover, they shared the belief that past US policies of intervention had undermined the reputation of the United States. In other words, convinced that they were serving the long-range interests of the United States by emphasizing the need for governments to be more respectful of their citizens' human rights, they also felt constrained from acting forcefully against regimes that were unwilling to promote human rights, for fear that such force would rekindle the image of the United States as an interventionist power.

This constraint did not permeate the perceptions of members of the second camp. Bowdler and Vaky shared with the members of the first camp the beliefs that it was critically important for the United States to promote its commitment to human rights and to erase the image, born of past actions, that it was an interventionist power. But in their minds – at least in Vaky's mind – this image had been the result not of a tendency by the United States to intervene but of a tendency to intervene militarily and unilaterally as a hegemon convinced that it need not consult and act with others. For members of the second camp, not all forms of intervention had to resemble those used against the Dominican Republic in 1965 and Chile between 1970 and 1973. They were fully convinced that with the United States at the lead, Costa Rica, Panama, and Venezuela would join forces to exert pressure on Somoza to exit from Nicaragua's political scene. Failure to act decisively against Somoza could have the same effect as that experienced by the Eisenhower administration in 1958 when it was reluctant to pressure Batista from power – the birth of a radical regime.

The battle between the two camps was consistently won by those who advocated a non-interventionist stand by the United States. Even the decision by the Carter administration that the United States become a member of the mediating team reflected the imparity in power between the two sides. This decision was arrived at reluctantly, only after it became obvious that without Washington's involvement the mediating effort by some concerned Central American leaders would fail, and only after it had been made clear that the United States would not force Somoza to resign.

When it finally became evident in 1979 that Somoza would not be able to continue controlling the reins of government much longer, a new issue divided the two groups. Vaky, sensing that the Sandinistas had gained the upper hand in Nicaragua's internal political battle, proposed that the United States pressure the Sandinista leaders to make room for moderates in any future government that would replace Somoza. But this had not been Vaky's preferred alternative. During the latter half of 1978, the assistant secretary of state for inter-American affairs had been promoting the idea of forcing Somoza from power in order to preempt the Sandinistas with a moderate political government (Pastor, 1987a: 97). By June 1979, however, Vaky had concluded that the latest show of military and political power by the Sandinistas had, for all practical purposes, nullified the viability of his original policy. His new hope was that with moderates ruling along with the Sandinistas, the United States would still be able to retain some degree of influence on Nicaragua's new government. Vaky's proposed policy was not discarded in its entirety. Christopher, believing that it might still be feasible to preempt the Sandinistas with the creation of a moderate government, proposed that the Carter administration pursue both objectives concurrently.

Christopher's plan was short-lived. Upon realizing that Vaky was indeed correct in estimating that it was too late to put together a coalition of moderates, the Carter administration sought to persuade the Sandinistas to broaden the ideological spectrum of the regime that would replace Somoza and not to fully dismantle the National Guard. The decision to try to avoid the full dismantling of the National Guard was rooted in an important historical precedent. In 1959, one of the first steps taken by Fidel Castro, following his victorious entrance into Havana, was to replace Batista's armed forces in its entirety with a military force committed to the defense and advancement of the revolution. Just as Castro had learned from Arbenz's experience in Guatemala some five years earlier that without the backing of the military a revolutionary regime has little chance of succeeding, the United States government learned from its experience in 1961 that it is nearly impossible to overturn a revolutionary regime that has the full backing of the military. Or, as stated by Robert Pastor, "the key issue after Somoza left would be who had the guns" (1987a: 156).

One last comment is in order as to why the Carter administration tried to convince the Sandinista leaders to incorporate Nicaraguan moderates into the new government. The rationale behind that decision had the same intellectual roots as did the decision in April 1979 to adopt a regional strategy toward the new ruling regime in Grenada. At that time, the Carter administration had convinced itself that there was little it could do to co-opt the Bishop regime to contour both its domestic and foreign policies along a moderate path. The most the leaders in Washington could aspire to was to ensure that other Caribbean states would not be tempted to duplicate Grenada's experience, and to guarantee that the Soviet Union and Cuba would not be seduced by the idea that they could use the Bishop regime to advance their own interests. In the minds of many US officials, the situation in Nicaragua was still in a state of flux. Although it was evident that the Sandinistas would play a very important role in whatever new government was formed after the demise of the Somoza regime, it was believed that they were not sufficiently powerful to refuse to work with some of Nicaragua's moderate leaders. These moderate leaders, the Carter administration hoped, would be instrumental in advancing domestic changes that corresponded with US views, while blocking attempts by the Sandinistas to foster the creation of a radical domestic structure.

The one central figure in the Carter administration who was not fully convinced that co-optation was the best alternative was Brzezinski. He felt that history should have taught the United States that the Sandinistas were likely to prevail after Somoza's departure and that the Carter administration might therefore have to resort to other alternatives: a multinational intervention in Nicaragua, preferably, or unilateral intervention as a measure of last resort. Brzezinski's rationale was in large measure guided by the firm belief that the 1965 intervention in the Dominican Republic had served the interests of the United States and was viewed positively by most Latin American leaders (Pastor, 1987a: 165). However, Brzezinski's interpretation of history did not carry the day.

The co-optation strategy of the Carter administration began on July 24, 1979, with the State Department announcing its formal recognition of the new government of Nicaragua. Four days later, Ambassador Pezzullo arrived in Managua on a transport plane loaded with food and medicine; other similar flights followed in the next few weeks. The overall strategy had three objectives. Its first objective was to help the revolution fulfill its original promises of promoting political pluralism and creating the structure for the development of a strong private sector. It was hoped that fulfillment of this objective would reduce the chances of the revolution becoming communist. The second objective was to deny the Sandinistas a reason for turning for help to the Cubans and Soviets. And the third objective was to signal to the new government in Nicaragua that good relations with the United States were contingent on the former's willingness not to interfere in the internal affairs of other Central American states (Pastor, 1987a: 194).

Nicaragua's new government was not impressed by President Carter's policy of co-optation and acted promptly to signal its determination to follow its own path. On July 26, Alfonso Robelo and Humberto Ortega traveled to Cuba, where they were treated as honored guests. Robelo, a moderate member of the junta, praised Castro and noted that there would be a special place for Cuba in Nicaragua's international policies (*Latin American Political Report*, August 3, 1979: 234). Castro responded by comparing Nicaragua's revolution with

Cuba's own struggle twenty years earlier, noting that the two were quite different in that the FSLN had had to compromise with different political factions in order to succeed, while he did not. On the following day, the two countries renewed full diplomatic relations (Christian, 1985: 137).

In the domestic arena, the FSLN wasted little time in setting its political agenda. In late July, the FSLN set three priorities for Nicaragua: economic reconstruction, mass organizing, and the creation of an army. Responsibility for the first task was left in the hands of the junta, while the second two were to be administered directly by the FSLN. It came as no surprise, therefore, when on July 28 the Sandinistas announced the creation of a "general command" that excluded Bernardino Larios, a former member of the National Guard, who had been named defense minister under the new post-Somoza regime. Instead, the members of the new command were Tomas Borge, from the "prolonged war" faction, Humberto Ortega, from the "Tercerista" faction, and Luis Carrion Cruz, from the "Proletarian" faction (Christian, 1985: 122–3). One of the first steps of the new command was to request weapons from the United States, with the warning that if conditions were attached to their provision, Nicaragua would turn to Europe, then to the socialist countries if the Europeans refused to cooperate. The extent to which the creation of the new command and the request for new weapons were influenced by Castro's own behavior in 1959 cannot be ascertained, because there is a lack of firm empirical evidence. On the other hand, it is quite doubtful that the new Nicaraguan regime was unaware that the same strategy had been implemented some twenty years earlier by Castro's regime.

In early August, the new Nicaraguan regime took two important steps. The FSLN created a network of mass organizations. The most important were the Sandinista defense committees, created for the purpose of setting up the "eyes, ears, and voice" of the revolution from the block level – through neighborhood councils, districts, and regions – to the national level. At the same time, the Junta of Reconstruction announced the nationalization of banks and foreign trade (Christian, 1985: 123–5).

By this time, a debate had begun within the Carter administration between the State Department and the White House on the one hand, and the Defense Department and the Central Intelligence Agency on the other hand. The Defense Department and the CIA contended that a clear military cordon needed to be established around Nicaragua to prevent the spread of Cuban and Soviet influence in Central America. The State Department – Cyrus Vance to be specific – countered that there was no evidence of any substantial increase in the Soviet military presence in Cuba over the past several years or of the presence of a Soviet military base (*Latin American Political Report*, August 10, 1979: 244). Thus, rather than restoring military aid to El Salvador and Guatemala, the White House and State Department proposed establishing good relations with Nicaragua's new regime and allowing events to unfold. Robert Pastor explained the rationale as follows:

> We weren't surprised when after the Sandinistas came in that they took so many anti-American steps. But we didn't believe that the game was over by a long shot!

We didn't believe that the entire leadership was Marxist–Leninist or even that those that considered themselves Marxist–Leninist were incapable of evolving within the most conducive climate. Thus, we thought that the policy that made the most sense for the United States was one which creates a climate that encourages those whose minds were not yet frozen to realize that to succeed in meeting the needs of their people ... they needed to reach an accommodation with the US. To have this relationship with the US they would have to dispense with their reflexive anti-Americanism and moderate their behavior. (Quoted in Moreno, 1987: 268)

The White House prevailed, and at the end of August the State Department began to consider submitting to Congress for approval the figure of $75 million in aid to Nicaragua.

In the meantime, the FSLN continued to maneuver very carefully. Just as members within the Carter administration were debating whether to extend aid to Nicaragua, Tomas Borge, in an attempt to ease some of the fears of Washington leaders concerning the intentions of the Nicaraguan regime, commented that "Revolutions ... cannot be exported. We believe we have helped these enough by carrying out our own revolution, by showing it is possible to fight and win. But we will not send any of our fighters..." (Christian, 1985: 145). The FSLN, however, had no intention of altering its ultimate goals. All along it recognized that its chances of survival depended on how successful it was in maintaining its alliance of convenience with the non-Marxist groups in Nicaragua. Its leaders believed that so long as they maintained a working relationship with the moderates, the United States would not consider intervening, and Western financial assistance would flow to Nicaragua. In other words, it was critical not to move too quickly or too radically in making changes (Christian, 1985: 129).

And yet, during this time the Sandinistas continued to make moves that did not endear them to Washington. In October and November, for instance, insurance and mining companies were nationalized. Moreover, while delivering a speech to the United Nations Assembly in New York, Daniel Ortega voiced several pro-Soviet, anti-US, and anti-Chinese statements. These actions were coupled with an announcement in early November that the creation of the Council of State – the thirty-three-member, quasi-legislative body proposed in the Plan of government – would be delayed until May of the following year. COSEP, Nicaragua's private sector umbrella group, concerned about the direction of the new government, voiced its unhappiness on November 14 and demanded certain guarantees.

Developments in Nicaragua placed the Carter administration in a difficult position. As noted by Vaky, most of its decision-makers assumed that the Sandinistas wanted to create a Cuban model in Nicaragua, but they also believed that the authority of the radicals could be undermined by helping the moderates augment their own power. To achieve this objective, it was important to provide economic aid to Nicaragua (Vaky, 1987). With this idea in mind, the State Department requested Congressional approval for $75 million in economic aid for Nicaragua. At the same time, however, the Carter administration concluded that it would not be wise to assume, as suggested by Tomas Borge, that Nicaragua had no intention of exporting revolution. To protect against this possibility, the Carter administration began to increase the military strength of El Salvador, Honduras, and Guatemala by supplying high performance aircraft to their governments. Of the three states, Honduras was perceived as being the keystone of US "bridgebuilding" in Central America.

The decision by the Carter administration to provide economic aid to a regime that had professed very little enthusiasm for the United States was structured, once again, on a very peculiar interpretation of history. On September 11, 1979, Viron Vaky argued before a House subcommittee that "While it is true that Marxist elements are well-positioned to exert power, they do not yet dominate the situation. Moderate democratic elements capable of exerting influence and power of their own also exist in key places in the Government and in society" (Pastor, 1987a: 208).

In a sense, Vaky, Pezzullo, Pastor, and other members of the Carter administration were placing the Cuban analogy used by previous administrations on its head. Richard Nixon had believed that the way to prevent a Latin American state from becoming another "Cuba" was by not giving the new radical regime time to consolidate its power. This was the policy he adopted toward Allende in Chile in the early 1970s and that would be resuscitated in the early 1980s by the Reagan administration. In 1979, however, the basic form of thinking was that although the "United States had not 'pushed' Castro to the left, ... the tough response to Castro's decision to gain control of Cuba's politics and economy had accelerated its revolution and hardened its anti-Yankee posture" (Pastor, 1987a: 193). Avoiding the same mistake required ignoring the nationalistic anti-US rhetoric of the new Nicaraguan government and trying to influence it by providing economic aid. In the long run, this type of policy would, it was hoped, undermine the political power of the most radical elements of the FSLN while encouraging the more moderate ones to advocate pragmatic accommodations with the United States (Moreno, 1987: 263–4, n. 42).

Between December 1979 and the end of May 1980, two new related scenarios unfolded – the first in Nicaragua, the second in Washington. Beginning in December, the FSLN started to take overt steps to consolidate its power and express its allegiance to the Soviet bloc. The first step taken was to appoint Humberto Ortega as Nicaragua's new defense minister, replacing Bernardino Larios, who had been appointed to that position to appease the Carter administration. In addition to Ortega's appointment, Henry Ruiz, a member of the GPP, was named minister of planning (Christian, 1985: 135). Some two months later, on February 26, Cuba announced that it was extending $50 million in economic aid to Nicaragua (*Latin American Weekly Report* [*LAWR*], March 7, 1980: 2–3).

There was an important rationale for making the announcement on that particular date. On January 29, 1980, the US Senate approved by a vote of 55 to 38 the Nicaraguan aid package requested by the Carter administration (*LAWR*, March 7, 1980: 26). And on February 25, a day before Cuba's announcement, the US House of Representatives gave its own stamp of approval to the aid package but by a margin of only five votes and with strict amendments. The amendments stipulated that aid be cut if Cuban or Soviet influence appeared to be on the rise or if it were revealed that Nicaragua was backing guerrilla activities in other countries of the area (*LAWR*, March 7, 1980: 3; Pastor, 1987a: 210). The passage of the economic bill was followed by the approval of $3.98 million in military aid to Honduras and El Salvador in early March (*NACLA*, 1985: 28).

Throughout March and April the FSLN continued to gain dominance in Nicaragua's political arena. On April 16, exactly a month after reaching a party-to-party agreement with the Soviet Communist Party, the FSLN submitted to the Junta of Reconstruction a proposal calling for an increase in the size of the Council of State to forty-seven members and a reapportionment of the seats in such a manner that the FSLN would be assured an absolute majority. Alfonso Robelo and Violeta Barrios de Chamorro, two of the members of the Junta of Reconstruction, opposed the proposal, contending that the FSLN had originally agreed not to be the sole ruling force in Nicaragua (Christian, 1985: 148). Three days after the proposal had been submitted, Mrs Chamorro resigned without mentioning the dispute. On April 22 Robelo followed in her footsteps, noting that since Somoza's overthrow "substantive changes have been imposed in our Plan of Government without the indispensable consensus, and steps have been taken that deviate from the aims of our revolution" (Christian, 1985: 149–50).

The resignations of Chamorro and Robelo incited strong reactions. In late April, Ambassador Pezzullo warned the FSLN that if the Junta were not reconstituted as originally created, the Carter administration would not disburse the $75 million in economic aid that had been targeted for Nicaragua. In addition, on May 1, COSEP leaders demanded that Chamorro and Robelo be replaced by two non-Marxists, that the Council of State be kept at its initial, intended size, and that a timetable for elections be set. A compromise between COSEP and the FSLN was reached on May 3 whereby the Council of State would be increased to the size wanted by the Sandinistas, and July 19 would be the date the timetable for elections would be announced (Christian, 1985: 155–7).

These latest developments in Nicaragua forced the Speaker of the US House of Representatives, Thomas O'Neill, to withdraw the economic aid package from the floor. O'Neill noted that Managua could expect aid only if the vacant posts on the ruling junta were filled by politically moderate figures (*LAWR*, May 23, 1980: 5).

The FSLN, presumably realizing that it could not afford to alienate the United States so rapidly, agreed to appoint as new junta members Arturo Cruz, a former president of Nicaragua's Central Bank, and Rafael Cordova Ruiz, a former justice of the Supreme Court. In early June, Arturo Cruz and Foreign Minister Miguel d'Escato visited Washington, hoping to persuade the leaders of the United States that the Junta was in favor of US involvement in the Nicaraguan reconstruction effort (*LAWR*, June 3, 1980: 2–3). These latest developments led the new assistant secretary of state for inter-American affairs, William Bowdler, to argue before the US Congress that "despite some contrary trends, Nicaragua remains a largely open society." and that US aid was crucial for maintaining democracy in Central America (Moreno, 1987: 272).

The US Congress, however, was not in any rush to reinstate the economic package. The Congressional delays frustrated the State Department, particularly Ambassador Pezzullo, who felt that the Cubans were winning the battle for the hearts and minds of the Nicaraguans. This viewpoint was expressed with great impatience by Secretary of State Cyrus Vance when he commented that:

> Those who are most concerned about the potential for radical revolution in Latin America and growing Cuban influence in the region should be the strongest supporters of efforts to help Nicaragua build a better future . . . Cuba's position in Nicaragua has only been strengthened by the delay. (Quoted in Moreno, 1987: 273–4)

The relationship between the United States and Nicaragua failed to improve through the remainder of 1980. President Carter, recognizing that presidential candidate Ronald Reagan had been successful at making economic assistance to Nicaragua a major campaign issue, decided to postpone the signing of the aid package. Disbursement of the funds was delayed until after a consortium of banks had successfully renegotiated Nicaragua's foreign debt in mid-September (*LAWR*, September 19, 1980: 12). By this time, however, the Carter administration was entering its political twilight. In early November the election of Ronald Reagan to the presidency signaled a dramatic shift in the foreign policy of the United States toward Nicaragua.

In January 1981, just as Carter was getting ready to relinquish his presidential authority, his administration acknowledged that it had compelling evidence that "Cuba, Vietnam, and the Soviet Union had begun channeling massive arms shipments into El Salvador via Nicaragua" (Moreno, 1987: 275). This type of evidence simply reinforced the commitment of the Reagan administration to structure differently the US policies toward Grenada and Nicaragua. From their first days in power, the leaders of the new administration made clear their belief that the immediate cause of political violence and unrest resided in the Soviet commitment to world domination and not, as assumed by the Carter administration, in the quest for equality by the people of the developing world. These new leaders believed that their predecessors had erred in not realizing that unless Washington firmly signaled its determination to respond to the Soviet challenge, Moscow would perceive the United States as a weak rival and would attempt to extend itself "beyond the natural limits of its own apparent interests and influence" (Haig, 1984: 26). To reaffirm its worldwide credibility, therefore, the United States first had to resolve the political crisis in its own backyard – Central America. President Reagan expressed this view very clearly when he stated:

> If Central America were to fall, what would the consequences be for our position in Asia and Europe and for alliances such as NATO? If the US cannot respond to threats near our border, why should Europeans or Asians believe we are seriously concerned about threats to them? If the Soviets can assume that nothing short of an actual attack on the US will provoke an American response, which ally, which friend will trust us then? (Quoted in Moreno, 1987: 325)

Accompanying Reagan into his new administration were several prominent critics of Carter's foreign policy toward Latin America. Roger Fontaine, General Gordon Summers, and Lewis Tambs, all of whom were appointed to the new administration, had participated in writing *The Report of the Committee of Santa Fe*. One of the report's central arguments was that the Soviets would use Central America as a platform to undermine US interests in the rest of Latin America. The report went on to propose that Carter's human rights policy be

> abandoned and replaced by a non-interventionist policy of political and ethical realism . . . [The human rights policy] has cost the United States friends and allies and lost us influence . . . The reality of the situations confronted by Latin American governments that are under attack . . . must be understood not just as a threat to some alleged oligarchy, but as a threat to the security interests of the United States. (Quoted in Pastor, 1987b: 362)

An equally critical analysis of the Carter administration was presented by Jeane Kirkpatrick, who would eventually become Reagan's UN ambassador. Carter's central mistake, noted Kirkpatrick, was in not realizing that most developing countries lack strong political and social structures capable of supporting the peaceful transformation from dictatorship to democracy. Thus, when an external party such as the United States weakens the power of the dictatorship, each faction seeks to become the dominant power by using whatever means it has at its disposal. It is under these conditions that the

> guerrilla enters, as well as groups trained by Cuba and linked to the plans and alliance of the Soviet Union. These forces use terrorism to destroy order, disorganize the economy and daily life, and demoralize the police and governments by demonstrating the latter's inability to protect personal political authority. With the arrival of the concept of terrorism as a form of revolution, the advent of the revolution need no longer await the masses. (Kirkpatrick, 1981: 130–1)

Guided by these beliefs, the Reagan administration came to power determined to pressure the political regimes of Grenada and Nicaragua to alter their domestic and international behavior. One of the first steps taken by the Reagan administration against the Bishop regime was to refuse to accredit its ambassador. Cognizant that diplomatic pressure would not by itself alter the structure of Grenada's political regime, the Reagan administration also resorted to economic and military pressure. In March 1981, a State Department official traveled to Brussels to convince members of the European community to stop providing economic aid to Grenada, because it was helping perpetuate communism in the region. In addition, a few months later, the Reagan administration warned the Caribbean Development Bank that unless it excluded Grenada from the countries receiving aid for domestic programs, the United States would cut its support to the institution. The Bank's Caribbean member states took a united, strong stand against the United States's threat, and their reaction led the Reagan administration to carry out its warning (Pastor, 1985: 38–9).

These economic measures were accompanied by a major military signal. In July the Senate Intelligence Committee rejected a Reagan administration proposal to launch a covert intelligence operation against Grenada. The following month, however, the United States coordinated the largest naval maneuver in the Caribbean since the Second World War. As part of the overall maneuver, the United States engaged in an operation code-named "Amber and the Amberines" – a direct allusion to Grenada and the Grenadines – involving the amphibious landing on Vieques, an island belonging to Puerto Rico (Hopple and Gilley, 1985: 61). If the action had any effect on the Bishop regime, it was only to fuel its determination to establish closer relations with the Soviet Union and Cuba. In December, Grenada's minister of national mobilization, Selwyn Strachan, announced that his government was granting Cuba and the Soviet Union full access to the international airport being built on the island. Strachan, in addition, acknowledged that the airport would be used by Cuba to fly troops to Angola (Germain, 1985: 154).

In Nicaragua, the litmus test of the revolutionary government's willingness not to undermine the interests of the United States in the Central American region would be its restraint in supporting the rebels in El Salvador. As explained by Secretary of State Alexander Haig: "our most important objective is to stop the large flow of arms through Nicaragua into El Salvador. We consider what is happening as part of the global communist campaign coordinated by Havana and Moscow to support the Marxist guerrillas in El Salvador" (*New York Times*, February 21, 1981). With this objective in mind, the Reagan administration immediately suspended $15 million of the $75 million in aid to Nicaragua until it could certify that the Sandinistas were not helping the guerrillas in El Salvador (Christian, 1985: 194). This action was followed, under Haig's recommendation, by the suspension of $10 million in PL-480 wheat credit.

About this time, US intelligence indicated that the shipment of weapons from Nicaragua to El Salvador had diminished considerably. The significance of this development was interpreted in two contrasting ways. For some State Department officials, particularly Ambassador Pezzullo, and the new head of the Latin American Bureau, Thomas Enders, the slowdown seemed to signal that the Sandinistas would not want to confront the United States and would be willing to negotiate. Haig, on the other hand, was convinced that the slowdown in the arms traffic resulted from a decrease in need for new weapons on the part of the Salvadoran guerrillas. Moreover, Haig argued that, since coming to power, the Sandinistas had been engaging in an unprecedented military buildup which was altering the balance of power in Central America (Moreno, 1987: 343–4). As noted by a senior White House official, "Nicaragua was on the verge of becoming a super power in Central American terms" (*New York Times*, December 3, 1981).

It took very little time for the FSLN to recognize that the election of Reagan as the new political leader of the United States had resulted in the quantum amplification of Nicaragua's problem, particularly on the economic front. Thus, in an attempt to moderate the actions of the United States, the Nicaraguan government in March appointed Arturo Cruz as its new ambassador to the United States. Cruz, a well-known and respected figure in banking circles, had served as a member of the Junta of Reconstruction and had acted as the symbol of understanding between the young revolutionaries and the private business sector, which controlled almost 60 percent of Nicaragua's productive capacity. The hope in Managua was that Cruz would be able to influence the foreign creditors not to alter the terms of Nicaragua's large foreign debt (*LAWR*, March 13, 1981: 1).

Managua, however, was not convinced that it would be able to appease the Reagan administration; nor was it willing to compromise its goals to the extent hoped by the colossus of the North. Afraid that Washington would attempt to strangle Nicaragua's economy and that this action would exacerbate internal tensions, the FSLN on March 31 called for all political and social groups to join in a "patriotic dialogue" (*LAWR*, April 1, 1981: 1). In addition, in June, Humberto Ortega declared that Marxism–Leninism was to be the guide of the Nicaraguan revolution (Christian, 1985: 196).

The Reagan administration, in the meantime, continued to exert economic and political pressure on Nicaragua. In early April, US officials ordered the cut of an $11 million loan for rural education and health; and at the end of the same month, they ordered the suspension of all aid, including an end to Export–Import Bank guarantees to finance US exports to Nicaragua (Maxfield and Stahler-Sholk, 1985: 258). At the start of the following month, the United States threatened to ban the import quota for Nicaraguan beef (*LAWR*, May 15, 1981: 16). And at the beginning of July, the US ambassador to El Salvador, Deane Hinton, accused the FSLN of providing weapons to the Salvadoran guerrillas and recommended that more arms and aid be extended to the Salvadoran military (*LAWR*, July 17, 1981: 3).

Hinton's recommendation reflected, in some ways, the distinct attitudes of the Carter and Reagan administrations toward using military aid as an instrument of US policy. For the most part, officials in the Carter administration had been inclined to reason that military aid, instead of contributing to stability, provoked instability by strengthening the power of the central actor in the Third World that opposed fundamental change – the military. This perception stood in stark contrast to the view of Reagan officials, who were convinced that military aid and force were valuable instruments for bringing about stability in Central America (Moreno, 1987: 363).

Although consensus existed in the Reagan administration regarding the effectiveness of military aid and force as an instrument of US policy, there was significant disagreement with respect to the role the US military should play. To a large degree, the variance in perceptions could be attributed to the lessons the competing parties believed should be derived from the US experience in the Vietnam War.

The leading figures of the two competing factions were Secretary of State Alexander Haig and Secretary of Defense Caspar Weinberger. Haig was convinced that the main reason Vietnam proved to be a major fiasco was the lack of commitment among the leaders in Washington to the use of the military resources necessary to succeed. This weakness of American will, believed Haig, had measurably undermined US credibility and had seduced the Soviet Union to extend itself "beyond the natural limits of its own apparent interests and influence" (Haig, 1984: 27). To regain US credibility, it was imperative that the leaders in Washington convey their willingness to use force in no uncertain terms when critical interests were at stake. In Haig's eyes, therefore, the situation in Central America called for active US military involvement. Haig brought this argument to the surface when he warned the US Congress that Nicaragua was threatening the interests of the United States and that the use of force by the United States to deal with the problem could not be ruled out (Haig, 1984: 129; Moreno, 1987: 364).

Weinberger was not convinced by Haig's reasoning. He might have agreed that the United States was outmaneuvered by North Vietnam because the leaders in Washington were not committed to an aggressive military policy. Weinberger, however, believed that the absence of this commitment was due to a lack of consensus. Thus, one of the critical lessons that had to be inferred from the Vietnam experience was that objectives must be defined by the president and the US Congress, with the support of the US public. Weinberger feared that, given the high degree of congressional and public opposition to direct US military involvement in El Salvador and Nicaragua, US money would be wasted in an unmanageable tropical war (Moreno, 1987: 364–5; see also Pastor, 1987b: 365–6).

Despite these differences, the Reagan administration was determined to provide military aid to allies of the United States in Central America to "arrest the spread of communism." The two major recipients of US military sales and aid were Honduras and El Salvador. Between 1950 and 1979, Honduras received $27.8 million and El Salvador $16 million in US military sales and aid; between 1980 and 1983, these figures increased to $95.1 million and $230.9 million, respectively (Moreno, 1987: 362).

The United States continued to apply pressure on Nicaragua throughout the remainder of 1981. On August 11, Thomas Enders arrived in Managua and submitted to the Nicaraguan leaders a proposal designed to break the impasse the two states had reached. In exchange for economic assistance and a promise that the United States would not help the exiles seeking to overthrow the Sandinista regime, Enders demanded that Nicaragua withdraw from arms-trafficking to El Salvador, cease its own arms buildup, open the political system, and temper its association with Cuba and the Soviet bloc in general (*LAWR*, August 21, 1981: 2–3; see also Pastor, 1987b: 365–6). To ensure that the Sandinistas fully understood that the United States was determined to act as strongly as was necessary to alter Nicaragua's behavior, the Reagan administration ordered AID, in mid-September, to suspend credit for $7 million targeted for reconstruction work (*LAWR*, September 25, 1981: 12). More importantly, during October 7 through 9, the United States, Honduras, and other Caribbean Basin states held joint military maneuvers off the Caribbean coast of eastern Honduras. Although these maneuvers were part of a yearly joint activity, their execution was designed to signal that the United States was in a position to intervene militarily if the FSLN did not acquiesce to the demands made by Enders during his visit to Managua in August (*LAWR*, October 9, 1981: 2). The FSLN was not intimidated by these United States actions. While the joint maneuvers were being held, the Nicaraguan leaders called for volunteers to patrol the Honduran border. More importantly, they rejected Enders's proposal, calling it a "sterile" attempt (United States Department of State, 1985: 23).

Between November and December 1981, the Reagan administration con-cluded that it would be necessary to take steps beyond applying economic pressure if it hoped to alter the policies of the FSLN. After having organized the necessary votes in the International Development Bank to block a $30 million fishery loan, the Reagan administration began to contemplate seriously the feasibility of engaging in extensive covert military intervention. On November 16, the National Security Council, pressed by Secretary of State Haig, proposed the implementation of a large-scale program to deal with opposition to US policies in the Caribbean Basin. The program included an increase in subversive activities inside Nicaragua, support for paramilitary operations against the Sandinistas from the outside, contingency planning for military intervention, increased propaganda efforts and intelligence activities, more military aid to El Salvador and more pressure on Cuba, and joint planning with friendly states in Latin America (McConnell, 1983: 185). These proposals were formalized in National Security Decision Directive No. 17, which was approved and signed by the president on the following day (Pastor, 1987b: 366). The directive also authorized the Central Intelligence Agency to contact dissident Nicaraguans in exile and to conduct political and military operations to interdict the shipment of weapons from Nicaragua to guerrillas in El Salvador. In the first stage, the United States was to spend some $19 million to create a 500-man, US-trained paramilitary force. Argentina would assume the responsibility for training an additional 1,000-man force. At this time, the overthrow of the FSLN was not actually contemplated, but there was an awareness that such a consequence could very easily follow (*Newsweek*, November 8, 1982; see also Pastor, 1987b: 366).

The commitment by the Reagan administration to pressure the Sandinista regime militarily increased over time. Many officials were convinced that if the United States continued to provide military help to the rebels fighting the Sandinista government, eventually the regime in Managua would be brought down. The provision of military support was closely accompanied by the exertion of economic pressure on Nicaragua. The battle against the Sandinistas continued to be portrayed as part of a global struggle against attempts by the Soviets and Cubans to augment their domination in Central America. "We must remember," noted President Reagan in April 1985, "that if the Sandinis-tas are not stopped now, they will, as they have sworn, attempt to spread communism to El Salvador, Costa Rica, Honduras and elsewhere" (*New York Times*, April 22, 1985). Reagan's concern was heightened by his belief that the Nicaraguans were shrewd adversaries who had been excellently trained by the Cubans. He once noted that

> Castro ... told them [the Sandinistas] to tell the world they were fighting for political democracy, not communism. But most important, he instructed them to form a broad alliance with the genuinely democratic opposition to the Somoza regime. Castro explained that this would deceive Western public opinion, confuse potential critics, and make it difficult for the Western democracies to oppose the Nicaraguan revolution without causing great dissent at home. (Quoted in Schoultz, 1987: 185)

While the struggle against the Sandinistas proved to be quite cumbersome, the fight against Grenada proved to be more rewarding. After a year in power the Reagan administration decided to increase its pressure on the Bishop regime. On February 8, 1982, in his annual report to the US Congress, Secretary of Defense Caspar Weinberger condemned the Grenadian government. Weinberger described Grenada as a "Cuban satellite" and contended that the Cubans were building air and naval facilities in the island which far exceeded their needs (United States Department of Defense, 1982).

A few weeks later, on February 24, President Reagan unveiled his Caribbean Basin Initiative. The plan was designed to deal with the region's instability, brought about by the latest rise in the price of petroleum and a decline in prices for tropical agricultural products (Schoultz, 1987: 97). To deal with the region's economic suffering, Reagan proposed the appropriation of $350 million in aid, the granting of tax-free status to exports entering the United States from the Caribbean Basin, and the extension of tax incentives to US firms investing in the region. But Reagan's rationale for proposing the Caribbean Basin Initiative was not defined by the region's economic predicament. As the president made clear during the unveiling, "the Caribbean region is a vital strategic and commercial artery for the United States . . . nearly half of our trade, two-thirds of our imported oil, and over half of our imported strategic materials pass through the Panama Canal or the Gulf of Mexico" (Schoultz, 1987: 202). The significance of this position was further substantiated by the revelation that Cuba, Nicaragua, and Grenada would be excluded from participation in the initative.

Toward the end of 1982 Bishop gave the first signal that his regime was suffering the effects of the steps taken by the United States and that he wanted to alleviate some of the pressure. At the CARICOM summit meeting held in November at Ocho Rios, Jamaica, the Caribbean states pressured the Bishop regime to carry out its human rights promises. Bishop agreed to release some political prisoners, permit some democratic reforms, and allow observers to verify that his regime was not training leftist guerrillas (Pastor, 1985: 44).

Bishop's willingness to compromise was momentarily derailed by new statements from Washington. On March 9, 1983, the deputy assistant secretary of defense for inter-American affairs, Nestor Sanchez, warned that "in Grenada, Cuban influence has reached such a high level that it can be considered a Cuban protégé" (quoted in Hopple and Gilley, 1985: 56). On the following day Reagan added fuel to the fire when he commented in a somewhat facetious manner that, "It isn't nutmeg that's at stake in the Caribbean and Central America. It is the US national security" (quoted in Pastor, 1985: 45).

Bishop reacted by throwing caution to the winds. On March 13, he accused Reagan of being a warmonger and referred to his aides as "the fascist clique in Washington." In addition, he warned the Grenadian people to get "ready for the ultimate sacrifice," because an invasion was forthcoming (Cypher, 1985: 48–9). Ten days later, while unveiling his Strategic Defense Initiative, Reagan disclosed satellite photographs of the airport being built in Port Salines to support his contention that the "Soviet–Cuban militarization of Grenada can only be seen as a power projection into the region" (quoted in Pastor, 1985: 45).

Bishop responded that same month by flying with Fidel Castro to the Seventh Summit of the Non-Aligned Nations held in New Delhi, India (Germain, 1985: 155). The following month, on April 14, Bishop traveled to North Korea, where it was announced that North Korea would build in Grenada a 15,000-seat stadium, a party headquarters, a fruit-processing plant, two fishing boats, and an irrigation system (1985: 155).

All along, however, Bishop did not lose sight of the fact that Washington was very displeased with the behavior of his regime. On May 31, he arrived in the United States to address the Sixth Annual Dinner of TransAfrica, to be held in Washington, DC. Bishop decided to use the trip to convey the message that Grenada had no ill intentions toward the United States. Initially, the Reagan administration refused to meet with the Grenadian leader. But after realizing that this stand made the administration look foolish, Bishop was granted a meeting on June 6 with National Security Advisor William Clark and Deputy Secretary of State Kenneth Dam. Clark, who left the meeting early, made it very clear that the United States would not accept Soviet influence in the region. Bishop, while meeting alone with Dam, assured the US official that Grenada did not pose any threat to the United States (Pastor, 1985: 50). He sought to substantiate his claim a few days after he returned to Grenada by announcing the formation of a five-member commission in charge of drafting a constitution that would in time be submitted to a popular referendum (Cypher, 1985: 49).

The Bishop regime, however, was not willing to sacrifice its ties with the Soviet Union and Cuba. In July, Cuba agreed to construct in Grenada thirty miles of road, fifty-seven bridges, an ice plant, and a national convention center (Germain, 1985: 156). The Soviet Union was authorized to build a ground communications station on the island as part of the Soviet Intersputnik satellite system (Cypher, 1985: 49).

Although on the surface the United States seemed to pose the greatest threat to the integrity of the Bishop regime, a much greater menace was smoldering within the regime itself. Since 1982, some members of the Central Committee of the New Jewel Movement had been worrying about their party's declining prestige. The internal problems of the NJM were further aggravated in early October of the same year when Bernard Coard resigned from both the Central Committee and the Politburo. His resignation introduced more confusion about the proper personality and role of the NJM in Grenada's political arena. Moreover, as time went by, disagreements over organization and leadership, particularly Bishop's role as leader of the party, intensified. These problems were addressed in a series of meetings held in September and October 1983, a few months after Bishop had returned from his trip to the United States.

The Coard faction proposed a joint leadership, with Coard responsible for strategy and organization, and Bishop, as prime minister, responsible for the public aspects of the party and the government (Croes, 1985: 19–20; Germain, 1985: 157–8). The proposal was approved on September 14 by a vote of nine to one, with three abstentions. Eleven days later, Bishop finally agreed to a joint leadership for the sake of party unity (Germain, 1985: 158).

But the proposed joint leadership, and Bishop's decision to accept it, did not calm the waters. Less than a month later, after returning from a trip to Moscow and Havana, Maurice Bishop was placed under house arrest at his official residence on Mount Royal by the Central Committee. Disclosure that Bishop had been arrested created intense public protest, which persuaded Coard to resign from his new leadership position. And yet, although it was evident that Bishop had overwhelming public support, the challengers to his rule, which included the army, were reluctant to compromise. Their attitude toward compromise suffered an almost immediate reversal when they learned that other West Indian politicians, including Fidel Castro, were very critical of their behavior. Thus, on October 18, the Central Committee agreed to allow Bishop to return to his post as prime minister on condition that he accept the Central Committee as Grenada's key political body.

Bishop conveyed his willingness to accept the agreement, but his response came too late (Thorndike, 1985: 158). The following day, a crowd of 15,000 people gathered to demand Bishop's release. Upon being released, the Grenadian leader went to Fort Rupert, where an armed confrontation ensued. Some sixty people were killed, and Bishop and seven of his supporters were captured and executed by members of the People's Revolutionary Army (1985: 162–3). That same day, General Hudson Austin announced that the People's Revolutionary Government was being dissolved, that the Revolutionary Military Council was in charge, and that a twenty-four-hour, four-day curfew was in effect (pp. 163–5).

On October 20, Fidel Castro reacted critically to the actions of the newly established government. He noted that Bishop had been one of the leaders best liked by the Cuban people and demanded that his executioners suffer the same fate they had inflicted. Austin, in turn, made special efforts to reassure the United States that the 1,000 US medical students on the island were safe and free to leave at any time (Payne, Sutton, and Thorndike, 1984: 63).

The Reagan administration, in the meantime, had been following these developments with some interest. One of the first steps taken by US officials had been to initiate informal discussions with Eastern Caribbean countries about the possibility of mounting an operation to rescue Bishop (Pearson, 1987: 16). After Bishop's assassination, concern within the Reagan administration intensified. On October 19 and 20, the assistant secretary of state for inter-American affairs, Langhorn Motley, and the assistant secretary of state for political affairs, Lawrence Eagleburger, recommended that contingency plans be prepared immediately for a full-scale invasion of the island. Eagleburger emphasized the need to ensure that the United States not be confronted a second time by an Iran-type hostage situation. The Pentagon, however, convinced that its engagement in Lebanon precluded the execution of a full-scale invasion, proposed a small-scale rescue operation (Hopple and Gilley, 1985: 58; Pearson, 1987: 16). Secretary of State George Schultz and President Reagan favored the option proposed by Motley and Eagleburger, and a naval task force bound for Lebanon was ordered to change course to Grenada (Gilmore, 1984: 33).

On October 21, leaders of Jamaica, Barbados, St Vincent, St Lucia, Dominica, St Kitts–Nevis, Antigua, and Barbuda met with US Ambassador

Milan Bish and Deputy Assistant Secretary of State for Caribbean Affairs Charles Gillespie to request that the Reagan administration organize a joint US–OECS–Barbadian–Jamaican invasion of Grenada (Payne, Sutton, and Thorndike, 1984: 151). The request provided the Reagan administration with the justification it needed to order the invasion. At a meeting of the National Security Council, chaired by Vice President George Bush, Pentagon officials once again voiced reservations about an invasion, but their objections were overruled.

Two possible obstacles to the US invasion plans surfaced on October 22. First, Trinidad, Guyana, Belize, and the Bahamas, announced they would not support the invasion. Second, that same day, Castro informed Washington he wanted to work with the United States to find a non-violent solution to the Grenadian crisis. Early the next morning, however, Reagan convened a meeting with his advisors and personally approved the invasion of Grenada, with October 25 designated as the landing date (Payne, Sutton, and Thorndike, 1984: 151). On October 24, the OECS asked Great Britain to participate in the invasion. Prime Minister Margaret Thatcher rejected the request and immediately telephoned President Reagan to try to persuade him to cancel the operation. The phone call arrived too late; that same day Reagan had signed a national security directive authorizing the invasion. On October 25, Operation Urgent Fury commenced. After three days of sporadic fighting, the invading forces had secured the island.

One of the most obvious and significant characteristics of the Reagan administration has been its willingness to revive lessons considered relevant by US leaders preceding the Carter administration. It is no secret that President Reagan was convinced that the United States should never forget one important lesson learned from the Cuban revolution – that the best time to confront a radical regime was at its conception (Pastor, 1987a: 231). Based on this rationale, Reagan used economic and political instruments to debilitate the Bishop and Sandinista regimes. But this part of the rationale was not particularly original; Nixon had used the same measures some ten years earlier to destabilize the Allende government. Of much greater significance is the fact that the Reagan administration linked the same rationale with a different lesson to justify the direct use of US military forces against the one regime but not against the other.

Besides rationalizing from the Cuban case that revolutionary regimes have to be destroyed at birth, Reagan agreed with Secretary of Defense Weinberger that there was one lesson from the Vietnam experience a president could not afford to forget – that the protracted use of US military forces in a campaign that could entail heavy costs could be approved only after securing a broad, solid consensus for the policy. Reagan also recognized that after garnishing a consensus, a political leader still faces the unenviable task of keeping it alive. Vietnam had proven too well that political leaders can be destroyed by the failure to retain the support of those who had pledged themselves in favour of military force.

Reagan and his advisors recognized that the overthrow of Bishop provided the United States with the perfect opportunity to act aggressively against the new Grenadian regime. To begin with, Grenada's political arena was in total disarray and was permeated by a power vacuum. Moreover, Castro, by voicing his displeasure regarding Bishop's assassination and by attempting to commit the Reagan administration to a peaceful resolution of the Grenadian crisis, had signaled his government's unwillingness to rise to the defense of Grenada's new regime if the country were to be invaded by the United States. In other words, Bishop's death and the power vacuum that immediately ensued enabled the Reagan administration to live up to its dictum that the best time to act aggressively against a regime is immediately after its birth.

The specter of Vietnam, on the other hand, became quite palpable during the consideration of whether to intervene directly with US forces against the Sandinista regime. The Reagan administration was well aware that the Sandinista government had erected a loyal, powerful, revolutionary force capable of turning any US invasion into a costly and protracted war. This reality gave the Vietnam syndrome renewed relevance, thus warning Reagan and his advisors that unless Nicaragua attempted overtly and indiscriminately to upset the existing political order in Central America, it would not be possible to consolidate a consensus behind a fully fledged US invasion.

REASONING AND LEARNING BY ANALOGY

The birth of the Carter administration introduced a new reasoning structure in the foreign policy of the United States. Many of its officials shared the belief that it was morally unacceptable for the United States to maintain close relationships with dictatorial regimes. These officials also surmised that since most of these regimes were destined to be toppled, it would be in the best interest of the United States not to be identified as one of their principal backers. These ideas did not take root without consideration of the international environment. The same decision-makers who advocated a more "humane" foreign policy believed that it was pressing to recognize that not all major challenges to US strategic and economic interests could be attributed to communism. The new reasoning can be depicted analogically as follows:

| Government in target state is dominated by anticommunists who oppose political, social, and economic reforms but face widespread domestic opposition. | : | Pressure government in target state to respect human rights. | : | International reputation of actor pressuring government in target state to respect human rights is enhanced. | :: |

| Government in target state is dominated by anticommunists who oppose political, social, and economic reforms but face widespread domestic opposition. | : | Do not pressure government in target state to respect human rights. | : | International reputation of actor pressuring government in target state to respect human rights is undermined. | |

The last analogical structure is incomplete, for it does not describe the type of pressure the Carter administration was willing to apply to Somoza so that he would begin to promote human rights in Nicaragua. Convinced that the willingness of past administrations to use military, political, and economic power to alter the behavior of foreign governments had vilified the reputation of the United States, the Carter administration committed itself to altering the image. The new reasoning structure assumed the following analogical contour:

Use diplomatic channels to persuade government in target state dominated by anticommunists who oppose political, economic, and social reforms but face widespread domestic opposition, to respect human rights.	:	Actor relying on diplomatic channels will be praised for its actions.

::

Use primarily economic, military, and political pressure to persuade government in target state dominated by anticommunists who oppose political, economic, and social reforms but face widespread domestic opposition, to respect human rights.	:	Actor relying primarily on economic, military, and political pressure will be accused of being interventionist.

An extremely important aspect of the reasoning process of some of the dominant figures in the Carter administration is that the logic of their argument remained fairly constant even while it was becoming evident that the Sandinistas were a viable political force determined to alter the nature of Nicaragua's political structure. The constancy of the analogical form even under significantly different environmental constraints can be captured as follows:

Use diplomatic channels to persuade government in target state dominated by anticommunists who oppose political, economic, and social reforms and face being toppled by suspected communist forces, to respect human rights and to relinquish power in favor of a moderate, preferably democratic government.	:	Actor relying on diplomatic channels will be praised for its actions.

::

Use primarily economic, military, and political pressure to persuade government in target state dominated by anticommunists who oppose political, economic, and social reforms and face being toppled by suspected communist forces, to respect human rights and relinquish power in favor of a moderate, preferably democratic government.	:	Actor relying primarily on economic, military, and political pressure will be accused of being interventionist.

Needless to say, not all members of the Carter administration agreed with the logic of this argument. Some argued that the same objectives could be achieved more effectively by using extensive political, economic, and diplomatic pressure, and eschewing military force and unilateral action. In analogical form, their argument adopted the following structure:

Join forces with other international actors and rely on every form of pressure, with the exception of the threat of military invasion, to persuade government in target state dominated by anticommunists who oppose political, economic, and social reforms and face being toppled by suspected communist forces, to respect human rights and relinquish power in favor of a moderate, preferably democratic, government.

: Actors who join forces with other international actors and rely on every form of pressure, with the exception of :: the threat of military invasion, will be praised for actions and will have a good chance of preempting the instatement of a government in target state dominated by communists.

Join forces with other international actors and rely primarily on diplomatic channels to persuade government in target state dominated by anticommunists who oppose reforms and face being toppled by suspected communist forces, to respect human rights and relinquish power in favor of a moderate, preferably democratic, government.

: Actors who join forces with other international actors and rely primarily on diplomatic channels will be criticized for lack of determination and will fail to preempt the instatement of a government in target state dominated by communists.

When those in the Carter administration who had opposed the use of non-diplomatic means to persuade Somoza to step down recognized that their strategy had failed, they faced a new set of choices. Initially, they had to react to a proposal made by the national security advisor, Zbigniew Brzezinski. Afraid that the United States might be confronted by a new anti-US radical regime in Latin America unless it acted decisively, Brzezinski proposed the reenactment of the 1965 Dominican Republic scenario. His rationale, structured in analogical form, was almost the same as that used by Johnson some fourteen years earlier:

Do not extend military support to military in target state dominated by anticommunists and facing the threat of being toppled by suspected communist forces.

: Instatement of government in target state dominated by communists is not preempted. ::

Extend extensive military support to military in target state dominated by anticommunists and facing the threat of being toppled by suspected communist forces.

: Instatement of government in target state dominated by communists is preempted.

Most members of the Carter administration, however, shared the conviction that the reputation of the United States would be damaged badly if it intervened militarily in Nicaragua to prevent a takeover by the Sandinistas. In fact, for most of them, there was a different lesson to be inferred from the Dominican Republic scenario. It was:

Do not extend military support to military in target state dominated by anticommunists and facing the threat of being toppled by suspected communist forces.	:	Actor who refuses to use military force is praised for decision by international community. ::
Extend military support to military in target state dominated by anticommunists and facing the threat of being toppled by suspected communist forces.	:	Actor who uses military force is criticized for decision by international community.

The rejection of military intervention opened the gates for consideration of new alternatives. Realizing that it must accept the fact that the Sandinistas had become the driving force in Nicaragua's political arena, the Carter administration initially sought to influence the composition of the post-Somoza regime. The leaders in Washington were greatly concerned that Nicaragua's National Guard not be demobilized and replaced by forces totally loyal to the Sandinista cause. These leaders had not forgotten Cuba; they knew how important it was to ensure that the guns not be controlled solely by the radical members of the revolution. In analogical form, this rationale was structured in the following way:

Permit revolutionary leaders to replace target state's armed forces with forces loyal to the revolution immediately after toppling government dominated by anticommunists.	:	Revolutionary leaders succeed in consolidating their power in the target state and in implementing radical domestic and foreign policies. ::
Do not permit revolutionary leaders to replace fully the target state's armed forces with forces loyal to the revolution immediately after toppling government dominated by anticommunists.	:	Revolutionary leaders have difficulty in consolidating their power in the target state and in implementing radical domestic and foreign policies.

A similar rationale drove the Carter administration to try to persuade the Sandinistas to incorporate Nicaraguan moderates into the government that would replace Somoza. It was assumed that, with moderates aboard, the Sandinistas would have difficulty in guiding Nicaragua on a radical path. Thus,

Permit revolutionary leaders to exclude moderates from the new government in target state.	:	Revolutionary leaders succeed in consolidating their power in target state and in implementing radical domestic and foreign policies. ::
Do not permit revolutionary leaders to exclude moderates from the new government in target state.	:	Revolutionary leaders have difficulty in consolidating their power in target state and in implementing radical domestic and foreign policies.

By the time the Sandinistas marched into Managua, the Carter administration had finally concluded that it had no option but to recognize the new political regime. Although the Sandinistas had refused to expand the junta, they had agreed to incorporate members of the National Guard into the new Nicaraguan army, and they had announced the creation of an eighteen-person cabinet, many of whom came from the moderate ranks. A common attitude among leaders in Washington was that rather than challenge the course of action of the new Nicaraguan regime at the outset, it would be better to attempt to impress upon it that in the long run it would be in Nicaragua's interests to pursue a moderate path and maintain a friendly relationship with the United States.

The strategy was not entirely without precedent. In 1945 and the early 1950s, the Truman administration believed that it could influence the Arévalo and Arbenz regimes, respectively, not to alter radically the political and economic structures of Guatemala and to continue accepting the United States as the dominant actor in the region. In other words, the Truman administration hoped to persuade the two regimes that the center was the most desirable intersection point in the ideological political spectrum. In 1959, the Eisenhower administration accepted the possibility that it would be unrealistic to expect the Castro regime to create in Cuba a center-oriented political environment; thus, it sought to ensure that the structure it erected would not be too distant in content from the middle.

There are, however, two critical differences between these three cases and the 1979 Nicaraguan scenario. In the first three instances, Washington assumed that the leaders in Guatemala and Cuba would have no difficulty in recognizing the tremendous obstacles that could be laid in their paths if they attempted to disregard the interests of the United States. This assumption did not guide the actions of the Carter administration with regard to the Sandinistas in 1979. The new leaders in Washington realized that the Sandinistas would initially be drawn closer to the Soviets and the Cubans. The main challenge faced by Washington was to accept the competition and prove to the Sandinistas that the benefits of working with the United States were significantly greater than the benefits of relying on the other two parties.

The second critical difference was time. The Carter administration believed that its policy of co-optation could work only if Washington was willing to be patient – to give time to the moderates in Nicaragua to develop a better-rooted and more solid political infrastructure, and time for the Sandinistas to ventilate their anti-US anger and to realize that Washington and Managua did not need to be at odds with one another. The Carter administration reasoned that in its handling of Cuba, the Eisenhower administration had not been patient. Although initially it adopted a "wait and see" attitude, the Eisenhower administration never seriously considered giving the new Cuban government time to learn that it had much to gain by working with the United States. Therein lay Eisenhower's mistake. The Cuban experience, thus, led the Carter administration to structure its thinking process according to the following analogical relationship:

Accept newly formed government in target state dominated by political leaders who are committed to political, social, and economic reforms, and express willingness to help so long as they avoid radical reforms.	: Political leaders in newly formed government in target state criticize offer and begin to implement radical reforms.	: Criticize political leaders in newly formed government in target state for their rhetoric and reforms, and begin to impose extensive political and diplomatic pressure, and economic sanctions.	: Political leaders in newly formed government in target state intensify their rhetoric and continue to implement radical reforms, and radical leaders become more powerful. ::
Accept newly formed government in target state dominated by political leaders who are committed to political, social, and economic reforms, and express willingness to help.	: Political leaders in newly formed government in target state criticize offer and begin to implement radical reforms.	: Do not criticize political leaders in newly formed government in target state, and extend economic assistance.	: Political leaders in newly formed government in target state slowly begin to temper their rhetoric and reforms, and moderate leaders become more powerful.

This is a good point to introduce in analogical form the reasoning process behind the Carter administration's decision not to co-opt the Bishop regime following the overthrow of Eric Gairy in Grenada in 1979. Two conditions persuaded Washington that it would be unreasonable for the United States to adopt such a strategy. First, it was concluded that in order for a co-optation strategy to be effective, the targeted regime had to have representatives of the country's political center among its leaders. A regime made up solely of communists would reject any suggestion of following a moderate path and would use whatever economic assistance it received to promote its own radical causes. Second, it was feared that implementation of a co-optation strategy toward a communist regime would send the wrong signal to other Caribbean actors – that the most effective way to receive assistance from the United States was by taunting its leaders with the specter of communism. Keeping in mind the structure of the last analogy, the difference between the Grenadian and the Nicaraguan cases can be delineated as follows:

Accept newly formed government in target state dominated entirely by communists, and express willingness to help.	: Political leaders in newly formed target state criticize offer and begin to implement radical reforms.	: Do not criticize political leaders in newly formed target state for their rhetoric and reforms, and extend economic assistance.	: Communist political leaders in newly formed government in target state intensify their rhetoric and continue to implement radical reforms. Other international actors in the region are tempted to echo the behavior of the government in the target state. ::
Accept newly formed government in target state led by a mixture of communists and moderates, and express willingness to help.	: Political leaders in newly formed target state criticize offer and begin to implement radical reforms.	: Do not criticize political leaders in newly formed target state for their rhetoric and reforms, and extend economic assistance.	: Moderate political leaders in newly formed government in target state slowly begin to temper rhetoric and reforms. Other international actors in the region are not tempted to engage in radical reforms.

The Carter administration did not begin to alter its outlook on the Sandinista regime until the latter part of 1980. But by then there was little it could do to change course. In January 1981, the Reagan administration took over the reins of government committed to a completely different reasoning structure, one driven by the idea that in order to set the foreign policy of the United States toward the Caribbean and Latin America on its proper course, it was imperative that US leaders derive the "right" lessons from history.

For the Reagan administration, the central error committed by Eisenhower in 1959 and Carter in 1979 was the failure to realize that the best time to confront a radical regime was at its conception. This lesson had been learned by President Nixon and applied with tremendous success against Allende in Chile between 1970 and 1973. There was, however, a factor that set the Reagan and Nixon administrations apart. President Nixon had concluded during his experience as vice president that if measures against a regime are administered overtly, as they were by Eisenhower against Castro, the affected party is likely to use them to help rally domestic support against the foreign aggressor. Thus, Nixon's choice was to apply domestic pressure covertly. Reagan, on the other hand, was determined to make sure that everybody understood very clearly that his administration was committed to using extraordinary means against any party that sought to undermine the interests of the United States. To convey this message meant that sanctions would often have to be imposed overtly. In other words, the second pair-relationship in Nixon's general analogical structure of:

Impose overt economic sanctions on government in target state suspected to be dominated by communists only after they have implemented radical political, social, and economic reforms.	:	Political leaders of government in target state succeed in creating a communist regime. ∷
Impose covert economic sanctions on government in target state suspected to be dominated by communists immediately after they have gained power.	:	Political leaders of government in target state fail to create a communist regime.

was given the following new format:

Impose *overt* economic sanctions on government in target state suspected to be dominated by communists immediately after they have gained power.	:	Political leaders of government in target state fail to create a communist regime. Other international actors in the region *are initially tempted* to echo the behavior of government in target state. ∷
Impose *covert* economic sanctions on government in target state suspected to be dominated by communists immediately after they have gained power.	:	Political leaders of government in target state fail to create a communist regime. Other international actors *are not tempted* to echo the behavior of government in target state.

The last issue that needs to be delineated in analogical form is the decision by the Reagan administration to use US troops against Grenada but not against Nicaragua. Vietnam taught US leaders not to use US military forces to affect the affairs of another state unless they are almost certain that the objective will be achieved at a relatively low cost, or unless they are sure that they can secure at home a broad, solid consensus for the policy if they estimate that the invasion will be a costly operation.[7] In analogical form, the relationship can be depicted as follows:

Military invasion to topple government in target state dominated by communists is likely to be a very costly operation. Support for operation among leaders of state contemplating aggressive action is likely to be weak and unstable.	:	Do not rely on military invasion to topple government in target state ∷

Military invasion to topple government in target state dominated by communists is likely to be a very costly operation. Support for operation among leaders of state contemplating aggressive action is likely to be broad and stable.	Seriously consider relying on military invasion to topple government in target state.

THE INTERPLAY BETWEEN INTERESTS, BELIEFS, AND COGNITIVE PROCESSES

The strategic and economic perspectives

History, in its own cruel and enigmatic way, is occasionally helpful to those who seek to unravel its secrets. Alienated in a global system no longer in awe of their country's might, and disillusioned by the realization that some of their political leaders had been unable to resist the allure of power, the American public sought comfort in 1976 in a president with the mind of an engineer and the heart of a missionary. When the experiment failed, and the belief took hold that a particular past would help rekindle the United States's withering greatness, the American voter placed in the White House in 1981 an individual driven by the notion that good things would follow from the use of power for righteous causes.

The analysis of the foreign policies of Jimmy Carter and Ronald Reagan toward Nicaragua and Grenada is a study in contrasts. Rarely is the student of US foreign policy given the opportunity to compare the actions of individuals with such distinctly conflicting values as those of Carter and Reagan as they dealt with the same set of targets. It is under this set of conditions that the strategic and economic explanations can be tested most effectively.

Challenges to these explanations can take three forms. Viewed through a wide-angle lens that captures US policies of intervention toward Nicaragua and Grenada, as well as the targets already considered, there is little doubt that there is no correspondence between the force resorted to by the leaders in Washington and the threats posed by the various developments in the Caribbean Basin and South America. Grenada in 1983, even with a communist regime, did not exert on the United States the threat imposed by Guatemala in 1954, Cuba in 1961, or Chile in 1970. When US actions toward Nicaragua are considered, still using a wide-angle perspective, the strategic explanation does not fare much better than it did earlier. Nicaragua in 1979 may have posed a smaller threat to the United States than did the Dominican Republic in 1965, but the discrepancy between the two Caribbean Basin states was not so monumental as to require the use of some 22,000 US marines against the Dominican Republic, but only covert means against Nicaragua.

The nature and direction of the argument remain unaltered as the comparison focuses solely on the capabilities of Nicaragua and Grenada and the policies their post-1979 regimes experienced from the United States. Both strategically and economically, Nicaragua was, and is, a much more consequential country to the United States than Grenada (see tables 8 and 9). And yet, Washington responded with more force against the small Caribbean island than it did against a country with greater ability to undermine US interests in Central America.

It will not do to argue, at this juncture, that the United States acted in a rational manner when its leaders chose not to use direct military intervention against Nicaragua. So long as the focus is on strategic and/or economic interests, the United States would be expected to act more forcefully against those actors with greater capability to imperil its interests. It goes without saying that had Washington tried to topple the Sandinista regime with the type of force it used against Grenada, it would have borne heavy costs. But such a price would have been justified, for failure to launch a similar operation against the Sandinistas could have been expected to enhance their chances of political survival and, as a result, their ability to jeopardize the long-term interests of the United States.

However effective these arguments against the strategic and economic perspectives might seem, they pale in comparison to the objections that can be produced by a comparison of the policies of the Carter and Reagan administrations. Because the threat generated by the government in Grenada in 1983 was not more intense than that bred by the Bishop regime in 1979 or 1980, it would not seem to have justified an overt military invasion. With respect to Nicaragua, the argument requires a more detailed analysis. Unwillingness to resort to some form of force in 1979 to topple the Sandinista regime could be attributed to uncertainty about its true nature. By 1980, however, the structure of the new government had been defined fairly well, and the most virulent articulators of anti-US sentiments had become the dominant governmental figures. Moreover, their political power was not undermined by the arrival in Washington of a new administration; most of those who had ruled in Managua in 1980 were still among the leadership in 1983. The single most important element that varied during this period was one that the Carter administration had known would change and could have acted to avert – the increase in size and power of Nicaragua's armed forces. In sum, since most of the conditions that defined Nicaragua's political and military power were in place in 1980, it cannot be argued that Reagan's decision in 1981 to authorize the CIA to initiate covert operations against the Sandinistas can be attributed to an increase in threat. To explain the change in foreign policy, one must focus on President Carter's and President Reagan's cognitive processes.

The cognitive perspectives

Little additional analysis is required to understand the structure of Carter's beliefs and the effect it had on US foreign policy. At first glance, his decision not to intervene more forcefully against Somoza might seem contradictory to his beliefs. As already shown, he came to power convinced that strong democracies lead to the formation of stable governments which, in turn, serve the interests of the United States. From this reasoning, it would be tempting to infer that it would have been quite natural for his administration to use the various resources available to the United States to dispose of Somoza in

Table 8 Measures of the strategic value to the United States of Nicaragua and Grenada[a]

	Distance between the US and:	Military capability		Population	Economic capability	Strategic raw material capability	Access to strategic maritime passages
		Armed forces	Population				
Nicaragua	Approximately 760 miles	13,000 (1979) 50,000 (1982)		2.54 m (1979)	$1,493.3 m (1979)	Zinc: 3.6 m tn Silver: 482 troy oz Gold: 73.9 troy oz Copper: 0.1 m tn Lead: 0.4 m tn (1978)	2
Grenada	Approximately 1,525 miles	1,000 (1983)		112,000 (1982)	N/A	N/A	4

[a] Data for this table were derived from the sources used for table 4. The explanatory notes for that table also apply here.

Table 9   *Measures of the economic value to the United States of Nicaragua and Grenada*[a]

	Imports from the US by:	Exports to the US by:	Total earnings from direct US investments in:	Economic interaction between the US and states adjacent to target states
Nicaragua $91 m (1979)	$190.9 m (1979)	N/A	$14.91 b (1985)	
Grenada	$26.83 m (1983)	$0.99 m (1983)	N/A	$15.03 b (1985)

[a] Data for this table were derived from the same source as table 5. The explanatory notes for that table also apply here.

Nicaragua and to instate in his place a democratic government.

The problem with this contention is that it overlooks two other critical beliefs of Carter. Early in his presidency he had emphasized that the United States must be freed of its past inordinate fear of communism. Furthermore, he truly believed that his personal moral standards were not values he could afford to renounce simple because he had become president. In his book, *Why Not the Best?*, he states: "Our personal problems are magnified when we assume different standards of morality and ethics in our own lives as we shift from one responsibility or milieu to another" (quoted in Glad, 1980: 477). And then he adds: "Public officials, the President, the Vice-President, members of Congress, Attorneys General, federal judges, the triad of the CIA, . . . ought to set a standard that is absolutely exemplary. We ought to be like Caesar's wife. We ought to be free of any criticism or allegation."

Intervention, for Carter, would have signified the reneging of one of his central values. It would have meant a return to the past, a willingness "to adopt the flawed and erroneous principles and tactics of our adversaries" and, in the process, "abandoning our own values." It was this belief that impelled Carter to use Vietnam as an analogy to justify his opposition to intervention. Vietnam, he believed, should be a lesson never forgotten by leaders who were contemplating intervening against a corrupt regime in order to replace it with a moderate government, or against a government such as the one in Grenada, which had fallen under the communist spell. In either case, the action would convey to the international arena that the United States was morally incapable of living according to its own principles. The ultimate effect of this type of action would be that those who might have been inclined to side with the United States would not now trust it.

The tone of the argument remains the same as one explains Carter's forbearance toward the Sandinista regime. But to account for his confidence that he could win the new Nicaraguan regime to the United States's side, one must go a step deeper in the analysis. As already noted, many members of the Carter administration had been critical of Eisenhower's lack of patience toward

Cuba's post-1959 governmental leaders. The same mistake, they felt, would be avoided by creating in Managua a "conducive climate," one that "encourages those whose minds were not yet frozen to realize that to succeed ... they needed to reach accommodation with the US." This attitude was not foreign to Carter, for as he once stated, "fire is better quenched with water," rather than with fire.

Few political leaders hold fully complementary beliefs. In some measure, rationality is a function of an individual's intellectual and emotional ability to identify and act upon the potential conflicts in some of his most central beliefs. Carter prided himself on being both an engineer and a moralist. From an engineer, one would generally expect awareness of the need to evaluate information carefully before defining the nature of a problem, and readiness to assess various alternatives in order to gauge the effect they might have on a set of critical interests. Did Carter approach foreign policy problems in this fashion? According to James Fallows, one of his speechwriters, Carter might not always have thought out carefully the effect a policy could have on different values.

> [Carter] holds explicit, thorough positions on every issue under the sun, but he has no large view of the relations between them, no line indicating which goals (reducing unemployment? human rights?) will take precedence over which (inflation control? a SALT treaty?) when the goals conflict ... values that others would find contradictory complement one another in his mind. (Quoted in Glad, 1980: 485)

Fallows's statement is very revealing, not because of what it says, but because of what it fails to consider. Inability to find contradictions between certain values is not always a sign of failure to decide which values will take precedence. In some cases, in fact, it is a sign that values are so unequally ranked that there will be no compulsion against sacrificing lower-rated goals. When Carter and some of his closest advisors arrived in Washington, they hoped to persuade Somoza to democratize Nicaragua's political system. Somoza's refusal to follow the suggested path could have been used to justify the use of interventionist means. But not by Carter, for he had given top priority to the need to create a new image for the United States. It was this deep, moral commitment that prevented the new president from intervening to overthrow Somoza, from warding off the Sandinista takeover of Managua, and from deposing both the Bishop and Sandinista regimes.

It is inappropriate, thus, to suggest that some of those who advocated non-intervenionist policies did not appreciate fully the significance of their stand. A more correct conclusion is that whenever a potential contradiction surfaced between non-intervention and other existing values, the contradiction was partially disposed of by placing an extraordinary amount of weight on non-intervention. There is, however, another important side to the argument. Adherence to a value and acting rationally on it signify an understanding of the various consequences that could result from implementing a policy. Understanding of potential outcomes, in turn, calls for careful analysis. It may be asked, therefore, what level of analytical sophistication pervaded the evaluative process of those unwilling to sacrifice non-intervention?

Decision-makers in the Carter administration were not driven by the need to maintain cognitive consistency; but nor were they steered by a desire to grasp as fully as they could the potential ramifications of their policies. When policies fail, it is often tempting to accuse their authors of committing a variety of errors. In the case of the Carter administration and its handling of the Nicaraguan case, the temptation is to argue that some of its policy-makers never fully understood the nature of the problem and, thus, that their responses had no chance of attaining positive outcomes. This form of criticism is generally unsound unless it is preceded by an analysis of the way in which the blamed parties tried to cope with uncertainty.

Uncertainty permeates almost all foreign policy problems. The Nicaraguan case was not an exception. The problem with the Carter administration was that its competing decision-making groups handled several of the Nicaraguan episodes as if they were embedded in very little uncertainty. During the earlier stages, for instance, those who wanted to promote human rights were accused by Todman of failing to consider the effect such a policy would have on other aspects of the relationship between the United States and Nicaragua. Viewed from a theoretical perspective, Todman's fear reflected a concern regarding the tendency, among decision-makers who are obsessed by the desire to promote one value or set of values, to place a problem, and its corresponding policy, in the context of simply defined categories, without carefully evaluating the policy's overall potential effectiveness. The latter form of evaluation would have called for a comparison of the effect that past, similar policies had, under a variety of conditions, on a broad set of critical values, with the effects brought about by alternative policies.

Addressing human rights from a simple, categorical perspective was not an atypical way of approaching foreign policy problems by the Carter administration. A similar process surfaces as the focus switches to the analyses of the decisions not to intervene to remove Somoza from power, and to try to entice the Sandinistas to consider US interests as they developed Nicaragua's domestic and foreign policies. Rather than appraising the various effects a policy of non-intervention might have on several interests by comparing its effects with those of other conceivable responses across a variety of cases, Carter and several of his advisors used the Vietnam experience to rationalize their stand against intervention. Moreover, instead of considering the alternative implications of attempting to seduce the Sandinistas to take into account US interests as they designed Nicaragua's future, the Carter administration reflected on the lessons taught by the Eisenhower administration's impatience with Castro's moves toward independence. In sum, those who ultimately influenced the course of US foreign policy in the Carter administration were not oblivious to the presence of several values. Some values, however, had been ranked so high that the process almost automatically diluted any form of conflict with lower-ranked goals. Core beliefs, furthermore, acted as mechanisms designed to determine which past cases were or were not relevant to the problem at hand, and to impose specific interpretations on those that were deemed pertinent.

Inasmuch as Carter's vision of the international arena was burdened by a sense of moral obligation, Reagan's perception of the same landscape was buoyed by a deep feeling of ideological infallibility. The end of 1980 marked the rebirth of the long-dead spirit of the 1950s when Reagan reaffirmed the conviction that behind every major international upheaval lurked communism, ready to assert its will, with the United States as the only actor in the international environment capable of withstanding and repelling the onslaught. Or, in the words of a former US ambassador to the United Nations, Jeane Kirkpatrick, Reagan brought about the "restoration of the conviction that American power is necessary for the survival of liberal democracy in the modern world." This return, she adds, coincided "with a period of unprecedented Soviet expansionism and power" (1983: 14).

The definition by Reagan and his advisors of the problems emanating from the Caribbean Basin reflects some of their core beliefs. The problems faced by some of the countries in the region were not indigenous, but the result of a "well-orchestrated Communist campaign" (LaFeber, 1989: 274) designed to transform internal crises into increasingly internationalized confrontations. For Reagan, as noted by Stephen Ambrose, the threat was that "Nicaragua would become another Cuba, providing the Russians with a base in Central America that they would use both to export revolution to their neighbors, north and south, and as a naval military base" (1988: 328).

Reagan's definition of the problem has been both praised and criticized. This is not the place to gauge which response is more deserving, or to reconcile their differences, for ultimately such a task would not serve this study's purpose. As in the previous cases, a more rewarding procedure is to focus on how the principal decision-makers handled information.

Data do not always facilitate the derivation of non-competing interpretations. The Reagan administration, like its predecessors, did not always have sufficient information to derive a clear, absolute interpretation. In mid-1981, for instance, after learning that the flow of weapons from Nicaragua to El Salvador had diminished, State Department officials forwarded different interpretations of the new development. Ambassador Pezzullo, who had been appointed by Carter and who had consistently advocated temperance in US dealings with the Sandinistas, interpreted the slowdown to mean that the Sandinistas were looking for ways to signal their willingness to negotiate. Haig, on the other hand, was still convinced that the Nicaraguan regime was a Soviet–Cuban surrogate, and he construed the development as a sign that the Salvadoran guerrillas needed fewer weapons.

This example sheds light on the role played by beliefs during the interpretation of data. Cognitive consistency theory, as already explained, proposes that decision-makers distill information that might challenge their innermost beliefs. The problem with this claim is that it can be tested only in instances in which the information at hand is so evident that only one meaning can be construed from it. When this is not the case – and it often is not in the realm of foreign affairs – the most that can be stated is that the presence of uncertainty clears the way for the decision-maker to impose on the data the meaning that is most closely attuned with his beliefs. This also means that such an individual possesses the freedom to discard as irrelevant that information which could pose a strong, but not certain, challenge to his initial diagnosis.

The Reagan administration, convinced that the time had come to recognize once again how great a threat communism posed to the United States, was drawn to interpretations of history that differed markedly from those of certain members of the Carter administration. For Reagan, Cuba in the late 1950s was an example of the fallacy of placing too much weight on the presence of political moderates in a government dominated by communists. The formation of the alliance with genuinely democratic leaders, contended Reagan, had been designed by Castro for the purpose of defusing any major international criticism and opposition. A similar development came to pass some twenty years later in Nicaragua. In other words, in the face of competing information, Reagan was free to rely fully on his beliefs in deciding which analogy corresponded with the Nicaraguan problem and which data to use to define it.

A similar process took place when it came time for the Reagan administration to select policies that would address the Nicaraguan problem. At this point, however, the analysis must focus on a different set of issues. In the face of uncertainty, it is often inappropriate to render a judgment on the quality of the policy selected by a group of decision-makers. It is not unsuitable, however, to evaluate the way in which the policy was selected.

The decision by the Reagan administration to engage in covert activities against the Sandinista regime did not result from the type of process assumed by attribution theory. Rather than trying to gauge the viability of the policy by assessing the degree to which a similar past policy affected a variety of actors and comparing it with other policies, the Reagan administration narrowed the range of policies to two and derived inferences about their effects principally from two cases. The principal focus was on whether to intervene covertly with paramilitary forces or overtly with US troops. Estimates of each policy's potential effect were not conducted systematically. It was not fear of criticism from Latin American leaders that led to rejection of overt military intervention by US troops. In fact, several members of the Reagan administration believed that direct military intervention would help persuade Latin American leaders, and others around the world, that the United States had regained the will to use force to protect its interests. Rather, trepidation concerning using such an instrument came about as a result of the Vietnam experience. Fearing that the United States might become embroiled in another protracted war, with a resulting loss in domestic presidential prestige, Reagan and his advisors concluded that by using economic instruments, along with covert paramilitary means, they would be able to control the risks more effectively. Once again, this appraisal did not stem from the conduct of a quasi-systematic evaluation. Chile was relied on as an example of how effective economic instruments can be when used to incite domestic turmoil. Domestic turmoil, however, does not bring a government down; a coercer is always needed. The Reagan administration, cognizant that it could not rely on Nicaragua's military to topple the Sandinista regime, estimated that such a goal could be achieved by paramilitary forces.

These calculations, however, did not consider that Nicaragua's domestic environment in the early 1980s might have differed markedly from Chile's internal milieu, and that toppling a regime backed by its own forces might be much more difficult than overthrowing one which is not.

Grenada, in turn, extended the Reagan administration the chance to promote fully its beliefs without seriously risking the possibility of undermining its own reputation. Distinctly unconcerned about possible criticism of an invasion of the island, Reagan viewed the situation in Grenada as a perfect opportunity to eliminate a communist regime at minimum cost.

In sum, this chapter has attempted to argue that Carter's and Reagan's diametrically opposite belief structures influenced the types of policies their respective administrations articulated and implemented. The threat posed by communism, the role the United States should play in the international arena, and the use of power were all viewed through different prisms which, in turn, brought about foreign policies that differed in terms of both content and intent. As significant as these differences are, they are watered down by the fact that the two major decision-makers concerned engaged in the same types of cognitive processes to define problems and select policies.

Neither leader experienced the threat of cognitive inconsistency, largely because their core beliefs had been valued so much higher than lesser beliefs that whenever a potential conflict between them surfaced, little introspection was required to abandon the fulfillment of the subordinate principles. Moreover, neither actor sought to delineate the nature of the various problems by breaking them into distinct, but interrelated, parts, or to evaluate the conditions required to implement effectively their prefered policies. Instead, in both cases there was a tendency to try to capture the nature of the divergent problems in the context of simple analogical categories expropriated from historical evidence. A similar process was manifested in their selection of policies.

10

Continuity and Change in US Policy of Intervention

INTRODUCTION

This study's fundamental objective was to derive an analogical theory of foreign policy-making that would explain the rationale behind the decisions by various US administrations to intervene in the domestic affairs of seven Caribbean and Latin American states. To achieve this end, it was imperative to demonstrate that alternative explanations of US intervention did not possess the theoretical reach expected from the analogical theory of foreign policy-making. Specifically, it was necessary to prove that existing strategic and economic explanations could not account for the various puzzles that surface as one attempts to give meaning to the steps taken by the United States in response to threats emanating from the political arenas of its southern neighbors. It was also critical to show that alternative cognitive theories of decision-making would be no more successful in unraveling the nature of these quandaries.

To place the results of the empirical analysis in an intelligible form, this chapter travels a fairly simple path. In its earlier stages it proves that strategic and economic theories of intervention that postulate parsimonious explanations tend to depict a world unrelated to the reality that comprises the environment of foreign affairs. The critical fallacy of these theories is to assume that foreign policy-makers' goals are always materialistic and are neatly ordered into one unitary pattern of desires, with either power or economic dominance at the top of the scale. As an alternative, this chapter suggests that decision-makers, like people in general, have dual natures.

Morality is what separates human beings from animals. As Amitai Etzioni notes, an individual's moral commitment and his desires often pull him in opposite directions. Much of human life, adds Etzioni, "can be explained in terms of the struggle between the two forces and the conditions under which one or the other prevails" (1988: 9). Cognitive models accept this view, and go a step further. They explain how decision-makers cope with their various values as they define problems and find ways to solve them.

The explanatory quality of the alternative cognitive theories is gauged in the second phase of this chapter. At the outset it is argued that attribution theory adheres to unrealistic assumptions about the decision-maker's ability to approach a problem in a semi-systematic fashion. It is noted that although this talent varied markedly from one individual to another, it is not a common form of behavior even among individuals who have the training for using a systematic approach.

Criticism of attribution theory should not be interpreted as an endorsement of cognitive consistency theory. Contrary to this theory's assumption, decision-makers rarely have difficulty recognizing the presence of multiple values as they seek to define the nature of certain international problems and find solutions for them. Those who define a problem and respond to it in the context of a single value are generally guided not by the belief that other values will not be affected, but by the conviction that they are much less important and thus can be sacrificed.

Cognitive consistency theory, as just implied, maintains that beliefs are important. This study substantiates that claim, in no small degree. Beliefs play decisive roles in the way goals are ranked, information processed, and analogies selected and interpreted. A discussion of how these three factors interact and affect the way decision-makers interpret and respond to problems, serves as the prelude to this chapter's principal section: the postulation of hypotheses bearing on US intervention in the Caribbean and Latin America. The purpose of these hypotheses is not to capture the overall underlying nature of the theory of reasoning and learning by analogy, but to depict its theoretical applicability in the context of a specific foreign policy issue area. The study closes with reflections about future research paths.

THE INAPPOSITENESS OF STRATEGIC AND ECONOMIC PARADIGMS

Bad habits never die easily. In the second half of the 1940s, Hans Morgenthau argued that the evidence of history bears out the assumption that "statesmen think and act in terms of interest defined as power." Burdened by the trauma that resulted from the fighting of the Second World War and the uncertainty brought about by the onset of the Cold War, a large number of US scholars embraced Morgenthau's testimony as an article of faith. In the 1960s, however, James March, a social scientist with limited training in international politics, wrote a thorough and devastating critique of models of social choice that rely on power as the critical predictive variable. After a detailed analysis of six social-choice models, four of which rely on power as the principal factor, March concluded that "the class of social-choice situations in which power is a significantly useful concept is much smaller than I previously believed ... Although *power* and *influence* are useful concepts for many kinds of situations, they have not greatly helped us to understand many of the natural social choice mechanisms to which they have traditionally been applied" (1966: 68).

March's warning received extensive attention. Many scholars recognized the need to break loose from the claims of realism and began to explore new ways of approaching the study of international politics and foreign policy. The concept of power, however, has always had a strong allure for students of international affairs; the conceptual and theoretical value assigned to it would be tempered temporarily, only to be resuscitated with new energy. In 1983, Robert Keohane, building on works by two eminent scholars, Kenneth Waltz and Robert Gilpin, tried to give power a more "realistic" face. Believing that it was imperative to achieve a more finely tuned understanding of how power affects behavior in the international arena, Keohane proposed altering two of its assumptions. First, he suggested discarding the assumption that the search for power constitutes an overriding interest in all cases, and substituting the premise that under different "systemic conditions states will define their self-interests differently." In addition, Keohane proposed that instead of assuming that power is fungible, it should be presumed that the "value of power resources for influencing behavior in world politics depends on the goals sought" (1983: 529).

Keohane's prescriptions come to naught when the empirical analysis focuses on US intervention in the Caribbean Basin and Latin America. He is quite correct in noting, as he does with regard to the first modification, that when the international environment is relatively benign, states will direct their energies to fulfilling goals other than maintaining their autonomy. This change in perspective, however, is of little theoretical value. The autonomy of the United States was never at stake in the cases considered in this study, and its foreign policy-makers reacted to the presence of regional problems in significantly different ways. Their responses, however, did not correspond to the power of the states posing the threats. Directly related to this point is Keohane's argument for modifying the second assumption. He proposes that the usefulness of a given set of power resources depends on the policy contingency frameworks within which it must be employed. True, it could be argued that economic, political, covert paramilitary, and overt military intervention were all part of one "policy-contingency framework" used to remove the threat posed to US interests by unstable non-communist governments or by regimes that were or risked being controlled by communist leaders. But the argument overlooks the fact that the use of these various instruments varied markedly, and not according to the power resources of the adversaries. Moreover, it fails to recognize that although the use of power resources varied according to the goals sought, such goals could not be identified a priori, but only with reference to the beliefs of the principal foreign policy-makers addressing the problems at hand.

Marxist theories of US intervention did not fare any better than the strategic paradigm. And their problem is no different. To evaluate the argument that the leaders in Washington intervened to protect either the broad economic interests of the United States in a region or those of some of its most powerful corporations, there must be a way to gauge the relationship between threats to economic interests and responses to offset the threats. This requirement might seem inappropriate to advocates of these theories. Even a casual study of the evidence, these analysts would contend, indicates that US foreign policy-makers place a great deal of value on economic interests. Any attempt to disregard this factor, they are likely to add, simply reflects an unwillingness to acknowledge that the economic system of the United States is so dominated by its capitalist nature that US leaders cannot escape being controlled by its structural needs.

This study finds such a claim totally unjustified. It acknowledges that Washington was determined to protect US economic interests from domestic instability in some critical countries and from unfriendly governments. But Washington's concerns were always of a much broader and deeper nature. Material interests were rarely embodied singularly in the minds of decision-makers; furthermore, they generally coexisted with less tangible, but equally significant, values. To understand how these concerns and others were dealt with, it is necessary to descend to the realm of cognitive theories.

ATTRIBUTION AND COGNITIVE CONSISTENCY THEORY

Attribution theory proved to be a major disappointment. Before depicting its main problems, however, a few clarifications are in order. According to Deborah Larson, attribution theorists "do not try to erect a grand theory deduced from a few underlying premises" (1985: 40). She also notes that attribution theory "is a general rubric used to tie together many different research studies that share certain basic assumptions" (p. 35).

Larson's contention is correct: attribution theory is indeed a general rubric encompassing a variety of types of research. But careful exploration of some of the studies that refer to attribution theory will also show that in some cases their basic postulates contradict one another. For instance, Richard Nisbett and Lee Ross propose that vivid information – information that is concrete, has an emotional effect on the individual, and is derived from personal experience or first hand knowledge – has a disproportionate effect on the way individuals judge and derive explanations (1980: 43–51). This conclusion is inconsistent with the notion that in attribution theory there are "no motivational constructs of any kind" (Larson, 1985: 35). Furthermore, it poses a direct challenge to Harold Kelley's central thesis that individuals, in formulating causal explanations, use information to gauge distinctiveness, consistency, and consensus. In using information for these three purposes, adds Kelley, the individual is, in some ways, conducting an "analysis of variance" not much different from that relied on by the trained social scientist (1967: 194). The trained social scientist, however, knows perfectly well that he cannot permit "vivid information" to have an exaggerated effect on his analysis.

Nisbett and Ross try to minimize the significance of this discrepancy by suggesting that the problem is not that individuals are emotionally committed to certain values, but that they lack the skills to conduct efficient analyses. But if this is the case, then how do they account for their discovery that information that has an emotional effect on individuals will have a magnified effect on their analyses? In other words, Nisbett and Ross fail to give sufficient weight to the strong possibility that information becomes "vivid information" because it touches on some central values.

This brief discourse has a major purpose. Because attribution theory, as just argued, cannot assimilate both Kelley's thesis and some of Nisbett and Ross's findings, a choice must be made between the two. The choice made here, as reflected by the nature of the empirical analysis, is to focus on the former. This decision should not be construed as an attempt to question Nisbett and Ross's work, for some of their findings parallel a few of this study's explanations, as will be shown. The decision, instead, was derived from the assumption that Kelley's interpretation of attribution theory would serve better this study's interest in comparing truly competing theories.

The simplest way to reflect on the explanatory reach of attribution theory is to postulate that none of the decision-makers considered in this study approached problems and sought solutions by using information in the manner delineated by Harold Kelley. Thomas Mann in 1951 did not contemplate the possibility that the presence of communists in Guatemala's government might *not* result in the birth of a communist regime. Moreover, when he recommended that the United States impose economic sanctions covertly on Guatemala, he did not compare the policy's potential effects with the possible impact of alternative policy instruments. The absence of a quasi-scientific approach to problem-solving is so evident throughout the remaining administrations that it is not necessary to identify once again the principal characters and their analytical misdeeds.

Of greater theoretical pertinence are the roles played by beliefs. The evidence establishes in a fairly conclusive manner that, with the exception of Kennedy, decision-makers had little difficulty defining a problem in the context of more than one value and responding accordingly. Thomas Mann's suggestion that Arbenz's regime be undermined via covert means, Eisenhower's decision to rely on covert paramilitary means in 1954, Nixon's wanting to use discretion in the imposition of economic sanctions on Chile in the early 1970s, and Reagan's unwillingness to use United States forces to invade Nicaragua in the first half of the 1980s – all reflect the belief by the decision-makers that more than one value bounded the problem they were attempting to resolve.

There were, however, instances in which a single value contextualized the nature of the problem. In 1961 Kennedy ordered US military forces to be on standby in case they were needed to avert a major domestic uprising in the Dominican Republic; four years later Johnson commanded that the same country be invaded to stave off the genesis of a communist regime; in 1970 Nixon demanded the CIA take whatever steps were necessary to obstruct Allende's rise to the presidency in Chile; in 1979 Carter refused to intervene against the Somoza and Bishop regimes; and in 1983 Reagan instructed US forces to land in Grenada and overthrow its newly created regime. Each of these decisions was prefaced by the recognition that other values might be affected and that such values might have to be sacrificed. Kennedy, Johnson, Nixon, and Reagan gambled that their decisions would not cause Latin American condemnation, but they were willing to absorb those costs, if necessary. Carter, on the other hand, though dedicated to the promotion of democracy, was more committed to persuading the world that the United States was not an interventionist power.

Values are not the only elements of the decision-making process affected by beliefs. In a world of uncertainty, pieces of conflicting information compete for attention. Decision-makers rarely pause to balance systematically the different signals they receive. Their analysis generally entails the assimilation of that information which corresponds with existing beliefs, and the rejection of that which does not.[1] Mann, for instance, was never bothered by the fact that only a few members of Arbenz's government were communists. In an environment in which information is rarely conclusive, and in which the costs of waiting for clearer signals can be devastating, Mann's beliefs took over his analytical process. The presence of a few communists, he inferred, reflected a government's commitment to their values or, at minimum, a willingness to tolerate them. Either scenario, reasoned Mann, would serve the interests of the communists; thus, it behoved the United States to ensure that their path to power was obstructed. Similarly, John Foster Dulles knew perfectly well in 1954 that he did not have the evidence necessary to prove to his Latin American counterparts that the Arbenz regime was governed by Moscow, but this did not dissuade him from promoting the view that it was. His beliefs were no different from Mann's. The pattern repeats itself in 1965. For Johnson it was irrelevant that most of Bosch's supporters were not communists; he believed that so long as some of them were communists, the threat could not be permitted to continue.

The discriminative nature of beliefs transcends ideological boundaries. In 1979 President Carter and his associates were quite convinced that the United States could reach an amicable compromise with the Sandinista regime if Washington showed tolerance and a willingness to help Nicaragua's new government. Originally, this decision was vilified by some and applauded by others. Neither side, however, ever truly attempted to comprehend fully the circumstances under which the choice was made. The decision was arrived at under extreme uncertainty. The Carter administration was aware that many of Nicaragua's new leaders were communists or communist sympathizers, but it had no way of ascertaining with complete certainty that they would become their country's principal force. At the same time, however, the weight placed by Carter and his associates on the moderates gaining the upper hand was not the result of the careful balance of the pertinent information. Another group of leaders, with a different set of beliefs, could easily have concluded that the only germane information was that which indicated that communists were the critical force in Nicaragua's new political reign.

The international environment is awash with historical incidents, but not all of them are important. The costs of bad past policies often linger in the minds of policy-makers for more than a generation. The general impressions derived from some of these incidents are known to be comparable even among individuals with disparate beliefs. Munich was a débâcle both to those who believe that the most effective way to offset a leader's imperialist dreams is with power, and to those who maintain that the heavy reliance on power must be sacrificed for the creation of an international organization with authority to address conflicts of interest between different international parties. Among individuals with different beliefs, however, agreement that a particularly past policy prompted excessive costs does not signify agreement on the causes of the problem. The nature of the disagreement, in fact, is most likely to be a reflection of the competing beliefs. In short, in the presence of uncertainty, beliefs will invariably determine which information is relevant and which is not, and they will influence the process of deciding which historical events are apposite and what lessons to infer from them.

At first glance, the argument just posited might seem to run opposite to schema theory's basic postulate that errors in judgement and decisions are the result of limited human intellectual capabilities. A more careful look will show that it does not. In a world in which the decision-maker sorts out what is important by developing categories into which experiences can be filed, beliefs help give form to the categories. Beliefs, in other words, aid in the definition of "problem-solving" spaces.

THE ANALOGICAL PRINCIPLE

Thus far a great deal has been said about the different facets of the decision-making process, but no attempt has been made to link the various arguments into a coherent explanatory framework. The fulfillment of this task is finally possible.

The US policy of intervention toward the Caribbean Basin and Latin American states has been the function of three factors: attitude toward communism, attitude toward intervention, and the results of past policies. The interaction between these three factors did not remain constant from one decision-maker to another. Every major US foreign policy-maker since 1945 has attempted, in some form or another, to ensure that none of the Caribbean Basin or Latin American states would be ruled by a communist regime. The time of response by the various policy-makers to prevent the genesis of such a regime, however, varied markedly. In some instances, steps were delayed until it became quite evident that the new Latin American or Caribbean regime had no intention of respecting US desires; in other cases measures were taken while a pro-US dictatorial regime was still in power but was beginning to experience the threat of increasing domestic turmoil. Furthermore, the policy instruments used by the United States also changed significantly. In some cases US policy-makers relied on limited covert means; on other occasions they ordered the invasion of the target state with US troops.

The relationship between the three factors can be explicated in the context of differentiated hypotheses logically linked. The first hypothesis must delineate the relationship betweeen costs, beliefs, and the use of historical analogies to define problems.

Hypothesis 1

The greater the costs attributed by US policy-makers to a past failure to prevent the genesis of a communist regime in a strategically and economically valuable state, and the stronger the belief that such costs could have been averted if the "true" conditions that brought the communists to power had been identified forthwith, the greater the tendency to place exceptionally high value on the assumed "true" conditions to define problems in states in which the communists are part of the political equation.

By not defining the nature of the "true" conditions, the hypothesis is broad enough to extend its explanatory reach over a diverse set of events. As delineated, the hypothesis accounts for the link between the failure by the United States to prevent the communist party from winning control over China's government in 1949, and subsequent attempts to apply lessons inferred from the incident to the definition of the Guatemalan problem; or the link between Washington's approach to the Cuban problem in 1960, and Carter's determination not to commit the same error as he tried to deal with the Sandinistas almost twenty years later.

Determination of "true" conditions in an uncertain world, however, is the function of a decision-maker's beliefs.[2] By giving context to beliefs, it is possible to infer their effects on a decision-maker's analysis of history and on the way he applies such lessons to contemporary events in a particular region:

Hypothesis 2

The stronger the belief among US policy-makers that communism is the principal cause of all major domestic uprisings, the greater their tendency to use past events in such a way that they help corroborate the view that problems in a Caribbean Basin or Latin American state had been given form by communists.

A strong inclination to believe that communism is a major threatening force does not translate automatically into a willingness to rely on interventionist means to remove the threat. As already explained, a decision-maker's disposition toward breaking the non-interventionist principle can also play an important role. Thus:

Hypothesis 3

The stronger the belief among US policy-makers that communism is the principal cause of all major domestic uprisings and that the United States is not always obligated to abide by its non-interventionist principle, the stronger their determination to use coercive means to prevent the genesis of a communist regime in a Caribbean Basin or Latin American state.

Careful reading of the last hypothesis will show that it helps explicate actions as diverse as Dean Acheson's opposition to military intervention in Guatemala, Jimmy Carter's decision not to move more aggressively against both the Somoza and the Sandinista regimes, and Ronald Reagan's decision in 1981 to approve the use of covert means against Nicaragua and in 1983 to invade Grenada. Still, as delineated, the hypotheses do not explain the effects that past experiences have had on the timing and form of intervention. The first relationship can be summarized as follows:

Hypothesis 4

The greater the costs US policy-makers believe were accrued during past attempts to prevent the genesis of a communist regime in a Caribbean Basin or Latin American state, the greater their determination not to delay intervention, even if it means acting against a dictatorial, pro-US regime.

In turn, the relationship between past experiences and means assumes the following form:

Hypothesis 5

The greater the degree of success by the United States in its latest attempt to prevent the genesis of a communist regime in a Caribbean Basin or Latin American state, the greater the likelihood that US policy-makers will rely on similar means to address a comparable problem.

The last two hypotheses are specific enough that they can be used, for instance, to shed light on why the United States took so long to intervene against Fidel Castro and relied only on paramilitary means, but moved so early with regular US forces against Juan Bosch as his supporters tried to return him to power.

The hypotheses presented in the last few pages depict a dynamic process that is captured by the interaction between beliefs and analogies. Foreign policy-makers use their beliefs to identify pertinent past events and decide what lessons to infer from them. With lessons accumulated from the past, policy-makers develop incrementally a problem-solving space. By referring to a familiar problem-solving space, foreign policy-makers compute the costs and effectiveness of past policy instruments to fulfill a set of preferred goals. Often, however, they refer to a problem-solving space developed in the past which, when applied to a present problem, results in the undermining of the values they were seeking to maximize. This type of action triggers a discrimination that constrains the range of applicability of the original problem-solving space, and a search process that transforms the old solution into one that satisfies the conditions created by the new problem. These changes are then expressed through the application of new policy means which, if successful, are made part of the new policy repertoire which has resulted from the development of the latest problem-solving space.

Rarely, however, will the value of a policy repertoire remain constant. In time, new costs are likely to surface, largely because some less obvious objectives were not properly addressed by the latest problem-solving space. In view of these new values, the foreign policy-makers will assess whether it might be justifiable to reassess some of the lessons inferred from the past and, possibly, alter the contours of the relevant problem-solving space. If it is decided that a change must take place, then a new policy repertoire is likely to be formalized. The chances that a change will survive the challenges of time are a function of how effective it is in balancing the fulfillment of the objectives sought initially, with the attainment of those that had been neglected.

It is critical to note that the formalization of a new policy repertoire, particularly if it is conducted by the same administration, is rarely conducted without accounting for the central beliefs shared by its members. For instance, when in the late 1950s the Eisenhower administration began to realize that it would have to rethink its policy of maintaining friendly relations with dictatorial regimes that had for years been supportive of the United States, the reassessment was conducted principally within the context of how continued support of such regimes was impairing US ability to effectively contain communist efforts in the Caribbean Basin and Latin America.

The formalization of a policy repertoire has a very specific content when it comes to intervention by the United States in the Caribbean Basin and Latin America. The foreign policy-makers in Washington sought, after 1945, to contain the spread of communism in the two regions without resorting to extraordinary means. Their first success reinforced the initial attitude that the fulfillment of the identified objective required minimum effort. But as this belief began to take root, a new danger surfaced – the possibility that support of dictatorial regimes might not necessarily be in the best interests of the United States. Guided by their initial attitude and their new awareness, the foreign policy-makers in Washington were faced by a new political regime that was suspected of being dominated by communists, and by the need to decide what to do with an old dictatorship. The crossing of the paths of these two attitudes regarding two different cases brought mixed results and, hence, a new set of lessons. Dictatorial regimes create domestic discontent and turmoil which can be exploited by the communists. Newly born political regimes dominated by communists must not be allowed to establish their power structures. From these two lessons it was inferred that the United States had to act more decisively against both types of regime.

The policy repertoire designed to deal with these two distinct conditions involved, depending on the circumstances, the extension of economic aid, the promotion of democracy as a preferred type of governmental structure, covert paramilitary and overt military intervention, and the denial of economic assistance. Success, however, can sometimes breed failure in some unexpected areas. The policy of intervention by the United States helped avert the birth, or at least the survival, of new communist regimes throughout the Americas. But it also helped undermine the international standing of the United States.

In the 1970s new beliefs began to capture the minds of some of Washington's foreign policy-makers: namely, that the United States could regain some of its world stature by being less interventionist, and that newly formed political regimes dominated by communists could be prevented from becoming communist regimes by relying on economic assistance and the political astuteness of those moderates who held positions of leadership. This policy repertoire failed to balance the original need to avert the creation of communist regimes, and the new need to brighten the international image of the United States. The end result was the rekindling of an old idea: behave aggressively against any attempt by a political group dominated by communists to create a political regime, and against any attempt by a political regime dominated by communists to consolidate its power.

CONCLUSION

By the mid-1970s the study of foreign policy had experienced what at that time might have seemed a critical metamorphosis. Scholars such as Robert Axelrod, Matthew Bonham, Alexander George, Robert Jervis, Michael Shapiro, John Steinbruner, and many others, posited powerful arguments for analyzing foreign policy not from the perspective of an objective reality ready to be grasped in its true context by decision-makers, but from the perspective of the cognitions of the decision-makers. These scholars' arguments, at least initially, did not fall on deaf ears. Many other analysts, excited by the theoretical implications of the new focus, responded to the challenge.

The excitement, however, was short-lived. It took little time to recognize that attempts to engage in sophisticated empirical analyses were bound to be frustrated by the presence of psychological theories that conflicted with one another significantly, and by the unavailability of reliable data (see Holsti, 1976: 39–52). Thus, as the 1980s moved along, the number of foreign policy studies that focused on the cognitive processes of decision-makers began to diminish, and less cumbersome approaches were presented.

This change in direction signified that parsimony became king of the mountain once again. But at what cost? The power structure of the international system is always a critical factor. Without reference to it, it is not possible to explain the nature of outcomes. However, to understand why one outcome resulted instead of another, it is essential to investigate the extent to which the obstacles imposed by the power structure were accounted for by the policy adopted by foreign policy-makers.

In a world in which information is rarely available in the quantity necessary to eliminate all risks, evaluating the effectiveness of a policy in overcoming the various barriers contained within the international structure requires understanding how leaders reason. For years analysts used, in some form or another, a conception of the decision process derived from rational choice models (Steinbruner, 1974: 8). The concept of rationality, like the concept of power, has not been easy to displace from the realm of foreign policy analysis, although its theoretical relevance has long been acknowledged to be meager.[3] Most troubling in this regard is the fact that we have tended to accept assumptions about human nature proposed by individuals who have rarely sought to understand human nature – economists and mathematicians.

One need not be cautious in deploring this blind commitment to the assumption of rationality. The concept, since it was first conceived, was promoted as an ideal. Ideals, as generally understood, can be sought, but never achieved. This dividing line, which philosophers throughout the centuries had little difficulty in drawing, began to lose its hue with the advent of modern science in the year 1600. Convinced that man had the intellectual tools to explain the universe that surrounded him, analysts imposed the assumption of rationality on the study of a broad variety of subjects, including economics. It did not take long for this conception to move into the realm of politics. The association between politics and rationality has taken various forms throughout the centuries, and this is not the place to describe it. It suffices to say, as explained earlier, that an obvious victim of this association has been the study of foreign policy. We have become so attached to the notion that rationality can become the cure to all major ills that we have great difficulty accepting that the "mind of man, for all its marvels, is a limited instrument" (Steinbruner, 1974: 13) and that, as a consequence, foreign policy-making is unlikely ever to become the product of a rational process.[4] In addition, we seem to have forgotten George Orwell's warning that politics, more than any other field of human interaction, is less an instrument for expressing thought than a means for "preventing thought" (1957: 157). When Orwell delivered his criticism, he had in mind the debasement of language. Indirectly, however, he was reminding us that since language reflects our thoughts, the absence of careful thought as we make political decisions, either as voters or as foreign policy-makers, signifies in no small measure the absence of rationality.

Discarding the rationality assumption could be interpreted as an attempt to promote the idea that we should lower our theoretical expectations as foreign policy analysts. Nothing could be further from the true goal that drives this argument. When scientists decided to investigate the behavior of the atom, they did not expect to derive a theory as parsimonious as that postulated to explain and predict the trajectory of a falling apple. But at the same time, they realized that existing arguments could not capture the more complex behavior of the atom.

A similar vision drives the present exhortation. Foreign policy is concerned with acts generally initiated by a small group of complex individuals, with a variety of interests and beliefs, that affect an array of human targets. To provide useful explanations of this process we must learn to theorize about how these individuals reason, and we must do so without being afraid to be burdened by the presence of complexity.[5]

The theory promoted throughout these pages does not attempt to run away from complexity, nor does it promote it for its own sake. Analogical thinking is not an easy process to structure, particularly in its linkage with an individual's beliefs. But although the association of both concepts complicates the nature of the explanation and the theory, the end result justifies the loss of parsimony. The obstacles to the conduct of solid empirical analysis are unlikely to become less cumbersome with time. The likelihood of greater complexity, however, rather than pulling us away from the analysis of the cognitive processes of decision-makers, ought to push us closer to it.

The field of social psychology is in a constant state of flux, with no single theory being able to act as the sole dominant force. How much we benefit from it depends on our willingness to look seriously at the various theories and test their explanatory reach across a range of cases. This endeavor is bound to bring significant benefits, along with some high costs. But if we are serious about our commitment to intellectual growth, then we must take the risk. As we ponder the potential costs of future failures, it might help to keep in mind Socrates' dictum that if we believe "that we must try to find out what is not known, we should be better, braver, and less idle . . ."

Notes

CHAPTER 1 THE NATURE OF THE PUZZLE

1 Here I am referring principally to the works by May, 1973; Jervis, 1976; Neustadt and May, 1986. These works have been extremely informative and helpful but have, for the most part, misapplied the concept of analogy. I will address this issue in some detail in chapter 2.

2 Some of the principal voices on the side of the strategic argument are Grant, 1955; Wriston, 1967; and Morgenthau, 1969. The economic argument has been proposed by Aybar, 1978; and Schlesinger and Kinzer, 1983.

3 For a more detailed discussion of the nature of the debate between "instrumentalist Marxists" and "structuralist Marxists," see Krasner, 1978.

4 This hypothesis is a logical derivation of Karl von Clausewitz's proposition that a state determined to defeat its enemies will "proportion [its] efforts to [its adversaries'] power of resistance" (see von Clausewitz, 1986: 299).

5 For a more detailed discussion of this argument, see chapter 2, n. 2.

6 Some of the major exceptions are the works by Vandenbroucke, 1984, on the Bay of Pigs; and to a lesser extent Lowenthal's 1972 study of the invasion of the Dominican Republic in 1965 by the United States; Immerman's 1982 account of the 1954 invasion of Guatemala; and Schoultz's 1987 study of the central beliefs that guided US foreign policy in Latin America.

7 For a detailed discussion of this theory and its applicability to foreign policy, see Steinbruner, 1974: 88–139; and Larson, 1985: 29–34. Larson's focus, however, is on cognitive dissonance theory and its relevance to the explanation of attitude change.

8 These four parts are discussed in some detail in chapter 3.

9 For a more formalized discussion of the process of differentiating operational objectives, see von Winterfeldt and Edwards, 1986.

10 A detailed explanation of why these cases were selected is presented toward the end of chapter 3.

CHAPTER 2   THE CALCULATION OF INTERESTS AND THE DEFINITION OF PROBLEMS

1 According to Bentham, since it is not possible to distinguish the merit of one man's demand for pleasure from that of any other man, all the pleasures of all men must be treated as equally valuable, and the maximization of these pleasures must be considered as the only rational standard of political might. See Bentham, 1834; Davidson, 1916.

2 The decision to limit the analysis to two additional cognitive theories is based on the recognition that they are among the perspectives most commonly used by foreign policy analysts who have sought to design foreign policy models, and on the belief that they reflect some of the most dissonant assumptions about how the individual, as an active agent, constructs meaning from the environment.

It might also be noted that I have purposely decided not to test the analogical theory against information-processing models such as the "operational code" or various versions of cognitive mapping. This decision is based on the contention that these models are not erected on specific theories. Alexander George's operational code is a case in point.

In 1969, George argued that although the concept "operational code" can be studied without reference to psychoanalytic hypotheses, the researcher can, if he so wishes, relate some of the beliefs delineated by the application of the code to motivational variables of a psychodynamic character. In 1979, upon having acknowledged that new research in psychology was moving away from the conception of man as a passive individual, and also was moving from the conception of man as a "consistency-seeker" to the view of man as a "problem-solver," George hinted that the operational code might be cast as a derivative of attribution theory.

George's supposed transition from psychoanalytic theory to attribution theory does not pose an insurmountable theoretical problem, at least regarding the issue of whether the individual should be perceived as a passive or an active agent. In both instances the decision-maker is viewed as an actor seeking to exercise some control over the outcome of social situations. Moreover, George makes it very clear that his conception of the policy-maker is not that of a "consistency-seeker" but that of a "problem-solver." What George overlooks is that attribution theory is not the only cognitive theory that beholds the individual as a problem-solver; schema theory imputes the same form of behavior. The critical difference between these two theories is that attribution theory assumes that when confronted by a decision problem the individual will weigh the relative influence of potential causes and formulate causal explanations as he searches for a solution, while schema theory contends that under the same circumstances the individual would structure and respond to the problem quickly and economically by reasoning analogically. See George, 1969, 1979; and Larson, 1985.

3 Cognitive dissonance theory should not be confused with cognitive consistency theory. Cognitive dissonance theory is built on the assumption that ego-defensive motivations lead the individual to avoid situations and information which would likely increase dissonance, and it has been designed to analyze only *post-decision* situations. Cognitive consistency theory, on the other hand, assumes the individual needs to develop simple rules for processing information in order to maintain consistency. The second theory, moreover, seeks to explain the process that takes place prior to and just at the time the decision is being made. See Jervis, 1976: 382–3, n. 2; and Lebow, 1981: 111.

4   March implicitly infers these changes when he contends that goals cannot be assumed to remain constant through time. See March, 1977.
5   "Analogy" will be referred to as "the similarity of relations," since it is difficult to assess the ratios between foreign policy concepts.
6   These similarities of relations are simple-minded. The sole purpose of presenting the relations in such simple forms is to facilitate the understanding behind analogical reasoning.
7   I hope that purists will forgive me for stating that a city makes inferences. It goes without saying that individuals, not cities, make inferences. References to cities, rather than decision-makers, are made merely as an attempt to add some variety to the text.

CHAPTER 3   METHODOLOGICAL CRITERIA

1   The four concepts are defined as follows: "direct combat involvement" refers to the intervention by the aggressor's regular forces in the affairs of the target; "indirect combat involvement" refers to the intervention by irregular troops under the intervener's command in the affairs of the target; "direct para-combat involvement" refers to the intervention by the aggressor with advisors and/or the supply of arms in the affairs of the target; "indirect para-combat involvement" refers to the intervention by the aggressor with financial support, armed blockade, and/or military training in the affairs of the target.
2   Here I am using Larson's study of four US foreign policy-makers as my principal criterion. See Larson, 1985.
3   One of the basic ideas behind the operational code is that in the analysis of the relationships between beliefs and decisions that pertain to foreign policy, the only beliefs that are important are the political ones. This study agrees with that position, and carries it a step further by contending that a careful analysis of the studies that have sought to identify the philosophical and instrumental beliefs of major foreign policy-makers will show that only a few of them need to be studied in order to predict foreign policy decisions. Walker's study of Henry Kissinger's operational code and how it influenced his decision not to pursue unreasonable goals in his negotiations with the North Vietnamese, is just one example. See Walker, 1977: 153.

CHAPTER 4   GUATEMALA: THE DESIGNING OF THE FUTURE

1   A similar argument is put forward by Schlesinger and Kinzer, 1983.
2   Confidential memorandum from John M. Cabot to Hull, December 4, 1940, NA814.00/12-440.
3   Message by US military attaché to War Deaprtment, September 23, 1944, M300-Warfare, Sec. 1. of "Warfare (Central America)," 1942–44, FDR papers.
4   Nelson Rockefeller to Edwin Kyle, 2, July 6, 1945, FRUS 9: 1084–6.
5   Of great concern to the US Embassy in Guatemala was the increased activity of labor movements.
6   "Communism in Guatemala," Wells to the Honorable Secretary of State, May 6, 1948, NA 814.00/B5-648.
7   Policy statement by US Department of State, August 17, 1948, NA 711.14/8-1748.
8   See especially Immerman's notes 19, 20, and 21, on p. 233.

9   See especially Immerman's notes 25, 60, 61, and 62, on pp. 233 and 237.
10 Notes of the Undersecretary's meeting, June 15, 1951, Foreign Relations of the United States, 1951, 2: 1440–3, 1445.
11 A more detailed, alternative, explanation of this decision is presented in chapter 7.
12 "Memorandum: the Guatemalan Problem in Central America," March 31, 1953, Berle Diary.
13 Milton Eisenhower, "Report to the President."
14 Although it is not known precisely when Eisenhower ordered the CIA to begin drafting a covert paramilitary plan, the general assumption is that he did sometime between July and August 1953. See Immerman, 1982: 134.
15 According to Kermit Roosevelt, Allan Dulles was so impressed by the operation that he offered him the opportunity to organize the Guatemalan plan.
16 See notes 19 and 20 in this chapter.
17 According to Ambrose, "the Eisenhower administration saw the arms shipment as an ominous indication of the future course of the Guatemalan revolutionary regime and a sign that the United States could not afford to tolerate the regime any longer" (Ambrose, 1984: 193). This section does not necessarily challenge Ambrose's conclusion, but instead proposes that the timing of the decision can better be explained by contending that the Czech arms shipment afforded the Eisenhower administration a great political opportunity. Eisenhower was already committed to overthrowing the Arbenz regime, but he also needed to ensure that if it were revealed that the operation had been designed and financed by the United States, public opinion would acknowledge the importance of relying on such means in view of the lastest developments that had transpired in Guatemala.
18 John Foster Dulles, "US Policy on Guatemala," Bulletin 30 (June 21, 1954): 950–1.
19 Statement appears in US State Department Memorandum of conversation, October 29, 1953, attached to AMEMBASSY, Guatemala, to Department of State, November 2, 1953, NA 611.14/11-253.
20 Report from Peurifoy to Secretary of State, November 19, 1953, NA 611.14/11-1953.

CHAPTER 5 CUBA: THE APPLICATION OF THE WRONG LESSON?

1   I am grateful to Jules Benjamin for letting me read his manuscript before it went to press. For this reason, I am unable to cite specific pages for note purposes.
2   Minutes of Cabinet meeting, March 11, 1955, Eisenhower Library (Microfilm): 1–3.
3   For a detailed explanation of this period, see Bonachea and Valdez, 1969; Dumont, 1970.
4   Minutes of Cabinet meeting, May 16, 1958, Eisenhower Library (Microfilm): 1–2.
5   The Department of State approved Pawley's mission only after the White House agreed that the ambassador would not be visiting Cuba as an official US representative.
6   Both Rubottom and Bonsal believed that it was inappropriate for US businesses to expect the State Department to protect their interests in foreign states. Their emphasis was on ensuring that foreign governments adhered to international practices toward foreign investments. See Starr and Lowenthal, 1988: 40.
7   Herter to Eisenhower, November 5, 1959. Memorandum can be found in Declassified Documents Quarterly, 1981, no. 356.

8 Letter from former National Security Advisor Gordon Gray to Dr Don Wilson, Assistant Director, Dwight D. Eisenhower Library, December 3, 1974. Gordon Gray papers, 1946–1976. See also Benjamin, 1989. I am grateful to Ms Pamela Starr for bringing to my attention the February 4 meeting between Dulles and Eisenhower.
9 Interview conducted by Ambrose with Bissell. A more detailed explanation regarding Eisenhower's attitude toward the use of military force overtly is presented in chapter 7.
10 Nixon had been advocating armed intervention by Cuban nationals, trained and financed by the CIA, since 1959. See Nixon, 1962:352.
11 On January 25, 1960, Eisenhower agreed with Herter that Latin American leaders would not tolerate the imposition of economic sanctions on Cuba and thus refused to approve the policy. It is also evident that he had yet to order the CIA to develop a paramilitary intervention plan.
12 A detailed analysis of this decision, and its relation to Kennedy's cognitive process, is presented in chapter 7.

CHAPTER 6 THE DOMINICAN REPUBLIC: THE FUTURE MUST NOT RESEMBLE THE PAST

1 Memorandum for the President by Christian Herter, April 14, 1960: 1.
2 Originally formed in 1955 as the 5412 Committee, and later renamed the Forty Committee, the Special Group's mandate was to oversee all covert operations. In theory, all covert operations needed the Special Group's approval before they could be implemented. The members of the Group were the national security advisor, the director of central intelligence, the under secretary of state, and the deputy secretary of defense (Ambrose, 1984: 506).
3 Memorandum for the President by Christian Herter, April 14, 1960.
4 Kennedy was in fact agreeing to implement the contingency plan drawn by Herter and approved by Eisenhower in April 1961.
5 For a detailed analysis of the events during the months preceding the elections, see Martin, 1966: 84–302; and Gleijeses, 1978: 65–85.
6 For a detailed analysis of the two-day struggle, see Gleijeses, 1978: 249–52.
7 Even Ambassador Martin, who in his first account of the invasion (Martin, 1966) contends that initially the US intervened in order to protect American lives and property, subsequently acknowledges that the real reason Johnson ordered the US Marines to land was to avert a "second Cuba." See Martin, 1978: 95.
8 By this I do not mean to suggest that governments always learn the correct lessons.

CHAPTER 7 THE INTERPLAY BETWEEN INTERESTS, BELIEFS, AND COGNITIVE PROCESSES

1 Here I am responding to Larson's interpretation of schema theory. See Larson, 1985: 51.
2 This argument must not be interpreted as a contention that the United States should have launched a military invasion. It only proposes that in order for the decision-making process to be considered "rational," such calculation had to have been conducted.

CHAPTER 8 PERU AND CHILE: DOES THE PAST HAVE MORE THAN ONE PATTERN?

1 Haya de la Torre missed the mark by 0.03 percentage point.
2 US Congress, P.L. 87-565, August 1, 1962, Sec. 620(e), 76 Sta. 260.
3 It is important to keep in mind, however, that President Kennedy had indicated a willingness to recognize the military regime that had toppled President Bosch in the Dominican Republic even before the new regime disclosed that it would call for new elections.
4 For a discussion on the military background of the members of the new military regime, see McClintock, 1983: 275. This argument will be presented in greater detail in this chapter's last section.
5 Although there is no data to substantiate this inference, it is important to keep in mind that in 1959, Nixon, after meeting with Castro, informed Eisenhower that the United States might be able to work with the Cuban leader. But it was also Nixon who pressured Eisenhower to act more forcefully against Castro as it became evident that the Cuban leader had no intention of allowing the United States to dictate Cuba's new political, economic, and social courses. It seems very unlikely that Nixon would have been disposed to take the same risk a second time.
6 For a succinct description of these steps, see Falcoff, 1984: 80–3.
7 Doherty's statement was made to a Senate subcommittee.
8 Description of the function of the joint military group by the chief of the US delegation to the group, Major General George S. Beatty.
9 Having discussed already the cognitive processes of Kennedy and Johnson, this chapter will not evaluate their relevance to explaining US actions toward Peru and Chile.

CHAPTER 9 NICARAGUA AND GRENADA: THE PAST HAS ONLY ONE FUTURE

1 In his analysis of the Carter policy, Schoultz focuses almost entirely on the period after the Sandinistas came to power, with very little reference to the earlier time.
2 For a biting criticism of Derian's viewpoint, see Muravchik, 1986: 53–73.
3 According to Muravchik, "the foreign policy team of the Carter administration included a network of individuals in key positions affecting human rights policy who shared a 'McGovernite' or 'left-liberal' world view and whose human rights passions were focused on the depravations of rightist regimes" (Muravchik, 1986: 14).
4 During this period Todman was being transferred to his new post as ambassador to Spain, while Vaky was still in the process of moving from Caracas to Washington.
5 According to Pastor, the letter was released to the press not by Somoza or Perez, but by a US State Department official who had opposed the sending of the letter.
6 This helps explain why the Bush administration waited until December 1989 to intervene in Panama to topple Manuel Noriega. By then, particularly after deciding not to intervene during an earlier coup attempt and being heavily criticized by the US Congress, the Bush administration knew quite well that an invasion would be widely supported in the United States.

CHAPTER 10   CONTINUITY AND CHANGE IN US POLICY OF INTERVENTION

1   As Steinbruner notes: "Pertinent information may enter the decision process or it may be screened out, depending on how it relates to the existing pattern of belief" (Steinbruner, 1974: 123).

2   Jervis and Steinbruner recognized this relationship in their respective studies. See Steinbruner, 1974; Jervis, 1976.

3   Steinbruner attributes this phenomenon to several factors. See Steinbruner, 1974: 9.

4   Ibid.: 13. For an excellent critique of rational choice theory, see the January 1989 issue of *World Politics*.

5   Complexity is automatically increased whenever analysts attempt to understand the frame of reference utilized by decision-makers as they address problems. But this analytical process is essential. As Richard Ned Lebow and Janice Gross Stein contend, the most important determinant of decisions is not "the process of choosing among options but the prior definition and the construction of the problem to be decided." See Lebow and Stein, 1989: 214. See also Simon, 1985: 295.

Bibliography

Alexander, Robert J. (1978) *The Tragedy of Chile*. Westport, CT: Greenwood Press.
Ambrose, Stephen (1981) *Ike's Spies*. New York: Doubleday.
Ambrose, Stephen (1984) *Eisenhower: The President*, vol. II. New York: Simon and Schuster.
Ambrose, Stephen (1988) *Rise to Globalism*. New York: Penguin Books.
Andriole, Stephen J. (1985) "A Theoretical Analysis of the Reagan Administration's Decision to Invade Grenada," in Peter M. Dunn and Bruce W. Watson (eds), *American Intervention in Grenada*. Boulder, CO: Westview Press.
Axelrod, Robert (1976) "The Analysis of Cognitive Maps," in Robert Axelrod (ed.), *Structure of Decision*. Princeton, NJ: Princeton University Press.
Aybar de Soto, Jose M. (1978) *Dependency and Intervention: The Case of Guatemala in 1954*. Boulder, CO: Westview Press.
Baklanoff, Eric N. (1971) "International Economic Relations," in Carmelo Mesa-Lago (ed.), *Revolutionary Change in Cuba*. Pittsburgh, PA: University of Pittsburgh Press.
Baldwin, David A. (1985) *Economic Statecraft*. Princeton, NJ: Princeton University Press.
Ball, George (1982) *The Past Has Another Pattern – Memoirs*. New York: W. W. Norton and Company.
Baran, Paul, and Sweezy, Paul (1966) *Monopoly Capital*. New York: Monthly Review Press.
Beard, Charles A. (1966) *The Idea of National Interest: An Analytical Study in American Foreign Policy*. Chicago: Quadrangle.
Bell, Ian (1981) *The Dominican Republic*. Boulder, CO: Westview Press.
Benjamin, Jules (1989) *The United States and the Origins of the Cuban Revolution*. Princeton, NJ: Princeton University Press.
Bentham, J. (1834) *Deontology*, arranged and edited by J. Bowring, vols I and II. London: Longman.
Biersteker, Thomas J. (1983) "The Logic of the Reagan Administration's Invasion of Grenada," Department of Political Science, Yale University (unpublished paper).
Blasier, Cole (1971) "The Elimination of United States Influence," in Carmelo Mesa-Lago (ed.), *Revolutionary Change in Cuba*. Pittsburgh, PA: University of Pittsburgh Press.
Blasier, Cole (1976) *The Hovering Giant*, Pittsburgh, PA: University of Pittsburgh Press.
Blasier, Cole (1985) *The Hovering Giant*, rev. edn. Pittsburgh, PA: University of Pittsburgh Press.

Blechman, Barry M., and Kaplan, Stephen S. (1978) *Force Without War*. Washington, DC: The Brookings Institute.

Bodenheimer, Sussane Jonas (1981) *Guatemala: Plan Piloto Para Continente*. Editorial Universitaria Centroamericana.

Bonachea, Ramon L., and San Martin, Marta (1974) *The Cuban Insurrection: 1952–1959*. New Brunswick: Transaction Books.

Bonachea, Rolando E., and Valdez, Nelson P. (1969) *Che. Selected Works of Ernesto Guevara*. Cambridge, MA: The MIT Press.

Bonham, G. Matthew, and Shapiro, Michael (1976) "Explanation of the Unexpected: The Syrian Intervention in Jordan in 1970," in Robert Axelrod (ed.), *Structure of Decision*. Princeton, NJ: Princeton University Press.

Bonsal, Philip W. (1971) *Cuba, Castro, and the United States*. Pittsburgh, PA: University of Pittsburgh Press.

Booth, John A. (1984) "The Revolution in Nicaragua: Through a Frontier of History," in Donald G. Schulz and Douglas H. Graham (eds), *Revolution and Counterrevolution in Central America and the Caribbean*. Boulder, CO: Westview Press.

Brodie, Bernard (1977) *A Guide to Naval Strategy*, 4th edn. Westport, CT: Greenwood Press.

Brzezinski, Zbigniew (1970) *Between Two Ages: America's Role in the Technocratic Era*. New York: Viking Press.

Brzezinski, Zbigniew (1983) *Power and Principle: Memoirs of the National Security Advisor, 1977–1981*. New York: Farrar, Straus, Giroux.

Burbach, Roger, and Herald, Marc (1984) "The US Economic Stake in Central America and the Caribbean," in Roger Burbach and Patricia Flynn (eds), *The Politics of Intervention*. New York: Monthly Review Press.

Cammarota, V. Anthony, Jr (1984) "American Dependency on Strategic Materials," in Gerald J. Mangone (ed.), *American Strategic Minerals*. New York: Crane Russak.

Carbonell, Jaime G. (1983) "Learning by Analogy: Formulating and Generalizing Plans from Past Experience," in Ryszarol S. Michalski, Jaime G. Carbonell, and Tom M. Mitchells (eds), *Machine Learning in Artificial Intelligence Approach*. Palo Alto, CA: Tioga Publishing Company.

Carter, Jimmy (1975) *Why Not the Best?* Nashville, Tenn.: Broadman Press.

Carter, Jimmy (1982) *Keeping-Faith: Memoirs of a President*. New York: Bantam Books.

Chadwin, Mark L. (1972) "Foreign Policy Report: Nixon's Expropriation Policy Seeks to Soothe Angry Congress," *National Journal*, January 22.

Challener, Richard D. (1986) "The National Security Policy from Truman to Eisenhower: Did the 'Hidden-Hand' Leadership Make Any Difference?," in Norman A. Graebner (ed.), *The National Security*. New York: Oxford University Press.

Child, John (1980) *Unequal Alliance: The Inter-American Military System, 1938–1978*. Boulder, CO: Westview Press.

Chomsky, Noam (1972) "The Pentagon Papers and US Imperialism in South East Asia," in *Spheres of Influence in the Age of Imperialism*. London: Spokesman.

Christian, Shirley (1985) *Nicaragua: Revolution in the Family*. New York: Random House.

CIA (1948) *Review of the World Situation*, 12 (May).

von Clausewitz, Karl (1986) "On the Nature of War," in John A. Vasquez (ed.), *Classics of International Relations*. Englewood Cliffs, NJ: Prentice-Hall.

Croes, Robertico (1985) "Sifting Through the Ashes: The Grenada Experience." Los Angeles, CA: School of International Relations, University of Southern California (unpublished paper).

Cypher, Dorothea (1985) "Grenada: Indications, Warning, and the US Response," in

Peter M. Dunn and Bruce W. Watson (eds), *American Intervention in Grenada.* Boulder, CO: Westview Press.

Davidson, W. L. (1916) *Political Thought in England. The Utilitarians from Bentham to J. T. Mill.* New York: Holt, Reinhart, and Winston, Inc.

Davis, Nathaniel (1985) *The Last Two Years of Salvador Allende.* London: I. B. Taurs and Company Ltd, Publishers.

Declassified Documents Quarterly (1976) "Memorandum for the President. Subject: Evaluation of the Unofficial Visit to Washington by Prime Minister Fidel Castro of Cuba," 23 April 1959, no. 58.

Declassified Documents Quarterly (1981) "Herter to Eisenhower," 5 November 1959, no. 3560.

Diederich, Bernard (1978) *Trujillo: The Death of the Goat.* Boston: Little, Brown, and Company.

Diederich, Bernard (1981) *Somoza.* New York: E. P. Dutton.

Dixon, Marlene (1985) "Reagan's Central American Policy: A New Somoza for Nicaragua," in Marlene Dixon (ed.), *On Trial: Reagan's War Against Nicaragua.* San Francisco: Synthesis Publications.

Draper, Theodore (1965) "The Dominican Revolt. A Case Study in American Policy," *Commentary* (December): 33–68.

Dugger, Ronnie (1982) *The Politician: The List and Times of Lyndon Johnson.* New York: W. W. Norton.

Dumont, Rene (1970) *Cuba: Socialism and Development,* translated by Helen R. Lane. New York: Grove Press, Inc.

Dunér, Bertil (1983) "The Many-Pronged Spear: External Military Intervention in Civil Wars in the 1970s," *Journal of Peace Research,* vol. 20, no. 1: 59–72.

Eckstein, Harry (1975) "Case Study and Theory in Political Science," in Fred Greenstein and Nelson Polsby (eds), *Handbook of Political Science,* vol. 7. Reading, MA: Addison–Wesley.

Einhorn, Jessica Pernitz (1974) *Expropriation Politics.* Lexington, MA: D. C. Heath and Company.

Eisenhower, Milton (1963) *The Wine is Bitter.* Garden City, NY: Doubleday.

Esper, E. A. (1973) *Analogy and Association in Linguistics and Psychology.* Athens: University of Georgia Press.

Etheredge, Lloyd S. (1985) *Can Governments Learn?* New York: Pergamon Press.

Etzioni, Amitai (1988) *The Moral Dimension.* New York: The Free Press.

Falcoff, Mark (1984) *Small Countries, Large Issues.* Washington, DC: American Enterprise Institute for Public Research.

Foreign Relations of the United States (1951) Washington, DC.

Freed, Donald, with Landis, Fred Simon (1980) *Death in Washington. The Murder of Orlando Letelier.* Westport, CT: Lawrence Hill and Company.

Gaddis, John Lewis (1982) *Strategies of Containment.* Oxford: Oxford University Press.

George, Alexander L. (1969) "The Operational Code: A Neglected Approach to the Study of Political Leaders and Decision-Making," *International Studies Quarterly* (June), vol. 13, no. 2: 190–222.

George, Alexander L. (1979) "Case Studies and Theory Development: The Method of Structured, Focused Comparison," in Paul G. Lauren (ed.), *Diplomacy: New Approaches in History, Theory, and Policy.* New York: The Free Press.

George, Alexander L. (1980) *Presidential Decision Making in Foreign Policy: The Effective Use of Information and Advice.* Boulder, CO: Westview Press.

George, Alexander L., and Smoke, Richard (1974) *Deterrence in American Foreign Policy.* New York: Columbia University Press.

Germain, Lawrence (1985) "A Chronology of Events Concerning Grenada," in Peter M. Dunn and Bruce W. Watson (eds), *American Intervention in Grenada*. Boulder, CO: Westview Press.

Geyelen, Philip (1966) *Lyndon B. Johnson and the World*. New York: Praeger.

Gilmore, William C. (1984) *The Grenada Intervention*. New York: Facts on File Publications.

Gilpin, Robert (1981) *War and Change in World Politics*. New York: Cambridge University Press.

Glad, Betty (1980) *Jimmy Carter*. New York: W. W. Norton.

Gleijeses, Piero (1978) *The Dominican Crisis – The 1965 Constitutionalist Revolt and American Intervention*. Baltimore: The Johns Hopkins University Press.

Goff, Fred, and Locker, Michael (1969) "The Violence of Domination: US Power and the Dominican Republic," in Irving L. Horowitz, Josue de Castro, and John Gerassi (eds), *Latin American Radicalism*. New York: Random House.

Goldman, Eric F. (1969) *The Tragedy of Lyndon Johnson*. New York: Alfred A. Knopf.

Gonzalez, Edward (1972) *Partners in Deadlock: The United States and Castro, 1959–1972*. The Southern California Arms Control and Foreign Policy Seminar.

Goodsell, Charles T. (1972) "Diplomatic Protection of US Business in Peru," in Daniel A. Sharp (ed.), *US Foreign Policy in Peru*. Austin: University of Texas Press.

Goodsell, Charles T. (1974) *American Corporations and Peruvian Politics*. Cambridge: Harvard University Press.

Goodwin, Richard (1969) "Letter From Peru," in *The New Yorker* (May 17): 41–109.

Gordon Gray Papers (1946–1976) Dwight Eisenhower Library.

Grabner, D. A. (1959) *Crisis Diplomacy: A History of US Intervention Policies and Practices*. Washington, DC: Public Affairs Press.

Grant, Donald (1955) "Guatemala and the United States Foreign Policy," *Journal of International Affairs*, vol. 9, no. 1: 64–81.

Greenstein, Fred I. (1982) *The Hidden-Hand Presidency*. New York: Basic Books.

Guasti, Laura (1983) "The Peruvian Military Government and the International Corporations," in Cynthia McClintock and Abraham Lowenthal (eds), *The Peruvian Experiment Reconsidered*. Princeton, NJ: Princeton University Press.

Haig, Alexander (1984) *Caveat*. New York: Macmillan.

Hayes, Margaret Daly (1984) *Latin America and the US National Interest*. Boulder, CO: Westview Press.

Hoagland, Steven W., and Walker, Stephen, G. (1979) "Operational Codes and Crisis Outcomes," in Lawrence S. Falkowski (ed.), *Psychological Models in International Politics*. Boulder, CO: Westview Press.

Hoffmann, Stanley (1960) *Contemporary Theory in International Relations*. Englewood Cliffs, NJ: Prentice Hall.

Hoffmann, Stanley (1980) *Primacy or World Order*. New York: McGraw-Hill.

Holsti, K. J. (1985) *The Dividing Discipline*. Boston: Allen and Unwin.

Holsti, Ole (1976) "Foreign Policy Formation Viewed Cognitively," in Robert Axelrod (ed.), *Structure of Decision*. Princeton, NJ: Princeton University Press.

Hopkins, Jack (ed.) (1981–84) *Latin American and Caribbean Contemporary Record*, vols 1–3. New York: Holmes and Meier.

Hopple, Gerald, and Gilley, Cynthia (1985) "Policy Without Intelligence," in Peter M. Dunn and Bruce W. Watson (eds), *American Intervention in Grenada*. Boulder, CO: Westview Press.

Horowitz, Irving (1967) "The Military Elites," in Seymour Martin Lipset and Aldo Solari (eds), *Elites in South America*. New York: Oxford University Press.

Hybel, Alex Roberto (1986) *The Logic of Surprise in International Conflict*. Lexington, MA: D. C. Heath.

Immerman, Richard (1982) *The CIA in Guatemala*. Austin: University of Texas Press.

Ingram, George M. (1974) *Expropriation of U.S. Property in Latin America*. New York: Praeger Publishers.

Janis, Irving L. (1976) *Groupthink*. Boston, MA: Houghton Mifflin, Co.

Jervis, Robert (1970) *The Logic of Images in International Relations*. Princeton, NJ: Princeton University Press.

Jervis, Robert (1976) *Perception and Misperception in International Politics*. Princeton, NJ: Princeton University Press.

Johnson, Lyndon B. (1971) *The Vantage Point: Perspectives of the Presidency 1963–1969*. New York: Holt, Rinehart, and Winston.

Jonas, Susanne (1983) "The New Cold War and the Nicaraguan Revolution: The Case of U.S. 'Aid' to Nicaragua," in Stanford Central American Action Network (eds), *Revolution in Central America*. Boulder, CO: Westview Press.

Jordan, Amos A., and Kilmarx, Robert A. (1979) *Strategic Mineral Dependence: The Stockpile Dilemma*. Beverly Hills, CA: Sage Publications, The Center for Strategic and International Studies.

Kahneman, Daniel, and Tversky, Adam (1973) "On the Psychology of Prediction," *Psychological Review*, 80: 237–51.

Kail, Robert, and Pellegrino, James W. (1985) *Human Intelligence. Perspectives and Prospects*. New York: W. H. Freeman and Co.

Keane, Mark (1985) "On Drawing Analogies When Solving Problems: A Theory and Test of Solution Generation in an Analogical Problem-Solving Task," *British Journal of Psychology*, 76: 449–58.

Kearns, Doris (1976) *Lyndon Johnson and the American Dream*. New York: Harper and Row.

Keeney, Ralph L., and Raiffa, Howard (1976) *Decisions with Multiple Objectives: Preferences and Value Tradeoffs*. New York: John Wiley and Sons.

Kelley, Harold H. (1967) "Attribution Theory in Social Psychology," in *Nebraska Symposium on Motivation*. Lincoln: University of Nebraska Press.

Kennan, George F. (1967) *Memoirs, 1925–1950*. Boston, MA: Little, Brown.

Kenner, Martin, and Petras, James (eds) (1969) *Fidel Castro Speaks*. New York: Grove Press, Inc.

Kenworthy, Eldon (1984) "Grenada As Theater," in *World Policy Journal* (Spring) 1.

Keohane, Robert (1983) "Theory of World Politics: Structural Realism and Beyond," in Ada W. Finifter (ed.), *Political Science: The State of the Discipline*. Washington, DC: The American Political Science Association.

Keohane, Robert O. (1984) *After Hegemony*. Princeton, NJ: Princeton University Press.

Kirkpatrick, Jeane (1981) "US Security and Latin America," *Commentary* (January).

Kirkpatrick, Jeane (1983) *The Reagan Phenomenon*. Washington, DC: American Enterprise Institute for Public Policy Research.

Kissinger, Henry (1979) *White House Years*. Boston, MA: Little, Brown and Company.

Kissinger, Henry (1982) *Years of Upheaval*. Boston, MA: Little, Brown and Company.

Klaiber, Jeffrey, L. (1977) *Religion and Revolution in Peru, 1824–1976*. Notre Dame, IN: University of Notre Dame Press.

Krasner, Stephen (1978) *Defending the National Interest*. Princeton, NJ: Princeton University Press.

Kuhn, Thomas S. (1970) *The Structure of Scientific Revolutions*. Chicago: The University of Chicago Press.

Kurth, James (1974) "Testing Theories of Economic Imperialism," in Steven J. Rosen and James R. Kurth (eds), *Testing Theories of Economic Imperialism*. Lexington, MA: D. C. Heath.

Kurth, James (1984) "The New Realism in US Latin American Relations: Principles for

314   *Bibliography*

a New US Foreign Policy," in Richard Newfarmer (ed.), *From Gunboats to Diplomacy.* Baltimore, MD: The Johns Hopkins University Press.

LaFeber, Walter (1983) *Inevitable Revolutions – The United States in Central America.* New York: W. W. Norton and Company.

LaFeber, Walter (1989) *The American Age.* New York: W. W. Norton.

Lakoff, George, and Johnson, Mark (1980) *Metaphors We Live By.* Chicago: Chicago University Press.

Lang, David (1985) "United States Policy Toward Peru, 1970–1973," Los Angeles: University of Southern California (unpublished paper).

Larson, Deborah W. (1985) *Origins of Containment.* Princeton, NJ: Princeton University Press.

Latin American Political Report (1979a) August 3.

Latin American Political Report (1979b) August 10.

Latin American Weekly Report: March 7, 1980; May 23, 1980; June 3, 1980; September 19, 1980; March 13, 1981; April 1, 1981; May 15, 1981; July 17, 1981; August 21, 1981; September 25, 1981; October 9, 1981.

Lebow, Richard Ned (1981) *Between Peace and War.* Baltimore, MD: The Johns Hopkins University Press.

Lebow, Richard Ned, and Stein, Janice Gross (1989) "Rational Deterrence Theory: I Think, Therefore I Deter," *World Politics*, vol. XLI (January), no. 2: 208–24.

Lehnert, Wendy, and Ringle, Martin (eds) (1982) *Strategies for Natural Language Processing.* Hillsdale, NJ: Lawrence Erlbaum.

Leites, Nathan (1953) *A Study of Bolshevism.* Glencoe, IL: The Free Press.

Lenin, V. I. (1982) *Imperialism: The Highest Stage of Capitalism.* New York: International Publishers.

LeoGrande, William (1983) "The Revolution in Nicaragua: Another Cuba?," in Stanford's *Revolution in Central America.* A complete version of LeoGrande's "The Revolution . . ." appears in *Foreign Affairs* (1979), vol. 58, no. 1: 28–50.

Levi, E. H. (1949) *An Introduction to Legal Reasoning.* Chicago: University of Chicago Press.

Lipson, Charles (1985) *Standing Guard.* Berkeley, CA: University of California Press.

Little, Richard (1975) *Intervention: External Involvement in Civil Wars.* London: Martin Robinson.

Lowenthal, Abraham (1972) *The Dominican Intervention.* Cambridge, MA: Harvard University Press.

Lowenthal, Abraham (1987) *Partners in Conflict.* Baltimore, MD: The Johns Hopkins University Press.

McCall, Richard (1984) "From Monroe to Reagan: An Overview of US–Latin American Relations," in Richard Newfarmer (ed.), *From Gunboats to Diplomacy.* Baltimore, MD: The Johns Hopkins University Press.

McClellan, David S. (1971) "The 'Operational Code' Approach to the Study of Political Leaders: Dean Acheson's Philosophical and Instrumental Beliefs," *Canadian Journal of Political Science* (March), vol. iv, no. 1: 52–75.

McClintock, Cynthia (1983) "Velasco, Officers, and Citizens: The Politics of Stealth," in Cynthia McClintock and Abraham Lowenthal (eds), *The Peruvian Experiment Reconsidered.* Princeton, NJ: Princeton University Press.

McConnell, Jeff (1983) "Counterrevolution in Nicaragua: the US Connection," in Peter Rosset and John Vandermeer (eds), *The Nicaraguan Reader.* New York: Grover Press, Inc.

McCormich, James M. (1985) *American Foreign Policy and American Values.* Itasca, IL: F. E. Peacock Publishers, Inc.

Mack, Andrew (1974) "Comparing Theories and Economic Imperialism," in Steven J. Rosen and James R. Kurth (eds), *Testing Theories of Economic Imperialism*. Lexington, MA: D. C. Heath and Company.

Madison, G. B. (1982) *Understanding: A Phenomenological-Pragmatic Analysis*. London: Greenwood Press.

March, James (1966) "The Power of Power," in David Easton (ed.), *Varieties of Political Theory*. Englewood Cliffs, NJ: Prentice-Hall: 39–70.

March, James (1977) "Bounded Rationality, Ambiguity and the Engineering of Choice," paper presented at Carnegie–Mellon University (October).

Marshall, A. (1920) *Principles of Economics*, 8th edn. London: Macmillan.

Martin, John Bartlow (1966) *Overtaken by Events*. New York: Doubleday.

Martin, John Bartlow (1978) *US Policy in the Caribbean*. Boulder, CO: Westview Press.

Marx, Karl, and Engels, Frederick (1977) "The Communist Manifesto," in David McLellan (ed.), *Karl Marx: Selected Writings*. Oxford: Oxford University Press.

Matthews, Herbert L. (1961) *The Cuban Story*. New York: George Braziller.

Maull, Hanns W. (1984) *Raw Materials, Energy and Western Security*. London: Macmillan.

Maxfield, Sylvia, and Stahler-Scholk, Richard (1985) "External Constraints," in Thomas W. Walker (ed.), *Nicaragua: The First Five Years*. New York: Praeger.

May, Ernest R. (1973) *"Lessons" of the Past. The Use and Misuse of History in American Foreign Policy*. New York: Oxford University Press.

Mecham, J. Lloyd (1961) *The United States and Inter-American Security, 1889–1960*. Austin: University of Texas Press.

Mefford, Dwain (1984) "Formulating Foreign Policy on the Basis of Historical Analogies: An Application of Developments in Artificial Intelligence," paper delivered at the 25th Annual Convention of the International Studies Association, Atlanta, GA (March).

Mefford, Dwain (1985) "Combining Historical Narrative and Game Theory in a Rule Based System," paper delivered at the Annual Meeting of the Western International Studies Association, Los Angeles, CA (October).

Mefford, Dwain (1986) "Using Political Narratives to Structure Decisions and Games: The Design for an Expert System Shell," paper delivered at the Annual Meeting of the International Studies Association, Anaheim, California (March).

Melanson, Richard A. (1987) "The Foundations of Eisenhower's Foreign Policy: Continuity, Community, and Consensus," in Richard A. Melanson and David Mayers (eds), *Reevaluating Eisenhower*. Urbana, IL: University of Illinois Press.

Mesquita, Bueno de (1981) *The War Trap*. New Haven, CT: Yale University Press.

Miroff, Bruce (1976) *Pragmatic Illusions*. New York: David McKay.

Mischel, Walter (1973) "Toward a Cognitive Social Learning: Reconceptualization of Personality," *Psychological Review*, 80: 252–83.

Molineu, Harold (1986) *US Policy Toward Latin America, From Regionalism to Globalism*. Boulder, CO: Westview Press.

Mommsen, Wolfgang J. (1977) *Theories of Imperialism*. Translated by P. S. Falla. Chicago: The University of Chicago Press.

Moreno, Dario (1987) "Ideology and United States Central American Policy under Carter and Reagan." Los Angeles: School of International Relations, University of Southern California (dissertation).

Morgenthau, Hans (1966) *Politics Among Nations*. New York: Alfred A. Knopf.

Morgenthau, Hans (1969) *A New Foreign Policy for the United States*. New York: Council on Foreign Relations, F. A. Praeger.

Morgenthau, Hans (1983) *Politics Among Nations*. New York: Alfred A. Knopf.

Morley, Morris (1983) "Reinterpreting the State–Class Relationship: American Corporations and U.S. Policy Toward Cuba, 1959–1960," *Comparative Politics* (October), vol. 16, no. 1: 67–83.

Morris, Roger (1977) *Uncertain Greatness*. New York: Harper and Row.

Munro, Dana G. (1974) *The United States and the Caribbean Republics, 1921–1933*. Princeton, NJ: Princeton University Press.

Muravchik, Joshua (1986) *The Uncertain Crusade*. New York: Hamilton Press.

NACLA, Report on the Americas (1985) May/June, vol. XIX, no. 3.

Nagel, E. (1939) *Principles of the Theory of Probability*, vol. I, no. 6. Chicago: University of Chicago Press.

Neustadt, Richard E., and May, Ernest R. (1986) *Thinking in Time: The Uses of History for Decision Makers*. New York: The Free Press.

New York Times: January 4, 1961; October 30, 1977; February 11, 1978; June 27, 1978; February 21, 1981; December 3, 1981; April 22, 1985.

Newell, Allen, and Simon, Herbert A. (1972) *Human Problem Solving*. Englewood Cliffs, NJ: Prentice-Hall.

Newsweek, November 8, 1982.

Nisbett, Richard E., Borgida, Eugene, Crandall, Rick, and Reed, Harvey (1976) "Popular Induction: Information Is Not Always Information," in John S. Carroll and John W. Payne (eds), *Cognition and Social Behavior*. Hillsdale, NJ: Lawrence Erlbaum Associates.

Nisbett, Richard E., and Ross, Lee (1980) *Human Inference: Strategies and Shortcomings of Social Judgment*. Englewood Cliffs, NJ: Prentice-Hall.

Nixon, Richard M. (1962) *Six Crises*. New York: Doubleday.

North, Liisa (1983) "Ideological Orientations of Peru's Military Rulers," in Cynthia McClintock and Abraham Lowenthal (eds), *The Peruvian Experiment Reconsidered*. Princeton, NJ: Princeton University Press.

Nunn, Frederick M. (1976) *The Military in Chilean History*. Albuquerque, NM: University of New Mexico Press.

Odell, John S. (1974) "Correlates of US Military Assistance and Military Intervention," in Steven J. Rosen and James R. Kurth (eds), *Testing Theories of Economic Imperialism*. Lexington, MA: D. C. Heath and Company.

Oppenheimer, Robert (1956) "Analogy in Science," *American Psychologist*, vol. II (March): 127–35.

Orwell, George (1957) "Politics and the English Language," in G. Orwell, *Selected Essays*. Harmondsworth: Penguin.

Parmet, Herbert S. (1983) *JFK*. New York: The Dial Press.

Pastor, Robert (1985) "The United States and the Grenada Revolution: Who Pushed First and Why?," paper delivered in San German, Puerto Rico, October 17–19.

Pastor, Robert (1987a) *Condemned to Repetition: The United States and Nicaragua*. Princeton, NJ: Princeton University Press.

Pastor, Robert (1987b) "The Reagan Administration and Latin America: Eagle Insurgent," in Kenneth A. Oye, Robert J. Lieber, and Donald Rothchild (eds), *Eagle Resurgent? The Reagan Era in American Foreign Policy*. Boston, MA: Little, Brown and Company.

Payne, Arnold (1968) *The Peruvian Coup d'Etat of 1962: The Overthrow of Manuel Prado*. Washington, DC: Institute for the Comparative Study of Political Systems.

Payne, Anthony, Sutton, Paul, and Thorndike, Tony (1984) *Grenada: Revolution and Invasion*. London: Croom Helm.

Pearson, Frederic S. and Baumann, Robert (1977) "Foreign Military Intervention and Changes in United States Business Activity," *Journal of Political and Military Sociology*, vol. 5 (Spring): 79–97.

Pearson, Phillip (1987) "The Grenada Invasion of October 1983: A Decision-Making Analysis." Los Angeles: School of International Relations, University of Southern California (unpublished paper).

Perkins, D. (1966) *The United States and the Caribbean*. Cambridge: Harvard University Press.

Petras, James F., and Morley, Morris H. (1975). *The United States and Chile*. New York: Monthly Review Press.

Petras, James F., and Morley, Morris H. (1983) "Economic Expansion, Political Crisis and US Policy in Central America," in Marlene Dixon and Sussane Jonas (eds), *Revolution and Intervention in Central America*. San Francisco: Synthesis Publications.

Philip, George D. E. (1978) *The Rise and Fall of the Peruvian Military Radicals, 1968–1976*. London: University of London, The Athlone Press.

Phillips, David (1977) *The Night Watch*. New York: Atheneum.

Pinelo, Adalberto J. (1973) *The Multinational Corporation as a Force in Latin American Politics*. New York: Praeger Publishers.

Polya, George (1954) *Mathematics and Plausible Reasoning: Patterns of Plausible Inference*, vol. II. Princeton, NJ: Princeton University Press.

Polya, George (1962) *Mathematical Discovery: On Understanding Learning, and Teaching Problem Solving*, vol. I. New York: John Wiley and Sons.

Rabe, Stephen G. (1988) *Eisenhower and Latin America*. Chapel Hill, NC: The University of North Carolina Press.

Raiffa, Howard (1968) *Decision Analysis: Introductory Lectures on Choices Under Uncertainty*. Reading, MA: Addison–Wesley.

Raiffa, Howard (1969) *Preferences for Multiattributed Alternatives* (Report No. RM-5868-D07/RC). Santa Monica, CA: Rand Corporation.

Roosevelt, Kermit (1979) *Countercoup: The Struggle for the Control of Iran*. New York: McGraw-Hill.

Rosen, Steven J. (1974) "The Open Door Imperative and US Foreign Policy," in Steven J. Rosen and James R. Kurth (eds), *Testing Theories of Economic Imperialism*. Lexington, MA: D. C. Heath and Company.

Rosenau, James N. (1969) "Intervention as a Scientific Concept, and a Postscript," in Richard A. Falk (ed.), *The Vietnam War and International Law*, vol. 2. Princeton, NJ: Princeton University Press.

Ross, Lee (1977) "The Intuitive Psychologist and his Shortcomings," in Leonard Berkowitz (ed.), *Advances in Experimental Social Psychology*, vol. 10. New York: Academic Press.

Roxborough, Ian, O'Brien, Philip, and Roddick, Jackie (1977) *Chile: The State and Revolution*. New York: Holmes and Meier Publishers.

Rubin, Barry (1987) *Secrets of State*. New York: Oxford University Press.

Rumelhart, D. E., and Abrahamson, A. A. (1973) "A Model for Analogical Reasoning," *Cognitive Psychology*, vol. 5: 1–28.

Safford, Jeffrey (1980) "The Nixon–Castro Meeting of 19 April 1959," *Diplomatic History*, vol. 4 (Fall): 425–31.

Sandford, Gregory, and Vigilante, Richard (1984) *Grenada: The Untold Story*. Lanham, MD: Madison Books.

Sartori, Giovanni, Riggs, Fred, and Tuene, Henry (1975) *The Tower of Babel: On the Definition and Analysis of Concepts in the Social Sciences*. International Studies Association, Occasional Paper, no. 6.

Schank, Roger C. (1982) *Dynamic Memory: A Theory of Reminding and Learning in Computers and People*. Cambridge: Cambridge University Press.

Schlesinger, Stephen, and Kinzer, Stephen (1983) *Bitter Fruit: The Untold Story of the American Coup in Guatemala*. Garden City, NY: Doubleday.

Schoultz, Lars (1981) *Human Rights and United States Policy Toward Latin America*. Princeton, NJ: Princeton University Press.

Schoultz, Lars (1987) *National Security and United States Policy Toward Latin America*. Princeton, NJ: Princeton University Press.

Schreiber, A. P. (1973) "Economic Coercion as an Instrument of Foreign Policy: US Economic Measures Against Cuba and the Dominican Republic," *World Politics*, vol. 25, no. 3: 387–413.

Schrodt, Philip A. (1986) "Pattern Matching, Set Prediction and Foreign Policy Analysis," in Stephen Cimbala (ed.), *Artificial Intelligence and National Security*. Lexington, MA: Lexington Books.

Schulz, Donald E. (1985) "Ten Theories in Search of Central American Reality," in Donald E. Schulz and Douglas H. Graham (eds), *Revolution and Counterrevolution in Central America and the Caribbean*. Boulder, CO: Westview Press.

Schurmann, Franz (1974) *The Logic of World Power: An Inquiry Into the Orgins, Currents and Contradictions of World Politics*. New York: Random House.

Semmel, Andrew T., and Minnix, Dean (1979) "Small-Group Dynamics on Foreign Policy Decision Making: An Experimental Approach," in Lawrence S. Falkowski (ed.), *Psychological Models in International Politics*. Boulder, CO: Westview Press.

Shalom, H., and Schlesinger, I. M. (1972) "Analogical Thinking: A Conceptual Analysis of Analogical Tests," in R. Reurstein, I. M. Sclesinger, H. Shalom, and H. Narrol (eds), *Studies in Cognitive Modifiability*, Report 1, vol. II. Jerusalem: Haddasah Wizo Canada Research Institute.

Sigmund, Paul E. (1974) "The 'Invisible Blockade' and the Overthrow of Allende," *Foreign Affairs* (January), vol. 52, no. 2: 322–40.

Sigmund, Paul E. (1977) *The Overthrow of Allende and the Politics of Chile, 1964–1976*. Pittsburgh: University of Pittsburgh Press.

Simon, Herbert A. (1957) *Models of Man*. New York: John Wiley and Sons.

Simon, Herbert A. (1985) "Human Nature in Politics: The Dialogue of Psychology with Political Science," *American Political Science Review*, 79 (June): 293–304.

Simon, Herbert A., with Hayes, John R. (1979) "The Understanding Process: Problem Isomorphs," in Herbert A. Simon (ed.), *Models of Thought*. New Haven, CT: Yale University Press.

Simon, Herbert A., and Kotovsky, K. (1963) "Human Acquisition of Concepts for Sequential Patterns," *Psychological Review*, 70: 534–46.

Slater, J. (1970) *Intervention and Negotiation: The United States and the Dominican Republic*. New York: Harper and Row.

Snyder, Glenn, and Diesing, Paul (1977) *Conflict Among Nations*. Princeton, NJ: Princeton University Press.

Starr, Pamela (1987) "The Semi-Rational Response to Revolution – The Influence of Rationality and Operational Codes in the U.S. Decision to Overthrow the Cuban Revolutionary Regime, 1959–1960." Los Angeles: School of International Relations, University of Southern California (unpublished paper).

Starr, Pamela K., and Lowenthal, Abraham F. (1988) "The United States and the Cuban Revolution, 1958–1960," Pew Diplomatic Training Project. Los Angeles: School of International Relations, University of Southern California.

Statistical Abstract of Latin America, vols 1–23 (1955–84). Los Angeles: University of California at Los Angeles Latin American Center Publications.

Steinbruner, John D. (1974) *The Cybernetic Theory of Decision*. Princeton, NJ: Princeton University Press.

Stepan, Alfred (1971) *The Military in Politics. Changing Patterns in Brazil*. Princeton, NJ: Princeton University Press.

Sternberg, Robert (1977) *Intelligence, Information Processing, and Analogical Reasoning.* Hillsdale, NJ: Lawrence Erlbaum.

Strasma, John (1972) "The United States and Agrarian Reform in Peru," in Daniel A. Sharp (ed.), *US Foreign Policy in Peru.* Austin: University of Texas Press.

Tambs, Lewis (ed.) (1980) *A New Inter-American Policy for the Eighties: Report of the Committee of Santa Fe.* Washington, DC.

Thomas, A. V. W., and Thomas, A. J. (1956) *Non-Intervention: The Law and its Imports in the Americas.* Dallas: Southern Methodist University Press.

Thomas, Caroline (1985) *New States, Sovereignty, and Intervention.* New York: St Martin's Press.

Thorndike, Tony (1985) *Grenada: Politics, Economics and Society.* Boulder, CO: Lynne Reinner Publishers, Inc.

Tversky, Amos, and Kahneman, Daniel (1981) "The Framing of Decisions and the Psychology of Choice," *Science,* 211 (January): 453–8.

United States Congress, House, Committee on Foreign Affairs, Inter-American Subcommittee (1975) *United States and Chile during the Allende Years, 1970–1973,* Hearings, 20 September 1973. Washington, DC: GPO no. 39-180.

United States Congress, Senate, Committee on Foreign Relations (1965) *Background Information Relating to the Dominican Republic.* Washington, DC: US Government Printing Office.

United States Department of Defense (1982) Special Report to the US Congress, February 1982.

United States Department of State (1985) Special Report no. 132, September 1985.

Vaky, Viron (1987) Personal interview, July 21.

Valenzuela, Arturo, and Kaufman, Robert (1984) "Chile: From Democracy to Authoritarianism," in Richard Newfarmer (ed.), *From Gunboats to Diplomacy.* Baltimore, MD: The Johns Hopkins University Press.

Vandenbroucke, Lucien (1984) "Anatomy of a Failure: The Decision to Land at the Bay of Pigs," *Political Science Quarterly,* vol. 99: 3 (Fall): 471–91.

Vicini, J. D. (1957) *La Isla del Azucar.* Ciudad Trujillo.

Villanueva, Victor (1963) *Un Año Bajo El Sable.* Lima, Peru: Empresa Grafica T. Scheuch S.A.

Vincent, R. J. (1974) *Nonintervention and International Order.* Princeton, NJ: Princeton University Press.

Viotti, Paul R., and Kauppi, Mark V. (1987) *International Relations Theory.* New York: Macmillan.

Vital Speeches (1977) no. 43, February 15.

Walker, Stephen (1977) "The Interface Between Beliefs and Behavior: Henry A. Kissinger's Operational Code and the Vietnam War," *Journal of Conflict Resolution* (March), vol. 21, no. 1: 129–68.

Walton, Richard J. (1972) *Cold War and Counterrevolution.* Baltimore, MD: Penguin Books.

Waltz, Kenneth (1979) *Theory of International Politics.* New York: Random House.

Washington Post: May 16, 1978; November 14, 1978.

Weisskopf, Thomas E. (1974) "Capitalism, Socialism, and the Sources of Imperialism," in Steven J. Rosen and James R. Kurth (eds), *Testing Theories of Imperialism.* Lexington, MA: D. C. Heath and Company.

Werlich, David P. (1978) *Peru: A Short History.* Carbondale, IL: Southern Illinois University Press.

The West Indies and Caribbean Yearbook, 1955–1967.

Wiarda, H. J. (1968) *Dictatorship and Development: The Methods of Control in Trujillo's*

Dominican Republic. Gainesville, FL: University of Florida Press.

Wiarda, H. J. (1975) *Dictatorship, Development and Disintegration*, vol. III. Ann Arbor, MI: Xerox University Microfilms.

von Winterfeldt, Detlof, and Edwards, Ward (1986) *Decision Analysis and Behavioral Research*. New York: Cambridge University Press.

Wood, Bryce (1985) *The Dismantling of the Good Neighbor Policy*. Austin: University of Texas Press.

Wriggins, Howard (1968) "Political Outcomes of Foreign Assistance: Influence, Involvement or Intervention?," *Journal of International Affairs*, vol. 22, no. 2: 217–30.

Wriston, Henry (1967) "A Historical Perspective," in John Plant (ed.), *Cuba and the United States*. Washington, DC: The Brookings Institution.

Wyden, Peter (1979) *Bay of Pigs: The Untold Story*. New York: Simon and Schuster.

Zagoria, Donald S. (1967) *Vietnam Triangle: Moscow, Peking, Hanoi*. New York: Pegasus.

Zakheim, Dov S. (1986) "The Grenada Operation and Superpower Relations: A Perspective from the Pentagon," in Jiri Valenta and Herbert J. Ellison (eds), *Grenada and Soviet/Cuba Policy*. Boulder, CO: Westview Press.

Zietlin, Maurice, and Scheer, Robert (1963) *Cuba: Tragedy in Our Hemisphere*. New York: Grove Press.

Index

Kennedy, (President) John F. – *cont.*
and plan to overthrow Trujillo, 110, 136–7, 162,
166–8; and Schlesinger's and Fulbright's warnings,
94, 165; and Trujillo's family, 119–20; and use of
military force, 119, 293
Kennedy, (Attorney General) Robert, 74
Keohane, Robert O., 15–16, 291
Kirkpatrick, (UN Ambassador) Jeane, 263, 286; and
Carter and dictatorships, 263
Kissinger, (National Security Advisor and Secretary of
State) Henry, 190; and Allende, 193, 218, 222; and
appearance of inferiority, 221; and Chilean situation
in 1973, 204–7; and communism, 173–221; and
comparison between Chile and Peru, 222; and
Council on International Economic Policy, 194,
196; and covert operation, 190–1, 221–2; and
economic embargo, 193, 198; and linkage politics,
223–4; and military aid to Chile, 194; and national
interest, 218, 220, 222; and negotiations, 221; and
Nixon, 220, 223; and NSDM, 93, 192; and Soviet
foreign policy, 221; and Velasco, 223
Korry, (Ambassador) Edward, 189, 191–3, 222
Krasner, Stephen, 16, 45
Khrushchev, (Premier) Nikita, 91, 163
Kyle, (Ambassador) Edwin Jackson, 55

La Brea y Pariñas, 178–80, 183–4
Lake, (Director of Policy Planning at the Department
of State) Anthony, 242
Larios, Bernardino, 258, 260
Larson, Deborah, W., 1, 6–7, 22–3, 42–3, 149–51,
292
Lavett, (Under-Secretary of State) Robert, 60
Leddy, Raymond, 65
Little, Richard, 33–5
Long, (Ambassador) Boaz, 52
Lopez, (General) Nicolas Lindley, 177
Lopez-Fresquet, (Finance Minister) Rufo, 85
Loret de Mola, Carlos, 184

McAuliffe, (Lieutenant General) Dennis, 245
McCoy, (Colonel) James L., 251
McElroy, (Secretary of Defense) Neil, 195
McGee, (Under-Secretary of State) George, 119
McNamara, (Secretary of Defense) Robert, 94, 132,
141, 195
Magalhães, (Foreign Minister) Juracy, 213
Mann, (Assistant Secretary of State for Inter-
American Affairs) Thomas, 57, 58, 126, 130, 138,
149, 182; and Arbenz, 57, 94, 150; and Belaunde,
179; and Bosch, 126; and communism, 150, 293,
294; and democracy, 126; and economic sanctions,
58, 150, 152; and letter proposing Trujillo's
assassination, 116; and non-intervention agreement,
58–9, 151; and paramilitary invasion of Cuba, 94;
and policy toward Guatemala, 153–4, 293; and
protection of US economic interests, 179–80; and
request for US assistance, 131, 133; and US
offensive power, 150
Marambio, (General) Turio, 188
Marriberón, (General) Angel Valdivia, 185
Marshall, (Secretary of State) George, 55
Martin, Edward, 152
Martin, (Ambassador) John Bartlow, 107, 119, 121;
and communism, 123; and coup attempt, 124; and
Dominican armed forces, 121; and Dominican
economic reforms, 123; and Dominican elections,
121; and US Marines, 124
Martínez, (President) Maximiliano Hernández, 51

Marxist-Leninist perspective, 5, 8, 11, 17–21, 31,
290–2; as applied to Chile, 216–19; as applied to
Cuba, 71–3, 147–8; as applied to the Dominican
Republic, 108, 147–8; as applied to Grenada, 280–
1; as applied to Guatemala, 50, 147–8; as applied to
Nicaragua, 228–9, 280–1; as applied to Peru, 174,
216–19; and class interests, 17–21; and
instrumental-Marxist perspective, 19–20; and
national interest, 18–21; and power, 17–19; and
rationality, 21; and structural-Marxist perspective,
19–21
Matos, (Vice-Admiral) Francisco Torres, 177
Mazzocco, William J., 197
Mercado, Sergio Ramírez (referred to also as Sergio
Ramírez), 243, 252
Mikoyan, (Soviet Deputy Chairman) Anastas, 89, 105
Miller, (Assistant Secretary of State for Inter-
American Affairs) Edward, 57–8, 149–50, 153
Miolán, Angel, 126
Moa Bay Mining Company, 89, 96
Mondale, (Vice-President) Walter, 254
Morales, Moises Hassan, 252
Morgenthau, Hans, 15, 33, 71, 97–8
Moscoso, Teodoro, 178
Mossadegh, (Prime Minister) Mohammed, 61–2, 67,
189
Motley, (Assistant Secretary of State for Inter-
American Affairs) Langhorn, 270
Moyar, (Major) Enrique Jimenez, 112
Moyers, Bill, 132–3, 141
Murphy, (Congressman) John, 244, 252

National Bank of New York, 194
Nehru, (Prime Minister) Jawaharlal, 72
New Jewel Movement (NJM), 227, 248–9, 269
Nisbett, Richard, and Ross, Lee, 22, 292
Nixon, (Vice-President and President) Richard M.,
47, 173, 192; and Allende as a second Castro, 192,
211; and Allende's election, 176, 191, 222–3, 293;
and anti-expropriation policy, 201; on Castro, 85;
and communism, 220–1; and comparison between
Chile and Peru, 222; and Council on International
Economic Policy, 194; and covert actions, 211–12,
278–9, 293; and dictators, 80–1; and economic
embargo on Chile, 193, 271; and Helms, 191; and
international affairs, 220; and Kissinger, 190, 220;
and Latin American tour, 78, 80; and Latin
America's economic needs, 80–1; and linkage
politics, 223–4; and negotiations with Peru, 186;
and 1960 presidential election, 92, 192; and reports
on Cuba and Guatemala, 78; and threat to cut aid to
Peru, 185; and Vietnam, 187, 189
Northern Indiana Company, 194
Northrop Aviation, 183
Odría, Manuel, 176
O'Neill, (Speaker of the House), Thomas, 261
Organization of American States (OAS), 87, 113,
115–16, 133, 156, 171, 186, 192, 193, 202, 241,
253, 255
Organization of Central American States, 61
Ortega, Daniel, 252, 259
Ortega, Humberto, 238, 251–2, 257–8, 260, 265
Ortiz, (Ambassador) Frank, 249–50
Osegueda, (Foreign Minister) Raul, 61

Pallais, Luis, 252
Pan American Airways, 53
Pastor, (Director of Latin American and Caribbean
Affairs) Robert, 231–3; and human rights, 255; and